Evolution of the Japanese
Social and Psychic
BY
SIDNEY L. GULICK

PREFACE

The present work is an attempt to interpret the characteristics of modern Japan in the light of social science. It also seeks to throw some light on the vexed question as to the real character of so-called race-nature, and the processes by which that nature is transformed. If the principles of social science here set forth are correct, they apply as well to China and India as to Japan, and thus will bear directly on the entire problem of Occidental and Oriental social intercourse and mutual influence.

The core of this work consists of addresses to American and English audiences delivered by the writer during his recent furlough. Since returning to Japan, he has been able to give but fragments of time to the completion of the outlines then sketched, and though he would gladly reserve the manuscript for further elaboration, he yields to the urgency of friends who deem it wise that he delay no longer in laying his thought before the wider public.

To Japanese readers the writer wishes to say that although he has not hesitated to make statements painful to a lover of Japan, he has not done it to condemn or needlessly to criticise, but simply to make plain what seem to him to be the facts. If he has erred in his facts or if his interpretations reflect unjustly on the history or spirit of Japan, no one will be more glad than he for corrections. Let the Japanese be assured that his ruling motive, both in writing about Japan and in spending his life in this land, is profound love for the Japanese people. The term "native" has been freely used because it is the only natural correlative for "foreign." It may be well to say that neither the one nor the other has any derogatory implication, although anti-foreign natives, and anti-native foreigners, sometimes so use them.

The indebtedness of the writer is too great to be acknowledged in detail. But whenever he has been conscious of drawing directly from any author for ideas or suggestions, effort has been made to indicate the source.

Since the preparation of the larger part of this work several important contributions to the literature on Japan have appeared which would have been of help to the writer, could he have referred to them during the progress of his undertaking. Rev. J.C.C. Newton's "Japan: Country, Court, and People"; Rev. Otis Cary's "Japan and Its Regeneration"; and Prof. J. Nitobe's "Bushido: The Soul of Japan," call for special mention. All are excellent works, interesting, condensed, informative, and well-balanced. Had the last named come to hand much earlier it would have received frequent reference and quotation in the body of this volume, despite the fact that it sets forth an ideal rather than the actual state of Old Japan.

Special acknowledgment should be made of the help rendered by my brothers, Galen M. Fisher and Edward L. Gulick, and by my sister, Mrs. F.F. Jewett, in reading and revising the manuscript. Acknowledgment should also be made of the invaluable criticisms and suggestions in regard to the general theory of social evolution advocated in these pages made by my uncle, Rev. John T. Gulick, well known to the scientific world for his contributions to the theory as well as to the facts of biological evolution.

S.L.G.

MATSUYAMA, JAPAN.

INTRODUCTION

The tragedy enacted in China during the closing year of the nineteenth century marks an epoch in the history of China and of the world. Two world-views, two types of civilization met in deadly conflict, and the inherent weakness of isolated, belated, superstitious and corrupt paganism was revealed. Moreover, during this, China's crisis, Japan for the first time stepped out upon the world's stage of political and military activity. She was recognized as a civilized nation, worthy to share with the great nations of the earth the responsibility of ruling the lawless and backward races.

The correctness of any interpretation as to the significance of this conflict between the opposing civilizations turns, ultimately, on the question as to what is the real nature of man and of society. If it be true, as maintained by Prof. Le Bon and his school, that the mental and moral character of a people is as fixed as its physiological characteristics, then the conflict in China is at bottom a conflict of races, not of civilizations.

The inadequacy of the physiological theory of national character may be seen almost at a glance by a look at Japan. Were an Oriental necessarily and unchangeably Oriental, it would have been impossible for Japan to have come into such close and sympathetic touch with the West.

The conflict of the East with the West, however, is not an inherent and unending conflict, because it is not racial, but civilizational. It is a conflict of world-views and systems of thought and life. It is a conflict of heathen and Christian civilizations. And the conflict will come to an end as soon as, and in proportion as, China awakes from her blindness and begins to build her national temple on the bedrock of universal truth and righteousness. The conflict is practically over in Japan because she has done this. In loyally accepting science, popular education, and the rights of every individual to equal protection by the government, Japan has accepted the fundamental conceptions of civilization held in the West, and has thus become an integral part of Christendom, a fact of world-wide significance. It proves that the most important differences now separating the great races of men are civilizational, not physiological. It also proves that European, American, and Oriental peoples may be possessed by the same great ideals of life and principles of action, enabling them to co-operate as nations in great movements to their mutual advantage.

While even we of the West may be long in learning the full significance of what has been and still is taking place in Japan and more conspicuously just now, because more tragically, in China, one thing is clear: steam and electricity have abolished forever the old isolation of the nations.

Separated branches of the human race that for thousands of years have been undergoing divergent evolution, producing radically different languages, customs, civilizations, systems of thought and world-views, and have resulted even in marked physiological and psychological differences, are now being brought into close contact and inevitable conflict. But at bottom it is a conflict of ideas, not of races. The age of isolation and divergent evolution is passing away, and that of international association and convergent social evolution has begun. Those races and nations that refuse to recognize the new social order, and oppose the cosmic process and its forces, will surely be pushed to the wall and cease to exist as independent nations, just as, in ancient times, the tribes that refused to unite with neighboring tribes were finally subjugated by those that did so unite.

Universal economic, political, intellectual, moral, and religious intercourse is the characteristic of the new æon on which we are entering. What are to be the final consequences of this wide intercourse? Can a people change its character? Can a nation fully possessed by one type of civilization reject it, and adopt one radically different? Do races have "souls" which are fixed and incapable of radical transformations? What has taken place in Japan, a profound, or only a superficial change in psychical character? Are the destinies of the Oriental races already unalterably determined?

The answers to these questions have already been suggested in the preceding paragraphs, in regard to what has already taken place in Japan. But we may add that that answer really turns on our conception as to the nature of the characteristics separating the East from the West. In proportion as national character is reckoned to be biological, will it be considered fixed and the national destiny predetermined. In proportion as it is reckoned to be sociological, will it be considered alterable and the national destiny subject to new social forces. Now that the intercourse of widely different races has begun on a scale never before witnessed, it is highly important for us to know its probable consequences. For this we need to gain a clear idea of the nature both of the individual man and of society, of the relation of the social order to individual and to race character, and of the law regulating and the forces producing social evolution. Only thus can we forecast the probable course and consequences of the free social intercourse of widely divergent races.

It is the belief of the writer that few countries afford so clear an illustration of the principles involved in social evolution as Japan. Her development has been so rapid and so recent that some principles have become manifest that otherwise might easily have escaped notice. The importance of understanding Japan, because of the light her recent transformations throw on the subject of social evolution and of national character and also because of the conspicuous rôle to which she is destined as the natural leader of the Oriental

2

races in their adoption of Occidental modes of life and thought, justifies a careful study of Japanese character. He who really understands Japan, has gained the magic key for unlocking the social mysteries of China and the entire East. But the Japanese people, with their institutions and their various characteristics, merit careful study also for their own sakes. For the Japanese constitute an exceedingly interesting and even a unique branch of the human race. Japan is neither a purgatory, as some would have it, nor a paradise, as others maintain, but a land full of individuals in an interesting stage of social evolution.

Current opinions concerning Japan, however, are as curious as they are contradictory. Sir Edwin Arnold says that the Japanese "Have the nature rather of birds or butterflies than of ordinary human beings." Says Mr. A.M. Knapp: "Japan is the one country in the world which does not disappoint ... It is unquestionably the unique nation of the globe, the land of dream and enchantment, the land which could hardly differ more from our own, were it located in another planet, its people not of this world." An "old resident," however, calls it "the land of disappointments." Few phenomena are more curious than the readiness with which a tourist or professional journalist, after a few days or weeks of sight-seeing and interviewing, makes up his mind in regard to the character of the people, unless it be the way in which certain others, who have resided in this land for a number of years, continue to live in their own dreamland. These two classes of writers have been the chief contributors of material for the omnivorous readers of the West.

It appears to not a few who have lived many years in this Far Eastern land, that the public has been fed with the dreams of poets or the snap-judgments of tourists instead of with the facts of actual experience. A recent editorial article in the *Japan Mail*, than whose editor few men have had a wider acquaintance with the Japanese people or language, contains the following paragraph:

"In the case of such writers as Sir Edwin Arnold and Mr. Lafcadio Hearn it is quite apparent that the logical faculty is in abeyance. Imagination reigns supreme. As poetic nights or outbursts, the works of these authors on Japan are delightful reading. But no one who has studied the Japanese in a deeper manner, by more intimate daily intercourse with all classes of the people than either of these writers pretends to have had, can possibly regard a large part of their description as anything more than pleasing fancy. Both have given rein to the poetic fancy and thus have, from a purely literary point of view, scored a success granted to few.... But as exponents of Japanese life and thought they are unreliable.... They have given form and beauty to much that never existed except in vague outline or in undeveloped germs in the Japanese mind. In doing this they have unavoidably been guilty of misrepresentation.... The Japanese nation of Arnold and Hearn is not the nation we have known for a quarter of a century, but a purely ideal one manufactured out of the author's brains. It is high time that this was pointed out. For while such works please a certain section of the English public, they do a great deal of harm among a section of the Japanese public, as could be easily shown in detail, did space allow."—*Japan Mail, May 7, 1898.*

But even more harmful to the reading public of England and America are the hastily formed yet, nevertheless, widely published opinions of tourists and newspaper correspondents. Could such writers realize the inevitable limitations under which they see and try to generalize, the world would be spared many crudities and exaggerations, not to say positive errors. The impression so common to-day that Japan's recent developments are anomalous, even contrary to the laws of national growth, is chiefly due to the superficial writings of hasty observers. Few of those who have dilated ecstatically on her recent growth have understood either the history or the genius of her people.

"To mention but one among many examples," says Prof. Chamberlain, "the ingenious Traveling Commissioner of the *Pall Mall Gazette*, Mr. Henry Norman, in his lively letters on Japan published nine or ten years ago, tells the story of Japanese education under the fetching title of 'A Nation at School'; but the impression left is that they have been their own schoolmasters. In another letter on 'Japan in Arms,' he discourses concerning 'The Japanese Military Re-organizers,' 'The Yokosuka dockyard,' and other matters, but omits to mention that the reorganizers were Frenchmen, and that the Yokosuka dockyard was also a French creation. Similarly, when treating of the development of the Japanese newspaper, he ignores the fact that it owed its origin to an Englishman, which surely, to a man whose object was

3

reality, should have seemed an object worth recording. These letters, so full and apparently so frank, really so deceptive, are, as we have said, but one instance among many of the way in which popular writers on Japan travesty history by ignoring the part which foreigners have played. The reasons for this are not far to seek. A wonderful tale will please folks at a distance all the better if made more wonderful still. Japanese progress, traced to its causes and explained by references to the means employed, is not nearly such fascinating reading as when represented in the guise of a fairy creation, sprung from nothing, like Aladdin's palace."—"*Things Japanese," p. 116.*

But inter-racial misunderstanding is not, after all, so very strange. Few things are more difficult than to accommodate one's self in speech, in methods of life, and even in thought, to an alien people; so identifying one's deepest interest with theirs as really to understand them. The minds of most men are so possessed by notions acquired in childhood and youth as to be unable to see even the plainest facts at variance with those notions. He who comes to Japan possessed with the idea that it is a dreamland and that its old social order was free from defects, is blind to any important facts invalidating that conception; while he who is persuaded that Japan, being Oriental, is necessarily pagan at heart, however civilized in form, cannot easily be persuaded that there is anything praiseworthy in her old civilization, in her moral or religious life, or in any of her customs.

If France fails in important respects to understand England; and England, Germany; and Germany, its neighbors; if even England and America can so misunderstand one another as to be on the verge of war over the boundary dispute of an alien country, what hope is there that the Occident shall understand the Orient, or the Orient the Occident?

Though the difficulty seems insurmountable, I am persuaded that the most fruitful cause of racial misunderstandings and of defective descriptions both of the West by Orientals, and of the East by Occidentals, is a well-nigh universal misconception as to the nature of man, and of society, and consequently of the laws determining their development. In the East this error arises from and rests upon its polytheism, and the accompanying theories of special national creation and peculiar national sanctity. On these grounds alien races are pronounced necessarily inferior. China's scorn for foreigners is due to these ideas.

Although this pagan notion has been theoretically abandoned in the West, it still dominates the thought not only of the multitudes, but also of many who pride themselves on their high education and liberal sentiments. They bring to the support of their national or racial pride such modern sociological theories as lend themselves to this view. Evolution and the survival of the fittest, degeneration and the arrest of development, are appealed to as justifying the arrogance and domineering spirit of Western nations.

But the most subtle and scholarly doctrine appealed to in support of national pride is the biological conception of society. Popular writers assume that society is a biological organism and that the laws of its evolution are therefore biological. This assumption is not strange, for until recent times the most advanced professional sociologists have been dominated by the same misconception. Spencer, for example, makes sociology a branch of biology. More recent sociological writers, however, such as Professors Giddings and Fairbanks, have taken special pains to assert the essentially psychic character of society; they reject the biological conception, as inadequate to express the real nature of society. The biological conception, they insist, is nothing more than a comparison, useful for bringing out certain features of the social life and structure, but harmful if understood as their full statement. The laws of psychic activity and development differ as widely from those of biologic activity and development as these latter do from those that hold in the chemical world. If the laws which regulate psychic development and the progress of civilization were understood by popular writers on Japan, and if the recent progress of Japan had been stated in the terms of these laws, there would not have been so much mystification in the West in regard to this matter as there evidently has been. Japan would not have appeared to have "jumped out of her skin," or suddenly to have escaped from the heredity of her past millenniums of development. This wide misunderstanding of Japan, then, is not simply due to the fact that "Japanese progress, traced to its causes and explained by reference to the means employed, is not nearly such fascinating reading as when represented in the guise of a fairy creation," but it is also due to the still current popular view that the social organism is biological, and subject therefore to the laws of biological evolution. On this assumption, some hold that the progress of Japan, however it may appear, is really superficial, while others represent it as somehow having evaded the laws regulating the development of other races. A nation's character and characteristics are conceived to be the product of brain-structure; these can change only as brain structure changes. Brain is held to determine civilization, rather than civilization brain. Hampered by this defective view, popular writers inevitably describe Japan to the West in terms that necessarily misrepresent her, and that at the same time pander to Occidental pride and prejudice.

But this misunderstanding of Japan reveals an equally profound misunderstanding in regard to ourselves. Occidental peoples are supposed to be what they are in civilization and to have reached their high attainments in theoretical and applied science, in philosophy and in practical politics, because of their unique brain-structures, brains secured through millenniums of biological evolution. The following statement may seem to be rank heresy to the average sociologist, but my studies have led me to believe that the main differences between the great races of mankind to-day are not due to biological, but to social conditions; they are not physico-psychological differences, but only socio-psychological differences. The Anglo-Saxon is what he is because of his social heredity, and the Chinaman is what he is because of his social heredity. The profound difference between social and physiological heredity and evolution is unappreciated except by a few of the most recent sociological writers. The part that association, social segregation, and social heredity take in the maintenance, not only of once developed languages and civilizations, but even in their genesis, has been generally overlooked.

But a still more important factor in the determination of social and psychic evolution, generally unrecognized by sociologists, is the nature and function of personality. Although in recent years it has been occasionally mentioned by several eminent writers, personality as a principle has not been made the core of any system of sociology. In my judgment, however, this is the distinctive characteristic of human evolution and of human association, and it should accordingly be the fundamental principle of social science. Many writers on the East have emphasized what they call its "impersonal" characteristics. So important is this subject that I have considered it at length in the body of this work.

Sociological phenomena cannot be fully expressed by any combination of exclusively physical, biological, and psychic terms, for the significant element of man and of society consists of something more than these—namely, personality. It is this that differentiates human from animal evolution. The unit of human sociology is a self-conscious, self-determinative being. The causative factor in the social evolution of man is his personality. The goal of that evolution is developed personality. Personality is thus at once the cause and the end of social progress. The conditions which affect or determine progress are those which affect or determine personality.

The biological evolution of man from the animal has been, it is true, frankly assumed in this work. No attempt is made to justify this assumption. Let not the reader infer, however, that the writer similarly assumes the adequacy of the so-called naturalistic or evolutionary origin of ethics, of religion, or even of social progress. It may be doubted whether Darwin, Wallace, Le Conte, or any exponent of biological evolution has yet given a complete statement of the factors of the physiological evolution of man. It is certain, however, that ethical, religious, and social writers who have striven to account for the higher evolution of man, by appealing to factors exclusively parallel to those which have produced the physiological evolution of man, have conspicuously failed. However much we may find to praise in the social interpretations of such eminent writers as Comte, Spencer, Ward, Fiske, Giddings, Kidd, Southerland, or even Drummond, there still remains the necessity of a fuller consideration of the moral and religious evolution of man. The higher evolution of man cannot be adequately expressed or even understood in any terms lower than those of personality.

EVOLUTION OF THE JAPANESE
I
PRELIMINARY CONSIDERATIONS

Said a well educated and widely read Englishman to the writer while in Oxford, "Can you explain to me how it is that the Japanese have succeeded in jumping out of their skins?" And an equally thoughtful American, speaking about the recent strides in civilization made by Japan, urged that this progress could not be real and genuine. "How can such a mushroom-growth, necessarily without deep roots in the past, be real and strong and permanent? How can it escape being chiefly superficial?" These two men are typical of much of the thought of the West in regard to Japan.

Seldom, perhaps never, has the civilized world so suddenly and completely reversed an estimate of a nation as it has that with reference to Japan. Before the recent war, to the majority even of fairly educated men, Japan was little more than a name for a few small islands somewhere near China, whose people were peculiar and interesting. To-day there is probably not a man, or woman, or child attending school in any part of the civilized world, who does not know the main facts about the recent war: how the small country and the men of small stature, sarcastically described by their foes as "Wojen," pygmy, attacked the army and navy of a country ten times their size.

Such a universal change of opinion regarding a nation, especially regarding one so remote from the centers of Western civilization as Japan, could not have taken place in any previous generation. The telegraph, the daily paper, the intelligent reporters and writers of books and magazine articles, the rapid steam travel and the many travelers—all these have made possible this sudden acquisition of knowledge and startling reversal of opinion.

There is reason, however, to think that much misapprehension and real ignorance still exists about Japan and her leap into power and world-wide prestige. Many seem to think that Japan has entered on her new career through the abandonment of her old civilization and the adoption of one from the West—that the victories on sea and land, in Korea, at Port Arthur, and a Wei-hai-wei, and more recently at Tientsin and Pekin, were solely due to her Westernized navy and army. Such persons freely admit that this process of Westernization had been going on for many years more rapidly than the world at large knew, and that consequently the reputation of Japan before the war was not such as corresponded with her actual attainments. But they assume that there was nothing of importance in the old civilization; that it was little superior to organized barbarism.

These people conceive of the change which has taken place in Japan during the past thirty years as a revolution, not as an evolution; as an abandonment of the old, and an adoption of the new, civilization. They conceive the old tree of civilization to have been cut down and cast into the fire, and a new tree to have been imported from the West and planted in Japanese soil. New Japan is, from this view-point, the new tree.

Not many months ago I heard of a wealthy family in Kyoto which did not take kindly to the so-called improvements imported from abroad, and which consequently persisted in using the instruments of the older civilization. Even such a convenience as the kerosene lamp, now universally adopted throughout the land of the Rising Sun, this family refused to admit into its home, preferring the old-style andon with its vegetable oil, dim light, and flickering flame. Recently, however, an electric-light company was organized in that city, and this brilliant illuminant was introduced not only into the streets and stores, but into many private houses. Shortly after its introduction, the family was converted to the superiority of the new method of illumination, and passed at one leap from the old-style lantern to the latest product of the nineteenth century. This incident is considered typical of the transformations characteristic of modern Japan. It is supposed that New Japan is in no proper sense the legitimate product through evolution of Old Japan.

In important ways, therefore, Japan seems to be contradicting our theories of national growth. We have thought that no "heathen" nation could possibly gain, much less wield, unaided by Westerners, the forces of civilized Christendom. We have likewise held that national growth is a slow process, a gradual evolution, extending over scores and centuries of years. In both respects our theories seem to be at fault. This "little nation of little people," which we have been so ready to condemn as "heathen" and "uncivilized," and thus to despise, or to ignore, has in a single generation leaped into the forefront of the world's attention.

6

Are our theories wrong? Is Japan an exception? Are our facts correct? We instinctively feel that something is at fault. We are not satisfied with the usual explanation of the recent history of Japan. We are perhaps ready to concede that "the rejection of the old and the adoption of Western civilization" is the best statement whereby to account for the new power of Japan and her new position among the nations, but when we stop to think, we ask whether we have thus explained that for which we are seeking an explanation? Do not the questions still remain—Why did the Japanese so suddenly abandon Oriental for Occidental civilization? And what mental and other traits enabled a people who, according to the supposition, were far from civilized, so suddenly to grasp and wield a civilization quite alien in character and superior to their own; a civilization ripened after millenniums of development of the Aryan race? And how far, as a matter of fact, has this assimilation gone? Not until these questions are really answered has the explanation been found, So that, after all, the prime cause which we must seek is not to be found in the external environment, but rather in the internal endowment.

An effort to understand the ancient history of Japan encounters the same problem as that raised by her modern history. What mental characteristics led the Japanese a thousand years ago so to absorb the Chinese civilization, philosophy, and language that their own suffered a permanent arrest? What religious traits led them so to take on a religion from China and India that their own native religion never passed beyond the most primitive development, either in doctrine, in ethics, in ritual, or in organization? On the other hand, what mental characteristics enabled them to preserve their national independence and so to modify everything brought from abroad, from the words of the new language to the philosophy of the new religions, that Japanese civilization, language, and religion are markedly distinct from the Chinese? Why is it that, though the Japanese so fell under the bondage of the Chinese language as permanently to enslave and dwarf their own beautiful tongue, expressing the dominant thought of every sentence with characters (ideographs) borrowed from China, yet at the same time so transformed what they borrowed that no Chinaman can read and understand a Japanese book or newspaper?

The same questions recur at this new period of Japan's national life. Why has she so easily turned from the customs of centuries? What are the mental traits that have made her respond so differently from her neighbor to the environment of the nineteenth-century civilization of the West Why is it that Japan has sent thousands of her students to these Western lands to see and study and bring back all that is good in them, while China has remained in stolid self-satisfaction, seeing nothing good in the West and its ways? To affirm that the difference is due to the environment alone is impossible, for the environment seems to be essentially the same. This difference of attitude and action must be traced, it would seem, to differences of mental and temperamental characteristics. Those who seek to understand the secret of Japan's newly won power and reputation by looking simply at her newly acquired forms of government, her reconstructed national social structure, her recently constructed roads and railroads, telegraphs, representative government, etc., and especially at her army and navy organized on European models and armed with European weapons, are not unlike those who would discover the secret of human life by the study of anatomy.

This external view and this method of interpretation are, therefore, fundamentally erroneous. Never, perhaps, has the progress of a nation been so manifestly an evolution as distinguished from a revolution. No foreign conquerors have come in with their armies, crushing down the old and building up a new civilization. No magician's wand has been waved over the land to make the people forget the traditions of a thousand years and fall in with those of the new régime. No rite or incantation has been performed to charm the marvelous tree of civilization and cause it to take root and grow to such lofty proportions in an unprepared soil.

In contrast to the defective views outlined above, one need not hesitate to believe that the actual process by which Old Japan has been transformed into New Japan is perfectly natural and necessary. It has been a continuous growth; it is not the mere accumulation of external additions; it does not consist alone of the acquisition of the machinery and the institutions of the Occident. It is rather a development from within, based upon already existing ideas and institutions. New Japan is the consequence of her old endowment and her new environment. Her evolution has been in progress and can be traced for at least a millennium and a half, during which she has been preparing for this latest step. All that was necessary for its accomplishment was the new environment. The correctness of this view and the reasons for it will appear as we proceed in our study of Japanese characteristics. But we need to note at this point the danger, into which many fall, of ascribing to Japan an attainment of western civilization which the facts will not warrant. She has secured much, but by no means all, that the West has to give.

We may suggest our line of thought by asking what is the fundamental element of civilization? Does it consist in the manifold appliances that render life luxurious; the railroad, the telegraph, the post office, the manufactures, the infinite variety of mechanical and other conveniences? Or is it not rather the social and intellectual and ethical state of a people? Manifestly the latter. The tools indeed of civilization may be imported into a half-civilized, or barbarous country; such importation, however, does not render the country civilized, although it may assist greatly in the attainment of that result. Civilization being mental, social, and ethical, can arise only through the growth of the mind and character of the vast multitudes of a nation. Now has Japan imported only the tools of civilization? In other words, is her new civilization only external, formal, nominal, unreal? That she has imported much is true. Yet that her attainments and progress rest on her social, intellectual, and ethical development will become increasingly clear as we take up our successive chapters. Under the new environment of the past fifty years, this growth, particularly in intellectual, in industrial, and in political lines, has been exceedingly rapid as compared with the growths of other peoples.

This conception of the rise of New Japan will doubtless approve itself to every educated man who will allow his thought to rest upon the subject. For all human progress, all organic evolution, proceeds by the progressive modification of the old organs under new conditions. The modern locomotive did not spring complete from the mind of James Watt; it is the result of thousands of years of human experience and consequent evolution, beginning first perhaps with a rolling log, becoming a rude cart, and being gradually transformed by successive inventions until it has become one of the marvels of the nineteenth century. It is impossible for those who have attained the view-point of modern science to conceive of discontinuous progress; of continually rising types of being, of thought, or ofmoral life, in which the higher does not find its ground and root and thus an important part of its explanation, in the lower. Such is the case not only with reference: to biological evolution; it is especially true of social evolution. He who would understand the Japan of to-day cannot rest with the bare statement that her adoption of the tools and materials of Western civilization has given her her present power and place among the nations. The student with historical insight knows that it is impossible for one nation, off-hand, without preparation, to "adopt the civilization" of another.

The study of the evolution of Japan is one of unusual interest; first, because of the fact that Japan has experienced such unique changes in her environment. Her history brings into clear light some principles of evolution which the visual development of a people does not make so clear.

In the second place, New Japan is in a state of rapid growth. She is in a critical period, resembling a youth, just coming to manhood, when all the powers of growth are most vigorous. The latent qualities of body and mind and heart then burst forth with peculiar force. In the course of four or five short years the green boy develops into a refined and noble man; the thoughtless girl ripens into the full maturity of womanhood and of motherhood. These are the years of special interest to those who would observe nature in her time of most critical activity.

Not otherwise is it in the life of nations. There are times when their growth is phenomenally rapid; when their latent qualities are developed; when their growth can be watched with special ease and delight, because so rapid. The Renaissance was such a period in Europe. Modern art, science, and philosophy took their start with the awakening of the mind of Europe at that eventful and epochal period of her life. Such, I take it, is the condition of Japan to-day. She is "being born again"; undergoing her "renaissance." Her intellect, hitherto largely dormant, is but now awaking. Her ambition is equaled only by her self-reliance. Her self-confidence and amazing expectations have not yet been sobered by hard experience. Neither does she, nor do her critics, know how much she can or cannot do. She is in the first flush of her new-found powers; powers of mind and spirit, as well as of physical force. Her dreams are gorgeous with all the colors of the rainbow. Her efforts are sure, to be noble in proportion as her ambitions are high. The growth of the past half-century is only the beginning of what we may expect to see.

Then again, this latest and greatest step in the evolution of Japan has taken place at a time unparalleled for opportunities of observation, under the incandescent light of the nineteenth century, with its thousands of educated men to observe and record the facts, many of whom are active agents in the evolution in progress. Hundreds of papers and magazines, native and European, read by tens of thousands of intelligent men and women, have kept the world aware of the daily and hourly events. Telegraphic dispatches and letters by the million have passed between the far East and the West. It would seem as if the modernizing of Japan had been providentially delayed until the last half of the nineteenth century with its steam and electricity, annihilators of space and time, in order that her evolution might be studied with a minuteness impossible in any previous age, or by any previous generation. It is almost as if one were conducting an experiment in human evolution in his own laboratory, imposing the conditions and noting the results.

For still another reason is the evolution of New Japan of special interest to all intelligent persons. To illustrate great things by small, and human by physical, no one who has visited Geneva has failed to see the beautiful mingling of the Arve and the Rhone. The latter flowing from the calm Geneva lake is of delicate blue, pure and limpid. The former, running direct from the glaciers of Mont Blanc and the roaring bed of Chamouni, bears along in its rushing waters powdered rocks and loosened soil. These rivers, though joined in one bed, for hundreds of rods are quite distinct; the one, turbid; the other, clear as crystal; yet they press each against the other, now a little of the Rhone's clear current forces its way into the Arve, soon to be carried off, absorbed and discolored by the mass of muddy water around it. Now a little of the turbid Arve forces its way into the clear blue Rhone, to lose there its identity in the surrounding waters. The interchange goes on, increasing with the distance until, miles below, the two-rivers mingle as one. No longer is it the Arve or the old Rhone, but the new Rhone.

In Japan there is going on to-day a process unique in the history of the human race. Two streams of civilization, that of the far East and that of the far West, are beginning to flow in a single channel. These streams are exceedingly diverse, in social structure, in government, in moral ideals and standards, in religion, in psychological and metaphysical conceptions. Can they live together? Or is one going to drive out and annihilate the other? If so, which will be victor? Or is there to be modification of both? In other words, is there to be a new civilization—a Japanese, an Occidento-Oriental civilization?

The answer is plain to him who has eyes with which to see. Can the Ethiopian change his skin or the leopard his spots? No more can Japan lose all trace of inherited customs of daily life, of habits of thought and language, products of a thousand years of training in Chinese literature, Buddhist doctrine, and Confucian ethics. That "the boy is father to the man" is true of a nation no less than of an individual. What a youth has been at home in his habits of thought, in his purpose and spirit and in their manifestation in action, will largely determine his after-life. In like manner the mental and moral history of Japan has so stamped certain characteristics on her language, on her thought, and above all on her temperament and character, that, however she may strive to Westernize herself, it is impossible for her to obliterate her Oriental features. She will inevitably and always remain Japanese.

Japan has already produced an Occidento-Oriental civilization. Time will serve progressively to Occidentalize it. But there is no reason for thinking that it will ever become wholly Occidentalized. A Westerner visiting Japan will always be impressed with its Oriental features, while an Asiatic will be impressed with its Occidental features. This progressive Occidentalization of Japan will take place according to the laws of social evolution, of which we must speak somewhat more fully in a later chapter.

An important question bearing on this problem is the precise nature of the characteristics differentiating the Occident and the Orient. What exactly do we mean when we say that the Japanese are Oriental and will always bear the marks of the Orient in their civilization, however much they may absorb from the West? The importance and difficulty of this question have led the writer to defer its consideration till toward the close of this work.

If one would gain adequate conception of the process now going on, the illustration already used of the mingling of two rivers needs to be supplemented by another, corresponding to a separate class of facts. Instead of the mingling of rivers, let us watch the confluence of two glaciers. What pressures! What grindings! What upheavals! What rendings! Such is the mingling of two civilizations. It is not smooth and Noiseless, but attended with pressure and pain. It is a collision in more ways than one. The unfortunates on whom the pressures of both currents are directed are often quite destroyed.

Comparison is often made between Japan and India. In both countries enormous social changes are taking place; in both, Eastern and Western civilizations are in contact and in conflict. The differences, however, are even more striking than the likenesses. Most conspicuous is the fact that whereas, in India, the changes in civilization are due almost wholly to the force and rule of the conquering race, in Japan these changes are spontaneous, attributable entirely to the desire and initiative of the native rulers. This difference is fundamental and vital. The evolution of society in India is to a large degree compulsory; in a true sense it is an artificial evolution. In Japan, on the other hand, evolution is natural. There has not been the slightest physical compulsion laid on her from without. With two rare exceptions, Japan has never heard the boom of foreign cannon carrying destruction to her people. During these years of change, there have been none but Japanese rulers, and such has been the case throughout the entire period of Japanese history. Their native rulers have introduced changes such as foreign rulers would hardly have ventured upon. The adoption of the Chinese language, literature, and religions from ten to twelve centuries ago, was not occasioned by a military occupancy of Japanese soil by invaders from China. It was due absolutely to the free choice of their versatile people, as free and voluntary as was the adoption by Rome of Greek literature and standards of learning. The modern choice of Western material civilization no doubt had elements of fear as motive power. But impulsion through a knowledge of conditions differs radically from compulsion exercised by a foreign military occupancy. India illustrates the latter; Japan, the former.

Japan and her people manifest amazing contrasts. Never, on the one hand, has a nation been so free from foreign military occupancy throughout a history covering more than fifteen centuries, and at the same time, been so influenced by and even subject to foreign psychical environment. What was the fact in ancient times is the fact to-day. The dominance of China and India has been largely displaced by that of Europe. Western literature, language, and science, and even customs, are being welcomed by Japan, and are working their inevitable effects. But it is all perfectly natural, perfectly spontaneous. The present choice by Japan of modern science and education and methods and principles of government and nineteenth-century literature and law,—in a word, of Occidental civilization,—is not due to any artificial pressure or military occupancy. But the choice and the consequent evolution are wholly due to the free act of the people. In this, as in several other respects, Japan reminds us of ancient Greece. Dr. Menzies, in his "History of Religion," says: "Greece was not conquered from the East, but stirred to new lifeby the communication of new ideas." Free choice has made Japan reject Chinese astronomy, surgery, medicine, and jurisprudence. The early choice to admit foreigners to Japan to trade may have been made entirely through fear, but is now accepted and justified by reason and choice.

The true explanation, therefore, of the recent and rapid rise of Japan to power and reputation, is to be found, not in the externals of her civilization, not in the pressure of foreign governments, but rather in the inherited mental and temperamental characteristics, reacting on the new and stimulating environment, and working along the lines of true evolution. Japan has not "jumped out of her skin," but a new vitality has given that skin a new color.

II
HISTORICAL SKETCH

How many of the stories of the Kojiki (written in 712 A.D.) and Nihongi (720 A.D.) are to be accepted is still a matter of dispute among scholars. Certain it is, however, that Japanese early history is veiled in a mythology which seems to center about three prominent points: Kyushu, in the south; Yamato, in the east central, and Izumo in the west central region. This mythological history narrates the circumstances of the victory of the southern descendants of the gods over the two central regions. And it has been conjectured that these three centers represent three waves of migration that brought the ancestors of the present inhabitants of Japan to these shores. The supposition is that they came quite independently and began their conflicts only after long periods of residence and multiplication.

Though this early record is largely mythological, tradition shows us the progenitors of the modern Japanese people as conquerors from the west and south who drove the aborigines before them and gradually took possession of the entire land. That these conquerors were not all of the same stock is proved by the physical appearance of the Japanese to-day, and by their language. Through these the student traces an early mixture of races—the Malay, the Mongolian, and the Ural-Altaic. Whether the early crossing of these races bears vital relation to the plasticity of the Japanese is a question which tempts the scholar.

Primitive, inter-tribal conflicts of which we have no reliable records resulted in increasing intercourse. Victory was followed by federation. And through the development of a common language, of common customs and common ideas, the tribes were unified socially and psychically. Consciousness of this unity was emphasized by the age-long struggle against the Ainu, who were not completely conquered until the eighteenth century.

With the dawn of authentic history (500-600 A.D.) we find amalgamation of the conquering tribes, with, however, constantly recurring inter-clan and inter-family wars. Many of these continued for scores and even hundreds of years—proving that, in the modern sense, of the word, the Japanese were not yet a nation, though, through inter-marriage, through the adoption of important elements of civilization brought from China and India via Korea, through the nominal acceptance of the Emperor as the divinely appointed ruler of the land, they were, in race and in civilization, a fairly homogeneous people.

The national governmental system was materially affected by the need, throughout many centuries, of systematic methods of defense against the Ainu. The rise of the Shogunate dates back to 883 A.D., when the chief of the forces opposing the Ainu was appointed by the Emperor and bore the official title, "The Barbarian-expelling Generalissimo." This office developed in power until, some centuries later, it usurped in fact, if not in name, all the imperial prerogatives.

It is probable that the Chinese written language, literature, and ethical teachings of Confucius came to Japan from Korea after the Christian era. The oldest known Japanese writings (Japanese written with Chinese characters) date from the eighth century. In this period also Buddhism first came to Japan. For over a hundred years it made relatively little progress. But when at last in the ninth and tenth centuries native Japanese Buddhists popularized its doctrines and adopted into its theogony the deities of the aboriginal religion, now known as Shinto, Buddhism became the religion of the people, and filled the land with its great temples, praying priests, and gorgeous rituals.

Even in those early centuries the contact of Japan with her Oriental neighbors revealed certain traits of her character which have been conspicuous in recent times —great capacity for acquisition, and readiness to adopt freely from foreign nations. Her contact with China, at that time so far in advance of herself in every element of civilization, was in some respects disastrous to her original growth. Instead of working out the problems of thought and life for herself, she took what China and Korea had to give. The result was an arrest in the development of everything distinctively native. The native religion was so absorbed by Buddhism that for a thousand years it lost all self-consciousness. Indeed the modern clear demarcation between the native and the imported religions is a matter of only a few decades,

11

due to the researches of native scholars during the latter part of the last and the early part of this century. Even now, multitudes of the common people know no difference between the various elements of the composite religion of which they are the heirs.

Moreover, early contact with China and her enormous literature checked the development of the native language and the growth of the native literature. The language suffered arrest because of the rapid introduction of Chinese terms for all the growing needs of thought and civilization. Modern Japanese is a compound of the original tongue and Japonicized Chinese. Native speculative thought likewise found little encouragement or stimulus to independent activity in the presence of the elaborate and in many respects profound philosophies brought from India and China.

From earliest times the government of Japan was essentially feudal. Powerful families and clans disputed and fought for leadership, and the political history of Japan revolves around the varying fortunes of these families. While the Imperial line is never lost to sight, it seldom rises to real power.

When, in the fifteenth and sixteenth centuries, Japan's conquering arm reached across the waters, to ravage the coast of China, to extend her influence as far south as Siam, and even to invade Korea with a large army in 1592, it looked as if she were well started on her career as a world-power. But that was not yet to be. The hegemony of her clans passed into the powerful and shrewd Tokugawa family, the policy of which was peace and national self-sufficiency.

The representatives of the Occidental nations (chiefly of Spain and Portugal) were banished. The Christian religion (Roman Catholic), which for over fifty years had enjoyed free access and had made great progress, was forbidden and stamped out, not without much bloodshed. Foreign travel and commerce were strictly interdicted. A particular school of Confucian ethics was adopted and taught as the state religion. Feudalism was systematically established and intentionally developed. Each and every man had his assigned and recognized place in the social fabric, and change was not easy. It is doubtful if any European country has ever given feudalism so long and thorough a trial. Never has feudalism attained so complete a development as it did in Japan under the Tokugawa régime of over 250 years.

During this period no influences came from other lands to disturb the natural development. With the exception of three ships a year from Holland, an occasional stray ship from other lands, and from fifteen to twenty Dutchmen isolated in a little island in the harbor of Nagasaki, Japan had no communication with foreign lands or alien peoples.

Of this period, extending to the middle of the present century, the ordinary visitor and even the resident have but a superficial knowledge. All the changes that have taken place in Japan, since the coming of Perry in 1854, are attributed by the easy-going tourist to the external pressure of foreign nations. But such travelers know nothing of the internal preparations that had been making for generations previous to the arrival of Perry. The tourist is quite ignorant of the line of Japanese scholars that had been undermining the authority of the military rulers, "the Tokugawa," in favor of the Imperial line which they had practically supplanted.

The casual student of Japan has been equally ignorant of the real mental and moral caliber of the Japanese. Dressed in clothing that appeared to us fantastic, and armed with cumbersome armor and old-fashioned guns, it was easy to jump to the conclusion that the people were essentially uncivilized. We did not know the intellectual discipline demanded of one, whether native or foreign, who would master the native language or the native systems of thought. We forgot that we appeared as grotesque and as barbarous to them as they to us, and that mental ability and moral worth are qualities that do not show on the surface of a nation's civilization. While they thought us to be "unclean," "dogs," "red-haired devils," we perhaps thought them to be clever savages, or at best half-civilized heathen, without moral perceptions or intellectual ability.

Of Old Japan little more needs to be said. Without external commerce, there was little need for internal trade; ships were small; roads were footpaths; education was limited to the samurai, or military class, retainers of the daimyo, "feudal lords"; inter-clan travel was limited and discouraged; Confucian ethics was the moral standard. From the beginning of the seventeenth century Christianity was forbidden by edict, and was popularly known as the "evil way"; Japan was thought to be especially sacred, and the coming of foreigners was supposed to pollute the land and to be the cause of physical evils. Education, as in China, was limited to the Chinese classics. Mathematics, general history, and science, in the modern sense, were of course wholly unknown. Guns and powder were brought from the West in the sixteenth century by Spaniards and Portuguese, but were never improved. Ship-building was the same in the middle of the nineteenth century as in the middle of the sixteenth, perhaps even less advanced. Architecture had received its great impulse from the introduction of Buddhism in the ninth and tenth centuries and had made no material improvement thereafter.

But while there was little progress in the external and mechanical elements of civilization, there was progress in other respects. During the "great peace," first arose great scholars. Culture became more general throughout the nation. Education was esteemed. The corrupt lives of the priests were condemned and an effort was made to reform life through the revival of a certain school of Confucian teachers known as "Shin-Gaku"—"Heart-Knowledge." Art also made progress, both pictorial and manual. It would almost seem as if modern artificers and painters had lost the skill of their forefathers of one or two hundred years ago.

Many reasons explain the continuance of the old political and social order: the lack of a foreign foe to compel abandonment of the tribal organisation; the mountainous nature of the country with its slow, primitive means of intercommunication; the absence of all idea of a completely centralized nation. Furthermore, the principle of complete subordination to superiors and ancestors had become so strong that individual innovations were practically impossible. Japan thus lacked the indispensable key to further progress, the principle of individualism. The final step in the development of her nationality has been taken, therefore, only in our own time.

Old Japan seemed absolutely committed to a thorough-going antagonism to everything foreign. New Japan seems committed to the opposite policy. What are the steps by which she has effected this apparent national reversal of attitude?

We should first note that the absolutism of the Tokugawa Shogunate served to arouse ever-growing opposition because of its stern repression of individual opinion. It not only forbade the Christian religion, but also all independent thought in religious philosophy and in politics. The particular form of Confucian moral philosophy which it held was forced on all public teachers of Confucianism. Dissent was not only heretical, but treasonable. Although, by its military absolutism, the Tokugawa rule secured the great blessing of peace, lasting over two hundred years, and although the curse of Japan for well-nigh a thousand preceding years had been fierce inter-tribal and inter-family wars and feuds, yet it secured that peace at the expense of individual liberty of thought and act. It thus gradually aroused against itself the opposition of many able minds. The enforced peace rendered it possible for these men to devote themselves to problems of thought and of history. Indeed, they had no other outlet for their energies. As they studied the history of the past and compared their results with the facts of the present, it gradually dawned on the minds of the scholars of the eighteenth century, that the Tokugawa family were exercising functions of government which had never been delegated to them; and that the Emperor was a poverty-stricken puppet in the hands of a family that had seized the military power and had gradually absorbed all the active functions of government, together with its revenues.

It is possible for us to see now that these early Japanese scholars idealized their ancient history, and assigned to the Emperor a place in ancient times which in all probability he has seldom held. But, however that may be, they thought their view correct, and held that the Emperor was being deprived of his rightful rule by the Tokugawa family.

These ideas, first formulated in secret by scholars, gradually filtered down, still in secrecy, and were accepted by a large number of the samurai, the military literati of the land. Their opposition to the actual rulers of the land, aroused by the individual-crushing absolutism of the Tokugawa rule, naturally allied itself to the religious sentiment of loyalty to the Emperor. Few Westerners can appreciate the full significance of this fact. Throughout the centuries loyalty to the Emperor has been considered a cardinal virtue. With one exception, according to the popular histories, no one ever acknowledged himself opposed to the Emperor. Every rebellion against the powers in actual possession made it the first aim to gain possession of the Emperor, and proclaim itself as fighting for him. When, therefore, the scholars announced that the existing government was in reality a usurpation and that the Emperor was robbed of his rightful powers, the latent antagonism to the Tokugawa rule began to find both intellectual and moral justification. It could and did appeal to the religious patriotism of the people. It is perhaps not too much to say that the overthrow of the Tokugawa family and the restoration of the Imperial rule to the Imperial family would have taken place even though there had been no interference of foreign nations, no extraneous influences. But equally certain is it that these antagonisms to the ruling family were crystallized, and the great internal changes hastened by the coming in of the aggressive foreign nations. How this external influence operated must and can be told in a few words.

When Admiral Perry negotiated his treaty with the Japanese, he supposed he was dealing with responsible representatives of the government. As was later learned, however, the Tokugawa rulers had not secured the formal assent of the Emperor to the treaty. The Tokugawa rulers and their counselors, quite as much as the clan-rulers, wished to keep the foreigners out of the country, but they realized their inability. The rulers of the clans, however, felt that the Tokugawa rulers had betrayed the land; they were, accordingly, in active opposition both to the foreigners and to the national rulers. When the foreigners requested the Japanese government, "the Tokugawa Shogunate," to carry out the treaties, it was unable to comply with the request because of the antagonism of the clan-rulers. When the clan-rulers demanded that the government annul the treaties and drive out the hated and much-feared foreigners, it found itself utterly unable to do so, because of the formidable naval power of the foreigners.

As a consequence of this state of affairs, a few serious collisions took place between the foreigners and the two-sworded samurai, retainers of the clan-rulers. The Tokugawa rulers apparently did their best to protect the foreigners, and, when there was no possible method of evasion, to execute the treaties they had made. But they could not control the clans already rebellious. A few murders of foreigners, followed by severe reprisals, and two bombardments of native towns by foreign gunboats, began to reveal to the military class at large that no individual or local action against the foreigners was at all to be thought of. The first step necessary was the unification of the Empire under the Imperial rule. This, however, could be done only by the overthrow of the Tokugawa Shogunate; which was effected in 1867-68 after a short struggle, marked by great clemency.

We thus realize that the overthrow of the Shogunate as also the final abolishment of feudalism with its clans, lords, and hereditary rulers, and the establishment of those principles of political and personal centralization which lie at the foundation of real national unity, not only were hastened by, but in a marked degree dependent on, the stimulus and contribution of foreigners. They compelled a more complete Japanese unity than had existed before, for they demanded direct relations with the national head. And when treaty negotiations revealed the lack of such a head, they undertook to show its necessity by themselves punishing those local rulers who did not recognize the Tokugawa headship.

With the establishment of the Emperor on the throne, began the modern era in Japanese history, known in Japan as "Meiji"—"Enlightened Rule."

But not even yet was the purpose of the nation attained, namely, the expulsion of the polluters of the sacred soil of Japan. As soon as the new government was established and had turned its attention to foreign affairs, it found itself in as great a dilemma as had its predecessors, the Tokugawa rulers. For the foreign governments insisted that the treaties negotiated with the old government should be accepted in full by the new. It was soon as evident to the new rulers as it had been to the old that direct and forcible resistance to the foreigners was futile. Not by might were they to be overcome. Westerners had, however, supplied the ideals whereby national, political unity was to be secured. Mill's famous work on "Representative Government" was early translated, and read by all the thinking men of the day. These ideas were also keenly studied in their actual workings in the West. The consequence was that feudalism was utterly rejected and the new ideas, more or less modified, were speedily adopted, even down to the production of a constitution and the establishment of local representative assemblies and a national diet. In other words, the theories and practices of the West in regard to the political organization of the state supplied Japan with those new intellectual variations which were essential to the higher development of her own national unity.

A further point of importance is the fact that at the very time that the West applied this pressure and supplied Japan with these political ideals she also put within her reach the material instruments which would enable her to carry them into practice. I refer to steam locomotion by land and sea, the postal and telegraphic systems of communication, the steam printing press, the system of popular education, and the modern organization of the army and the navy. These instruments Japan made haste to acquire. But for these, the rapid transformation of Old Japan into New Japan would have been an exceedingly long and difficult process. The adoption of these tools of civilization by the central authority at once gave it an immense superiority over any local force. For it could communicate speedily with every part of the Empire, and enforce its decisions with a celerity and a decisiveness before unknown. It became once more the actual head of the nation.

We have thus reached the explanation of one of the most astonishing changes in national attitude that history has to record, and the new attitude seems such a contradiction of the old as to be inexplicable, and almost incredible. But a better knowledge of the facts and a deeper understanding of their significance will serve to remove this first impression.

What, then, did the new government do? It simply said, "For us to drive out these foreigners is impossible; but neither is it desirable. We need to know the secrets of their power. We must study their language, their science, their machinery, their steamboats, their battle-ships. We must learn all their secrets, and then we shall be able to turn them out without difficulty. Let us therefore restrict them carefully to the treaty ports, but let us make all the use of them we can."

This has virtually been the national policy of Japan ever since. And this policy gained the acceptance of the people as a whole with marvelous readiness, for a reason which few foreigners can appreciate. Had this policy been formulated and urged by the Tokugawa rulers, there is no probability that it would have been accepted. But because it was, ostensibly at least, the declared will of the Emperor, loyalty to him, which in Japan is both religion and patriotism, led to a hearty and complete acceptance which could hardly have been realized in any other land. During the first year of his "enlightened" rule (1868), the Emperor gave his sanction to an Edict, the last two clauses of which read as follows:

"The old, uncivilized way shall be replaced by the eternal principles of the universe.

"The best knowledge shall be sought throughout the world, so as to promote the Imperial welfare."

It is the wide acceptance of this policy, which, however, is in accord with the real genius of the people, that has transformed Japan. It has sent hundreds of its young men to foreign lands to learn and bring back to Japan the secrets of Western power and wealth; it has established roads and railways, postal and telegraphic facilities, a public common-school system, colleges and a university in which Western science, history, and languages have been taught by foreign and foreign-trained instructors; daily, weekly, and monthly papers and magazines; factories, docks, drydocks; local and foreign commerce; representative government—in a word, all the characteristic features of New Japan. The whole of New Japan is only the practical carrying out of the policy adopted at the beginning of the new era, when it was found impossible to cast out the foreigners by force. Brute force being found to be out of the question, resort was thus made to intellectual force, and with real success.

The practice since then has not been so much to retain the foreigner as to learn of him and then to eliminate him. Every branch of learning and industry has proved this to be the consistent Japanese policy. No foreigner may hope to obtain a permanent position in Japanese employ, either in private firms or in the government. A foreigner is useful not for what he can do, but for what he can teach. When any Japanese can do his work tolerably well, the foreigner is sure to be dropped.

The purpose of this volume does not require of us a minute statistical statement of the present attainments of New Japan. Such information may be procured from Henry Norman's "Real Japan," Ransome's "Japan in Transition," and Newton's "Japan: Country, Court, and People." It is enough for us to realize that Japan has wholly abandoned or profoundly modified all the external features of her old, her distinctively Oriental civilization and has replaced them by Occidental features. In government, she is no longer arbitrary, autocratic, and hereditary, but constitutional and representative. Town, provincial, and national legislative assemblies are established, and in fairly good working order, all over the land. The old feudal customs have been replaced by well codified laws, which are on the whole faithfully administered according to Occidental methods. Examination by torture has been abolished. The perfect Occidentalization of the army, and the creation of an efficient navy, are facts fully demonstrated to the world. The limited education of the few—— and in exclusively Chinese classics—has given place to popular education. Common schools number over 30,000, taught by about 100,000 teachers (4278 being women), having over 4,500,000 pupils (over 1,500,000 being girls). The school accommodation is insufficient; it is said that 30,000 additional teachers are needed at once. Middle and high schools throughout the land are rejecting nearly one-half of the student applicants for lack of accommodation.

Feudal isolation, repression, and seclusion have given way to free travel, free speech, and a free press. Newspapers, magazines, and books pour forth from the universal printing press in great profusion. Twenty dailies issue in the course of a year over a million copies each, while two of them circulate 24,000,000 and 21,000,000 copies, respectively.

Personal, political, and religious liberty has been practically secure now for over two decades, guaranteed by the constitution, and enforced by the courts.

Chinese medical practice has largely been replaced by that from the West, although many of the ignorant classes still prefer the old methods. The government enforces Western hygienic principles in all public matters, with the result that the national health has improved and the population is growing at an alarming rate. While in 1872 the people numbered 33,000,000, in 1898 they numbered 45,000,000. The general scale of living for the common people has also advanced conspicuously. Meat shops are now common throughout the land—a thing unknown in pre-Meiji times—and rice, which used to be the luxury of the wealthy few, has become the staple necessity of the many.

Postal and telegraph facilities are quite complete. Macadamized roads and well-built railroads have replaced the old footpaths, except in the most mountainous districts. Factories of many kinds are appearing in every town and city. Business corporations, banks, etc., which numbered only thirty-four so late as 1864 are now numbered by the thousand, and trade flourishes as in no previous period of Japanese history. Instead of being a country of farmers and soldiers, Japan is to-day a land of farmers and merchants. Wealth is growing apace. International commerce, too, has sprung up and expanded phenomenally. Japanese merchant steamers may now be seen in every part of the world.

All these changes have taken place within about three decades, and so radical have they been,—so productive of new life in Japan,—that some have urged the re-writing of Japanese history, making the first year of Meiji (1868) the year one of Japan, instead of reckoning from the year in which Jimmu Tenno is said to have ascended the throne, 2560 years ago (B.C. 660).

The way in which Japanese regard the transformations produced by the "restoration" of the present Emperor, upon the overthrow of the "Bakufu," or "Curtain Government," may be judged from the following graphic paragraph from *The Far East*:

"The Restoration of Meiji was indeed the greatest of revolutions that this island empire ever underwent. Its magic wand left nothing untouched and unchanged. It was the Restoration that overthrew the Tokugawa Shogunate, which reigned supreme for over two centuries and a half. It was the Restoration that brought us face to face with the Occidentals. It was the Restoration that pulled the demigods of the Feudal lords down to the level of the commoners. It was the Restoration that deprived the samurai of their fiefs and reduced them to penury. It was the Restoration that taught the people to build their houses of bricks and stones and to construct ships and bridges of iron instead of wood. It was the Restoration that informed us that eclipses and comets are not to be feared, and that earthquakes are not caused by a huge cat-fish in the bottom of the earth. It was the Restoration that taught the people to use the "drum-backing" thunder as their messenger, and to make use of the railroad instead of the palanquin. It was the Restoration that set the earth in motion, and proved that there is no rabbit in the moon. It was the Restoration that bestowed on Socrates and Aristotle the chairs left vacant by Confucius and Mencius. It was the Restoration that let Shakspere and Goethe take the place of Bakin and Chikamatsu. It was the Restoration that deprived the people of the swords and topnots. In short, after the Restoration a great change took place in administration, in art, in science, in literature, in language spoken and written, in taste, in custom, in the mode of living, nay in everything" (p. 541).

A natural outcome of the Restoration is the exuberant patriotism that is so characteristic a feature of New Japan. The very term "ai-koku-shin" is a new creation, almost as new as the thing. This word is an incidental proof of the general correctness of the contention of this chapter that true nationality is a recent product in Japan. The term, literally translated, is "love-country heart"; but the point for us to notice particularly is the term for country, "koku"; this word has never before meant the country as a whole, but only the territory of a clan. If I wish to ask a Japanese what part of Japan is his native home, I must use this word. And if a Japanese wishes to ask me which of the foreign lands I am a native of, he must use the same word. The truth is that Old Japan did not have any common word corresponding to the English term, "My country." In ancient times, this could only mean, "My clan-territory." But with the passing away of the clans the old word has taken on a new significance. The new word, "ai-koku-shin," refers not to love of clan, but to love of the whole nation. The conception of national unity has at last seized upon the national mind and heart, and is giving the people an enthusiasm for the nation, regardless of the parts, which they never before knew. Japanese patriotism has only in this generation come to self-consciousness. This leads it to many a strange freak. It is vociferous and imperious, and often very impractical and Chauvinistic. It frequently takes the form of uncompromising disdain for the foreigner, and the most absolute loyalty to the Emperor of Japan; it demands the utmost respect of expression in regard to him and the form of government he has graciously granted the nation. The slightest hint or indirect suggestion of defect or ignorance, or even of limitation, is most vehemently resented.

A few illustrations of the above statements from recent experience will not be out of place. In August, 1891, the Minister of Education, Mr. Y. Osaki, criticising the tendency in Japan to pay undue respect to moneyed men, said, in the course of a long speech, "You Japanese worship money even more reverently than the Americans do. If you had a republic as they have, I believe you would nominate an Iwazaki or a Mitsui to be president, whereas they don't think of nominating a Vanderbilt or a Gould." It was not long before a storm was raging around his head because of this reference to a republican form of government as a possibility in Japan. The storm became so fierce that he was finally compelled to resign his post and retire, temporarily, from political life.

In October, 1898, the High Council of Education was required to consider various questions regarding the conduct of the educational department after the New Treaties should come into force. The most important question was whether foreigners should be allowed to have a part in the education of Japanese youth. The general argument, and that which prevailed, was that this should not be allowed lest the patriotism of the children be weakened. So far as appears but one voice was raised for a more liberal policy. Mr. Y. Kamada maintained that "patriotism in Japan was the outcome of foreign intercourse. Patriotism, that is to say, love of country—not merely of fief—and readiness to sacrifice everything for its sake, was a product of the Meiji era."

In 1891 a teacher in the Kumamoto Boys' School gave expression to the thought in a public address that, as all mankind are brothers, the school should stand for the principle of universal brotherhood and universal good-will to men. This expression of universalism was so obnoxious to the patriotic spirit of so large a number of the people of Kumamoto Ken, or Province, that the governor required the school to dismiss that teacher. There is to-day a strong party in Japan which makes "Japanism" their cry; they denounce all expressions of universal good-will as proofs of deficiency of patriotism. There are not wanting those who see through the shallowness of such views and who vigorously oppose and condemn such narrow patriotism. Yet the fact that it exists to-day with such force must be noted and its natural explanation, too, must not be forgotten. It is an indication of self-conscious nationality.

That this love of country, even this conception of country, is a modern thing will appear from two further facts. Until modern times there was no such thing as a national flag. The flaming Sun on a field of white came into existence as a national flag only in 1859. The use of the Sun as the symbol for the Emperor has been in vogue since 700 A.D., the custom having been adopted from China. "When in 1859 a national flag corresponding to those of Europe became necessary, the Sun Banner naturally stepped into the vacant place."[A]

The second fact is the recent origin of the festival known as "Kigensetsu." It occurs on February 11 and celebrates the alleged accession of Jimmu Tenno, the first Emperor of Japan, to the throne 2560 years ago (660 B.C.). The festival itself, however, was instituted by Imperial decree ten years ago (1890).

The transformation which has come over Japan in a single generation requires interpretation. Is the change real or superficial? Is the new social order "a borrowed trumpery garment, which will soon be rent by violent revolutions," according to the eminent student of racial psychology, Professor Le Bon, or is it of "a solid nature" according to the firm belief of Mr. Stanford Ransome, one of the latest writers on Japan?

This is the problem that will engage our attention more or less directly throughout this work. We shall give our chief thought to the nature and development of Japanese racial characteristics, believing that this alone gives the light needed for the solution of the problem.[B]

III
THE PROBLEM OF PROGRESS

What constitutes progress? And what is the true criterion for its measurement? In adopting Western methods of life and thought, is Japan advancing or receding? The simplicity of the life of the common people, their freedom from fashions that fetter the Occidental, their independence of furniture in their homes, their few wants and fewer necessities—these, when contrasted with the endless needs and demands of an Occidental, are accepted by some as evidences of a higher stage of civilization than prevails in the West.

The hedonistic criterion of progress is the one most commonly adopted in considering the question as to whether Japan is the gainer or the loser by her rapid abandonment of old ways and ideas and by her equally rapid adoption of Western ones in their place. Yet this appeal to happiness seems to me a misleading because vague, if not altogether false, standard of progress. Those who use it insist that the people of Japan are losing their former happiness under the stress of new conditions. Now there can be no doubt that during the "Kyu-han jidai," the times before the coming in of Western waves of life, the farmers were a simple, unsophisticated people; living from month to month with little thought or anxiety. They may be said to have been happy. The samurai who lived wholly on the bounty of the daimyo led of course a tranquil life, at least so far as anxiety or toil for daily rice and fish was concerned. As the fathers had lived and fought and died, so did the sons. To a large extent the community had all things in common; for although the lord lived in relative luxury, yet in such small communities there never was the great difference between classes that we find in modern Europe and America. As a rule the people were fed, if there was food. The socialistic principle was practically universal. Especially was emphasis laid on kinship. As a result, save among the outcast classes, the extremes of poverty did not exist.

Were we to rest our inquiries at this point, we might say that in truth the Japanese had attained the summit of progress; that nothing further could be asked. But pushing our way further, we find that the peace and quiet of the ordinary classes of society were accompanied by many undesirable features.

Prominent among them was the domineering spirit of the military class. They alone laid claim to personal rights, and popular stories are full of the free and furious ways in which they used their swords. The slightest offense by one of the swordless men would be paid for by a summary act of the two-sworded swashbucklers, while beggars and farmers were cut down without compunction, sometimes simply to test a sword. In describing those times one man said to me, "They used to cut off the heads of the common people as farmers cut off the head of the daikon" (a variety of giant radish). I have frequently asked my Japanese friends and acquaintances, whether, in view of the increasing difficulties of life under the new conditions, the country would not like to return to ancient times and customs. But none have been ready to give me an affirmative reply. On detailed questioning I have always found that the surly, domineering methods, the absolutism of the rulers, and the defenselessness of the people against unjust arbitrary superiors would not be submitted to by a people that has once tasted the joy arising from individual rights and freedom and the manhood that comes from just laws for all.

A striking feature of those Japanese who are unchanged by foreign ways is their obsequious manner toward superiors and officials. The lordly and oftentimes ruthless manner of the rulers has naturally cowed the subject. Whenever the higher nobility traveled, the common people were commanded to fall on the ground in obeisance and homage. Failure to do so was punishable with instant death at the hands of the retainers who accompanied the lord. During my first stay in Kumamoto I was surprised that farmers, coming in from the country on horseback, meeting me as I walked, invariably got down from their horses, unfastened the handkerchiefs from their heads, and even took off their spectacles if there were nothing else removable. These were signs of respect given to all in authority. Where my real status began to be generally known, these signs of politeness gave place to rude staring. It is difficult for the foreigner to appreciate the extremes of the high-handed and the obsequious spirit which were developed by the ancient form of government. Yet it is comparatively easy to distinguish between the evidently genuine humility of the non-military classes and the studied deference of the dominant samurai.

Another feature of the old order of things was the emptiness of the lives of the people. Education was rare. Limited to the samurai, who composed but a fraction of the population, it was by no means universal even among them. And such education as they had was confined to the Chinese classics. Although there were schools in connection with some of the temples, the people as a whole did not learn to read or write. These were accomplishments for the nobility and men of leisure. The thoughts of the people were circumscribed by the narrow world in which they lived, and this allowed but an occasional glimpse of other clans through war or a chance traveler. For, in those times, freedom of travel was not generally allowed. Each man, as a rule, lived and labored and died where he was born. The military classes had more freedom. But when we contrast the breadth of thought and outlook enjoyed by the nation to-day, through newspapers and magazines, with the outlook and knowledge of even the most progressive and learned of those of ancient times, how contracted do their lives appear!

A third feature of former times is the condition of women during those ages. Eulogizers of Old Japan not only seem to forget that working classes existed then, but also that women, constituting half the population, were essential to the existence of the nation. Though allowing more freedom than was given to women in other Oriental nations, Japan did not grant such liberty as is essential to the full development of her powers. "Woman is a man's plaything" expresses a view still held in Japan. "Woman's sole duty is the bearing and rearing of children for her husband" is the dominant idea that has determined her place in the family and in the state for hundreds of years. That she has any independent interest or value as a human being has not entered into national conception. "The way in which they are treated by the men has hitherto been such as might cause a pang to any generous European heart.... A woman's lot is summed up in what is termed 'the three obediences,' obedience, while yet unmarried, to a father; obedience, when married, to a husband; obedience, when widowed, to a son. At the present moment the greatest duchess or marchioness in the land is still her husband's drudge. She fetches and carries for him, bows down humbly in the hall when my lord sallies forth on his good pleasure."[G] "The Greater Learning for Women," by Ekken Kaibara (1630-1714), an eminent Japanese moralist, is the name of a treatise on woman's duties which sums up the ideas common in Japan upon this subject. For two hundred years or more it has been used as a text-book in the training of girls. It enjoins such abject submission of the wife to her husband, to her parents-in-law, and to her other kindred by marriage, as no self-respecting woman of Western lands could for a moment endure. Let me prove this through a few quotations.

"A woman should look on her husband as if he were Heaven itself and never weary of thinking how she may yield to her husband, and thus escape celestial castigation." "Woman must form no friendships and no intimacy, except when ordered to do so by her parents or by the middleman. Even at the peril of her life, must she harden her heart like a rock or metal, and observe the rules of propriety." "A woman has no particular lord. She must look to her husband as her lord andmust serve him with all reverence and worship, not despising or thinking lightly of him. The great life-long duty of a woman is obedience.... When the husband issues his instructions, the wife must never disobey them.... Should her husband be roused to anger at any time, she must obey him, with fear and trembling." Not one word in all these many and specific instructions hints at love and affection. That which to Western ears is the sweetest word in the English language, the foundation of happiness in the home, the only true bond between husband and wife, parents and children—LOVE—does not once appear in this the ideal instruction for Japanese women.

Even to this day divorce is the common occurrence in Japan. According to Confucius there are seven grounds of divorce: disobedience, barrenness, lewd conduct, jealousy, leprosy or any other foul or incurable disease, too much talking, and thievishness. "In plain English, a man may send away his wife whenever he gets tired of her."

Were the man's duties to the wife and to her parents as minutely described and insisted on as are those of the wife to the husband and to his parents, this "Greater Learning for Women" would not seem so deficient; but such is not the case. The woman's rights are few, yet she bears her lot with marvelous patience. Indeed, she has acquired a most attractive and patient and modest behavior despite, or is it because of, centuries of well-nigh tyrannical treatment from the male sex. In some important respects the women of Japan are not to be excelled by those of any other land. But that this lot has been a happy one I cannot conceive it possible for a European, who knows the meaning of love or home, to contend. The single item of one divorce for every three marriages tells a tale of sorrow and heartache that is sad to contemplate. Nor does this include those separations where tentative marriage takes place with a view to learning whether the parties can endure living together. I have known several such cases. Neither does this take account of the great number of concubines that may be found in the homes of the higher classes. A concubine often makes formal divorce quite superfluous.

I by no means contend that the women of Old Japan were all and always miserable. There was doubtless much happiness and even family joy; affection between husband and wife could assuredly have been found in numberless cases. But the hardness of life as a whole, the low position held by woman in her relations to man, her lack of legal rights,[1] and her menial position, justify the assertion that there was much room for improvement.

These three conspicuous features of the older life in Japan help us to reach a clear conception as to what constitutes progress. We may say that true progress consists in that continuous, though slow, transformation of the structure of society which, while securing its more thorough organization, brings to each individual the opportunity of a larger, richer, and fuller life, a life which increasingly calls forth his latent powers and capacities. In other words, progress is a growing organization of society, accompanied by a growing liberty of the individual resulting in richness and fullness of life. It is not primarily a question of unreflecting happiness, but a question of the wide development of manhood and womanhood. Both men and women have as yet unmeasured latent capacities, which demand a certain liberty, accompanied by responsibilities and cares, in order for their development. Intellectual education and a wide horizon are likewise essential to the production of such manhood and womanhood. In the long run this is seen to bring a deeper and a more lasting happiness than was possible to the undeveloped man or woman.

The question of progress is confused and put on a wrong footing when the consciousness of happiness or unhappiness, is made the primary test. The happiness of the child is quite apart from that of the adult. Regardless of distressing circumstances, the child is able to laugh and play, and this because he is a child; a child in his ignorance of actual life, and in his inability to perceive the true conditions in which he lives. Not otherwise, I take it, was the happiness of the vast majority in Old Japan. Theirs was the happiness of ignorance and simple, undeveloped lives. Accustomed to tyranny, they did not think of rebellion against it. Familiar with brutality and suffering, they felt nothing of its shame and inhumanity. The sight of decapitated bodies, the torture of criminals, the despotism of husbands, the cringing obedience of the ruled, the haughtiness of the rulers, the life of hard toil and narrow outlook, were all so usual that no thought of escape from such an order of society ever suggested itself to those who endured it.

From time to time wise and just rulers did indeed strive to introduce principles of righteousness into their methods of government; but these men formed the exception, not the rule. They were individuals and not the system under which the people lived. It was always a matter of chance whether or not such men were at the head of affairs, for the people did not dream of the possibility of having any voice in their selection. The structure of society was and always had been absolute militarism. Even under the most benevolent rulers the use of cruel torture, not only on convicted criminals, but on all suspected of crime, was customary. Those in authority might personally set a good example, but they did not modify the system. They owned not only the soil but practically the laborers also, for these could not leave their homes in search of others that were better. They were serfs, if not slaves, and the system did not tend to raise the standard of life or education, of manhood or womanhood among the people. The happiness of the people in such times was due in part to their essential inhumanity of heart and lack of sympathy with suffering and sorrow. Each individual bore his own sorrow and pain alone. The community, as such, did not distress itself over individuals who suffered. Sympathy, in its full meaning, was unknown in Old Japan. The barbarous custom of casting out the leper from the home, to wander a lonely exile, living on the charity of strangers, is not unknown even to this day. We are told that in past times the "people were governed by such strong aversion to the sight of sickness that travelers were often left to die by the roadside from thirst, hunger, or disease; and householders even went the length of thrusting out of doors and abandoning to utter destitution servants who suffered from chronic maladies." So universal was this heartlessness that the government at one time issued proclamations against the practices it allowed. "Whenever an epidemic occurred the number of deaths was enormous." Seven men of the outcast, "the Eta," class were authoritatively declared equal in value to one common man. Beggars were technically called "hi-nin," "not men."

Those who descant on the happiness of Old Japan commit the great error of overlooking all these sad features of life, and of fixing their attention exclusively on the one feature of the childlike, not to say childish, lightness of heart of the common people. Such writers are thus led to pronounce the past better than the present time. They also overlook the profound happiness and widespread prosperity of the present era. Trade, commerce, manufactures, travel, the freest of intercommunication, newspapers, and international relations, have brought into life a richness and a fullness that were then unknown. But in addition, the people now enjoy a security of personal interests, a possession of personal rights and property, and a personal liberty, that make life far more worthy and profoundly enjoyable, even while they bring responsibilities and duties and not a few anxieties. This explains the fact that no Japanese has expressed to me the slightest desire to abandon the present and return to the life and conditions of Old Japan.

Let me repeat, therefore, with all possible emphasis, that the problem of progress is not primarily one of increasing light-heartedness, pure and simple, nor yet a problem of racial unification or of political centralization; it is rather a problem of so developing the structure of society that the individual may have the fullest opportunity for development.

The measure of progress is not the degree of racial unification, of political centralization, or of unreflective happiness, but rather the degree and the extent of individual personality. Racial unification, political centralization, and increasing happiness are in the attainment of progress, but they are not to be viewed as sufficient ends. Personality, can alone be that end. The wide development of personality, therefore, is at once the goal and the criterion of progress.

IV
THE METHOD OF PROGRESS

Progress as an ideal is quite modern in its origin. For although the ancients were progressing, they did it unconsciously, blindly, stumbling on it by chance, forced to it, as we have seen, by the struggle for existence. True of the ancient civilizations of Europe and Western Asia and Africa, this is emphatically true of the Orient. Here, so far from seeking to progress, the avowed aim has been not to progress; the set purpose has been to do as the fathers did; to follow their example even in customs and rites whose meaning has been lost in the obscurity of the past. This blind adherence was the boast of those who called themselves religious. They strove to fulfill their duties to their ancestors.

Under such conditions how was progress possible? And how has it come to pass that, ruled by this ideal until less than fifty years ago, Japan is now facing quite the other way? The passion of the nation to-day is to make the greatest possible progress in every direction. Here is an anomaly, a paradox; progress made in spite of its rejection; and, recently, a total volte-face. How shall we explain this paradox?

In our chapter on the Principles of National Evolution,[1] we see that the first step in progress was made through the development of enlarging communities by means of extending boundaries and hardening customs. We see that, on reaching this stage, the great problem was so to break the "cake of custom" as to give liberty to individuals whereby to secure the needful variations. We do not consider how this was to be accomplished. We merely show that, if further progress was to be made, it could only be through the development of the individualistic principle to which we give the more exact name communo-individualism. This problem as to how the "cake of custom" is successfully broken must now engage our attention.

Mr. Bagehot contends that this process consisted, as a matter of history, in the establishment of government by discussion. Matters of principle came to be talked over; the desirability of this or that measure was submitted to the people for their approval or disapproval. This method served to stimulate definite and practical thought on a wide scale; it substituted the thinking of the many for the thinking of the few; it stimulated independent thinking and consequently independent action. This is, however, but another way of saying that it stimulated variation. A government whose action was determined after wide discussion would be peculiarly fitted to take advantage of all useful variations of ideas and practice. Experience shows, he continues, that the difficulty of developing a "cake of custom" is far more easily surmounted than that of developing government by discussion; i.e., that it is far less difficult to develop communalism than communo-individualism. The family of arrested civilizations, of which China and India and Japan, until recent times, are examples, was caught in the net of what had once been the source of their progress. The tyranny of their laws and customs was such that all individual variations were nipped in the bud. They failed to progress because they failed to develop variations. And they failed in this because they did not have government by discussion.

No one will dispute the importance of Mr. Bagehot's, contribution to this subject. But it may be doubted whether he has pointed out the full reason for the difficulty of breaking the "cake of custom" or manifested the real root of progress. To attain progress in the full sense, not merely of an oligarchy or a caste, but of the whole people, there must not only be government by discussion, but the responsibilities of the government must be snared more or less fully by all the governed.

History, however, shows that this cannot take place until a conception of intrinsic manhood and womanhood has arisen, a conception which emphasizes their infinite and inherent worth. This conception is not produced by government by discussion, while government by discussion is the necessary consequence of the wide acceptance of this conception. It is therefore the real root of progress.

As I look over the history of the Orient, I find no tendency to discover the inherent worth of man or to introduce the principle of government by discussion. Left to themselves, I see no probability that any of these nations would ever have been able to break the thrall of their customs, and to reach that stage of development in which common individuals could be trusted with a large measure of individual liberty. Though I can conceive that Japan might have secured a thorough-going political centralization under the old *régime*, I cannot see that

that centralization would have been accompanied by growing liberty for the individual or by such constitutional rights for the common man as he enjoys to-day. Whatever progress she might have made in the direction of nationality it would still have been a despotism. The common man would have remained a helpless and hopeless slave. Art might have prospered; the people might have remained simple-minded and relatively contented. But they could not have attained that freedom and richness of life, that personality, which we saw in our last chapter to be the criterion and goal of true progress.

If the reader judges the above contention correct and agrees with the writer that the conception of the inherent value of a human being could not arise spontaneously in Japan, he will conclude that the progress of Japan depended on securing this important conception from without. Exactly this has taken place. By her thorough-going abandonment of the feudal social order and adoption of the constitutional and representative government of Christendom, whether she recognizes it or not, she has accepted the principles of the inherent worth of manhood and womanhood, as well as government by discussion. Japan has thus, by imitation rather than by origination, entered on the path of endless progress.

So important, however, is the step recently taken that further analysis of this method of progress is desirable for its full comprehension. We have already noted quite briefly[1] how Japan was supplied by the West with the ideal of national unity and the material instruments essential to its attainment. In connection with the high development of the nation as a whole, these two elements of progress, the ideal and the material, need further consideration.

We note in the first place that both begin with imitation, but if progress is to be real and lasting, both must grow to independence.

The first and by far the most important is the psychical, the introduction of new ideas. So long as the old, familiar ideas hold sway over the mind of a nation, there is little or no stimulus to comparison and discussion. Stagnation is well-nigh complete. But let new ideas be so introduced as to compel attention and comprehension, and the mind spontaneously awakes to wonderful activity. The old stagnation is no longer possible. Discussion is started; and in the end something must take place, even if the new ideas are not accepted wholly or even in part. But they will not gain attention if presented simply in the abstract, unconnected with real life. They must bring evidence that, if accepted and lived, they will be of practical use, that they will give added power to the nation.

Exactly this took place in 1854 when Admiral Perry demanded entrance to Japan. The people suddenly awoke from their sleep of two and a half centuries to find that new nations had arisen since they closed their eyes, nations among which new sets of ideas had been at work, giving them a power wholly unknown to the Orient and even mysterious to it. Those ideas were concerned, not alone with the making of guns, the building of ships, the invention of machinery, the taming and using of the forces of nature, but also with methods of government and law, with strange notions, too, about religion and duty, about the family and the individual, which the foreigners said were of inestimable value and importance. It needed but a few years of intercourse with Western peoples to convince the most conservative that unless the Japanese themselves could gain the secret of their power, either by adopting their weapons or their civilization, they themselves must fade away before the stronger nations. The need of self-preservation was the first great stimulus that drove new thoughts into unwilling brains.

There can be no doubt that the Japanese were right in this analysis of the situation. Had they insisted on maintaining their old methods of national life and social order and ancient customs, there can be no doubt as to the result. Africa and India in recent decades and China and Korea in the most recent years tell the story all too clearly. Those who know the course of treaty conferences and armed collisions, as at Shimonoseki and Kagoshima between Japan and the foreign nations, have no doubt that Japan, divided into clans and persisting in her love of feudalism, would long since have become the territory of some European Power. She was saved by the possession of a remarkable combination of national characteristics,—the powers of observation, of appreciation, and of imitation. In a word, her sensitiveness to her environment and her readiness to respond to it proved to be her salvation.

23

But the point on which I wish to lay special emphasis is that the prime element of the form in which the deliverance came was through the acquisition of numerous new ideas. These were presented by persons who thoroughly believed in them and who admittedly had a power not possessed by the Japanese themselves. Though unable to originate these ideas, the Japanese yet proved themselves capable of understanding and appreciating them—in a measure at least. They were at first attracted to that which related chiefly to the externals of civilization, to that which would contribute immediately to the complete political centralization of the nation. With great rapidity they adopted Western ideas about warfare and weapons. They sent their young men abroad to study the civilization of the foreign nations. At great expense they also employed many foreigners to teach them in their own land the things they wished to learn. Thus have the Japanese mastered so rapidly the details of those ideas which, less than fifty years ago, were not only strange but odious to them.

Under their influence, the conditions which history shows to be the most conducive to the continuous growth of civilization have been definitely accepted and adopted by the people, namely, popular rights, the liberty of individuals to differ from the past so far as this does not interfere with national unity, and the direct responsibility and relation of each individual to the nation without any mediating group. These rights and liberties are secured to the individual by a constitution and by laws enacted by representative legislatures. Government by discussion has been fairly inaugurated.

During these years of change the effort has been to leave the old social order as undisturbed as possible. For example, it was hoped that the reorganization of the military and naval forces of the Empire would be sufficient without disturbing the feudal order and without abolishing the feudal states. But this was soon found ineffectual. For a time it was likewise thought that the adoption of Western methods of government might be made without disturbing the old religious ideas and without removing the edicts against Christianity. But experience soon showed that the old civilization was a unit. No part could be vitally modified without affecting the whole structure. Having knocked over one block in the long row that made up their feudal social order, it was found that each successive block was touched and fell, until nothing was left standing as before. It was found also that the old ideas of education, of travel, of jurisprudence, of torture and punishment, of social ranks, of the relation of the individual to the state, of the state to the family, and of religion to the family, were more or less defective and unsuited to the new civilization. Before this new movement all obstructive ideas, however, sanctioned by antiquity, have had to give way. The Japanese of to-day look, as it were, upon a new earth and a new heaven. Those of forty years ago would be amazed, not only at the enormous changes in the externals, life and government, but also at the transformation which has overtaken every element of the older civilization. Putting it rather strongly, it is now not the son who obeys the father, but the father the son. The rulers no longer command the people, but the people command the rulers. The people do not now toil to support the state; but the state toils to protect the people.

Whether the incoming of these new ideas and practices be thought to constitute progress or not will depend on one's view of the aim of life. If this be as maintained in the previous chapter, then surely the transformation of Japan must be counted progress. That, however, to which I call attention is the fact that the essential requisite of progress is the attainment of new ideas, whatever be their source. Japan has not only taken up a great host of these, but in doing so she has adopted a social structure to stimulate the continuous production of new ideas, through the development of individuality. She is thus in the true line of continuously progressive evolution. Imitating the stronger nations, she has introduced into her system the life-giving blood of free discussion, popular education, and universal individual rights and liberty. In a word, she has begun to be an individualistic nation. She has introduced a social order fitted to a wide development of personality.

The importance of the second line of progress, the physical, would seem to be too obvious to call for any detailed consideration. But so much has been said by both graceful and able writers on Japan as to the advantages she enjoys from her simple non-mechanical civilization, and the mistake she is making in adopting the mechanical civilization of the

West, that it may not be amiss to dwell for a few moments upon it. I wish to show that the second element of progress consists in the *increasing use of mechanisms*.

The enthusiastic admirer of Japan hardly finds words wherewith sufficiently to praise the simplicity of her pre-Meiji civilization. No furniture brings confusion to the room; no machinery distresses the ear with its groanings or the eye with its unsightliness. No factories blacken the sky with smoke. No trains screeching through the towns and cities disturb sleepers and frighten babies. The simple bed on the floor, the straw sandal on the foot, wooden chopsticks in place of knives and forks, the small variety of foods and of cooking utensils, the simple, homespun cotton clothing, the fascinating homes, so small and neat and clean—in truth all that pertains to Old Japan finds favor in the eyes of the enthusiastic admirer from the Occident. One such writer, in an elaborate paper intended to set forth the superiority of the original Japanese to the Occidental civilization, uses the following language: "Ability to live without furniture, without impedimenta, with the least possible amount of neat clothing, shows more than the advantage held by the Japanese race in the struggle of life; it shows also the real character of some of the weaknesses in our own civilization. It forces reflection upon the useless multiplicity of our daily wants. We must have meat and bread and butter; glass windows and fire; hats, white shirts, and woolen underwear; boots and shoes; trunks, bags, and boxes; bedsteads, mattresses, sheets, and blankets; all of which a Japanese can do without, and is really better off without."[G] Surely one finds much of truth in this, and there is no denying the charm of the simpler civilization, but the closing phrase of the quotation is the assumption without discussion of the disputed point. Are the Japanese really better off without these implements of Western civilization? Evidently they themselves do not think so. For, in glancing through the list as given by the writer quoted, one realizes the extent of Japanese adoption of these Western devices. Hardly an article but is used in Japan, and certainly with the supposition of the purchaser that it adds either to his health or his comfort. In witness are the hundreds of thousands of straw hats, the glass windows everywhere, and the meat-shops in each town and city of the Empire. The charm of a foreign fashion is not sufficient explanation for the rapidly spreading use of foreign inventions.

That there are no useless or even evil features in our Western civilization is not for a moment contended. The stiff starched shirt may certainly be asked to give an account of itself and justify its continued existence, if it can. But I think the proposition is capable of defense that the vast majority of the implements of our Occidental civilization have their definite place and value, either in contributing directly to the comfort and happiness of their possessor, or in increasing his health and strength and general mental and physical power. What is it that makes the Occidental longer-lived than the Japanese? Why is he healthier? Why is he more intelligent? Why is he a more developed personality? Why are his children more energetic? Or, reversing the questions, why has the population of Japan been increasing with leaps and bounds since the introduction of Western civilization and medical science? Why is the rising generation so free from pockmarks? Why is the number of the blind steadily diminishing? Why are mechanisms multiplying so rapidly—the jinrikisha, the railroads, the roads, the waterworks and sewers, the chairs, the tables, the hats and umbrellas, lamps, clocks, glass windows and shoes? A hundred similar questions might be asked, to which no definite answers are needful.

Further discussion of details seems unnecessary. Yet the full significance of this point can hardly be appreciated without a perception of the great principle that underlies it. The only way in which man has become and continues to be increasingly superior to animals is in his use of mechanisms. The animal does by brute force what man accomplishes by various devices. The inventiveness of different races differs vastly. But everywhere, the most advanced are the most powerful. Take the individual man of the more developed race and separate him from his tools and machines, and it is doubtless true that he cannot in some selected points compete with an individual of a less developed race. But let ten thousand men of the higher development compete with ten thousand of the lower, each using the mechanisms under his control, and can there be any doubt as to which is the superior?

In other words, the method of human progress consists, in no small degree, in the progressive mastery of nature, first through understanding her and then through the use of her immense forces by means of suitable mechanisms. All the machines and furniture, and tools and clothing, and houses and canned foods, and shoes and boots, and railroads and telegraph lines, and typewriters and watches, and the ten thousand other so-called "impedimenta" of the Occidental civilization are but devices whereby Western man has sought to increase his health, his wealth, his knowledge, his comfort, his independence, his capacity of travel—in a word, his well-being. Through these mechanisms he masters nature. He extracts a rich living from nature; he annihilates time and space; he defies the storms; he tunnels the mountains; he extracts precious ores and metals from the rock-ribbed hills; with a magic touch he loosens the grip of the elements and makes them surrender their gold, their silver, and, more precious still, their iron; with these he builds his spacious cities and parks, his railroads and ocean steamers; he travels the whole world around, fearing neither beast nor alien man; all are subject to his command and will. He investigates and knows the constitution of stellar worlds no less than that of the world in which he lives. By his instruments he explores the infinite depths of heaven and the no less infinite depths of the microscopic world. All these reviled "impedimenta" thus bring to the race that has them a wealth of life both physical and psychical, practical and ideal, that is otherwise unattainable. By them he gains and gives external expression to the reality of his inner nature, his freedom, his personality. True, instead of bringing health and long life, knowledge and deep enjoyment, they may become the means of bitterest curses. But the lesson to learn from this fact is how to use these powers aright, not how to forbid their use altogether. They are not to be branded as hindrances to progress.

The defect of Occidental civilization to-day is hot its multiplicity of machinery, but the defective view that still blinds the eyes of the multitude as to the true nature and the legitimate goal of progress. Individual, selfish happiness is still the ideal of too many men and women to permit of the ideal which carries the Golden Rule into the markets and factories, into the politics of parties and nations, which is essential to the attainment of the highest progress. But no one who casts his eyes over the centuries of struggle and effort through which man has been slowly working his way upward from the rank of a beast to that of a man, can doubt that progress has been made. The worth of character has been increasingly seen and its possession desired. The true end of effort and development was never more clear than it is at the close of the nineteenth century. Never before were the conditions of progress so bright, not only for the favored few in one or two lands, but for the multitudes the world over. Isolation and separation have passed from this world forever. Free social intercourse between the nations permits wide dissemination of ideas and their application to practical life in the form of social organization and mechanical invention. This makes it possible for nations more or less backward in social and civilizational development to gain in a relatively short time the advantages won by advanced nations through ages of toil and under favoring circumstances. Nation thus stimulates nation, each furnishing the other with important variations in ideas, customs, institutions, and mechanisms resulting from long-continued divergent evolution. The advantages slowly gained by advanced peoples speedily accrues through social heredity to any backward race really desiring to enter the social heritage.

Thus does the paradox of Japan's recent progress become thoroughly intelligible.

V
JAPANESE SENSITIVENESS TO ENVIRONMENT

With this chapter we begin a more detailed study of Japanese social and psychic evolution. We shall take up the various characteristics of the race and seek to account for them, showing their origin in the peculiar nature of the social order which so long prevailed in Japan. This is a study of Japanese psychogenesis. The question to which we shall continually return is whether or not the characteristic under consideration is inherent and congenital and therefore inevitable. Not only our interpretation of Japanese evolution, past, present, and future, but also our understanding of the essential nature of social evolution in general, depends upon the answer to this question.

We naturally begin with that characteristic of Japanese nature which would seem to be more truly congenital than any other to be mentioned later. I refer to their sensitiveness to environment. More quickly than most races do the Japanese seem to perceive and adapt themselves to changed conditions.

The history of the past thirty years is a prolonged illustration of this characteristic. The desire to imitate foreign nations was not a real reason for the overthrow of feudalism, but there was, rather, a more or less conscious feeling, rapidly pervading the whole people, that the feudal system would be unable to maintain the national integrity. As intimated, the matter was not so much reasoned out as felt. But such a vast illustration is more difficult to appreciate than some individual instances, of which I have noted several.

During a conversation with Drs. Forsythe and Dale, of Cambridge, England, I asked particularly as to their experience with the Japanese students who had been there to study. They both remarked on the fact that all Japanese students were easily influenced by those with whom they customarily associated; so much so that, within a short time, they acquired not only the cut of coats and trousers, but also the manner and accent, of those with whom they lived. It was amusing, they said, to see what transformations were wrought in those who went to the Continent for their long vacations. From France they returned with marked French manners and tones and clothes, while from Germany they brought the distinctive marks of German stiffness in manner and general bearing. It was noted as still more curious that the same student would illustrate both variations, provided he spent one summer in Germany and another in France.

Japanese sensitiveness is manifested in many unexpected ways. An observant missionary lady once remarked that she had often wondered how such unruly, self-willed children as grow up under Japanese training, or its lack, finally become such respectable members of society. She concluded that instead of being punished out of their misbehaviors they were laughed out of them. The children are constantly told that if they do so and so they will be laughed at—a terrible thing.

The fear of ridicule has thus an important sociological function in maintaining ethical standards. Its power may be judged by the fact that in ancient times when a samurai gave his note to return a borrowed sum, the only guarantee affixed was the permission to be laughed at in public in case of failure. The Japanese young man who is making a typewritten copy of these pages for me says that, when still young, he heard an address to children which he still remembers. The speaker asked what the most fearful thing in the world was. Many replies were given by the children—"snakes," "wild beasts," "fathers," "gods," "ghosts," "demons," "Satan," "hell," etc. These were admitted to be fearful, but the speaker told the children that one other thing was to be feared than all else, namely, "to be laughed at." This speech, with its vivid illustrations, made a lasting impression on the mind of the boy, and on reading what I had written he realized how powerful a motive fear of ridicule had been in his own life; also how large a part it plays in the moral education of the young in Japan.

Naturally enough this fear of being laughed at leads to careful and minute observation of the clothing, manners, and speech of one's associates, and prompt conformity to them, through imitation. The sensitiveness of Japanese students to each new environment is thus easily understood. And this sensitiveness to environment has its advantages as well as its disadvantages. I have already referred to the help it gives to the establishment of individual conformity to ethical standards. The phenomenal success of many reforms in Japan may easily be traced to the national sensitiveness to foreign criticism. Many instances of this will be given in the course of this work, but two may well be mentioned at this point. According to the older customs there was great, if not perfect, freedom as to the use of clothing by the people. The apparent indifference shown by them in the matter of nudity led foreigners to call the nation uncivilized. This criticism has always been a galling one, and not without reason. In many respects their civilization has been fully the equal of that of any other nation; yet in this respect it is true that they resembled and still do resemble semi-civilized peoples. In response to this foreign criticism, however, a law was passed, early in the Meiji era, prohibiting nudity in cities. The requirement that public bathing houses be divided into two separate compartments, one for men and one for women, was likewise due to foreign opinion. That this is the case may be fairly inferred from the fact that the enforcement of these laws has largely taken places where foreigners abound, whereas, in the interior towns and villages they receive much less attention. It must be acknowledged, however, that now at last, twenty-five years after their passage, they are almost everywhere beginning to be enforced by the authorities.

My other illustration of sensitiveness to foreign opinion is the present state of Japanese thought about the management of Formosa. The government has been severely criticised by many leading papers for its blunders there. But the curious feature is the constant reference to the contempt into which such mismanagement will bring Japan in the sight of the world—as if the opinion of other nations were the most important issue involved, and not the righteousness and probity of the government itself. It is interesting to notice how frequently the opinion of other nations with regard to Japan is a leading thought in the mind of the people.

In this connection the following extract finds its natural place:

In a very large number of schools throughout the country special instructions have been given to the pupils as to their behavior towards foreigners. From various sources we have culled the following orders bearing on special points, which we state as briefly as possible.

(1) Never call after foreigners passing along the streets or roads.

(2) When foreigners make inquiries, answer them politely. If unable to make them understand, inform the police of the fact.

(3) Never accept a present from a foreigner when there is no reason for his giving it, and never charge him anything above what is proper.

(4) Do not crowd around a shop when a foreigner is making purchases, thereby causing him much annoyance. The continuance of this practice disgraces us as a nation.

(5) Since all human beings are brothers and sisters, there is no reason for fearing foreigners. Treat them as equals and act uprightly in all your dealings with them. Be neither servile nor arrogant.

(6) Beware of combining against the foreigner and disliking him because he is a foreigner; men are to be judged by their conduct and not by their nationality.

(7) As intercourse with foreigners becomes closer and extends over a series of years, there is danger that many Japanese may become enamored of their ways and customs and forsake the good old customs of their forefathers. Against this danger you must be on your guard.

(8) Taking off your hat is the proper way to salute a foreigner. The bending of the body low is not be commended.

(9) When you see a foreigner be sure and cover up naked parts of the body.

(10) Hold in high regard the worship of ancestors and treat your relations with warm cordiality, but do not regard a person as your enemy because he or she is a Christian.

(11) In going through the world you will often find a knowledge of a foreign tongue absolutely essential.

(12) Beware of selling your souls to foreigners and becoming their slaves. Sell them no houses or lands.

(13) Aim at not being beaten in your competition with foreigners. Remember that loyalty and filial piety are our most precious national treasures and do nothing to violate them.

Many of the above rules are excellent in tone. Number 7, however, which hails from Osaka, is somewhat narrow and prejudiced. The injunction not to sell houses to foreigners is, as the *Jiji Shimpo* points out, absurd and mischievous.[11]

The sensitiveness of the people also works to the advantage of the nation in the social unity which it helps to secure. Indeed I cannot escape the conviction that the striking unity of the Japanese is largely due to this characteristic. It tends to make their mental and emotional activities synchronous. It retards reform for a season, to be sure, but later it accelerates it. It makes it difficult for individuals to break away from their surroundings and start out on new lines. It leads to a general progress while it tends to hinder individual progress. It tends to draw back into the general current of national life those individuals who, under exceptional conditions, may have succeeded in breaking away from it for a season. This, I think, is one of the factors of no little power at work among the Christian churches in Japan. It is one, too, that the Japanese themselves little perceive; so far as I have observed, foreigners likewise fail to realize its force.

Closely connected with this sensitiveness to environment are other qualities which make it effective. They are: great flexibility, adjustability, agility (both mental and physical), and the powers of keen attention to details and of exact imitation.

As opposed to all this is the Chinese lack of flexibility. Contrast a Chinaman and a Japanese after each has been in America a year. The one to all appearances is an American; his hat, his clothing, his manner, seem so like those of an American that were it not for his small size, Mongolian type of face, and defective English, he could easily be mistaken for one. How different is it with the Chinaman! He retains his curious cue with a tenacity that is as intense as it is characteristic. His hat is the conventional one adopted by all Chinese immigrants. His clothing likewise, though far from Chinese, is nevertheless entirely un-American. He makes no effort to conform to his surroundings. He seems to glory in his separateness.

The Japanese desire to conform to the customs and appearances of those about him is due to what I have called sensitiveness; his success is due to the flexibility of his mental constitution.

But this characteristic is seen in multitudes of little ways. The new fashion of wearing the hair according to the Western styles; of wearing Western hats, and Western clothing, now universal in the army, among policemen, and common among officials and educated men; the use of chairs and tables, lamps, windows, and other Western things is due in no small measure to that flexibility of mind which readily adopts new ideas and new ways; is ready to try new things and new words, and after trial, if it finds them convenient or useful or even amusing, to retain them permanently, and this flexibility is, in part, the reason why the Japanese are accounted a fickle people. They accept new ways so easily that those who do not have this faculty have no explanation for it but that of fickleness. A frequent surprise to a missionary in Japan is that of meeting a fine-looking, accomplished gentleman whom he knew a few years before as a crude, ungainly youth. I am convinced that it is the possession of this set of characteristics that has enabled Japan so quickly to assimilate many elements of an alien civilization.

Yet this flexibility of mind and sensitiveness to changed conditions find some apparently striking exceptions. Notable among these are the many customs and appliances of foreign nations which, though adopted by the people, have not been completely modified to suit their own needs. In illustration is the Chinese ideograph, for the learning of which even in the modern common-school reader, there is no arrangement of the characters in the order of their complexity. The possibility of simplifying the colossal task of memorizing these uncorrelated ideographs does not seem to have occurred to the Japanese; though it is now being attempted by the foreigner. Perhaps a partial explanation of this apparent exception to the usual flexibility of the people in meeting conditions may be found in their relative lack of originality. Still I am inclined to refer it to a greater sensitiveness of the Japanese to the personal and human, than to the impersonal and physical environment.

The customary explanation of the group of characteristics considered in this chapter is that they are innate, due to brain and nerve structure, and acquired by each generation through biological heredity. If closely examined, however, this is seen to be no explanation at all. Accepting the characteristics as empirical inexplicable facts, the real problem is evaded, pushed into prehistoric times, that convenient dumping ground of biological, anthropological, and sociological difficulties.

Japanese flexibility, imitativeness, and sensitiveness to environment are to be accounted for by a careful consideration of the national environment and social order. Modern psychology has called attention to the astonishing part played by imitation, conscious and unconscious, in the evolution of the human race, and in the unification of the social group. Prof. Le Tarde goes so far as to make this the fundamental principle of human evolution. He has shown that it is ever at work in the life of every human being, modifying all his thoughts, acts, and feelings. In the evolution of civilization the rare man thinks, the millions imitate.

A slight consideration of the way in which Occidental lands have developed their civilization will convince anyone that imitation has taken the leading part. Japan, therefore, is not unique in this respect. Her periods of wholesale imitation have indeed called special notice to the trait. But the rapidity of the movement has been due to the peculiarities of her environment. For long periods she has been in complete isolation, and when brought into contact with foreign nations, she has found them so far in advance of herself in many important respects that rapid imitation was the only course left her by the inexorable laws of nature. Had she not imitated China in ancient times and the Occident in modern times, her independence, if not her existence, could hardly have been maintained.

Imitation of admittedly superior civilizations has therefore been an integral, conscious element of Japan's social order, and to a degree perhaps not equaled by the social order of any other race.

The difference between Japanese imitation and that of other nations lies in the fact that whereas the latter, as a rule, despise foreign races, and do not admit the superiority of alien civilizations as a whole, imitating only a detail here and there, often without acknowledgment and sometimes even without knowledge, the Japanese, on the other hand, have repeatedly been placed in such circumstances as to see the superiority of foreign civilizations as a whole, and to desire their general adoption. This has produced a spirit of imitation among all the individuals of the race. It has become a part of their social inheritance. This explanation largely accounts for the striking difference between Japanese and Chinese in the Occident. The Japanese go to the West in order to acquire all the West can give. The Chinaman goes steeled against its influences. The spirit of the Japanese renders him quickly susceptible to every change in his surroundings. He is ever noting details and adapting himself to his circumstances. The spirit of the Chinaman, on the contrary, renders him quite oblivious to his environment. His mind is closed. Under special circumstances, when a Chinaman has been liberated from the prepossession of his social inheritance, he has shown himself as capable of Occidentalization in clothing, speech, manner, and thought as a Japanese. Such cases, however, are rare.

But a still more effective factor in the development of the characteristics under consideration is the nature of Japanese feudalism. Its emphasis on the complete subordination of the inferior to the superior was one of its conspicuous features. This was a factor always and everywhere at work in Japan. No individual was beyond its potent influence. Attention to details, absolute obedience, constant, conscious imitation, secretiveness, suspiciousness, were all highly developed by this social system. Each of these traits is a special form of sensitiveness to environment. From the most ancient times the initiative of superiors was essential to the wide adoption by the people of any new idea or custom. Christianity found ready acceptance in the sixteenth century and Buddhism in the eighth, because they had been espoused by exalted persons. The superiority of the civilization of China in early times, and of the West in modern times, was first acknowledged and adopted by a few nobles and the Emperor. Having gained this prestige they promptly became acceptable to the rank and file of people who vied with each other in their adoption. A peculiarity of the Japanese is the readiness with which the ideas and aims of the rulers are accepted by the people. This is due to the nature of Japanese feudalism. It has made the body of the nation conspicuously subject to the ruling brain and has conferred on Japan her unique sensitiveness to environment.

Susceptibility to slight changes in the feelings of lords and masters and corresponding flexibility were important social traits, necessary products of the old social order. Those deficient in these regards would inevitably lose in the struggle for social precedence, if not in the actual struggle for existence. These characteristics would, accordingly, be highly developed.

Bearing in mind, therefore, the character of the factors that have ever been acting on the Japanese psychic nature, we see clearly that the characteristics under consideration are not to be attributed to her inherent race nature, but may be sufficiently accounted for by reference to the social order and social environment.

VI

WAVES OF FEELING—ABDICATION

It has long been recognized that the Japanese are emotional, but the full significance of this element of their nature is far from realized. It underlies their entire life; it determines the mental activities in a way and to a degree that Occidentals can hardly appreciate. Waves of feeling have swept through the country, carrying everything before them in a manner that has oftentimes amazed us of foreign lands. An illustration from the recent political life of the nation comes to mind in this connection. For months previous to the outbreak of the recent war with China, there had been a prolonged struggle between the Cabinet and the political parties who were united in their opposition to the government, though in little else. The parties insisted that the Cabinet should be responsible to the party in power in the Lower House, as is the case in England, that thus they might stand and fall together. The Cabinet, on the other hand, contended that, according to the constitution, it was responsible to the Emperor alone, and that consequently there was no need of a change in the Cabinet with every change of party leadership. The nation waxed hot over the discussion. Successive Diets were dissolved and new Diets elected, in none of which, however, could the supporters of the Cabinet secure a majority; the Cabinet was, therefore, incapable of carrying out any of its distinctive measures. Several times the opposition went so far as to decline to pass the budget proposed by the Cabinet, unless so reduced as to cripple the government, the reason constantly urged being that the Cabinet was not competent to administer the expenditure of such large sums of money. There were no direct charges of fraud, but simply of incompetence. More than once the Cabinet was compelled to carry on the government during the year under the budget of the previous year, as provided by the constitution. So intense was the feeling that the capital was full of "soshi,"—political ruffians,—and fear was entertained as to the personal safety of the members of the Cabinet. The whole country was intensely excited over the matter. The newspapers were not loath to charge the government with extravagance, and a great explosion seemed inevitable, when, suddenly, a breeze from a new quarter arose and absolutely changed the face of the nation.

War with China was whispered, and then noised around. Events moved rapidly. One or two successful encounters with the Chinese stirred the warlike passion that lurked in every breast. At once the feud with the Cabinet was forgotten. When, on short notice, an extra session of the Diet was called to vote funds for a war, not a word was breathed about lack of confidence in the Cabinet or its incompetence to manage the ordinary expenditures of the government; on the contrary, within five minutes from the introduction of the government bill asking a war appropriation of 150,000,000 yen, the bill was unanimously passed.

Such an absolute change could hardly have taken place in England or America, or any land less subject to waves of emotion. So far as I could learn, the nation was a unit in regard to the war. There was not the slightest sign of a "peace party." Of all the Japanese with whom I talked only one ever expressed the slightest opposition to the war, and he on religious grounds, being a Quaker.

The strength of the emotional element tends to make the Japanese extremists. If liberals, they are extremely liberal; if conservative, they are extremely conservative. The craze for foreign goods and customs which prevailed for several years in the early eighties was replaced by an almost equally strong aversion to anything foreign.

This tendency to swing to extremes has cropped out not infrequently in the theological thinking of Japanese Christians. Men who for years had done effective work in upbuilding the Church, men who had lifted hundreds of their fellow-countrymen out of moral and religious darkness into light and life, have suddenly, as it has appeared, lost all appreciation of the truths they had been teaching and have swung off to the limits of a radical rationalism, losing with their evangelical faith their power of helping their fellow-men, and in some few cases, going over into lives of open sin. The intellectual reasons given by them to account for their changes have seemed insufficient; it will be found that the real explanation of these changes is to be sought not in their intellectual, but in their emotional natures.

Care must be taken, however, not to over-emphasize this extremist tendency. In some respects, I am convinced that it is more apparent than real. The appearance is due to the silent passivity even of those who are really opposed to the new departure. It is natural that the advocates of some new policy should be enthusiastic and noisy. To give the impression to an outsider that the new enthusiasm is universal, those who do not share it have simply to keep quiet. This takes place to some degree in every land, but particularly so in Japan. The silence of their dissent is one of the striking characteristics of the Japanese. It seems to be connected with an abdication of personal responsibility. How often in the experience of the missionary it has happened that his first knowledge of friction in a church, wholly independent and self-supporting and having its own native pastor, is the silent withdrawal of certain members from their customary places of worship. On inquiry it is learned that certain things are being done or said which do not suit them and, instead of seeking to have these matters righted, they simply wash their hands of the whole affair by silent withdrawal.

The Kumi-ai church, in Kumamoto, from being large and prosperous, fell to an actual active membership of less than a dozen, solely because, as each member became dissatisfied with the high-handed and radical pastor, he simply withdrew. Had each one stood by the church, realizing that he had a responsibility toward it which duty forbade him to shirk, the conservative and substantial members of the church would soon have been united in their opposition to the radical pastor and, being in the majority, could have set matters right. In the case of perversion of trust funds by the trustees of the Kumamoto School, many Japanese felt that injustice was being done to the American Board and a stain was being inflicted on Japan's fair name, but they did nothing either to express their opinions or to modify the results. So silent were they that we were tempted to think them either ignorant of what was taking place, or else indifferent to it. We now know, however, that many felt deeply on the matter, but were simply silent according to the Japanese custom.

But silent dissent does not necessarily last indefinitely, though it may continue for years. As soon as some check has been put upon the rising tide of feeling, and a reaction is evident, those who before had been silent begin to voice their reactionary feeling, while those who shortly before had been in the ascendant begin to take their turn of silent dissent. Thus the waves are accentuated, both in their rise and in their relapse, by the abdicating proclivity of the people.

Yet, in spite of the tendency of the nation to be swept from one extreme to another by alternate waves of feeling, there are many well-balanced men who are not carried with the tide. The steady progress made by the nation during the past generation, in spite of emotional actions and reactions, must be largely attributed to the presence in its midst of these more stable natures. These are the men who have borne the responsibilities of government. So far as we are able to see, they have not been led by their feelings, but rather by their judgments. When the nation was wild with indignation over Europe's interference with the treaty which brought the China-Japanese war to a close, the men at the helm saw too clearly the futility of an attempt to fight Russia to allow themselves to be carried away by sentimental notions of patriotism. Theirs was a deeper and truer patriotism than that of the great mass of the nation, who, flushed with recent victories by land and by sea, were eager to give Russia the thrashing which they felt quite able to administer.

Abdication is such an important element in Japanese life, serving to throw responsibility on the young, and thus helping to emphasize the emotional characteristics of the people, that we may well give it further attention at this point. In describing it, I can do no better than quote from J.H. Gubbins' valuable introduction to his translation of the New Civil Code of Japan.[1]

"Japanese scholars who have investigated the subject agree in tracing the origin of the present custom to the abdication of Japanese sovereigns, instances of which occur at an early period of Japanese history. These earlier abdications were independent of religious influences, but with the advent of Buddhism abdication entered upon a new phase. In imitation, it would seem, of the retirement for the purpose of religious contemplation of the Head Priests of Buddhist monasteries, abdicating sovereigns shaved their heads and entered the priesthood, and when subsequently the custom came to be employed for political purposes, the cloak of religion was retained. From the throne the custom spread to Regents and high officers of state, and so universal had its observance amongst officials of the high ranks become in the twelfth century that, as Professor Shigeno states, it was almost the rule for such persons to retire from the world at the age of forty or fifty, and nominally enter the priesthood, both the act and the person performing it being termed 'niu do.' In the course of time, the custom of abdication ceased to be confined to officials, and extended to feudal nobility and the military class generally, whence it spread through the nation, and at this stage of its transition its connection with the phase it finally assumed becomes clear. But with its extension beyond the circle of official dignitaries, and its consequent severance from tradition and religious associations, whether real or nominal abdication changed its name. It was no longer termed 'niu do,' but 'in kio,' the old word being retained only in its strict religious meaning, and 'inkyo' is the term in use to-day.

"In spite of the religious origin of abdication, its connection with religion has long since vanished, and it may be said without fear of contradiction that the Japanese of to-day, when he or she abdicates, is in no way actuated by the feeling which impelled European monarchs in past times to end their days in the seclusion of the cloister, and which finds expression to-day in the Irish phrase, 'To make one's soul.' Apart from the influence of traditional convention, which counts for something and also explains the great hold on the nation which the custom has acquired, the motive seems to be somewhat akin to that which leads people in some Western countries to retire from active life at an age when bodily infirmity cannot be adduced as the reason. But with this great difference, that in the one case, that of Western countries, it is the business or profession, the active work of life, which is relinquished, the position of the individual vis-à-vis the family being unaffected; in the other case, it is the position of head of the family which is relinquished, with the result of the complete effacement of the individual so far as the family is concerned. Moreover, although abdication usually implies the abandonment of the business, or profession, of the person who abdicates, this does not necessarily follow, abdication being in no way incompatible with the continuation of the active pursuits in which the person-in question is engaged. And if an excuse be needed in either case, there would seem to be more for the Japanese head of family, who, in addition to the duties and responsibilities incumbent upon his position, has to bear the brunt of the tedious ceremonies and observances which characterize family life in Japan, and are a severe tax upon time and energies, while at the same time he is fettered by the restrictions upon individual freedom of action imposed by the family system. That in many cases the reason for abdication lies in the wish to escape from the tyrannical calls of family life, rather than in mere desire for idleness and ease, is shown by the fact that just as in past times the abdication of an Emperor, a Regent, or a state dignitary, was often the signal for renewed activity on his part, so in modern Japanese life the period of a person's greatest activity not infrequently dates from the time of his withdrawal from the headship of his family."

The abdicating proclivities of the nation in pre-Meiji times are well shown by the official list of daimyos published by the Shogunate in 1862. To a list of 268 ruling daimyos is added a list of 104 "inkyo."

In addition to what we may call political and family abdication, described above, is personal abdication, referred to on a previous page.

Are the traits of Japanese character considered in this chapter inherent and necessary? Already our description has conclusively shown them to be due to the nature of the social order. This was manifestly the case in regard to political and family abdication. The like origin of personal abdication is manifest to him who learns how little there was in the ancient training tending to give each man a "feeling of independent responsibility to his own conscience in the sight of Heaven." He was taught devotion to a person rather than to a principle. The duty of a retainer was not to think and decide, but to do. He might in silence disapprove and as far as possible he should then keep out of his lord's way; should he venture to think and to act contrary to his lord's commands, he must expect and plan to commit "harakiri" in the near future. Personal abdication and silent disapproval, therefore, were direct results of the social order.

VII

HEROES AND HERO-WORSHIP

If a clew to the character of a nation is gained by a study of the nature of the gods it worships, no less valuable an insight is gained by a study of its heroes. Such a study confirms the impression that the emotional life is fundamental in the Japanese temperament. Japan is a nation of hero-worshipers. This is no exaggeration. Not only is the primitive religion, Shintoism, systematic hero-worship, but every hero known to history is deified, and has a shrine or temple. These heroes, too, are all men of conspicuous valor or strength, famed for mighty deeds of daring. They are men of passion. The most popular story in Japanese literature is that of "The Forty-seven Ronin," who avenged the death of their liege-lord after years of waiting and plotting. This revenge administered, they committed harakiri in accordance with the etiquette of the ethical code of feudal Japan. Their tombs are to this day among the most frequented shrines in the capital of the land, and one of the most popular dramas presented in the theaters is based on this same heroic tragedy.

The prominence of the emotional element may be seen in the popular description of national heroes. The picture of an ideal Japanese hero is to our eyes a caricature. His face is distorted by a fierce frenzy of passion, his eyeballs glaring, his hair flying, and his hands hold with a mighty grip the two-handed sword wherewith he is hewing to pieces an enemy. I am often amazed at the difference between the pictures of Japanese heroes and the living Japanese I see. This difference is manifestly due to the idealizing process; for they love to see their heroes in their passionate moods and tenses.

The craving for heroes, even on the part of those who are familiar with Western thought and customs, is a feature of great interest. Well do I remember the enthusiasm with which educated, Christian young men awaited the coming to Japan of an eminent American scholar, from whose lectures impossible things were expected. So long as he was in America and only his books were known, he was a hero. But when he appeared in person, carrying himself like any courteous gentleman, he lost his exalted position.

Townsend Harris showed his insight into Oriental thought never more clearly than by maintaining his dignity according to Japanese standards and methods. On his first entry into Tokyo he states, in his journal, that although he would have preferred to ride on horseback, in order that he might see the city and the people, yet as the highest dignitaries never did so, but always rode in entirely closed "norimono" (a species of sedan chair carried by twenty or thirty bearers), he too would do the same; to have ridden into the limits of the city on horseback would have been construed by the Japanese as an admission that he held a far lower official rank than that of a plenipotentiary of a great nation.

It is not difficult to understand how these ideals of heroes arose. They are the same in every land where militarism, and especially feudalism, is the foundation on which the social order rests.

Some of the difficulties met by foreign missionaries in trying to do their work arise from the fact that they are not easily regarded as heroes by their followers. The people are accustomed to commit their guidance to officials or to teachers or advisers whom they can regard as heroes. Since missionaries are not officials and do not have the manners of heroes, it is not to be expected that the Japanese will accept their leadership.

A few foreigners have, however, become heroes in Japanese eyes. President Clark and Rev. S.R. Brown had great influence on groups of young men in the early years of Meiji, while giving them secular education combined with Christian instruction. The conditions, however, were then extraordinarily exceptional, and it is a noticeable fact that neither man remained long in Japan at that time. Another foreigner who was exalted to the skies by a devoted band of students was a man well suited to be a hero—for he had the samurai spirit to the full. Indeed, in absolute fearlessness and assumption of superiority, he out-samuraied the samurai. He was a man of impressive and imperious personality. Yet it is a significant fact that when he was brought back to Japan by his former pupils, after an absence of about eighteen years, during which they had continued to extol his merits and revere his memory, it was not long before they discovered that he was not the man their imagination had created. Not many months were needed to remove him from his pedestal. It would hardly be a fair statement of the whole case to leave the matter here. So far as I know, President Clark and

34

Rev. S.R. Brown have always retained their hold on the imagination of the Japanese. The foreigner who of all others has perhaps done the most for Japan, and whose services have been most heartily acknowledged by the nation and government, was Dr. Guido F. Verbeck, who began his missionary work in 1859; he was the teacher of large numbers of the young men who became leaders in the transformation of Japan; he alone of foreigners was made a citizen and was given a free and general pass for travel; and his funeral in 1898 was attended by the nobility of the land, and the Emperor himself made a contribution toward the expenses. Dr. Verbeck is destined to be one of Japan's few foreign heroes.

Among the signs of Japanese craving for heroes may be mentioned the constant experience of missionaries when search is being made for a man to fill a particular place. The descriptions of the kind of man desired are such that no one can expect to meet him. The Christian boys' school in Kumamoto, and the church with it, went for a whole year without principal and pastor because they could not secure a man of national reputation. They wanted a hero-principal, who would cut a great figure in local politics and also be a hero-leader for the Christian work in the whole island of Kyushu, causing the school to shine not only in Kumamoto, but to send forth its light and its fame throughout the Empire and even to foreign lands. The unpretentious, unprepossessing-looking man who was chosen temporarily, though endowed with common sense and rather unusual ability to harmonize the various elements in the school, was not deemed satisfactory. He was too much like Socrates. At last they found a man after their own heart. He had traveled and studied long abroad; was a dashing, brilliant fellow; would surely make things hum; so at least said those who recommended him (and he did). But he was still a poor student in Scotland; his passage money must be raised by the school if he was to be secured. And raised it was. Four hundred and seventy-five dollars those one hundred and fifty poor boys and girls, who lived on two dollars a month, scantily clothed and insufficiently warmed, secured from their parents and sent across the seas to bring back him who was to be their hero-principal and pastor. The rest of the story I need not tell in detail, but I may whisper that he was more of a slashing hero than they planned for; in three months the boys' school was split in twain and in less than three years both fragments of the school had not only lost all their Christian character, but were dead and gone forever. And the grounds on which the buildings stood were turned into mulberry fields.

Talking not long since to a native friend, concerning the hero-worshiping tendency of the Japanese, I had my attention called to the fact that, while what has been said above is substantially correct as concerns a large proportion of the people, especially the young men, there is nevertheless a class whose ideal heroes are not military, but moral. Their power arises not through self-assertion, but rather through humility; their influence is due entirely to learning coupled with insight into the great moral issues of life. Such has been the character of not a few of the "moral" teachers. I have recently read a Japanese novel based upon the life of one such hero. Omi Seijin, or the "Sage of Omi," is a name well known among the people of Japan; and his fame rests rather on his character than on his learning. If tradition is correct, his influence on the people of his region was powerful enough to transform the character of the place, producing a paradise on earth whence lust and crime were banished. Whatever the actual facts of his life may have been, this is certainly the representation of his character now held up for honor and imitation. There are also indications that the ideal military hero is not, for all the people, the self-assertive type that I have described above, though this is doubtless the prevalent one. Not long since I heard the following couplet as to the nature of a true hero:

"Makoto				no		Ei-yu;
Sono	yo,	aizen	to	shite	shumpu	no	gotoshi;
Sono	shin,	kizen	to	shite	kinseki	no	gotoshi.

"The			true			Hero;
In	appearance,	charming	like	the	spring	breeze.

In heart, firm as a rock."

Another phrase that I have run across relating to the ideal man is, "I atte takakarazu," which means in plain English, "having authority, but not puffed up." In the presence of these facts, it will not do to think that the ideal hero of all the Japanese is, or even in olden times was, only a military hero full of swagger and bluster; in a military age such would, of necessity, be a popular ideal; but just in proportion as men rose to higher forms of learning, and character, so would their ideals be raised.

It is not to be lightly assumed that the spirit of hero-worship is wholly an evil or a necessarily harmful thing. It has its advantages and rewards as well as its dangers and evils. The existence of hero-worship in any land reveals a nature in the people that is capable of heroic actions. Men appreciate and admire that which in a measure at least they are, and more that which they aspire to become. The recent war revealed how the capacity for heroism of a warlike nature lies latent in every Japanese breast and not in the descendants of the old military class alone. But it is more encouraging to note that popular appreciation of moral heroes is growing.

Education and religion are bringing forth modern moral heroes. The late Dr. Neesima, the founder of the Doshisha, is a hero to many even outside the Church. Mr. Ishii, the father of Orphan Asylums in Japan, promises to be another. A people that can rear and admire men of this character has in it the material of a truly great nation.

The hero-worshiping characteristic of the Japanese depends on two other traits of their nature. The first is the reality of strong personalities among them capable of becoming heroes; the second is the possession of a strong idealizing tendency. Prof. G.T. Ladd has called them a "sentimental" people, in the sense that they are powerfully moved by sentiment. This is a conspicuous trait of their character appearing in numberless ways in their daily life. The passion for group-photographs is largely due to this. Sentimentalism, in the sense given it by Prof. Ladd, is the emotional aspect of idealism.

The new order of society is reacting on the older ideal of a hero and is materially modifying it. The old-fashioned samurai, girded with two swords, ready to kill a personal foe at sight, is now only the ideal of romance. In actual life he would soon find himself deprived of his liberty and under the condemnation not only of the law, but also of public opinion. The new ideal with which I have come into most frequent contact is far different. Many, possibly the majority, of the young men and boys with whom I have talked as to their aim in life, have said that they desired to secure first of all a thorough education, in order that finally they might become great "statesmen" and might guide the nation into paths of prosperity and international power. The modern hero is one who gratifies the patriotic passion by bringing some marked success to the nation. He must be a gentleman, educated in science, in history, and in foreign languages; but above all, he must be versed in political economy and law. This new ideal of a national hero has been brought in by the order of society, and in proportion as this order continues, and emphasis continues to be laid on mental and moral power, rather than on rank or official position, on the intrinsic rather than on the accidental, will the old ideal fade away and the new ideal take its place. Among an idealizing and emotional people, such as the Japanese, various ideals will naturally find extreme expression. As society grows complex also and its various elements become increasingly differentiated, so will the ideals pass through the same transformations. A study of ideals, therefore, serves several ends; it reveals the present character of those whose ideals they are; it shows the degree of development of the social organism in which they live; it makes known, likewise, the degree of the differentiation that has taken place between the various elements of the nation.

VIII
LOVE FOR CHILDREN

An aspect of Japanese life widely remarked and praised by foreign writers is the love for children. Children's holidays, as the third day of the third moon and the fifth day of the fifth moon, are general celebrations for boys and girls respectively, and are observed with much gayety all over the land. At these times the universal aim is to please the children; the girls have dolls and the exhibition of ancestral dolls; while the boys have toy paraphernalia of all the ancient and modern forms of warfare, and enormous wind-inflated paper fish, symbols of prosperity and success, fly from tall bamboos in the front yard. Contrary to the prevailing opinion among foreigners, these festivals have nothing whatever to do with birthday celebrations. In addition to special festivals, the children figure conspicuously in all holidays and merry-makings. To the famous flower-festival celebrations, families go in groups and make an all-day picnic of the joyous occasion.

The Japanese fondness for children is seen not only at festival times. Parents seem always ready to provide their children with toys. As a consequence toy stores flourish. There is hardly a street without its store.

A still further reason for the impression that the Japanese are especially fond of their children is the slight amount of punishment and reprimand which they administer. The children seem to have nearly everything their own way. Playing on the streets, they are always in evidence and are given the right of way.

That Japanese show much affection for their children is clear. The question of importance, however, is whether they have it in a marked degree, more, for instance, than Americans? And if so, is this due to their nature, or may it be attributed to their family life as molded by the social order? It is my impression that, on the whole, the Japanese do not show more affection for their children than Occidentals, although they may at first sight appear to do so. Among the laboring classes of the %est, the father, as a rule, is away from home all through the hours of the day, working in shop or factory. He seldom sees his children except upon the Sabbath. Of course, the father has then very little to do with their care or education, and little opportunity for the manifestation of affection. In Japan, however, the industrial organization of society is still such that the father is at home a large part of the time. The factories are few as yet; the store is usually not separate from the home, but a part of it, the front room of the house. Family life is, therefore, much less broken in upon by the industrial necessities of civilization, and there are accordingly more opportunities for the manifestation of the father's affection for the children. Furthermore, the laboring-people in Japan live much on the street, and it is a common thing to see the father caring for children. While I have seldom seen a father with an infant tied to his back, I have frequently seen them with their infant sons tucked into their bosoms, an interesting sight. This custom gives a vivid impression of parental affection. But, comparing the middle classes of Japan and the West, it is safe to say that, as a whole, the Western father has more to do by far in the care and education of the children than the Japanese father, and that there is no less of fondling and playing with children. If we may judge the degree of affection by the signs of its demonstrations, we must pronounce the Occidental, with his habits of kissing and embracing, as far and away more affectionate than his Oriental cousin. While the Occidental may not make so much of an occasion of the advent of a son as does the Oriental, he continues to remember the birthdays of all his children with joy and celebrations, as the Oriental does not. Although the Japanese invariably say, when asked about it, that they celebrate their children's birthdays, the uniform experience of the foreigner is that birthday celebrations play a very insignificant part in the joys and the social life of the home.

It is not difficult to understand why, apart from the question of affection, the Japanese should manifest special joy on the advent of sons, and particularly of a first son. The Oriental system of ancestral worship, with the consequent need, both religious and political, of maintaining the family line, is quite enough to account for all the congratulatory ceremonies customary on the birth of sons. The fact that special joy is felt and manifested on the birth of sons, and less on the birth of daughters, clearly shows that the dominant conceptions of the social order have an important place in determining even so fundamental a trait as affection for offspring.

Affection for children is, however, not limited to the day of their birth or the period of their infancy. In judging of the relative possession by different races of affection for children, we must ask how the children are treated during all their succeeding years. It must be confessed that the advantage is then entirely on the side of the Occidental. Not only does this appear in the demonstrations of affection which are continued throughout childhood, often even throughout life, but more especially in the active parental solicitude for the children's welfare, striving to fit them for life's duties and watching carefully over their mental and moral education. In these respects the average Occidental is far in advance of the average Oriental.

I have been told that, since the coming in of the new civilization and the rise of the new ideas about woman, marriage, and home, there is clearly observable to the Japanese themselves a change in the way in which children are being treated. But, even still, the elder son takes the more prominent place in the affection of the family, and sons precede daughters.

A fair statement of the case, therefore, is somewhat as follows: The lower and laboring classes of Japan seem to have more visible affection for their children than the same classes in the Occident. Among the middle and upper classes, however, the balance is in favor of the West. In the East, while, without doubt, there always has been and is now a pure and natural affection, it is also true that this natural affection has been more mixed with utilitarian considerations than in the West. Christian Japanese, however, differ little from Christian Americans in this respect. The differences between the East and the West are largely due to the differing industrial and family conditions induced by the social order.

The correctness of this general statement will perhaps be better appreciated if we consider in detail some of the facts of Japanese family life. Let us notice first the very loose ties, as they seem to us, holding the Japanese family together. It is one of the constant wonders to us Westerners how families can break up into fragments, as they constantly do. One third of the marriages end in divorce; and in case of divorce, the children all stay with the father's family. It would seem as if the love of the mother for her children could not be very strong where divorce under such a condition is so common. Or, perhaps, it would be truer to say that divorce would be far more frequent than it is but for the mother's love for her children. For I am assured that many a mother endures most distressing conditions rather than leave her children. Furthermore, the way in which parents allow their children to leave the home and then fail to write or communicate with them, for months or even years at a time, is incomprehensible if the parental love were really strong. And still further, the way in which concubines are brought into the home, causing confusion and discord, is a very striking evidence of the lack of a deep love on the part of the father for the mother of his children and even for his own legitimate children. One would expect a father who really loved his children to desire and plan for their legitimacy; but the children by his concubines are not "ipso facto" recognized as legal. One more evidence in this direction is the frequency of adoption and of separation. Adoption in Japan is largely, though by no means exclusively, the adoption of an adult; the cases where a child is adopted by a childless couple from love of children are rare, as compared with similar cases in the United States, so far, at least, as my observation goes. I recently heard of a conversation on personal financial matters between a number of Christian evangelists. After mutual comparisons they agreed that one of their number was more fortunate than the rest in that he did not have to support his mother. On inquiring into the matter, the missionary learned that this evangelist, on becoming a Buddhist priest many years before, had secured from the government, according to the laws of the land, exemption from this duty. When he became a Christian it did not seem to occur to him that it was his duty and his privilege to support his indigent mother. I may add that this idea has since occurred to him and he is acting upon it.

Infanticide throws a rather lurid light on Japanese affection. First, in regard to the facts: Mr. Ishii's attention was called to the need of an orphan asylum by hearing how a child, both of whose parents had died of cholera, was on the point of being buried alive with its dead mother by heartless neighbors when it was rescued by a fisherman. Certain parts of Japan have been notorious from of old for this practice. In Tosa the evil was so rampant that a society for its prevention has been in existence for many years. It helps support children of poor parents who might be tempted to dispose of them criminally. In that province from January to March, 1898, I was told that "only" four cases of conviction for this crime were reported. The registered annual birth rate of certain villages has increased from 40-50 to 75-80, and this without any immigration from outside. The reason assigned is the diminution of infanticide.

In speaking of infanticide in Japan, let us not forget that every race and nation has been guilty of the same crime, and has continued to be guilty of it until delivered by Christianity.

Widespread infanticide proves a wide lack of natural affection. Poverty is, of course, the common plea. Yet infanticide has been practiced not so much by the desperately poor as by small land-holders. The amount of farming land possessed by each family was strictly limited and could feed only a given number of mouths. Should the family exceed that number, all would be involved in poverty, for the members beyond that limit did not have the liberty to travel in search of new occupation. Infanticide, therefore, bore direct relation to the rigid economic nature of the old social order.

Whatever, therefore, be the point of view from which we study the question of Japanese affection for children, we see that it was intimately connected with the nature of the social order. Whether we judge such affection or its lack to be a characteristic trait of Japanese nature, we must still maintain that it is not an inherent trait of the race nature, but only a characteristic depending for its greater or less development on the nature of the social order.

IX
MARITAL LOVE

If the Japanese are a conspicuously emotional race, as is commonly believed, we should naturally expect this characteristic to manifest itself in a marked degree in the relation of the sexes. Curiously enough, however, such does not seem to be the case. So slight a place does the emotion of sexual love have in Japanese family life that some have gone to the extreme of denying it altogether. In his brilliant but fallacious volume, entitled "The Soul of the Far East," Mr. Percival Lowell states that the Japanese do not "fall in love." The correctness of this statement we shall consider in connection with the argument for Japanese impersonality. That "falling in love" is not a recognized part of the family system, and that marriage is arranged regardless not only of love, but even of mutual acquaintance, are indisputable facts.

Let us confine our attention here to Japanese post-marital emotional characteristics. Do Japanese husbands love their wives and wives their husbands? We have already seen that in the text-book for Japanese women, the "Onna Daigaku," not one word is said about love. It may be stated at once that love between husband and wife is almost as conspicuously lacking in practice as in precept. In no regard, perhaps, is the contrast between the East and the West more striking than the respective ideas concerning woman and marriage. The one counts woman the equal, if not the superior of man; the other looks down upon her as man's inferior in every respect; the one considers profound love as the only true condition of marriage; the other thinks of love as essentially impure, beneath the dignity of a true man, and not to be taken into consideration when marriage is contemplated; in the one, the two persons most interested have most to say in the matter; in the other, they have the least to say; in the one, a long and intimate previous acquaintance is deemed important; in the other, the need for such an acquaintance does not receive a second thought; in the one, the wife at once takes her place as the queen of the home; in the other, she enters as the domestic for her husband and his parents; in the one, the children are hers as well as his; in the other, they are his rather than hers, and remain with him in case of divorce; in the one, divorce is rare and condemned; in the other, it is common in the extreme; in the one, it is as often the woman as the man who seeks the divorce; in the other, until most recent times, it is the man alone who divorces the wife; in the one, the reasons for divorce are grave; in the other, they are often trivial; in the one, the wife is the "helpmate"; in the other, she is the man's "plaything"; or, at most, the means for continuing the family lineage; in the one, the man is the "husband"; in the other, he is the "danna san" or "teishu" (the lord or master); in the ideal home of the one, the wife is the object of the husband's constant affection and solicitous care; in the ideal home of the other, she ever waits upon her lord, serves his food for him, and faithfully sits up for him at night, however late his return may be; in the one, the wife is justified in resenting any unfaithfulness or immorality on the part of her husband;

in the other, she is commanded to accept with patience whatever he may do, however many concubines he may have in his home or elsewhere; and however immoral he may be, she must not be jealous. The following characterization of the women of Japan is presumably by one who would do them no injustice, having himself married a Japanese wife (the editor of the *Japan Mail*).

"The woman of Japan is a charming personage in many ways—gracious, refined, womanly before everything, sweet-tempered, unselfish, virtuous, a splendid mother, and an ideal wife from the point of view of the master. But she is virtually excluded from the whole intellectual life of the nation. Politics, art, literature, science, are closed books to her. She cannot think logically about any of these subjects, express herself clearly with reference to them, or take an intellectual part in conversations relating to them. She is, in fact, totally disqualified to be her husband's intellectual companion, and the inevitable result is that he despises her."[1]

In face of all these facts, it is evident that the emotional element of character which plays so large a part in the relation of the sexes in the West has little, if any, counterpart in the Far East. Where the emotional element does come in, it is under social condemnation. There are doubtless many happy marriages in Japan, if the wife is faithful in her place and fills it well; and if the master is honorable according to the accepted standards, steady in his business, not given to wine or women. But even then the affection must be different from that which prevails in the West. No Japanese wife ever dreams of receiving the loving care from her husband which is freely accorded her Western sister by her husband.[K]

I wish, however, to add at once that this is a topic about which it is dangerous to dogmatize, for the customs of Japan demand that all expressions of affection between husband and wife shall be sedulously concealed from the outer world. I can easily believe that there is no little true affection existing between husband and wife. A Japanese friend with whom I have talked on this subject expresses his belief that the statement made above, to the effect that no Japanese wife dreams of receiving the loving care which is expected by her Western sister, is doubtless true of Old Japan, but that there has been a great change in this respect in recent decades; and especially among the Christian community. That Christians excel the others with whom I have come in contact, has been evident to me. But that even they are still very different from Occidentals in this respect, is also clear. Whatever be the affection lavished on the wife in the privacy of the home, she does not receive in public the constant evidence of special regard and high esteem which the Western wife expects as her right.

How much affection can be expressed by low formal bows? The fact is that Japanese civilization has striven to crush out all signs of emotion; this stoicism is exemplified to a large degree even in the home, and under circumstances when we should think it impossible. Kissing was an unknown art in Japan, and it is still unknown, except by name, to the great majority of the people. Even mothers seldom kiss their infant children, and when they do, it is only while the children are very young.

The question, however, which particularly interests us, is as to the explanation for these facts. Is the lack of demonstrative affection between husband and wife due to the inherent nature of the Japanese, or is it not due rather to the prevailing social order? If a Japanese goes to America or. England, for a few years, does he maintain his cold attitude toward all women, and never show the slightest tendency to fall in love, or exhibit demonstrative affection? These questions almost answer themselves, and with them the main question for whose solution we are seeking.

A few concrete instances may help to illustrate the generalization that these are not fixed because racial characteristics, but variable ones dependent on the social order. Many years ago when the late Dr. Neesima, the founder, with Dr. Davis, of the Doshisha, was on the point of departure for the United States on account of his health, he made an address to the students. In the course of his remarks he stated that there were three principal considerations that made him regret the necessity for his departure at that time; the first was that the Doshisha was in a most critical position; it was but starting on its larger work, and he felt that all its friends should be on hand to help on the great undertaking. The second was that he was compelled to leave his aged parents, whom he might not find living on his return to Japan. The third was his sorrow at leaving his beloved wife. This public reference to his wife, and especially to his love for her, was so extraordinary that it created no little comment, not to say scandal; especially obnoxious was it to many, because he mentioned her after having mentioned his parents. In the reports of this speech given by his friends to the public press no reference was made to this expression of love for his wife. And a few months after his death, when Dr. Davis prepared a short biography of Dr. Neesima, he was severely criticised by some of the Japanese for reproducing the speech as Dr. Neesima gave it.

Shortly after my first arrival in Japan, I was walking home from church one day with an English-speaking Japanese, who had had a good deal to do with foreigners. Suddenly, without any introduction, he remarked that he did not comprehend how the men of the West could endure such tyranny as was exercised over them by their wives. I, of course, asked what he meant. He then said that he had seen me buttoning my wife's shoes. I should explain that on calling on the Japanese, in their homes, it is necessary that we leave our shoes at the door, as the Japanese invariably do; this is, of course, awkward for foreigners who wear shoes; especially so is the necessity of putting them on again. The difficulty is materially increased by the invariably high step at the front door. It is hard enough for a man to kneel down on the step and reach for his shoes and then put them on; much more so is it for a woman. And after the shoes are on, there is no suitable place on which to rest the foot for buttoning and tying. I used, therefore, very gladly to help my wife with hers. Yet, so contrary to Japanese precedent was this act of mine that this well-educated gentleman and Christian, who had had much intercourse with foreigners, could not see in it anything except the imperious command of the wifeand the slavish obedience of the husband. His conception of the relation between the Occidental husband and wife is best described as tyranny on the part of the wife.

One of the early shocks I received on this general subject was due to the discovery that whenever my wife took my arm as we walked the street to and from church, or elsewhere, the people looked at us in surprised displeasure. Such public manifestation of intimacy was to be expected from libertines alone, and from these only when they were more or less under the influence of drink. Whenever a Japanese man walks out with his wife, which, by the way, is seldom, he invariably steps on ahead, leaving her to follow, carrying the parcels, if there are any. A child, especially a son, may walk at his side, but not his wife.

Let me give a few more illustrations to show how the present family life of the Japanese checks the full and free development of the affections. In one of our out-stations I but recently found a young woman in a distressing condition. Her parents had no sons, and consequently, according to the custom of the land, they had adopted a son, who became the husband of their eldest daughter; the man proved a rascal, and the family was glad when he decided that he did not care to be their son any longer. Shortly after his departure a child was born to the daughter; but, according to the law, she had no husband, and consequently the child must either be registered as illegitimate, or be fraudulently registered as the child of the mother's father. There is much fraudulent registration, the children of concubines are not recognized as legitimate; yet it is common to register such children as those of the regular wife, especially if she has few or none of her own.

An evangelist who worked long in Kyushu was always in great financial trouble because of the fact that he had to support two mothers, besides giving aid to his father, who had married a third wife. The first was his own mother, who had been divorced, but, as she had no home, the son took her to his. When the fatherdivorced his second wife, the son was induced to take care of her also. Another evangelist, with whom I had much to do, was the adopted son of a scheming old man; it seems that in the earlier part of the present era the eldest son of a family was exempt from military draft. It often happened, therefore, that families who had no sons could obtain large sums of money from those who had younger sons whom they wished to have adopted for the purpose of escaping the draft. This evangelist, while still a boy, was adopted into such a family, and a certain sum was fixed upon to be paid at some time in the future. But the adopted son proved so pleasing to the adopting father that he did not ask for the money; by some piece of legerdemain, however, he succeeded in adopting a second son, who paid him the desired money. After some years the first adopted son became a Christian, and then an evangelist, both steps being taken against the wishes of the adopting father. The father finally said that he would forego all relations to the son, and give him back his original name, provided the son would pay the original sum that had been agreed on, plus the interest, which altogether would, at that time, amount to several hundred yen. This was, of course, impossible. The negotiations dragged on for three or four years. Meanwhile, the young man fell in love with a young girl, whom he finally married; as he was still the son of his adopting father, he could not have his wife registered as his wife, for the old man had another girl in view for him and would not consent to this arrangement. And so the matter dragged for several months more. Unless the matter could be arranged, any children born to them must be registered as illegitimate. At this point I was consulted and, for the first time, learned the details of the case. Further consultations resulted in an agreement as to the sum to be paid; the adopted son was released, and re-registered under his newly acquired name and for the first time his marriage became legal. The confusion and suffering brought into the family by this practice of adoption and of separation are almost endless.

The number of cases in which beautiful and accomplished young women have been divorced by brutal and licentious husbands is appalling. I know several such. What wonder that Christians and others are constantly laying emphasis, in public lectures and sermons and private talks, on the crying need of reform in marriage and in the home?

Throughout the land the newspapers are discussing the pros and cons of monogamy and polygamy. In January of 1898 the *Jiji Shimpo,* one of the leading daily papers of Tokyo, had a series of articles on the subject from the pen of one of the most illustrious educators of New Japan, Mr. Fukuzawa. His school, the "Keio Gijiku," has educated more thousands of young men than any other, notwithstanding the fact that it is a private institution. Though not a Christian himself, nor making any professions of advocating Christianity, yet Mr. Fukuzawa has come out strongly in favor of monogamy. His description of the existing social and family life is striking, not to say sickening. If I mistake not, it is he who tells of a certain noble lady who shed tears at the news of the promotion of her husband in official rank; and when questioned on the matter she confessed that, with added salary, he would add to the number of his concubines and to the frequency of his intercourse with famous dancing and singing girls.

The distressing state of family life may also be gathered from the large numbers of public and secret prostitutes that are to be found in all the large cities, and the singing girls of nearly every town. According to popular opinion, their number is rapidly increasing. Though this general subject trenches on morality rather than on the topic immediately before us, yet it throws a lurid light on this question also. It lets us see, perhaps, more clearly than we could in any other way, how deficient is the average home life of the people. A professing Christian, a man of wide experience and social standing, not long since seriously argued at a meeting of a Young Men's Christian Association that dancing and singing girls are a necessary part of Japanese civilization to-day. He argued that they supply the men with that female element in social life which the ordinary woman cannot provide; were the average wives and daughters sufficiently accomplished to share in the social life of the men as they are in the West, dancing and singing girls, being needless, would soon cease to be.

One further question in this connection merits our attention. How are we to account for an order of society that allows so little scope for the natural affections of the heart, unless by saying that that order is the true expression of their nature? Must we not say that the element of affection in the present social order is deficient because the Japanese themselves are naturally deficient? The question seems more difficult than it really is.

In the first place, the affectionate relation existing between husbands and wives and between parents and children, in Western lands, is a product of relatively recent times. In his exhaustive work on "The History of Human Marriage," Westermarck makes this very plain. Wherever the woman is counted a slave, is bought and sold, is considered as merely a means of bearing children to the family, or in any essential way is looked down upon, there high forms of affection are by the nature of the case impossible, though some affection doubtless exists; it necessarily attains only a rudimentary development. Now it is conspicuous that the conception of the nature and purpose of woman, as held in the Orient, has always been debasing to her. Though individual women might rise above their assigned position the whole social order, as established by the leaders of thought, was against her. The statement that there was a primitive condition of society in Japan in which the affectionate relations between husband and wife now known in the West prevailed, is, I think, a mistake.

We must remember, in the second place, what careful students of human evolution have pointed out, that those tribes and races in which the family was most completely consolidated, that is to say, those in which the power of the father was absolute, were the ones to gain the victory over their competitors. The reason for this is too obvious to require even a statement. Every conquering race has accordingly developed the "patria potestas" to a greater or less degree. Now one general peculiarity of the Orient is that that stage of development has remained to this day; it has not experienced those modifications and restrictions which have arisen in the West. The national government dealt with families and clans, not with individuals, as the final social unit. In the West, however, the individual has become the civil unit; the "patria potestas" has thus been all but lost. This, added to religious and ethical considerations, has given women and children an ever higher place both in society and in the home. Had this loss of authority by the father been accompanied with a weakening of the nation, it would have been an injury; but, in the West, his authority has been transferred to the nation. These considerations serve to render more intelligible and convincing the main proposition of these chapters, that the distinctive emotional characteristics of the Japanese are not inherent; they are the results of the social and industrial order; as this order changes, they too will surely change. The entire civilization of a land takes its leading, if not its dominant, color from the estimate set by the people as a whole on the value of human life. The relatively late development of the tender affections, even in the West, is due doubtless to the extreme slowness with which the idea of the inherent value of a human being, as such, has taken root, even though it was clearly taught by Christ. But the leaven of His teaching has been at work for these hundreds of years, and now at last we are beginning to see its real meaning and its vital relation to the entire progress of man. It may be questioned whether Christ gave any more important impetus to the development of civilization than by His teaching in regard to the inestimable worth of man, grounding it, as He did, on man's divine sonship. Those nations which insist on valuing human life only by the utilitarian standard, and which consequently keep woman in a degraded place, insisting on concubinage and all that it implies, are sure to wane before those nations which loyally adopt and practice the higher ideals of human worth. The weakness of heathen lands arises in no slight degree from their cheap estimate of human life.

In Japan, until the Meiji era, human life was cheap. For criminals of the military classes, suicide was the honorable method of leaving this world; the lower orders of society suffered loss of life at the hands of the military class without redress. The whole nation accepted the low standards of human value; woman was valued chiefly, if not entirely, on a utilitarian basis, that, namely, of bearing children, doing house and farm work, and giving men pleasure. So far as I know, not among all the teachings of Confucius or Buddha was the supreme value of human life, as such, once suggested, much less any adequate conception of the worth and nature of woman. The entire social order was constructed without these two important truths.

By a great effort, however, Japan has introduced a new social order, with unprecedented rapidity. By one revolution it has established a set of laws in which the equality of all men before the law is recognized at least; for the first time in Oriental history, woman is given the right to seek divorce. The experiment is now being made on a great scale as to whether the new social order adopted by the rulers can induce those ideas among the people at large which will insure its performance. Can the mere legal enactments which embody the principles of human equality and the value of human life, regardless of sex, beget those fundamental conceptions on which alone a steady and lasting government can rest? Can Japan really step into the circle of Western nations, without abandoning her pagan religions and pushing onward into Christian monotheism with all its corollaries as to the relations and mutual duties of man? All earnest men are crying out for a strengthening of the moral life of the nation through the reform of the family and are proclaiming the necessity of monogamy; but, aside from the Christians, none appear to see how this is to be done.

Even Mr. Fukuzawa says that the first step in the reform of the family and the establishment of monogamy is to develop public sentiment against prostitution and plural or illegal marriage; and the way to do this is first to make evil practices secret. This, he says, is more important than to give women a higher education. He does not see that Christianity with its conceptions of immediate responsibility of the individual to God, the loving Heavenly Father, and of the infinite value of each human soul, thus doing away with the utilitarian scale for measuring both men and women, together with its conceptions of the relations of the sexes and of man to man, can alone supply that foundation for all the elements of the new social order, intellectual and emotional, which will make it workable and permanent, and of which monogamy is but one element.[1] He does not see that representative government and popular rights cannot stand for any length of time on any other foundation.

X
CHEERFULNESS—INDUSTRY—TRUTHFULNESS—SUSPICIOUSNESS

Many writers have dwelt with delight on the cheerful disposition that seems so common in Japan. Lightness of heart, freedom from all anxiety for the future, living chiefly in the present, these and kindred features are pictured in glowing terms. And, on the whole, these pictures are true to life. The many flower festivals are made occasions for family picnics when all care seems thrown to the wind. There is a simplicity and a freshness and a freedom from worry that is delightful to see. But it is also remarked that a change in this regard is beginning to be observed. The coming in of Western machinery, methods of government, of trade and of education, is introducing customs and cares, ambitions and activities, that militate against the older ways. Doubtless, this too is true. If so, it but serves to establish the general proposition of these pages that the more outstanding national characteristics are largely the result of special social conditions, rather than of inherent national character.

The cheerful disposition, so often seen and admired by the Westerner, is the cheerfulness of children. In many respects the Japanese are relatively undeveloped. This is due to the nature of their social order during the past. The government has been largely paternal in form and fully so in theory. Little has been left to individual initiative or responsibility. Wherever such a system has been dominant and the perfectly accepted order, the inevitable result is just such a state of simple, childish cheerfulness as we find in Japan. It constitutes that golden age sung by the poets of every land. But being the cheerfulness of children, the happiness of immaturity, it is bound to change with growth, to be lost with coming maturity.

Yet the Japanese are by no means given up to a cheerful view of life. Many an individual is morose and dejected in the extreme. This disposition is ever stimulated by the religious teachings of Buddhism. Its great message has been the evanescent character of the present life. Life is not worth living, it urges; though life may have some pleasures, the total result is disappointment and sorrow. Buddhism has found a warm welcome in the hearts of many Japanese. For more than a thousand years it has been exercising a potent influence on their thoughts and lives. Yet how is this consistent with the cheerful disposition which seems so characteristic of Japan? The answer is not far to seek. Pessimism is by its very nature separative, isolating, silent. Those oppressed by it do not enter into public joys. They hide themselves in monasteries, or in the home. The result is that by its very nature the actual pessimism of Japan is not a conspicuous feature of national character. The judgment that all Japanese are cheerful rests on shallow grounds. Because, forsooth, millions on holidays bear that appearance, and because on ordinary occasions the average man and woman seem cheerful and happy, the conclusion is reached that all are so. No effort is made to learn of those whose lives are spent in sadness and isolation. I am convinced that the Japan of old, for all its apparent cheer, had likewise its side of deep tragedy. Conditions of life that struck down countless individuals, and mental conditions which made Buddhism so popular, both point to this conclusion.

44

Again I wish to call attention to the fact that the prominence of children and young people is in part the cause of the appearance of general happiness. The Japanese live on the street as no Western people do. The stores and workshops are the homes; when these are open, the homes are open. When the children go out of the house to play they use the streets, for they seldom have yards. Here they gather in great numbers and play most enthusiastically, utterly regardless of the passers-by, for these latter are all on foot or in jinrikishas, and, consequently, never cause the children any alarm.

The Japanese give the double impression of being industrious and diligent on the one hand, and, on the other, of being lazy and utterly indifferent to the lapse of time. The long hours during which they keep at work is a constant wonder to the Occidental. I have often been amazed in Fukuoka to find stores and workshops open, apparently in operation, after ten and sometimes even until eleven o'clock at night, while blacksmiths and carpenters and wheelwrights would be working away as if it were morning. Many of the factories recently started keep very long hours. Indeed most of the cotton mills run day and night, having two sets of workers, who shift their times of labor every week. Those who work during the night hours one week take the day hours the following week. In at least one such factory, with which I am acquainted, the fifteen hundred girls who work from six o'clock Saturday evening until six o'clock Sunday morning, are then supposed to have twenty-four hours of rest before they begin their day's work Monday morning; but, as a matter of fact, they must spend three or four and sometimes five hours on Sunday morning cleaning up the factory.

In a small silk-weaving factory that I know the customary hours for work were from five in the morning until nine at night, seven days in the week. The wife, however, of the owner became a Christian. Through her intervention time for rest was secured on Sunday long enough for a Bible class, which the evangelist of the place was invited to teach. After several months of instruction a number of the hands became Christian, and all were sufficiently interested to ask that the whole of the Sabbath be granted to them for rest; but in order that the master might not lose thereby, they agreed to begin work at four each morning and to work on until ten at night. With such hours one would have expected them to fall at once into their beds when the work of the day was over. But for many months, at ten o'clock in the evening, my wife and I heard them singing a hymn or two in their family worship before retiring for the night.

In certain weaving factories I have been told that the girls are required to work sixteen hours a day; and that on Sundays they are allowed to have some rest, being then required to work but ten hours! The diligence of mail deliverers, who always run when on duty, the hours of consecutive running frequently performed by jin-irikisha men (several have told me that they have made over sixty miles in a single day), the long hours of persistent study by students in the higher schools, and many kindred facts, certainly indicate a surprising capacity for work.

But there are equally striking illustrations of an opposite nature. The farmers and mechanics and carpenters, among regular laborers, and the entire life of the common people in their homes, give an impression of indifference to the flight of time, if not of absolute laziness. The workers seem ready to sit down for a smoke and a chat at any hour of the day. In the home and in ordinary social life, the loss of time seems to be a matter of no consequence whatever. Polite palaver takes unstinted hours, and the sauntering of the people through the street emphasizes the impression that no business calls oppress them.

In my opinion these characteristics, also, are due to the conditions of society, past and present, rather than to the inherent nature of the people. The old civilization was easy-going; it had no clocks; it hardly knew the time of day; it never hastened. The hour was estimated and was twice as long as the modern hour. The structure of society demanded the constant observance of the forms of etiquette; this, with its numberless genuflections and strikings of the head on the floor, always demanded time. Furthermore, the very character of the footgear compelled and still compels a shuffling, ambling gait when walking the streets. The clog is a well-named hindrance to civilization in the waste of time it compels. The slow-going, time-ignoring characteristics of New Japan are social inheritances from feudal times, characteristics which are still hampering its development. The industrious spirit that is to be found in so many quarters to-day is largely the gift of the new civilization. Shoes are taking the place of clogs. The army and all the police, on ordinary duty, wear shoes. Even the industry of the students is largely due to the new conditions of student life. The way in which the Japanese are working to-day, and the feverish haste that some of them evince in their work, shows that they are as capable as Occidentals of acquiring the rush of civilization.

The home life of the people gives an impression of listlessness that is in marked contrast to that of the West. This is partly due to the fact that the house work is relatively light, there being no furniture to speak of, the rooms small, and the cooking arrangements quite simple. Housewives go about their work with restful deliberation, which is trying, however, to one in haste. It is the experience of the housekeepers from the West that one Japanese domestic is able to accomplish from a third to a half of what is done by a girl in America. This is not wholly due to slowness of movement, however, but also to smallness of stature and corresponding lack of strength. On the other hand, the long hours of work required of women in the majority of Japanese homes is something appalling. The wife is expected to be up before the husband, to prepare his meals, and to wait patiently till his return at night, however late that may be. In all except the higher ranks of society she takes entire care of the children, except for the help which her older children may give her. During much of the time she goes about her work with an infant tied to her back. Though she does not work hard at any one time (and is it to be wondered at?) yet she works long. Especially hard is the life of the waiting girls in the hotels. I have learned that, as a rule, they are required to be up before daylight and to remain on duty until after midnight. In some hotels they are allowed but four or five hours out of the twenty-four. The result is, they are often overcome and fall asleep while at service. Sitting on the floor and waiting to serve the rice, with nothing to distract their thoughts or hold their attention, they easily lose themselves for a few moments.

Two other strongly contrasted traits are found in the Japanese character, absolute confidence and trustfulness on the one hand, and suspicion on the other. It is the universal testimony that the former characteristic is rapidly passing away; in the cities it is well-nigh gone. But in the country places it is still common. The idea of making a bargain when two persons entered upon some particular piece of work, the one as employer, the other as employed, was entirely repugnant to the older generation, since it was assumed that their relations as inferior and superior should determine their financial relations; the superior would do what was right, and the inferior should accept what the superior might give without a question or a murmur. Among the samurai, where the arrangement is between equals, bargaining or making fixed and fast terms which will hold to the end, and which may be carried to the courts in case of differences, was a thing practically unknown in the older civilization. Everything of a business nature was left to honor, and was carried on in mutual confidence.

A few illustrations of this spirit of confidence from my own experience may not be without interest. On first coming to Japan, I found it usual for a Japanese who wished to take a jinrikisha to call the runner and take the ride without making any bargain, giving him at the end what seemed right. And the men generally accepted the payment without question. I have found that recently, unless there is some definite understanding arrived at before the ride, there is apt to be some disagreement, the runner presuming on the hold he has, by virtue of work done, to get more than is customary. This is especially true in case the rider is a foreigner. Another set of examples in which astonishing simplicity and confidence were manifested was in the employment of evangelists. I have known several instances in which a full correspondence with an evangelist with regard to his employment was carried on, and the settlement finally concluded, and the man set to work without a word said about money matters. It need hardly be said that no foreigner took part in that correspondence.

The simple, childlike trustfulness of the country people is seen in multiplied ways; yet on the whole I cannot escape the conviction that it is a trustfulness which is shown toward each other as equals. Certain farmers whom I have employed to care for a cow and to cultivate the garden, while showing a trustful disposition towards me, have not had the same feelings toward their fellows apparently.

This confidence and trustfulness were the product of a civilization resting on communalistic feudalism; the people were kept as children in dependence on their feudal

46

lord; they had to accept what he said and did; they were accustomed to that order of things from the beginning and had no other thought; on the whole too, without doubt, they received regular and kindly treatment. Furthermore, there was no redress for the peasant in case of harshness; it was always the wise policy, therefore, for him to accept whatever was given without even the appearance of dissatisfaction. This spirit was connected with the dominance of the military class. Simple trustfulness was, therefore, chiefly that of the non-military classes. The trustfulness of the samurai sprang from their distinctive training. As already mentioned, when drawing up a bond in feudal times, in place of any tangible security, the document would read, "If I fail to do so and so, you may laugh at me in public."

Since the overthrow of communal feudalism and the establishment of an individualistic social order, necessitating personal ownership of property, and the universal use of money, trustful confidence is rapidly passing away. Everything is being more and more accurately reduced to a money basis. The old samurai scorn for money seems to be wholly gone, an astonishing transformation of character. Since the disestablishment of the samurai class many of them have gone into business. Not a few have made tremendous failures for lack of business instinct, being easily fleeced by more cunning and less honorable fellows who have played the "confidence" game most successfully; others have made equally great successes because of their superior mental ability and education. The government of Japan is to-day chiefly in the hands of the descendants of the samurai class. They have their fixed salaries and everything is done on a financial basis, payment being made for work only. The lazy and the incapable are being pushed to the wall. Many of the poorest and most pitiable people of the land to-day are the proud sons of the former aristocracy, who glory in the history of their ancestors, but are not able or willing to change their old habits of thought and manner of life.

The American Board has had a very curious, not to say disastrous, experience with the spirit of trustful confidence that was the prevailing business characteristic of the older civilization. According to the treaties which Japan had made with foreign nations, no foreigner was allowed to buy land outside the treaty ports. As, however, mission work was freely allowed by the government and welcomed by many of the people in all parts of the land, and as it became desirable to have continuous missionary work in several of the interior towns, it seemed wise to locate missionaries in those places and to provide suitable houses for them. In order to do this, land was bought and the needed houses erected, and the title was necessarily held in the names of apparently trustworthy native Christians. The government was, of course, fully aware of what was being done and offered no objection. It was well understood that the property was not for the private ownership of the individual missionary, but was to be held by the Christians for the use of the mission to which the missionary belonged. For many years no questions were raised and all moved along smoothly. The arrangement between the missionaries and the Christian or Christians in whose names the property might be held was entirely verbal, no document being of any legal value, to say nothing of the fact that in those early days the mention of documentary relationships would have greatly hurt the tender feelings of honor which were so prominent a part of samurai character. The financial relations were purely those of honor and trust.

Under this general method, large sums of money were expended by the American Board for homes for its missionaries in various parts of Japan, and especially in Kyoto. Here was the Doshisha, which grew from a small English school and Evangelists' training class to a prosperous university with fine buildings. Tens of thousands of dollars were put into this institution, besides the funds needful for the land and the houses for nine foreign families. An endowment was also raised, partly in Japan, but chiefly in America. In a single bequest, Mr. Harris of New London gave over one hundred thousand dollars for a School of Science. It has been estimated that, altogether, the American Board and its constituency have put into the Doshisha, including the salaries of the missionary teachers, toward a million dollars.

In the early nineties the political skies were suddenly darkened. The question of treaty revision loomed up black in the heavens. The politicians of the land clamored for the absolute refusal of all right of property ownership by foreigners. In their political furore they soon began to attack the Japanese Christians who were holding the property used by the various missions. They accused them of being traitors to the country. A proposed law was drafted and presented in the National Diet, confiscating all such property. The Japanese holders naturally became nervous and desirous of severing the relationships with the foreigners as soon as possible. In the case of corporate ownership the trustees began to make assumptions of absolute ownership, regardless of the moral claims of the donors of the funds. In the earlier days of the trouble frequent conferences on the question were held by the missionaries of the American Board with the leading Christians of the Empire, and their constant statement was, "Do not worry; trust us; we are samurai and will do nothing that is not perfectly honorable." So often were these sentiments reiterated, and yet so steadily did the whole management of the Doshisha move further and further away from the honorable course, that finally the "financial honor of the samurai" came to have an odor far from pleasant. A deputation of four gentlemen, as representatives of the American Board, came from America especially to confer with the trustees as to the Christian principles of the institution, and the moral claims of the Board, but wholly in vain. The administration of the Doshisha became so distinctly non-Christian, to use no stronger term, that the mission felt it impossible to co-operate longer with the Doshisha trustees; the missionary members of the faculty accordingly resigned. In order to secure exemption from the draft for its students the trustees of the Doshisha abrogated certain clauses of the constitution relating to the Christian character of the institution, in spite of the fact that these clauses belonged to the "unchangeable" part of the constitution which the trustees, on taking office, had individually sworn to maintain. Again the Board sent out a man, now a lawyer vested with full power to press matters to a final issue. After months of negotiations with the trustees in regard to the restoration of the substance of the abrogated clauses, without result, he was on the point of carrying the case into the courts, when the trustees decided to resign in a body. A new board of trustees has been formed, who bid fair to carry on the institution in accord with the wishes of its founders and benefactors, as expressed in the original constitution. At one stage of the proceedings the trustees voted magnanimously, as they appeared to think, to allow the missionaries of the Board to live for fifteen years, rent free, in the foreign houses connected with the Doshisha; this, because of the many favors it had received from the Board! By this vote they maintained that they had more than fulfilled every requirement of honor. That they were consciously betraying the trust that had been reposed in them is not for a moment to be supposed.

It would not be fair not to add that this experience in Kyoto does not exemplify the universal Japanese character. There are many Japanese who deeply deplore and condemn the whole proceeding. Some of the Doshisha alumni have exerted themselves strenuously to have righteousness done.

Passing now from the character of trustful confidence, we take up its opposite, suspiciousness. The development of this quality is a natural result of a military feudalism such as ruled Japan for hundreds of years. Intrigue was in constant use when actual war was not being waged. In an age when conflicts were always hand to hand, and the man who could best deceive his enemy as to his next blow was the one to carry off his head, the development of suspicion, strategy, and deceit was inevitable. The most suspicious men, other things being equal, would be the victors; they, with their families, would survive and thus determine the nature of the social order. The more than two hundred and fifty clans and "kuni," "clan territory," into which the land was divided, kept up perpetual training in the arts of intrigue and subtlety which are inevitably accompanied by suspicion.

Modern manifestations of this characteristic are frequent. Not a cabinet is formed, but the question of its make-up is discussed from the clannish standpoint. Even though it is now thirty years since the centralizing policy was entered upon and clan distinctions were effectually broken down, yet clan suspicion and jealousy is not dead.

The foreigner is impressed with the constant need of care in conversation, lest he be thought to mean something more or other than he says. When we have occasion to criticise anything in the Japanese, we have found by experience that much more is inferred than is said. Shortly after my arrival in Japan I was advised by one who had been in the land many years to be careful in correcting a domestic or any other person sustaining any relation to myself, to say not more than one-tenth of what I meant, for the other nine-tenths would be inferred. Direct and perfectly frank criticism and suggestion, such as prevail among Anglo-Americans at least, seem to be rare among the Japanese.

In closing, it is in order to note once again that the emotional characteristics considered in this chapter, although customarily thought to be deep-seated traits of race nature, are, nevertheless, shown to be dependent on the character of the social order. Change the order, and in due season corresponding changes occur in the national character, a fact which would be impossible were that character inherent and essential, passed on from generation to generation by the single fact of biological heredity.

<h1 style="text-align:center">XI</h1>

JEALOUSY—REVENGE—HUMANE FEELINGS

According to the teachings of Confucius, jealousy is one of the seven just grounds on which a woman may be divorced. In the "Greater Learning for Women,"[M]occur the following words: "Let her never even dream of jealousy. If her husband be dissolute, she must expostulate with him, but never either render her countenance frightful or her accents repulsive, which can only result in completely alienating her husband from her, and making her intolerable in his eyes." "The five worst maladies that afflict the female mind are indocility, discontent, slander, jealousy, and silliness. Without any doubt, these five maladies infest seven or eight out of every ten women, and it is from these that arises the inferiority of women to men ... Neither when she blames and accuses and curses innocent persons, nor when in her jealousy of others she thinks to set herself up alone, does she see that she is her own enemy, estranging others and incurring their hatred."

The humiliating conditions to which women have been subjected in the past and present social order, and to which full reference has been made in previous chapters, give sufficient explanation of the jealousy which is recognized as a marked, and, as might appear, inevitable characteristic of Japanese women. Especially does this seem inevitable when it is remembered how slight is their hold on their husbands, on whose faithfulness their happiness so largely depends. Only as this order changes and the wife secures a more certain place in the home, free from the competition of concubines and harlots and dancing girls, can we expect the characteristic to disappear. That it will do so under such conditions, there is no reason to question. Already there are evidences that in homes where the husband and the wife are both earnest Christians, and where each is confident of the loyalty of the other, jealousy is as rare as it is in Christian lands.

But is jealousy a characteristic limited to women? or is it not also a characteristic of men? I am assured from many quarters that men also suffer from it. The jealousy of a woman is aroused by the fear that some other woman may supplant her in the eyes of her husband; that of a man by the fear that some man may supplant him in rank or influence. Marital jealousy of men seems to be rare. Yet I heard not long since of a man who was so afraid lest some man might steal his wife's affections that he could not attend to his business, and finally, after three months of married wretchedness, he divorced her. A year later he married her again, but the old trouble reappeared, and so he divorced her a second time. If marital jealousy is less common among men than among women, the explanation is at hand in the lax moral standard for man. The feudal order of society, furthermore, was exactly the soil in which to develop masculine jealousy. In such a society ambition and jealousy go hand in hand. Wherever a man's rise in popularity and influence depends on the overthrow of someone already in possession, jealousy is natural. Connected with the spirit of jealousy is that of revenge. Had we known Japan only during her feudal days, we should have pronounced the Japanese exceedingly revengeful. Revenge was not only the custom, it was also the law of the land and the teaching of moralists. One of the proverbs handed down from the hoary past is: "Kumpu no ada to tomo ni ten we itadakazu." "With the enemy of country, or father, one cannot live under the same heaven." The tales of heroic Japan abound in stories of revenge. Once when Confucius was asked about the doctrine of Lao-Tse that one should return good for evil, he replied, "With what then should one reward good? The true doctrine is to return good for good, and evil with justice." This saying of Confucius has nullified for twenty-four hundred years that pearl of truth enunciated by Lao-

Tse, and has caused it to remain an undiscovered diamond amid the rubbish of Taoism. By this judgment Confucius sanctified the rough methods of justice adopted in a primitive order of society. His dictum peculiarly harmonized with the militarism of Japan. Being, then, a recognized duty for many hundred years, it would be strange indeed were not revengefulness to appear among the modern traits of the Japanese.

But the whole order of society has been transformed. Revenge is now under the ban of the state, which has made itself responsible for the infliction of corporal punishment on individual transgressors. As a result conspicuous manifestations of the revengeful spirit have disappeared, and, may we not rightly say, even the spirit itself? The new order of society leaves no room for its ordinary activity; it furnishes legal methods of redress. The rapid change in regard to this characteristic gives reason for thinking that if the industrial and social order could be suitably adjusted, and the conditions of individual thought and life regulated, this, and many other evil traits of human character, might become radically changed in a short time. Intelligent Christian Socialism is based on this theory and seems to have no little support for its position.

Are Japanese cruel or humane? The general impression of the casual tourist doubtless is that they are humane. They are kind to children on the streets, to a marked degree; the jinrikisha runners turn out not only for men, women, and children, but even for dogs. The patience, too, of the ordinary Japanese under trying circumstances is marked; they show amazing tolerance for one another's failings and defects, and their mutual helpfulness in seasons of distress is often striking. To one traveling through New Japan there is usually little that will strike the eye as cruel.

But the longer one lives in the country, the more is he impressed with certain aspects of life which seem to evince an essentially unsympathetic and inhuman disposition. I well remember the shock I received when I discovered, not far from my home in Kumamoto, an insane man kept in a cage. He was given only a slight amount of clothing, even though heavy frost fell each night. Food was given him once or twice a day. He was treated like a wild animal, not even being provided with bedding. This is not an exceptional instance, as might, perhaps, at first be supposed. The editor of the *Japan Mail*, who has lived in Japan many years, and knows the people well, says: "Every foreigner traveling or residing in Japan must have been shocked from time to time by the method of treating lunatics. Only a few months ago an imbecile might have been seen at Hakone confined in what was virtually a cage, where, from year's end to year's end, he received neither medical assistance nor loving tendance, but was simply fed like a wild beast in a menagerie. We have witnessed many such sights with horror and pity. Yet humane Japanese do not seem to think of establishing asylums where these unhappy sufferers can find refuge. There is only one lunatic asylum in Tokyo. It is controlled by the municipality, its accommodation is limited, and its terms place it beyond the reach of the poor." And the amazing part is that such sights do not seem to arouse the sentiment of pity in the Japanese.

The treatment accorded to lepers is another significant indication of the lack of sympathetic and humane sentiments among the people at large. For ages they have been turned from home and house and compelled to wander outcasts, living in the outskirt of the villages in rude booths of their own construction, and dependent on their daily begging, until a wretched death gives them relief from a more wretched life. So far as I have been able to learn, the opening of hospitals for lepers did not take place until begun by Christians in recent times. This casting out of leper kindred was not done by the poor alone, but by the wealthy also, although I do hot affirm or suppose that the practice was universal. I am personally acquainted with the management of the Christian Leper Hospital in Kumamoto, and the sad accounts I have heard of the way in which lepers are treated by their kindred would seem incredible, were they not supported by the character of my informants, and by many other facts of a kindred nature.

A history of Japan was prepared by Japanese scholars under appointment from the government and sent to the Columbian Exposition in 1893; it makes the following statement, already referred to on a previous page: "Despite the issue of several proclamations ... people were governed by such strong aversion to the sight of sickness that travelers were often left to die by the roadside from thirst, hunger, or disease, and householders even went to the length of thrusting out of doors and abandoning to utter destitution servants who suffered from chronic maladies.... Whenever an epidemic occurred, the number of deaths that resulted was enormous."[N] This was the condition of things after Buddhism, with its civilizing and humanizing influences, had been at work in the land for about four hundred years, and Old Japan was at the height of her glory, whether considered from the standpoint of her government, her literature, her religious development, or her art.

Of a period some two hundred years earlier, it is stated that, by the assistance of the Sovereign, Buddhism established a charity hospital in Nara, "where the poor received medical treatment and drugs gratis, and an asylum was founded for the support of the destitute. Measures were also taken to rescue foundlings, and, in general, to relieve poverty and distress" (p. 92). The good beginning made at that time does not seem to have been followed up. As nearly as I can make out, relying on the investigations of Rev. J.H. Pettee and Mr. Ishii, there are to-day in Japan fifty orphan asylums, of which eleven are of non-Christian, and thirty-nine of Christian origin, support, and control. Of the non-Christian, five are in Osaka, two in Tokyo, four in Kyoto, and one each in Nagoya, Kumamoto, and Matsuye. Presumably the majority of these are in the hands of Buddhists. Of the Christian asylums twenty are Roman Catholic and nineteen are Protestant. It is a noteworthy fact that in this form of philanthropy and religious activity, as in so many others, Christians are the pioneers and Buddhists are the imitators. In a land where Buddhism has been so effective as to modify the diet of the nation, leading them in obedience to the doctrines of Buddha, as has been stated, to give up eating animal food, it is exceedingly strange that the people apparently have no regard for the pain of living animals. Says the editor of the *Mail* in the article already quoted: "They will not interfere to save a horse from the brutality of its driver, and they will sit calmly in a jinrikisha while its drawer, with throbbing heart and straining muscles, toils up a steep hill." How often have I seen this sight! How the rider can endure it, I cannot understand, except it be that revolt at cruelty and sympathy with suffering do not stir within his heart. Of course, heartless individuals are not rare in the West also. I am speaking here, however, not of single individuals, but of general characteristics.

But a still more conspicuous evidence of Japanese deficiency of sympathy is the use, until recently, of public torture. It was the theory of Japanese jurisprudence that no man should be punished, even though proved guilty by sufficient evidence, until he himself confessed his guilt; consequently, on the flimsiest evidence, and even on bare suspicion, he was tortured until the desired confession was extracted. The cruelty of the methods employed, we of the nineteenth century cannot appreciate. Some foreigner tells how the sight of torture which he witnessed caused him to weep, while the Japanese spectators stood by unmoved. The methods of execution were also refined devices of torture. Townsend Harris says that crucifixion was performed as follows: "The criminal is tied to a cross with his arms and legs stretched apart as wide as possible; then a spear is thrust through the body, entering just under the bottom of the shoulder blade on the left side, and coming out on the right side, just by the armpit. Another is then thrust through in a similar manner from the right to the left side. The executioner endeavors to avoid the heart in this operation. The spears are thrust through in this manner until the criminal expires, but his sufferings are prolonged as much as possible. Shinano told me that a few years ago a very strong man lived until the eleventh spear had been thrust through him."

From these considerations, which might be supported by a multitude of illustrations, we conclude that in the past there has certainly been a great amount of cruelty exhibited in Japan, and that even to this day there is in this country far less sympathy for suffering, whether animal or human, than is felt in the West.

But we must not be too quick to jump to the conclusion that in this regard we have discovered an essential characteristic of the Japanese nature. With reference to the reported savagery displayed by Japanese troops at Port Arthur, it has been said and repeated that you have only to scratch the Japanese skin to find the Tartar, as if the recent development of human feelings were superficial, and his real character were exhibited in his most cruel moments. To get a true view of the case let us look for a few moments at some other parts of the world, and ask ourselves a few questions.

How long is it since the Inquisition was enforced in Europe? Who can read of the tortures there inflicted without shuddering with horror? It is not necessary to go back to the times of the Romans with their amphitheaters and gladiators, and with their throwing of Christians to wild animals, or to Nero using Christians as torches in his garden. How long is it since witches were burned, not only in Europe by the thousand, but in enlightened and Christian New England? although it is true that the numbers there burned were relatively few and the reign of terror brief. How long is it since slaves were feeling the lash throughout the Southern States of our "land of freedom"? How long is it since fiendish mobs have burned or lynched the objects of their rage? How long is it since societies for preventing cruelty to animals and to children were established in England and America? Is it not a suggestive fact that it was needful to establish them and that it is still needful to maintain them? The fact is that the highly developed humane sense which is now felt so strongly by the great majority of people in the West is a late development, and is not yet universal. It is not for us to boast, or even to feel superior to the Japanese, whose opportunities for developing this sentiment have been limited.

Furthermore, in regard to Japan, we must not overlook certain facts which show that Japan has made gradual progress in the development of the humane feelings and in the legal suppression of cruelty. The Nihon Shoki records that, on the death of Yamato Hiko no Mikoto, his immediate retainers were buried alive in a standing position around the grave, presumably with the heads alone projecting above the surface of the ground. The Emperor Suijin Tenno, on hearing the continuous wailing day after day of the slowly dying retainers, was touched with pity and said that it was a dreadful custom to bury with the master those who had been most faithful to him when alive. And he added that an evil custom, even though ancient, should not be followed, and ordered it to be abandoned. A later record informs us that from this time arose the custom of burying images in the place of servants. According to the ordinary Japanese chronology, this took place in the year corresponding to 1 B.C. The laws of Ieyasu (1610 A.D.) likewise condemn this custom as unreasonable, together with the custom in accordance with which the retainers committed suicide upon the master's death. These same laws also refer to the proverb on revenge, given in the third paragraph of this chapter, and add that whoever undertakes thus to avenge himself or his father or mother or lord or elder brother must first give notice to the proper office of the fact and of the time within which he will carry out his intention; without such a notice, the avenger will be considered a common murderer. This provision was clearly a limitation of the law of revenge. These laws of Ieyasu also describe the old methods of punishing criminals, and then add: "Criminals are to be punished by branding, or beating, or tying up, and, in capital cases, by spearing or decapitation; but the old punishments of tearing to pieces and boiling to death are not to be used." Torture was finally legally abolished in Japan only as late as 1877.

It has already become quite clear that the prevalence of cruelty or of humanity depends largely upon the social order that prevails. It is not at all strange that cruelty, or, at least, lack of sympathy for suffering in man or beast, should be characteristic of an order based on constant hand-to-hand conflict. Still more may we expect to find a great indifference to human suffering wherever the value of man as man is slighted. Not until the idea of the brotherhood of man has taken full possession of one's heart and thought does true sympathy spring up; then, for the first time, comes the power of putting one's self in a brother's place. The apparently cruel customs of primitive times, in their treatment of the sick, and particularly of those suffering from contagious diseases, is the natural, not to say necessary, result of superstitious ignorance. Furthermore, it was often the only ready means to prevent the spread of contagious or epidemic diseases.

In the treatment of the sick, the first prerequisite for the development of tenderness is the introduction of correct ideas as to the nature of disease and its proper treatment. As soon as this has been effectually done, a great proportion of the apparent indifference to human suffering passes away. The cruelty which is to-day so universal in Africa needs but a changed social and industrial order to disappear. The needed change has come to Japan. Physicians trained in modern methods of medical practice are found all over the land. In

1894 there were 597 hospitals, 42,551 physicians, 33,921 nurses and midwives, 2869 pharmacists, and 16,106 druggists, besides excellent schools of pharmacy and medicine.[0]

It is safe to say that nearly all forms of active cruelty have disappeared from Japan; some amount of active sympathy has been developed, though, as compared to that of other civilized lands, it is still small. But there can be no doubt that the rapid change which has come over the people during the past thirty years is not a change in essential innate character, but only in the idea of the social order. As soon as the idea takes root that every man has a mission of mercy, and that the more cruel are not at liberty to vent their barbarous feelings on helpless creatures, whether man or beast, a strong uprising of humane activity will take place which will demand the formation of societies for the prevention of cruelty and for carrying active relief to the distressed and wretched. Lepers will no longer need to eke out a precarious living by exhibiting their revolting misery in public; lunatics will no longer be kept in filthy cages and left with insufficient care or clothing. The stream of philanthropy will rise high, to be at once a blessing and a glory to a race that already has shown itself in many ways capable of the highest ideals of the West.

XII
AMBITION—CONCEIT

Ambition is a conspicuous characteristic of New Japan. I have already spoken of the common desire of her young men to become statesmen. The stories of Neesima and other young Japanese who, in spite of opposition and without money, worked their way to eminence and usefulness, have fired the imagination of thousands of youths. They think that all they need is to get to America, when their difficulties will be at an end. They fancy that they have but to look around to find some man who will support them while they study.

Not only individuals, but the people as a whole, have great ambitions. Three hundred years ago the Taiko, Hideyoshi, the Napoleon of Japan, and the virtual ruler of the Empire, planned, after subjugating Korea, to conquer China and make himself the Emperor of the East. He thought he could accomplish this in two years. During the recent war, it was the desire of many to march on to Pekin. Frequent expression was given to the idea that it is the duty of Japan to rouse China from her long sleep, as America roused Japan in 1854. It is frequently argued, in editorial articles and public speeches, that the Japanese are peculiarly fitted to lead China along the path of progress, not only indirectly by example, as they have been doing, but directly by teaching, as foreigners have led Japan. "The Mission of Japan to the Orient" is a frequent theme of public discourse. But national ambitions do not rest here. It is not seldom asserted that in Japan a mingling of the Occidental and Oriental civilizations is taking place under such favorable conditions that, for the first time in history, the better elements of both are being selected; and that before long the world will sit to learn at her feet. The lofty ambition of a group of radical Christians is to discover or create a new religion which shall unite the best features of Oriental and Occidental religious thought and experience. The religion of the future will be, not Christianity, nor Buddhism, but something better than either, more consistent, more profound, more universal; and this religion, first developed in Japan, will spread to other lands and become the final religion of the world.

A single curious illustration of the high-flying thoughts of the people may well find mention here. When the Kumamoto Boys' School divided over the arbitrary, tyrannical methods of their newly secured, brilliant principal, already referred to in a previous chapter, the majority of the trustees withdrew and at once established a new school for boys. For some time they struggled for a name which should set forth the principles for which the school stood, and finally they fixed on that of "To-A Gakko." Translated into unpretentious English, this means "Eastern Asia School"; the idea was that the school stood for no narrow methods of education, and that its influence was to extend beyond the confines of Japan. This interpretation is not an inference, but was publicly stated oil various occasions. The school began with twenty-five boys, if my memory is correct, and never reached as many as fifty. In less than three years it died an untimely death through lack of patronage.

The young men of the island of Kyushu, especially of Kumamoto and Kagoshima provinces, are noted for their ambitious projects. The once famous "Kumamoto Band"

53

consisted entirely of Kyushu boys. Under the masterful influence of Captain Jaynes those high-spirited sons of samurai, who had come to learn foreign languages and science, in a school founded to combat Christianity and to upbuild Buddhism, became impressed with the immense superiority of foreign lands, which superiority they were led to attribute to Christianity. They accordingly espoused the Christian cause with great ardor, and, in their compact with one another, agreed to work for the reform of Japan. I have listened to many addresses by the Kumamoto schoolboys, and I have been uniformly impressed with the political and national tendencies of their thought.

Accompanying ambition is a group of less admirable qualities, such as self-sufficiency and self-conceit. They are seldom manifested with that coarseness which in the West we associate with them, for the Japanese is usually too polished to be offensively obtrusive. He seldom indulges in bluster or direct assertion, but is contented rather with the silent assumption of superiority.

I heard recently of a slight, though capital, illustration of my point. Two foreign gentlemen were walking through the town of Tadotsu some years since and observed a sign in English which read "Stemboots." Wondering what the sign could mean they inquired the business of the place, and learning that it was a steamboat office, they gave the clerk the reason for their inquiry, and at his request made the necessary correction. A few days later, however, on their return, they noticed that the sign had been re-corrected to "Stem-boats," an assumption of superior knowledge on the part of some tyro in English. The multitude of signboards in astonishing English, in places frequented by English-speaking people, is one of the amusing features of Japan. It would seem as if the shopkeepers would at least take the pains to have the signs correctly worded and spelled, by asking the help of some foreigner or competent Japanese. Yet they assume that they know all that is needful.

Indications of perfect self-confidence crop out in multitudes of ways far too numerous to mention. The aspiring ambition spoken of in the immediately preceding pages is one indication of this characteristic. Another is the readiness of fledglings to undertake responsibilities far beyond them. Young men having a smattering of English, yet wholly unable to converse, set up as teachers. Youths in school not infrequently undertake to instruct their teachers as to what courses of study and what treatment they should receive. Still more conspicuous is the cool assumption of superiority evinced by so many Japanese in discussing intellectual and philosophical problems. The manner assumed is that of one who is complete master of the subject. The silent contempt often poured on foreigners who attempt to discuss these problems is at once amusing and illustrative of the characteristic of which I am speaking.[1]

We turn next to inquire for the explanation of these characteristics. Are they inherent traits of the race? Or are they the product of the times? Doubtless the latter is the true explanation. It will be found that those individuals in whom these characteristics appear are descendants of the samurai. A small class of men freed from heavy physical toil, given to literature and culture, ever depending on the assumption of superiority for the maintenance of their place in society and defending their assumption by the sword—such a class, in such a social order, would develop the characteristics in question to a high degree. Should we expect an immediate change of character when the social order has been suddenly changed?

In marked contrast to the lofty assumptions of superiority which characterized the samurai of Old Japan, was the equally marked assumption of inferiority which characterized the rest of the people, or nineteen-twentieths of the nation. I have already sufficiently dwelt on this aspect of national character. I here recur to it merely to enforce the truth that self-arrogation and self-abnegation, haughtiness and humility, proud, high-handed, magisterial manners, and cringing, obsequious obedience, are all elements of character that depend on the nature of the social order. They are passed on from generation to generation more by social than by biological heredity. Both of these sets of contrasted characteristics are induced by a full-fledged feudal system, and must remain for a time as a social inheritance after that system has been overthrown, particularly if its overthrow is sudden. In proportion as the principles of personal rights and individual worth on the basis ofmanhood become realized by the people and incorporated into the government and customs of the land, will abnegating obsequiousness, as well as haughty lordliness, be replaced by a straightforward manliness, in which men of whatever grade of society will frankly face each other, eye to eye.

But what shall we say in regard to the assumption made by young Japan in its attitude to foreigners? Are the assumptions wholly groundless? Is the self-confidence unjustified? Far from it. When we study later the intellectual elements of Japanese character, we shall see some reasons for their feeling of self-reliance. The progress which the nation has made in many lines within thirty years shows that it has certain kinds of power and, consequently, some ground for self-reliance. Furthermore, self-reliance, if fairly supported by ability and zeal, is essential in the attainment of any end whatever. Faint heart never won fair lady. Confidence in self is one form of faith. No less of peoples than individuals is it true, that without faith in themselves they cannot attain their goal. The impression of undue self-confidence made by the Japanese may be owing partly to their shortness of stature. It is a new experience for the West to see a race of little people with large brains and large plans. Especially does it seem strange and conceited for a people whose own civilization is so belated to assume a rôle of such importance in the affairs of the world. Yet we must learn to dissociate physical size from mental or spiritual capacity. The future alone will disclose what Japanese self-reliance and energy can produce.

The present prominence of this characteristic in Japan is still further to be accounted for by her actual recent history. The overthrow of the Shogunate was primarily the work of young men; the introduction of almost all the sweeping reforms which have transformed Japan has been the work of young men who, though but partly equipped for their work, approached it with energy and perfect confidence, not knowing enough perhaps to realize the difficulties they were undertaking. They had to set aside the customs of centuries; to do this required startling assumptions of superiority to their ancestors and their immediate parents. The young men undertook to dispute and doubt everything that stood in the way of national re-organization. In what nation has there ever been such a setting aside of parental teaching and ancestral authority? These heroic measures secured results in which the nation glories. Is it strange, then, that the same spirit should show itself in every branch of life, even in the attitude of the people to the Westerners who have brought them the new ways and ideas?

The Japanese, however, is not the only conceited nation. Indeed, it would be near the truth to say that there is no people without this quality. Certainly the American and English, French and German nations cannot presume to criticise others. The reason why we think Japan unique in this respect is that in the case of these Western nations we know more of the grounds for national self-satisfaction than in the case of Japan. Yet Western lands are, in many respects, truly provincial to this very day, in spite of their advantages and progress; the difficulty with most of them is that they do not perceive it. The lack of culture that prevails among our working classes is in some respects great. The narrow horizon still bounding the vision of the average American or Briton is very conspicuous to one who has had opportunities to live and travel in many lands. Each country, and even each section of a country, is much inclined to think that it has more nearly reached perfection than any other.

This phase of national and local feeling is interesting, especially after one has lived in Japan a number of years and has had opportunities to mingle freely with her people. For they, although self-reliant and self-conceited, are at the same time surprisingly ready to acknowledge that they are far behind the times. Their open-mindedness is truly amazing. In describing the methods of land tenure, of house-building, of farming, of local government, of education, of moral instruction, of family life, indeed, of almost anything in the West that has some advantageous feature, the remark will be dropped incidentally that these facts show how uncivilized Japan still is. In their own public addresses, if any custom is attacked, the severest indictment that can be brought against it is that it is uncivilized. In spite, therefore, of her self-conceit, Japan is in a fairer way of making progress than many a Western nation, because she is also so conscious of defects. A large section of the nation has a passion for progress. It wishes to learn of the good that foreign lands have attained, and to apply the knowledge in such wise as shall fit most advantageously into the national life. Although Japan is conceited, her conceit is not without reason, nor is it to be attributed to her inherent race nature. It is manifestly due to her history and social order past and present.

XIII

PATRIOTISM—APOTHEOSIS—COURAGE

No word is so dear to the patriotic Japanese as the one that leaps to his lips when his country is assailed or maligned, "Yamato-Damashii." In prosaic English this means "Japan Soul." But the native word has a flavor and a host of associations that render it the most pleasing his tongue can utter. "Yamato" is the classic name for that part of Japan where the divinely honored Emperor, Jimmu Tenno, the founder of the dynasty and the Empire, first established his court and throne. "Damashii" refers to the soul, and especially to the noble qualities of the soul, which, in Japan of yore, were synonymous with bravery, the characteristic of the samurai. If, therefore, you wish to stir in the native breast the deepest feelings of patriotism and courage, you need but to call upon his "Yamato-Damashii."

There has been a revival in the use of this word during the last decade. The old Japan-Spirit has been appealed to, and the watchword of the anti-foreign reaction has been "Japan for the Japanese." Among English-speaking and English-reading Japanese there has been a tendency to give this term a meaning deeper and broader than the historic usage, or even than the current usage, will bear. One Japanese writer, for instance, defines the term as meaning, "a spirit of loyalty to country, conscience, and ideal." An American writer comes more nearly to the current usage in the definition of it as "the aggressive and invincible spirit of Japan." That there is such a spirit no one can doubt who has the slightest acquaintance with her past or present history.

Concerning the recent rise of patriotism I have spoken elsewhere, perhaps at sufficient length. Nor is it needful to present extensive evidence for the statement that the Japanese have this feeling of patriotism in a marked degree. One or two rather interesting items may, however, find their place here.

The recent war with China was the occasion of focusing patriotism and fanning it into flame. Almost every town street, and house, throughout the Empire, was brilliantly decked with lanterns and flags, not on a single occasion only, but continuously. Each reported victory, however small, sent a thrill of delight throughout the nation. Month after month this was kept up. In traveling through the land one would not have fancied that war was in progress, but rather, that a long-continued festival was being observed.

An incident connected with sending troops to Korea made a deep impression on the nation. The Okayama Orphan Asylum under the efficient management of its founder, Mr. Ishii, had organized the older boys into a band, securing for them various kinds of musical instruments. These they learned to use with much success. When the troops were on the point of leaving, Mr. Ishii went with his band to the port of Hiroshima, erected a booth, prepared places for heating water, and as often as the regiments passed by, his little orphans sallied forth with their teapots of hot tea for the refreshment of the soldiers. Each regiment was also properly saluted, and if opportunity offered, the little fellows played the national anthem, "Kimi-ga yo," which has been thus translated: "May Our Gracious Sovereign reign a thousand years, reign till the little stone grow into a mighty rock, thick velveted with ancient moss." And finally the orphans would raise their shrill voices with the rhythmical national shout, "Tei-koku Ban-zai, Tei-koku Ban-zai"; "Imperial-land, a myriad years, Imperial-land, a myriad years." This thoughtful farewell was maintained for the four or five days during which the troops were embarking for the seat of war, well knowing that some would never return, and that their children would be left fatherless even as were these who saluted them. So deep was the impression made upon the soldiers that many of them wept and many a bronzed face bowed in loving recognition of the patriotism of these Christian boys. It is said that the commander-in-chief of the forces himself gave the little fellows the highest military salute in returning theirs.

Throughout the history of Japan, the aim of every rebellious clan or general was first to get possession of the Emperor. Having done this, the possession of the Imperial authority was unquestioned. Whoever was opposed to the Emperor was technically called "Cho-teki," the enemy of the throne, a crime as heinous as treason in the West. The existence of this sentiment throughout the Empire is an interesting fact. For, at the very same time, there was the most intense loyalty to the local lord or "daimyo." This is a fine instance of a certain characteristic of the Japanese of which I must speak more fully in another connection, but which, for convenience, I term "nominality." It accepts and, apparently at least, is satisfied with a nominal state of affairs, which may be quite different from the real. The theoretical aspect of a question is accepted without reference to the actual facts. The real power may be in the hands of the general or of the daimyo, but if authority nominally proceeds from the throne, the theoretical demands are satisfied. The Japanese themselves describe this state as "yumei-mujitsu." In a sense, throughout the centuries there has been a genuine loyalty to the throne, but it has been of the "yumei-mujitsu" type, apparently satisfied with the name only. In recent times, however, there has been growing dissatisfaction with this state of affairs. Some decades before Admiral Perry appeared there were patriots secretly working against the Tokugawa Shogunate. Called in Japanese "Kinnoka," they may be properly termed in English "Imperialists." Their aim was to overthrow the Shogunate and restore full and direct authority to the Emperor. Not a few lost their lives because of their views, but these are now honored by the nation as patriots.

There is a tendency among scholars to-day to magnify the patriotism and loyalty of preceding ages, also to emphasize the dignity and Imperial authority of the Emperor. The patriotic spirit is now so strong that it blinds their eyes to many of the salient facts of their history. Their patriotism is more truly a passion than an idea. It is an emotion rather than a conception. It demands certain methods of treatment for their ancient history that Western scholarship cannot accept. It forbids any really critical research into the history of the past, since it might cast doubt on the divine descent of the Imperial line. It sums itself up in passionate admiration, not to say adoration, of the Emperor. In him all virtues and wisdom abound. No fault or lack in character can be attributed to him. I question if any rulers have ever been more truly apotheosized by any nation than the Emperors of Japan. The essence of patriotism to-day is devotion to the person of the Emperor. It seems impossible for the people to distinguish between the country and its ruler. He is the fountain of authority. Lower ranks gain their right and their power from him alone. Power belongs to the people only because, and in proportion as, he has conferred it upon them. Even the Constitution has its authority only because he has so determined. Should he at any time see fit to change or withdraw it, it is exceedingly doubtful whether one word of criticism or complaint would be publicly uttered, and as for forcible opposition, of such a thing no one would dream.

Japanese patriotism has had some unique and interesting features. In some marked respects it is different from that of lands in which democratic thought has held sway. For 1500 years, under the military social order, loyalty has consisted of personal attachment to the lord. It has ever striven to idealize that lord. The "yumei-mujitsu" characteristic has helped much in this idealizing process, by bridging the chasm between the prosaic fact and the ideal. Now that the old form of feudalism has been abruptly abolished, with its local lords and loyalty, the old sentiment of loyalty naturally fixes itself on the Emperor. Patriotism has perhaps gained intensity in proportion as it has become focalized. The Emperor is reported to be a man of commanding ability and good sense. It is at least true that he has shown wisdom in selecting his councilors. There is general agreement that he is not a mere puppet in the hands of his advisers, but that he exercises a real and direct influence on the government of the day. During the late war with China it was currently reported that from early morning until late at night, week after week and month after month, he worked upon the various matters of business that demanded his attention. No important move or decision was made without his careful consideration and final approval. These and other noble qualities of the present Emperor have, without doubt, done much toward transferring the loyalty of the people from the local daimyo to the national throne.

An event in the political world has recently occurred which illustrates pointedly the statements just made in regard to the enthusiastic loyalty of the people toward the Emperor. In spite of the fact that the national finances are in a distressing state of confusion, and notwithstanding the struggle which has been going on between successive cabinets and political parties, the former insisting on, and the latter refusing, any increase in the land tax, no sooner was it suggested by a small political party, to make a thank-offering to the Emperor of 20,000,000 yen out of the final payment of the war indemnity lately received, than the proposal was taken up with zeal by both of the great and utterly hostile political parties, and immediately by both houses of the Diet. The two reasons assigned were, "First, that the victory over China would never have been won, nor the indemnity obtained, had not the Emperor been the victorious, sagacious Sovereign that he is, and that, therefore, it is only right that a portion of the indemnity should be offered to him; secondly, that His Majesty is in need of money, the allowance granted by the state for the maintenance of the Imperial Household being insufficient, in view of the greatly enhanced prices of commodities and the large donations constantly made by His Majesty for charitable purposes."[Q] This act of the Diet appeals to the sentiment of the people as the prosaic, business-like method of the Occident would not do. The significance of the appropriation made by the Diet will be better realized if it is borne in mind that the post-bellum programme for naval and military expansion which was adopted in view of the large indemnity (being, by the way, 50,000,000 yen), already calls for an expenditure in excess of the indemnity. Either the grand programme must be reduced, or new funds be raised, yet the leading political parties have been absolutely opposed to any substantial increase of the land tax, which seems to be the only available source of increase even to meet the current expenses of the government, to say nothing of the post-bellum programme. So has a burst of sentiment buried all prudential considerations. This is a species of loyalty that Westerners find hard to appreciate. To them it would seem that the first manifestation of loyalty would be to provide the Emperor's Cabinet and executive officers with the necessary funds for current expenses; that the second would be to give the Emperor an allowance sufficient to meet his actual needs, and the third,—if the funds held out,—to make him a magnificent gift. This sentimental method of loyalty to the Emperor, however, is matched by many details of common life. A sentimental parting gift or speech will often be counted as more friendly than thoroughly business-like relations. The prosaic Occidental discounts all sentiment that has not first satisfied the demands of business and justice. Such a standard, however, seems to be repugnant to the average Japanese mind.

The theory that all authority resides in the Emperor is also enforced by recent history. For the constitution was not wrung from an unwilling ruler by an ambitious people, but was conferred by the Emperor of his own free will, under the advice of his enlightened and progressive councilors.

As an illustration of some of the preceding statements let me quote from a recent article by Mr. Yamaguchi, Professor of History in the Peeresses' School and Lecturer in the Imperial Military College. After speaking of the abolition of feudalism and the establishment of a constitutional monarchy, he goes on to say: "But we must not suppose that the sovereign power of the state has been transferred to the Imperial Diet. On the contrary, it is still in the hands of the Emperor as before.... The functions of the government are retained in the Emperor's own hands, who merely delegates them to the Diet, the Government (Cabinet), and the Judiciary, to exercise the same in his name. The present form of government is the result of the history of a country which has enjoyed an existence of many centuries. Each country has its own peculiar characteristics which differentiate it from others. Japan, too, has her history, different from that of other countries. Therefore we ought not to draw comparisons between Japan and other countries, as if the same principles applied to all indiscriminately. The Empire of Japan has a history of 3000 [!] years, which fact distinctly marks out our nationality as unique. The monarch, in the eyes of the people, is not merely on a par with an aristocratic oligarchy which rules over the inferior masses, or a few nobles who equally divide the sovereignty among themselves. According to our ideas, the monarch reigns over and governs the country in his own right, and not by virtue of rights conferred by the constitution.... Our Emperor possesses real sovereignty and also exercises it. He is quite different from other rulers who possess but a partial sovereignty.... He has inherited the rights of sovereignty from his ancestors. Thus it is quite legitimate to think that the rights of sovereignty exist in the Emperor himself.... The Empire of Japan shall be reigned over and governed by a line of Emperors unbroken for ages eternal. (Constitution, Art. LXXIII.) ... The sovereign power of the state cannot be dissociated from the Imperial Throne. It lasts forever, along with the Imperial line of succession, unbroken for ages eternal. If the Imperial house cease to exist, the Empire falls."

In a land where adopted sons are practically equivalent to lineal descendants (another instance of the "yumei-mujitsu" type of thought), and where marriage is essentially polygamous, and where the "yumei-mujitsu" spirit has allowed the sovereignty to be usurped in fact, though it may not be in name, it is not at all wonderful that the nation can boast of a longer line of Emperors than any other land. But when monogamy becomes the rule in Japan, as it doubtless will some day, and if lineal descent should be considered essential to inheritance, as in the Occident, it is not at all likely that the Imperial line will maintain itself unbroken from father to son indefinitely. Although the present Emperor has at least five concubines besides his wife, the Empress, and has had, prior to 1896, no less than thirteen children by them, only two of these are still living, both of them the offspring of his concubines; one of these is a son born in 1879, proclaimed the heir in 1887, elected Crown Prince in 1889, and married in 1900; he is said to be in delicate health; the second child is a daughter born in 1890. Since 1896 several children have been born to the Emperor and two or three have died, so that at present writing there are but four living children. These are all offspring of concubines.[R]

In speaking, however, of the Japanese apotheosis of their Emperor, we must not forget how the "divine right of kings" has been a popular doctrine, even in enlightened England, until the eighteenth century, and is not wholly unknown in other lands at the present day. Only in recent times has the real source of sovereignty been discovered by historical and political students. That the Japanese are not able to pass at one leap from the old to the new conception in regard to this fundamental element of national authority is not at all strange. Past history, together with that which is recent, furnishes a satisfactory explanation for the peculiar nature of Japanese patriotism. This is clearly due to the nature of the social order.

A further fact in this connection is that, in a very real sense, the existence of Japan as a unified nation has depended on apotheosis. It is the method that all ancient nations have adopted at one stage of their social development for expressing their sense of national unity and the authority of national law. In that stage of social development when the common individual counts for nothing, the only possible conception of the authority of law is that it proceeds from a superior being—the highest ruler. And in order to secure the full advantage of authority, the supreme ruler must be raised to the highest possible pinnacle, must be apotheosized. That national laws should be the product of the unvalued units which compose the nation was unthinkable in an age when the worth of the individual was utterly unrecognized. The apotheosis of the Emperor was neither an unintelligible nor an unreasonable practice. But now that an individualistic, democratic organization of society has been introduced resting on a principle diametrically opposed to that of apotheosis, a struggle of most profound importance has been inaugurated. Does moral or even national authority really reside in the Emperor? The school-teachers are finding great difficulty in teaching morality as based exclusively on the Imperial Edict. The politicians of Japan are not content with leaving all political and state authority to the Emperor. Not long ago (June, 1898), for the first time in Japan, a Cabinet acknowledging responsibility to a political party took the place of one acknowledging responsibility only, to the Emperor. For this end the politicians have been working since the first meeting of the national Diet. Which principle is to succeed, apotheosis and absolute Imperial sovereignty, or individualism with democratic sovereignty? The two cannot permanently live together. The struggle is sure to be intense, for the question of authority, both political and moral, is inevitably involved.

The parallel between Japanese and Roman apotheosis is interesting. I can present it no better than by quoting from that valuable contribution to social and moral problems, "The Genesis of the Social Conscience," by Prof. H.S. Nash: "Yet Rome with all her greatness could not outgrow the tribal principle.... We find something that reveals a fundamental fault in the whole system. It is the apotheosis of the Emperors. The process of apotheosis was something far deeper than servility in the subject conspiring with vanity in the ruler. It was a necessity of the state. There was no means of insuring the existence of the state except religion. In the worship of the Cæsars the Empire reverenced its own law. There was no other way in which pagan Rome could guarantee the gains she had made for civilization. Yet the very thing that was necessary to her was in logic her undoing.... The worship of the Emperor undid the definition of equality the logic of the Empire demanded. Again apotheosis violated the divine unity of humanity upon which alone the Empire could securely build."[9]

That the final issue of Japan's experience will be like that of Rome I do not believe. For her environment is totally different. But the same struggle of the two conflicting principles is already on. Few, even among the educated classes, realize its nature or profundity. The thinkers who adhere to the principle of apotheosis do so admittedly because they see no other way in which to secure authority for law, whether political or moral. Here we see the importance of those conceptions of God, of law, of man, which Christianity alone can give.

From patriotism we naturally pass to the consideration of courage. Nothing was more prized and praised in Old Japan. In those days it was the deliberate effort of parents and educators to develop courage in children. Many were their devices for training the young in bravery. Not content with mere precept, they were sent alone on dark stormy nights to cemeteries, to houses reputed to be haunted, to dangerous mountain peaks, and to execution grounds. Many deeds were required of the young whose sole aim was the development of courage and daring. The worst name you could give to a samurai was "koshinuke" (coward). Many a feud leading to a fatal end has resulted from the mere use of this most hated of all opprobrious epithets. The history of Japan is full of heroic deeds. I well remember a conversation with a son of the old samurai type, who told me, with the blood tingling in his veins, of bloody deeds of old and the courage they demanded. He remarked incidentally that, until one had slain his first foe, he was ever inclined to tremble. But once the deed had been done, and his sword had tasted the life blood of a man, fear was no more. He also told me how for the sake of becoming inured to ghastly sights under nerve-testing circumstances, the sons of samurai were sent at night to the execution grounds, there, by faint moonlight to see, stuck on poles, the heads of men who had been recently beheaded.

The Japanese emotion of courage is in some respects peculiar. At least it appears to differ from that of the Anglo-Saxon. A Japanese seems to lose all self-control when the supreme moment comes; he throws himself into the fray with a frenzied passion and a fearless madness allied to insanity. Such is the impression I have gathered from the descriptions I have heard and the pictures I have seen. Even the pictures of the late war with China give evidence of this.

But their courage is not limited to fearlessness in the face of death; it extends to complete indifference to pain. The honorable method by which a samurai who had transgressed some law or failed in some point of etiquette, might leave this world is well known to all, the "seppuku," the elegant name for the vulgar term "hara-kiri" or "belly-cutting." To one who is sensitive to tales of blood, unexpurgated Japanese history must be a dreadful thing. The vastness of the multitudes who died by their own hands would be incredible, were there not ample evidence of the most convincing nature. It may be said with truth that suicide becameapotheosized, a condition that I suppose cannot be said to have prevailed in any other land.

In thus describing the Japanese sentiment in regard to "seppuku," there is, however, some danger of misrepresenting it. "Seppuku" itself was not honored, for in the vast majority of cases those who performed it were guilty of some crime or breach of etiquette. And not infrequently those who were condemned to commit "seppuku" were deficient in physical courage; in such cases, some friend took hold of the victim's hand and forced him to cut himself. Such cowards were always despised. To be condemned to commit "seppuku" was a disgrace, but it was much less of a disgrace than to be beheaded as a common man, for it permitted the samurai to show of what stuff he was made. It should be stated further that in the case of "seppuku," as soon as the act of cutting the abdomen had been completed, always by a single rapid stroke, someone from behind would, with a single blow, behead the victim. The physical agony of "seppuku" was, therefore, very brief, lasting but a few seconds.

I can do no better than quote in this connection a paragraph from the "Religions of Japan" by W.E. Griffis:

"From the prehistoric days when the custom of 'Junshi,' or dying with the master, required the interment of living retainers with their dead lord, down through all the ages to the Revolution of 1868, when at Sendai and Aidzu scores of men and boys opened their bowels, and mothers slew their infant sons and cut their own throats, there has been flowing a river of suicides' blood having its springs in devotion of retainers to masters, and of soldiers to a lost cause.... Not only a thousand, but thousands of thousands of soldiers hated their parents, wife, child, friend, in order to be disciples to the supreme loyalty. They sealed their creed by emptying their own veins.... The common Japanese novels read like records of slaughter-houses. No Molech or Shivas won more victims to his shrine than has this idea of Japanese loyalty, which is so beautiful in theory but so hideous in practice ... Could the statistics of the suicides during this long period be collected, their publication would excite in Christendom the utmost incredulity."⬚

I well remember the pride, which almost amounted to glee, with which a young blood gave me the account of a mere boy, perhaps ten or twelve years old, who cut his bowels in such a way that the deed was not quite complete, and then tying his "obi" or girdle over it, walked into the presence of his mother, explained the circumstances which made it a point of honor that he should commit "seppuku," and forthwith untied his "obi" and died in her presence.

These are the ideals of courage and loyalty that have been held up before Japanese youth for centuries. Little comment is needful. From the evolutionary standpoint, it is relatively easy to understand the rise of these ideas and practices. It is clear that they depend entirely on the social order. With the coming in of the Western social order, feudal lords and local loyalty and the carrying of swords were abolished. Are the Japanese any less courageous now than they were thirty years ago? The social order has changed and the ways of showing courage have likewise changed. That is all that need be said.

Are we to say that the Japanese are more courageous than other peoples? Although no other people have manifested such phenomena as the Japanese in regard to suicide for loyalty, yet any true appreciation of Western peoples will at once dispel the idea that they lack courage. Manifestations of courage differ according to the nature of the social order, but no nation could long maintain itself, to say nothing of coming into existence, without a high degree of this endowment.

But Japanese courage is not entirely of the physical order, although that is the form in which it has chiefly shown itself thus far. The courage of having and holding one's own convictions is known in Japan as elsewhere. There has been a long line of martyrs. During the decades after the introduction of Buddhism, therewas such opposition that it required much courage for converts to hold to their beliefs. So, too, at the time of the rise of the new Buddhist sects, there was considerable persecution, especially with the rise of the Nichiren Shu. And when the testing time of Christianity came, under the edict of the Tokugawas by which it was suppressed, tens of thousands were found who preferred death to the surrender of their faith. In recent times, too, much courage has been shown by the native Christians.

As an illustration is the following: When an eminent American teacher of Japanese youth returned to Japan after a long absence, his former pupils gathered around him with warm admiration. They had in the interval of his absence become leaders among the trustees and faculty of the most prosperous Christian college in Japan. He was accordingly invited to deliver a course of lectures in the Chapel. It was generally known that he was no longer the earnest Christian that he had once been, when, as teacher in an interior town, he had inspired a band of young men who became Christians under his teaching and a power for good throughout the land. But no one was prepared to hear such extreme denunciations of Christianity and Christian missions and missionaries as constituted the substance of his lectures. At first the matter was passed over in silence. But, by the end of the second lecture, the missionaries entered a protest, urging that the Christian Chapel should not again be used for such lectures. The faculty, however, were not ready to criticise their beloved teacher. The third lecture proved as abusive as the others; the speaker seemed to have no sense of propriety. A glimpse of his thought, and method of expression may be gained from a single sentence: "I have been commissioned, gentlemen, by Jesus Christ, to tell you that there is no such thing as a soul or a future life." Although the missionary members of the faculty urged it, the Japanese members, most of whom were his former pupils, were unwilling to take any steps whatever to prevent the continuation of the blasphemous lectures. The students of the institution accordingly held a mass-meeting, in which the matter was discussed, and it was decided to inform the speaker that the students did not care to hear any more such lectures. The question then arose as to who would deliver the resolution. There was general hesitancy, and anyone who has seen or known the lecturer, and has heard him speak, can easily understand this feeling; for he is a large man with a most impressive and imperious manner. The young man, however, who had perhaps been most active in agitating the matter, and who had presented the resolution to the meeting, volunteered to go. He is slight and rather small, even for a Japanese. Going to the home of the lecturer, he delivered calmly the resolution of the students. To the demand as to who had drawn up and presented the resolution to the meeting, the reply was: "I, sir." That ended the conversation, but not the matter. From that day the idolized teacher was gradually lowered from his pedestal. But the moral courage of the young man who could say in his enraged presence, "I, sir," has not been forgotten. Neither has that of the young man who had acted as interpreter for the first lecture; not only did he decline to act in that capacity any longer, but, taking the first public opportunity, at the chapel service the following day, which proved to be Sunday, he went to the platform and asked forgiveness of God and of men that he had uttered such language as he had been compelled to use in his translating. Here, too, was moral courage of no mean order.

XIV
FICKLENESS—STOLIDITY—STOICISM

A frequent criticism of the Japanese is that they are fickle; that they run from one fad to another, from one idea to another, quickly tiring of each in turn. They are said to lack persistence in their amusements no less than in the most serious matters of life.

None will deny the element of truth in this charge. In fact, the Japanese themselves recognize that of late their progress has been by "waves," and not a few lament it. A careful study of school attendance will show that it has been subject to alternate waves of popularity and disfavor. Private schools glorying in their hundreds of pupils have in a short time lost all but a few score. In 1873 there was a passion for rabbits, certain varieties of which were then for the first time introduced into Japan. For a few months these brought fabulous prices, and became a subject of the wildest speculation. In 1874-75 cock-fighting was all the rage. Foreign waltzing and gigantic funerals were the fashion one year, while wrestling was the fad at another time, even the then prime minister, Count Kuroda, taking the lead. But the point of our special interest is as to whether fickleness is an essential element of Japanese character, and so dominant that wherever the people may be and whatever their surroundings, they will always be fickle; or whether this trait is due to the conditions of their recent history. Let us see.

Prof. Basil H. Chamberlain says, "Japan stood still so long that she has to move quickly and often now to make up for lost time." This states the case pretty well. Had we known Japan only through her Tokugawa period, the idea of fickleness would not have occurred to us; on the contrary, the dominant impression wouldhave been that of the permanence and fixity of her life and customs. This quality or appearance of fickleness is, then, a modern trait, due to the extraordinary circumstances in which Japan finds herself. The occurrence of wave after wave of fresh fashions and fads is neither strange nor indicative of an essentially fickle disposition. Glancing below the surface for a moment, we shall see that there is an earnestness of purpose which is the reverse of fickle.

What nation, for example, ever voluntarily set itself to learn the ways and thoughts and languages of foreign nations as persistently as Japan? That there has been fluctuation of intensity is not so surprising as that, through a period of thirty years, she has kept steadily at it. Tens of thousands of her young men are now, able to read the English language with some facility; thousands are also able to read German and French. Foreign languages are compulsory in all the advanced schools. A regulation going into force in September, 1900, requires the study of two foreign languages. This has been done at a cost of many hundred thousands of dollars. There has been a fairly permanent desire and effort to learn all that the West has to teach. The element of fickleness is to be found chiefly in connection with the methods rather than in connection with the ends to be secured. From the moment when Japan discovered that the West had sources of power unknown to herself, and indispensable if she expected to hold her own with the nations of the world, the aim and end of all her efforts has been to master the secrets of that power. She has seen that education is one important means. That she should stumble in the adoption of educational methods is not strange. The necessary experience is being secured. But for a lesson of this sort, more than one generation of experience is required of a nation. For some time to come Japan is sure to give signs of unsteadiness, of lack of perfect balance.

A pitiful sight in Japan is that of boys not more than five or six years of age pushing or pulling with all their might at heavily loaded hand-carts drawn by their parents. Yet this is typical of one aspect of Japanese civilization. The work is largely done by young people under thirty, and vast multitudes of the workers are under twenty years of age. This is true not only of menial labor, but also in regard to labor involving more or less responsibility. In the post offices, for instance, the great majority of the clerks are mere boys. In the stores one rarely sees a man past middle age conducting the business or acting as clerk. Why are the young so prominent? Partly because of the custom of "abdication." As "family abdication" is frequent, it has a perceptible effect on the general character of the nation, and accounts in part for rash business ventures and other signs of impetuosity and unbalanced judgment. Furthermore, under the new civilization, the older men have become unfitted to do the required work. The younger and more flexible members of the rising generation can quickly adjust themselves to the new conditions, as in the schools, where the older men, who had received only the regular training in Chinese classics, were utterly incompetent as teachers of science. Naturally, therefore, except for instruction in these classics, the common-school teachers, during the earlier decades, were almost wholly young boys. The extreme youthfulness of school-teachers has constantly surprised me. In the various branches of government this same phenomenon is equally common. Young men have been pushed forward into positions with a rapidity and in numbers unknown in the West, and perhaps unknown in any previous age in Japan.

The rise and decline of the Christian Church in Japan has been instanced as a sign of the fickleness of the people. It is a mistaken instance, for there are many other causes quite sufficient to account for the phenomenon in question. Let me illustrate by the experience of an elderly Christian. He had been brought to Christ through the teachings of a young man of great brilliancy, whose zeal was not tempered with full knowledge—which, however, was not strange, in view of his limited opportunities for learning. His instruction was therefore narrow, not to say bigoted. Still the elderly gentleman found the teachings of the young man sufficiently strong and clear to upset all his old ideas of religion, his polytheism, his belief in charms, his worship of ancestors, and all kindred ideas. He accepted the New Testament in simple unquestioning faith. But, after six or eight years, the young instructor began to lose his own primitive and simple faith. He at once proceeded to attack that which before he had been defending and expounding. Soon his whole theological position was changed. Higher criticism and religious philosophy were now the center of his preaching and writing. The result was that this old gentleman was again in danger of being upset in his religious thinking. He felt that his new faith had been received in bulk, so to speak, and if a part of it were false, as his young teacher now asserted, how could he know that any of it was true? Yet his heart's experience told him that he had secured something in this faith that was real; he was loath to lose it; consequently, for some years now, he has systematically stayed away from church services, and refrained from reading magazines in which these new and destructive views have been discussed; he has preferred to read the Bible quietly at home, and to have direct communion with God, even though, in many matters of Biblical or theoretical science, he might hold his mistaken opinions. A surface view of this man's conduct might lead one to think of him as fickle; but a deeper consideration will lead to the opposite conclusion.

The fluctuating condition of the Christian churches is not cause for astonishment, nor is it to be wholly, if at all, attributed to the fickleness of the national character, but rather, in a large degree, to the peculiar conditions of Japanese life. The early Christians had much to learn. They knew, experimentally, but little of Christian truth. The whole course of

Christian thought, the historical development of theology, with the various heresies, the recent discussions resting on the so-called "higher criticism" of the Bible, together with the still more recent investigations into the history and philosophy of religion in general, were of course wholly unknown to them. This was inevitable, and they were blameless. All could not be learned at once.

Nor is there any blame attached to the missionaries. It was as impossible for them to impart to young and inexperienced Christians a full knowledge of these matters as it was for the latter to receive such information. The primary interest of the missionaries was in the practical and everyday duties of the Christian life, in the great problem of getting men and women to put away the superstitions and narrowness and sins springing from polytheism or practical atheism, and getting them started in ways of godliness. The training schools for evangelists were designed to raise up practical workers rather than speculative theologians. Missionaries considered it their duty (and they were beyond question right) to teach religion rather than the science and philosophy of religion. When, therefore, the evangelists discovered that they had not been taught these advanced branches of knowledge, it is not strange that some should rush after them, and, in their zeal for that which they supposed to be important, hasten to criticise their former teachers. As a result, they undermined both their own faith and that of many who had become Christians through their teaching.

The dullness of the church life, so conspicuous at present in many of the churches, is only partly due to the fact that the Christians are tired of the services. It is true that these services no longer afford them that mental and spiritual stimulus which they found at the first, and that, lacking this, they find little inducement to attend. But this is only a partial explanation. Looking over the experience of the past twenty-five years, we now see that the intense zeal of the first few years was a natural result of a certain narrowness of view. It is an interesting fact that, during one of the early revivals in the Doshisha, the young men were so intense and excited that the missionaries were compelled to restrain them. These young Christians felt and said that the missionaries were not filled with the Holy Spirit; they accordingly considered it their duty to exhort their foreign leaders, even to chide them for their lack of faith. The extraordinary expectations entertained by the young Japanese workers of those days and shared by the missionaries, that Japan was to become a Christian nation before the end of the century, was due in large measure to an ignorance alike of Christianity, of human nature, and of heathenism, but, under the peculiar conditions of life, this was well-nigh inevitable. And that great and sudden changes in feeling and thought have come over the infant churches, in consequence of the rapid acquisition of new light and new experience, is equally inevitable. These changes are not primarily attributable to fickleness of nature, but to the extraordinary additions to their knowledge.

There is good reason to think, however, that the period of these rapid fluctuations is passing away. All the various fads, fancies, and follies, together with the sciences, philosophies, ologies, and isms of the Western world, have already come to Japan, and are fairly well known. No essentially new and sudden experiences lie before the people.

Furthermore, the young men are year by year growing older. Experience and age together are giving a soberness and a steadiness otherwise unattainable. In the schools, in the government, in politics, and in the judiciary, and in the churches, men of years and of training in the new order are becoming relatively numerous, and erelong they will be in the majority. We may expect to see Japan gradually settling down to a steadiness and a regularity that have been lacking during the past few decades. The newcomer to Japan is much impressed with the expressionless character of so many Japanese faces. They appear like the images of Buddha, who is supposed to be so absorbed in profound meditation that the events of the passing world make no impression upon him. I have sometimes heard the expression "putty face" used to describe the appearance of the common Japanese face. This immobility of the Oriental is more conspicuous to a newcomer than to one who has seen much of the people and who has learned its significance. But though the "putty" effect wears off, there remains an impression of stoicism that never fades away. These two features, stolidity and stoicism, are so closely allied in appearance that they are easily mistaken, yet they are really distinct. The one arises from stupidity, from dullness of mind. The other is the product of elaborate education and patient drill. Yet it is often difficult to determine where the one ends and the other begins.

The stolidity of stupidity is, of course, commonest among the peasant class. For centuries they have been in closest contact with the soil; nothing has served to awaken their intellectual faculties. Reading and writing have remained to them profound mysteries. Their lives have been narrow in the extreme. But the Japanese peasant is not peculiar in this respect. Similar conditions in other lands produce similar results, as in France, according to Millet's famous painting, "The Man with the Hoe."

It is an interesting fact, however, that this stolidity of stupidity can be easily removed. I have often heard comments on the marked change in the facial expression of those adults who learn to read the Bible. Their minds are awakened; a new light is seen in their eyes as new ideas are started in their minds.

The impression of stolidity made on the foreigner is, due less, however, to stupidity than to a stoical education. For centuries the people have been taught to repress all expression of their emotions. It has been required of the inferior to listen quietly to his superior and to obey implicitly. The relations of superior and inferior have been drilled into the people for ages. The code of a military camp has been taught and enforced in all the homes. Talking in the presence of a superior, or laughter, or curious questions, or expressions of surprise, anything revealing the slightest emotion on the part of the inferior was considered a discourtesy.

Education in these matters was not confined to oral instruction; infringements were punished with great rigor. Whenever a daimyo traveled to Yedo, the capital, he was treated almost as a god by the people. They were required to fall on their knees and bow their faces to the ground, and the death penalty was freely awarded to those who failed to make such expressions of respect.

One source, then, of the systematic repression of emotional expression is the character of the feudal order of society that so long prevailed. The warrior who had best control of his facial expression, who could least expose to his foe or even to his ordinary friends the real state of his feelings, other things being equal, would come off the victor. In further explanation of this repression is the religion of Buddha. For 1200 years it has helped to mold the middle and the lower classes of the people. According to its doctrine, desire is the great evil; from it all other evils spring. For this reason, the aim of the religious life is to suppress all desire, and the most natural way to accomplish this is to suppress the manifestation of desire; to maintain passive features under all circumstances. The images of Buddha and of Buddhist saints are utterly devoid of expression. They indicate as nearly as possible the attainment of their desire, namely, freedom from all desire. This is the ambition of every earnest Buddhist. Being the ideal and the actual effort of life, it does affect the faces of the people. Lack of expression, however, does not prove absence of desire.

Every foreigner has had amusing proof of this. A common experience is the passing of a group of Japanese who, apparently, give no heed to the stranger. Neither by the turn of the head nor by the movement of a single facial muscle do they betray any curiosity, yet their eyes take in each detail, and involuntarily follow the receding form of the traveler. In the interior, where foreigners are still objects of curiosity, young men have often run up from behind, gone to a distance ahead of me, then turned abruptly, as though remembering something, and walked slowly back again, giving me, apparently, not the slightest attention. The motive was the desire to get a better look at the foreigner. They hoped to conceal it by a ruse, for there must be no manifestation of curiosity.

Phenomena which a foreigner may attribute to a lack of emotion of, at least, to its repression, may be due to some very different cause. Few things, for instance, are more astonishing to the Occidental than the silence on the part of the multitude when the Emperor, whom they all admire and love, appears on the street. Undercircumstances which would call forth the most enthusiastic cheers from Western crowds, a Japanese crowd will maintain absolute silence. Is this from lack of emotion? By no means. Reverence dominates every breast. They would no more think of making noisy demonstrations of joy in the presence of the Emperor than a congregation of devout Christians would think of doing the same during a religious service. This idea of reverence for superiors has pervaded the social order —the intensity of the reverence varying with the rank of the superior. But a change has already begun. Silence is no longer enforced; no profound bowings to the ground are now demanded before the nobility; on at least one occasion during the recent China-Japan war the enthusiasm of the populace found audible expression when the Emperor made a public appearance. Even the stoical appearance of the people is passing away under the influence of the new order of society, with its new, dominant ideas. Education is bringing the nation into a large and throbbing life. Naturalness is taking the place of forced repression. A sense of the essential equality of man is springing up, especially among the young men, and is helping to create a new atmosphere in this land, where, for centuries, one chief effort has been to repress all natural expression of emotion.

While touring in Kyushu several years ago, I had an experience which showed me that the stolidity, or vivacity, of a people is largely dependent on the prevailing social order rather than on inherent nature. Those who have much to do with the Japanese have noted the extreme quiet and reserve of the women. It is a trait that has been lauded by both native and foreign writers. Because of this characteristic it is difficult for a stranger, to carry on conversation with them. They usually reply in monosyllables and in low tones. The very expression of their faces indicates a reticence, a calm stolidity, and a lack of response to the stimulus of social intercourse that is striking and oppressive to an Occidental. I have always found it a matter of no little difficulty to become acquainted with the women, and especially with the young women, in the church with which I have been connected. With the older women this reticence is not so marked. Now for my story:

One day I called on a family, expecting to meet the mother, with whom I was well acquainted. She proved to be out; but a daughter of whom I had not before heard was at home, and I began to talk with her. Contrary to all my previous experience, this young girl of less than twenty years looked me straight in the face with perfect composure, replied to my questions with clear voice and complete sentences, and asked questions in her turn without the slightest embarrassment. I was amazed. Here was a Japanese girl acting and talking with the freedom of an American. How was this to be explained? Difficult though it appeared, the problem was easily solved. The young lady had been in America, having spent several years in Radcliffe College. There it was that her Japanese demureness was dropped and the American frankness and vivacity of manner acquired. It was a matter simply of the prevailing social customs, and not of her inherent nature as a Japanese.

And this conclusion is enforced by the further fact that there is a marked increase in vivacity in those who become Christian. The repressive social restraints of the old social order are somewhat removed. A freedom is allowed to individuals of the Christian community, in social life, in conversation between men and women, in the holding of private opinions, which the non-Christian order of society did not permit. Sociability between the sexes was not allowed. The new freedom naturally results in greater vivacity and a far freer play of facial expression than the older order could produce. The vivacity and sociability of the geisha (dancing and singing girls), whose business it is to have social relations with the men, freely conversing with them, still further substantiates the view that the stolid, irrepressive features of the usual Japanese woman are social, not essential, characteristics. The very same girls exhibit alternately stolidity and vivacity according as they are acting as geisha or as respectable members of society.

This completes our direct study of the various elements characterizing the emotional nature of the Japanese. It is universally admitted that the people are conspicuously emotional. We have shown, however, that their feelings are subject to certain remarkable suppressions.

It remains to be asked why the Japanese are more emotional than other races? One reason doubtless is that the social conditions were such as to stimulate their emotional rather than their intellectual powers. The military system upon which the social structure rested kept the nation in its mental infancy. Twenty-eight millions of farmers and a million and a half of soldiers was the proportion during the middle of the nineteenth century. Education was limited to the soldiers. But although they cultivated their minds somewhat, their very occupation as soldiers required them to obey rather than to think; their hand-to-hand conflicts served mightily to stimulate the emotions. The entire feudal order likewise was calculated to have the same effect. The intellectual life being low, its inhibitions were correspondingly weak. When, in the future, the entire population shall have become fairly educated, and taught to think independently; and when government by the people shall have become much more universal, throwing responsibility on the people as never before, and stimulating discussion of the general principles of life, of government, and of law, then must the emotional features of the nation become less conspicuous.

It is a question of relative development. As children run to extremes of thought and action on the slightest occasion, simply because their intellects have not come into full activity, weeping at one moment and laughing at the next, so it is with national life. Where the general intellectual development of a people is retarded, the emotional manifestations are of necessity correspondingly conspicuous.

Even so fundamental a racial trait, then, as the emotional, is seen to be profoundly influenced by the prevailing social order. The emotional characteristics which distinguish the Japanese from other races are due, in the last analysis, to the nature of their social order rather than to their inherent nature or brain structure.

XV
ÆSTHETIC CHARACTERISTICS

In certain directions, the Japanese reveal a development of æsthetic taste which no other nation has reached. The general appreciation of landscape-views well illustrates this point. The home and garden of the average workman are far superior artistically to those of the same class in the West. There is hardly a home without at least a diminutive garden laid out in artistic style with miniature lake and hills and winding walks. And this garden exists solely for the delight of the eye.

The general taste displayed in many little ways is a constant delight to the Western "barbarian" when he first comes to Japan. Nor does this delight vanish with time and familiarity, though it is tempered by a later perception of certain other features. Indeed, the more one knows of the details of their artistic taste, the more does he appreciate it. The "toko-no-ma," for example, is a variety of alcove usually occupying half of one side of a room. It indicates the place of honor, and guests are always urged to sit in front of it. The floor of the "toko-no-ma" is raised four or five inches above the level of the room and should never be stepped upon. In this "toko-no-ma" is usually placed some work of art, or a vase with flowers, and on the wall is hung a picture or a few Chinese characters, written by some famous calligraphist, which are changed with the seasons. The woodwork and the coloring of this part of the room is of the choicest. The "toko-no-ma" of the main room of the house is always restful to the eye; this "honorable spot" is found in at least one room in every house; and if the owner has moderate means, there are two or three such rooms. Only the homes of the poorest of the poor are without this ornament.

The Japanese show a refined taste in the coloring and decoration of rooms; natural woods, painted and polished, are common; every post and board standing erect must stand in the position in which it grew. A Japanese knows at once whether a board or post is upside down, though it would puzzle a Westerner to decide the matter. The natural wood ceilings and the soft yellows and blues of the walls are all that the best trained Occidental eye could ask. Dainty decorations called the "ramma," over the neat "fusuma," consist of delicate shapes and quaint designs cut in thin boards, and serve at once as picture and ventilator. The drawings, too, on the "fusuma" (solid thick paper sliding doors separating adjacent rooms or shutting off the closet) are simple and neat, as is all Japanese pictorial art.

Japanese love for flowers reveals a high æsthetic development. Not only are there various flower festivals at which times the people flock to suburban gardens and parks, but sprays, budding branches, and even large boughs are invariably arranged in the homes and public halls. Every church has an immense vase for the purpose. The proper arrangement of flowers and of flowering sprays and boughs is a highly developed art. It is often one of the required studies in girls' schools. I have known two or three men who made their entire living by teaching this art. Miniature flowering trees are reared with consummate skill. An acquaintance of mine glories in 230 varieties of the plum tree, all in pots, some of them between two and three hundred years old. Shinto and Buddhist temples also reveal artistic qualities most pleasing to the eye.

But the main point of our interest lies in the explanation of this characteristic. Is the æsthetic sense more highly developed in Japan than in the West? Is it more general? Is it a matter of inherent nature, or of civilization?

In trying to meet these problems, I note, first of all, that the development of the Japanese æsthetic taste is one-sided; though advanced in certain respects it is belated in others. In illustration is the sense of smell. It will not do to say that "the Japanese have no use for the nose," and that the love of sweet smells is unknown. Sir Rutherford Alcock's off-quoted sentence that "in one of the most beautiful and fertile countries in the whole world the flowers have no scent, the birds no song, and the fruit and vegetables no flavor," is quite misleading, for it has only enough truth to make it the more deceptive. It is true that the cherry blossom has little or no odor, and that its beauty lies in its exquisite coloring and abounding luxuriance, but most of the native flowers are praised and prized by the Japanese for their odors, as well as for their colors, as the plum, the chrysanthemum, the lotus, and the rose. The fragrance of flowers is a frequent theme in Japanese poetry. Japanese ladies, like those of every land, are fond of delicate scents. Cologne and kindred wares find wide sale in Japan, and I am told that expensive musk is not infrequently packed away with the clothing of the wealthy.

But in contrast to this appreciation is a remarkable indifference to certain foul odors. It is amazing what horrid smells the cultivated Japanese will endure in his home. What we conceal in the rear and out of the way, he very commonly places in the front yard; though this is, of course, more true of the country than of large towns or cities. It would seem as if a high æsthetic development should long ago have banished such sights and smells. As a matter of fact, however, the æsthetics of the subject does not seem to have entered the national mind, any more than have the hygienics of the same subject.

In explanation of these facts, may it not be that the Japanese method of agriculture has been a potent hindrance to the æsthetic development of the sense of smell? In primitive times, when wealth was small, the only easy method which the people had of preserving the fertilizing properties of that which is removed from our cities by the sewer-system was such as we still find in use in Japan to-day. Perhaps the necessities of the case have toughened the mental, if not the physical, sense of the people. Perhaps the unæsthetic character of the sights and smells has been submerged in the great value of fertilizing materials. Then, too, with the Occidental, the thought is common that such odors are indications of seriously unhealthful conditions. We are accordingly offended not simply by the odor itself, but also by the associations of sickness and death which it suggests. Not so the unsophisticated Oriental. Such a correlation of ideas is only now arising in Japan, and changes are beginning to be made, as a consequence.

I cannot leave this point without drawing attention to the fact that the development of the sense of smell in these directions is relatively recent, even in the West. Of all the non-European nations and races, I have no doubt Japan is most free from horrid smells and putrid odors. And in view of our own recent emancipation it is not for us to marvel that others have made little progress. Rather is it marvelous that we should so easily forget the hole from which we have been so recently digged.

In turning to study certain features of Japanese pictorial art, we notice that a leading characteristic is that of simplicity. The greatest results are secured with the fewest possible strokes. This general feature is in part due to the character of the instrument used, the "fude," "brush." This same brush answers for writing. It admits of strong, bold outlines; and a large brush allows the exhibition of no slight degree of skill. As a result, "writing" is a fine art in Japan. Hardly a family that makes any pretense at culture but owns one or more framed specimens of writing. In Japan these rank as pictures do or mottoes in the West, and are prized not merely for the sentiment expressed, but also for the skill displayed in the use of the brush. Skillful writers become famous, often receiving large sums for small "pictures" which consist of but two or three Chinese characters.

No doubt the higher development of appreciation for natural scenery among the people in general is largely due to the character of the scenery itself. Steep hills and narrow valleys adjoin nearly every city in the land. Seas, bays, lakes, and rivers are numerous; reflected mountain scenes are common; the colors are varied and marked. Flowering trees of striking beauty are abundant. Any people living under these physical conditions, and sufficiently advanced in civilization to have leisure and culture, can hardly fail to be impressed with such wealth of beauty in the scenery itself.

In the artistic reproduction of this scenery, however, Japanese artists are generally supposed to be inferior to those of the West.

As often remarked, Japanese art has directed its chief endeavor to animals and to nature, thus failing to give to man his share of attention. This curious one-sidedness shows itself particularly in painting and in sculpture. In the former, when human beings are the subject, the aim has apparently been to extol certain characteristics; in warriors, the military or heroic spirit; in wise men, their wisdom; in monks and priests, their mastery over the passions and complete attainment of peace; in a god, the moral character which he is supposed to represent. Art has consequently been directed to bringing into prominence certain ideal features which must be over-accentuated in order to secure recognition; caricatures, rather than lifelike forms, are the frequent results. The images of multitudes of gods are frightful to behold; the aim being to show the character of the emotion of the god in the presence of evil. These idols are easily misunderstood, for we argue that the more frightful he is, the more vicious must be the god in his real character; not so the Oriental. To him the more frightful the image, the more noble the character. Really evil gods, such as demons, are always represented, I think, as deformed creatures, partly human and partly beast. It is to be remembered, in this connection, that idols are an imported feature of Japanese religion; Shinto to this day has no "graven image." All idols are Buddhistic. Moreover, they are but copies of the hideous idols of India; the Japanese artistic genius has added nothing to their grotesque appearance. But the point of interest for us is that the æsthetic taste which can revel in flowers and natural scenery has never delivered Japanese art from truly unæsthetic representations of human beings and of gods.

Standing recently before a toy store and looking at the numberless dolls offered for sale, I was impressed afresh with the lack of taste displayed, both in coloring and in form; their conventionality was exceedingly tiresome; their one attractive feature was their absurdity. But the moment I turned away from the imitations of human beings to look at the imitations of nature, the whole impression was changed. I was pleased with the artistic taste displayed in the perfectly imitated, delicately colored flowers. They were beautiful indeed.

Why has Japanese art made so little of man as man? Is it due to the "impersonality" of the Orient, as urged by some? This suggests, but does not give, the correct interpretation of the phenomenon in question. The reason lies in the nature of the ruling ideas of Oriental civilization. Man, as man, has not been honored or highly esteemed. As a warrior he has been honored; consequently, when pictured or sculptured as a warrior, he has worn his armor; his face, if visible, is not the natural face of a man, but rather that of a passionate victor, slaying his foe or planning for the same. And so with the priests and the teachers, the emperors and the generals; all have been depicted, not for what they are in themselves, but for the rank which they have attained; they are accordingly represented with their accouterments and robes and the characteristic attitudes of their rank. The effort to preserve their actual appearance is relatively rare. Manhood and womanhood, apart from social rank, have hardly been recognized, much less extolled by art. This feature, then, corresponds to the nature of the Japanese social order. The art of a land necessarily reveals the ruling ideals of its civilization. As Japan failed to discover the inherent nature and value of manhood and womanhood, estimating them only on a utilitarian basis, so has her art reflected this failure.

Apparently it has never attempted to depict the nude human form. This is partly explained, perhaps, by the fact that the development of a perfect physical form through exercise and training has not been a part of Oriental thought. Labor of every sort has been regarded as degrading. Training for military skill and prowess has indeed been common among the military classes; but the skill and strength themselves have been the objects of thought, rather than the beauty of the muscular development which they produce. When we recall the prominent place which the games of Greece took in her civilization previous to her development of art, and the stress then laid on perfect bodily form, we shall better understand why there should be such difference in the development of the art of these two lands. I have never seen a Japanese man or youth bare his arm to show with pride the development of his biceps; and so far as I have observed, the pride which students in the United States feel over well-developed calves has no counterpart in Japan—this, despite the fact that the average Japanese has calves which would turn the American youth green with envy.

From the absence of the nude in Japanese art it has been urged that Japan herself is far more morally pure than the West. Did the moral life of the people correspond to their art in this respect, the argument would have force. Unfortunately, such does not seem to be the case. It is further suggested as a reason that the bodily form of Oriental peoples is essentially unæsthetic; that the men are either too fat or too lean, and the women too plump when in the bloom of youth and too wrinkled and flabby when the first bloom is over. The absurdity of this suggestion raises a smile, and a query as to the experience which its author must have had. For any person who has lived in Japan must have seen individuals of both sexes, whom the most fastidious painter or sculptor would rejoice to secure as models.

It might be thought that a truly artistic people, who are also somewhat immoral, would have developed much skill in the portrayal of the nude female form. But such an attempt does not seem to have been made until recent times, and in imitation of Western art. At least such attempts have not been recognized as art nor have they been preserved as such. I have never seen either statue or picture of a nude Japanese woman. Even the pictures of famous prostitutes are always faultlessly attired. The number and size of the conventional hairpins, and the gaudy coloring of the clothing, alone indicate the immoral character of the woman represented.

It is not to be inferred, however, that immoral pictures have been unknown in Japan, for the reverse is true. Until forcibly suppressed by the government under the incentive of Western criticism, there was perfect freedom to produce and sell licentious and lascivious pictures. The older foreign residents in Japan testify to the frequency with which immoral scenes were depicted and exposed for sale. Here I merely say that these were not considered works of art; they were reproduced not in the interests of the æsthetic sense, but wholly to stimulate the taste for immoral things.

The absence of the nude from Japanese art is due to the same causes that led to the relative absence of all distinctively human nature from art. Manhood and womanhood, as such, were not the themes they strove to depict.

A curious feature of the artistic taste of the people is the marked fondness for caricature. It revels in absurd accentuations of special features. Children with protruding foreheads; enormously fat little men; grotesque dwarf figures in laughable positions; these are a few common examples. Nearly all of the small drawings and sculpturings of human figures are intentionally grotesque. But the Japanese love of the grotesque is not confined to its manifestation in art. It also reveals itself in other surprising ways. It is difficult to realize that a people who revel in the beauties of nature can also delight in deformed nature; yet such is the case. Stunted and dwarfed trees, trees whose branches have been distorted into shapes and proportions that nature would scorn—these are sights that the Japanese seem to enjoy, as well as "natural" nature. Throughout the land, in the gardens of the middle and higher classes, may be found specimens of dwarfed and stunted trees which have required decades to raise. The branches, too, of most garden shrubs and trees are trimmed in fantastic shapes. What is the charm in these distortions? First, perhaps, the universal human interest in anything requiring skill. Think of the patience and persistence and experimentation necessary to rear a dwarf pear tree twelve or fifteen inches high, growing its full number of years and bearing full-size fruit in its season! And second is the no less universal human interest in the strange and abnormal. All primitive people have this interest. It shows itself in their religions. Abnormal stones are often objects of religious devotion. Although I cannot affirm that such objects are worshiped in Japan to-day, yet I can say that they are frequently set up in temple grounds and dedicated with suitable inscriptions. Where nature can be made to produce the abnormal, there the interest is still greater. It is a living miracle. Witness the cocks of Tosa, distinguished by their two or three tail feathers reaching the extraordinary length of ten or even fifteen feet, the product of ages of special breeding.

According to the ordinary use of the term, æsthetics has to do with art alone. Yet it also has intimate relations with both speech and conduct. Poetry depends for its very existence on æsthetic considerations. Although little conscious regard is paid to æsthetic claims in ordinary conversation, yet people of culture do, as a matter of fact, pay it much unconscious attention. In conduct too, æsthetic ideas are often more dominant than we suppose. The objection of the cultured to the ways of the boorish rests on æsthetic grounds. This is true in every land. In the matter of conduct it is sometimes hard to draw the line between æsthetics and ethics, for they shade imperceptibly into one another; so much so that they are seen to be complementary rather than contradictory. Though it is doubtless true that conduct æsthetically defective may not be defective ethically, still is it not quite as true that conduct bad from the ethical is bad also from the æsthetical standpoint?

In no land have æsthetic considerations had more force in molding both speech and conduct than in Japan. Not a sentence is uttered by a Japanese but has the characteristic marks of æstheticism woven into its very structure. By means of "honorifics" it is seldom necessary for a speaker to be so pointedly vulgar as even to mention self. There are few points in the language so difficult for a foreigner to master, whether in speaking himself, or in listening to others, as the use of these honorific words. The most delicate shades of courtesy and discourtesy may be expressed by them. Some writers have attributed the relative absence of the personal pronouns from the language to the dominating force of impersonal pantheism. I am unable to take this view for reasons stated in the later chapters on personality.

Though the honorific characteristics of the language seem to indicate a high degree of æsthetic development, a certain lack of delicacy in referring to subjects that are ruled out of conversation by cultivated people in the West make the contrary impression upon the uninitiated. Such language in Japan cannot be counted impure, for no such idea accompanies the words. They must be described simply as æsthetically defective. Far be it from me to imply that there is no impure conversation in Japan. I only say that the particular usages to which I refer are not necessarily a proof of moral tendency. A realistic baldness prevails that makes no effort to conceal even that which is in its nature unpleasant and unæsthetic. A spade is called a spade without the slightest hesitation. Of course specific illustrations of such a point as this are out of place. Æsthetic considerations forbid.

And how explain these unæsthetic phenomena? By the fact that Japan has long remained in a state of primitive development. Speech is but the verbal expression of life. Every primitive society is characterized by a bald literalism shocking to the æsthetic sense of societies which represent a higher stage of culture. In Japan, until recently, little effort has been made to keep out of sight objects and acts which we of the West have considered disagreeable and repulsive. Language alters more slowly than acts. Laws are making changes in the latter, and they in time will take effect in the former. But many decades will doubtless pass before the cultivated classes of Japan will reach, in this respect, the standard of the corresponding classes of the West.

As for the æsthetics of conduct in Japan, enough is indicated by what has been said already concerning the æsthetics of speech. Speech and conduct are but diverse expressions of the same inner life. Japanese etiquette has been fashioned on the feudalistic theory of society, with its numberless gradations of inferior and superior. Assertive individualism, while allowed a certain range among the samurai, always had its well-marked limits. The mass of the people were compelled to walk a narrow line of respectful obedience and deference both in form and speech. The constant aim of the inferior was to please the superior. That individuals of an inferior rank had any inherent rights, as opposed to those of a superior rank, seldom occurred to them. Furthermore, this whole feudal system, with its characteristic etiquette of conduct and speech, was authoritatively taught by moralists and religious leaders, and devoutly believed by the noblest of the land. Ethical considerations, therefore, combined powerfully with those that were social and æsthetic to produce "the most polite race on the face of the globe." Recent developments of rudeness and discourtesy among themselves and toward foreigners have emphasized my general contention that these characteristics are not due to inherent race nature, but rather to the social order.

71

How are we to account for the wide æsthetic development of all classes of the Japanese? As already suggested, the beautiful scenery explains much. But I pass at once to the significant fact that although the classes of Japanese society were widely differentiated in social rank, yet they lived in close proximity to each other. There was no spatial gulf of separation preventing the lower from knowing fully and freely the thoughts, ideals, and customs of the upper classes. The transmission of culture was thus an easy matter, in spite of social gradations.

Moreover, the character of the building materials, and the methods of construction used by the more prosperous among the people, were easily imitated in kind, if not in costliness, by the less prosperous. Take, for example, the structure of the room; it is always of certain fixed proportions, that the uniform mats may be easily fitted to it. The mats themselves are always made of a straw "toko," "bed," and an "omote," "surface," of woven straw; they vary greatly in value, but, of whatever grade, may always be kept neat and fresh at comparatively small cost. The walls of the average houses are made of mud wattles. The outer layers of plaster consist of selected earth and tinted lime. Whether put up at large or small expense, these walls may be neat and attractive. So, too, with other parts of the house.

The utter lack of independent thinking throughout the middle and lower classes, and the constant desire of the inferior to imitate the superior, have also helped to make the culture of the classes the possession of the masses. This subserviency and spirit of imitation has been further stimulated by the enforced courtesy and deference and obedience of the common people.

In this connection it should be noted, however, that the universality of culture in Japan is more apparent than real. The appearance is due in part to the lack of furniture in the homes. Without chairs or tables, bedsteads or washstands, and the multitude of other things invariably found in the home of the Occidental, it is easy for the Japanese housewife to keep her home in perfect order. No special culture is needful for this.

How it came about that the Japanese people adopted their own method of sitting on the feet, I cannot say; neither have I heard any plausible explanation of the practice. Yet this habit has relieved them of all necessity for heavy furniture. Given the custom of sitting on the feet, and a large part of the furniture of the house will be useless. Already is the introduction of furniture after Western patterns producing changes in the homes of the people; and it will be interesting to see whether the æsthetic sense of the Japanese will be able to assimilate and harmonize with itself these useful, but bulky and unæsthetic, elements of Occidental civilization.

That no part of the fine taste of the Japanese is due to the general civilization, rather than to the individual possession of the æsthetic faculty, may be inferred from many little signs. In spite of the fact that, following the long-established social fashions, the women usually display good taste in the choice of colors for their clothing, it sometimes happens that they also manifest not the slightest sense of the harmony of colors. Daughters of wealthy families will array themselves in brilliant discordant hues, yet apparently without causing the wearers or their friends the slightest æsthetic discomfort. Little children are arrayed in clothing that would doubtless put Joseph's coat of many colors quite out of countenance. Combinations and brilliancy that to the Western eye of culture seem crude and gaudy, typical of barbaric splendor, are in constant use, and are apparently thought to be fine. The Japanese display both taste and its lack in the choice of colors for clothing; this contradiction is the more striking in view of the taste manifest in the decorations of the homes of all classes of the people. Few sights are more ludicrously unæsthetic than the red, yellow, and blue worsted crocheted caps and shawls for infants, which shock all our ideas of æsthetic harmony.

In connection with Western ways or articles of clothing, the native æsthetic faculty often seems to take its flight. In a foreign house many a Japanese seems to lose his sense of fitness. I have had schoolboys, and even gentlemen, enter my home with hobnailed muddied boots, without wiping their feet on the conspicuous door mat, which is the more remarkable since, in their own homes, they invariably take off their shoes on entering. I have frequently noticed that in railway cars the first comers monopolize the seats, and the later ones receive not the slightest notice, being often compelled to stand for an hour at a time, although, with a little moving, there would be abundant room for all. I have noticed this so often that I cannot think it an exceptional occurrence. I do not believe it to be intentional rudeness, but to be due simply to a lack of real heart politeness. Yet a true and deep æsthetic development, so far at least as relates to conduct, to say nothing of the spirit of altruism, would not permit such indifference to another's discomfort.

My explanation for this, and for all similar defects in etiquette, is somewhat as follows. Etiquette is popularly conceived as consisting of rules of conduct, rather than as the outward expression of the state of the heart. From time immemorial rules for the ordinary affairs of life have been formulated by superiors and have been taught the people. In all usual and conventional relations, therefore, the average farmer and peasant know how to express perfect courtesy. But in certain situations, as in foreign houses and the railroad car, where there are no precedents to follow, or rules to obey, all evidence of politeness takes its flight. The old rules do not fit the new conditions. Not being grounded on the inner principles of etiquette, the people are not able to formulate new rules for new conditions. To the Westerner, on the other hand, these seem to follow from the simplest principles of common sense and kindliness. The general collapse of etiquette in Japan, which native writers note and deplore, is due, therefore, not only to the withdrawal of feudal pressure, but also to introduction of strange circumstances for which the people have no rules, and to the fact that the people have not been taught those underlying principles of high courtesy which are applicable on all occasions.

An impression seems to have gained currency in the United States that the unæsthetic features seen in Japan to-day are due to the debasing influences of Western art and Occidental intercourse. There can be no doubt that a certain type of tourist, ignorant of Japanese art, by greedily buying strange, gaudy things at high prices, has stimulated a morbid production of truly unæsthetic pseudo-Japanese art. But this accounts for only a small part of the grossly inartistic features of Japan. The instances given of hideous worsted bibs for babes and collars for dogs, combining in the closest proximity the most uncomplementary and mutually repellent colors, has nothing whatever to do with foreign art or foreign intercourse. What foreigner ever decorated a little lapdog with a red-green-yellow-blue-and-purple crocheted collar, four or five inches wide?

Westerners have been charmed with the exquisite colored photographs produced in Japan. It is strange, yet true, that the same artistic hand that produces these beautiful effects will also, by a slight change of tints, produce the most unnatural and spectral views. Yet the strangest thing is, not that he produces them, but that he does not seem conscious of the defect, for he will put them on sale in his own shop or send them to purchasers in America, without the slightest apparent hesitation. The constant care of the purchaser in selection and his insistence on having only truly artistic work are what keep the Japanese artist up to the standard.

If other evidence is needed of æsthetic defect in the still unoccidentalized Japanese taste let the doubter go to any popular second-grade Shinto shrine or Buddhist temple. Here unæsthetic objects and sights abound. Hideous idols, painted and unpainted, big and little, often decorated with soiled bibs; decaying to-rii; ruined sub-shrines; conglomerate piles of cast-off paraphernalia, consisting of broken idols, old lanterns, stones, etc., filthy towels at the holy-water basins, piously offered to the gods and piously used by hundreds of dusty pilgrims; equally filthy bell-ropes hung in front of the main shrines, pulled by ten thousand hands to call the attention of the deity; travel-stained hands, each of which has left its mark on the once beautiful enormous tasselated cord; ex-voto tufts of human hair; scores of pictures, where the few may be counted works of art while the rest are hideous beyond belief; frightful faces of tengu, with their long noses and menacing teeth, decorated with scores of spit-balls or even ones with mud-balls; these are some of the more conspicuous unæsthetic features of multitudes of popular shrines and temples. And none of these can be attributed to the debasing influence of Western art. And these inartistic features will be found accompanying scrupulous neatness in well-swept walks, new sub-shrines, floral decorations, and much that pleases the eye—a strange compound of the beautiful and the ugly. Truly the æsthetic development of the Japanese is curiously one-sided.

A survey of Japanese musical history leads to the conclusion that while the people are fairly developed in certain aspects of the æsthetics of music, such as rhythm, they are certainly undeveloped in other directions—in melody, for example, and in harmony. Their instrumental music is primitive and meager. They have no system of musical notation. The love of music, such as it is, is well-nigh universal. Their solo-vocal music, a semi-chanting in minors, has impressive elements; but these are due to the passionate outbursts and plaintive wails, rather than to the musically æsthetic character of the melodies. The universal twanging samisen, a species of guitar, accompanied by the shrill, hard voices of the geisha (singing girls), marks at once the universality of the love of music and the undeveloped quality of the musical taste, both vocal and instrumental. But in comparing the musical development of Japan with that of the West, we must not forget how recent is that of the former.

The conditions which have served to develop musical taste in the West have but recently come to Japan. Sufficient time has not yet elapsed for the nation to make much visible progress in the lines of Occidental music. But it has already done something. The popularity of brass bands, the wide introduction of organs, their manufacture in this land, their use in all public schools, the exclusive use of Occidental music in Christian churches, the ability of trained individuals in foreign vocal and instrumental music—all these facts go to show that in time we may expect great musical evolution in Japan. Those who doubt this on the ground of inherent race nature may be reminded of the evolution which has taken place among the Hawaiians during the past two generations. From being a race manifesting marked deficiency in music they have developed astonishing musical taste and ability. During a recent visit to these islands after an absence of twenty-seven years, I attended a Sunday-school exhibition, which was largely a musical contest; the voices were sweet and rich; and the difficulty of the part songs, easily carried through by children and adults, revealed a musical sense that surpasses any ordinary Sunday school of the United States or England with which I am acquainted.

The development of Japanese literature likewise conspicuously reflects the ruling ideas of the social order, and reveals the dependence of literary taste on the order. As in other aspects in Japanese æsthetic development, so in this do we see marked lack of balance. "It is wonderful what felicity of phrase, melody of versification, and true sentiment can be compressed within the narrow limits (of the Tanka). In their way nothing can be more perfect than some of these little poems."[1] The deficiencies of Japanese poetry have been remarked by the foreigners most competent to judge. The following general characterization from the volume just quoted merits attention.

"Narrow in its scope and resources, it is chiefly remarkable for its limitations—for what it has not, rather than what it has. In the first place there are no long poems. There is nothing which even remotely resembles an epic—no Iliad or Divina Commedia—not even a Nibelungen Lied or Chevy Chase. Indeed, narrative poems of any kind are short and very few, the only ones which I have met with being two or three ballads of a sentimental cast. Didactic, philosophical, political, and satirical poems are also conspicuously absent. The Japanese muse does not meddle with such subjects, and it is doubtful whether, if it did, the native Pegasus possesses sufficient staying power for them to be dealt with adequately. For dramatic poetry we have to wait until the fourteenth century. Even then there are no complete dramatic poems, but only dramas containing a certain poetical element.

"Japanese poetry is, in short, confined to lyrics, and what, for want of a better word, may be called epigrams. It is primarily an expression of emotion. We have amatory verse poems of longing for home and absent dear ones, praise of love and wine, elegies on the dead, laments over the uncertainty of life. A chief place is given to the seasons, the sound of purling streams, the snow of Mount Fuji, waves breaking on the beach, seaweed drifting to the shore, the song of birds, the hum of insects, even the croaking of frogs, the leaping of trout in a mountain stream, the young shoots of fern in spring, the belling of deer in autumn, the red tints of the maple, the moon, flowers, rain, wind, mist; these are among the favorite subjects which the Japanese poets delight to dwell upon. If we add some courtly and patriotic effusions, a vast number of conceits more or less pretty, and a very few poems of a religious cast, the enumeration is tolerably complete. But, as Mr. Chamberlain has observed, there are curious omissions. War songs—strange to say—are almost wholly absent. Fighting and bloodshed are apparently not considered fit themes for poetry."[V]

The drama and the novel have both achieved considerable development, yet judged from Occidental standards, they are comparatively weak and insipid. They, of course, conspicuously reflect the characteristics of the social order to which they belong. Critics call repeated attention to the lack of sublimity in Japanese literature, and ascribe it to their inherent race nature. While the lack of sublimity in Japanese scenery may in fact account for the characteristic in question, still a more conclusive explanation would seem to be that in the older social order man, as such, was not known. The hidden glories of the soul, its temptations and struggles, its defects and victories, could not be the themes of a literature arising in a completely communal social order, even though it possessed individualism of the Buddhistic type.[VI] These are the themes that give Western literature—poetic, dramatic, and narrative—its opportunity for sustained power and sublimity. They portray the inner life of the spirit.

The poverty of poetic form is another point of Western criticism. Mr. Aston has shown how this poverty is directly due to the phonetic characteristics of the language. Diversities of both rhyme and rhythm are practically excluded from Japanese poetry by the nature of the language. And this in turn has led to the "preference of the national genius for short poems." But language is manifestly the combined product of linguistic heredity and the social order, and can in no sense be ascribed to inherent race nature. Thus directly are social heredity and social order determinative of the literary characteristics and æsthetic tastes of a nation.

Even more manifestly may Japanese architectural development be traced to the social heredity derived from China and India. The needs of the developing internal civilization have determined its external manifestation. So far as Japanese differs from Chinese architecture, it may be attributed to Japan's isolation, to the different demands of her social order, to the difference of accessible building materials, and to the different social heredity handed down from prehistoric times. That the distinguishing characteristics of Japanese architecture are due to the inherent race nature cannot for a moment be admitted.

We conclude that the Japanese are not possessed of a unique and inherent æsthetic taste. In some respects they are as certainly ahead of the Occidental as they are behind him in other respects. But this, too, is a matter of social development and social heredity, rather than of inherent race character, of brain structure. If æsthetic nature were a matter of inherited brain structure, it would be impossible to account for rapid fluctuations in æsthetic judgment, for the great inequality of æsthetic development in the different departments of life, or for the ease of acquiring the æsthetic development of alien races.[IX]

XVI.
MEMORY—IMITATION

The differences which separate the Oriental from the Occidental mind are infinitesimal as compared with the likenesses which unite them. This is a fact that needs to be emphasized, for many writers on Japan seem to ignore it. They marvel at the differences. The real marvel is that the differences are so few and so superficial. The Japanese are a race whose ancestors were separated from their early home nearly three thousand years ago; during this period they have been absolutely prevented from intermarriage with the parent stock. Furthermore, that original stock was not the Indo-European race. And no one has ventured to suggest how long before the migration of the ancestors of the Japanese to Japan their ancestors parted from those who finally became the progenitors of modern Occidental peoples. For thousands of years, certainly, the Japanese and Anglo-Saxon races have had no ancestry in common. Yet so similar is the entire structure and working of their minds that the psychological textbooks of the Anglo-Saxon are adopted and perfectly understood by competent psychological students among the Japanese. I once asked a professor of psychology in the Matsuyama Normal School if he had no difficulty in teaching his classes the psychological system of Anglo-Saxon thinkers, if there were not peculiarities of the Anglo-Saxon mind which a Japanese could not understand, and if there were not psychological phenomena of the Japanese mind which were ignored in Anglo-Saxon psychological text-books. The very questions surprised him; to each he gave a negative reply. The mental differences that characterize races so dissimilar as the Japanese and the Anglo-Saxon, I venture to repeat, are insignificant as compared with their resemblances.

Our discussions shall have reference, not to those general psychological characteristics which all races have in common, but only to those which may seem to stamp the Japanese people as peculiar. We wish to understand the distinguishing features of the Japanese mind. We wish to know whether they are due to brain structure, to inherent race nature, or whether they are simply the result of education, of social heredity. This is our ever-recurring question.

First, in regard to Japanese brain development. Travelers have often been impressed with the unusual size of the Japanese head. It has sometimes been thought, however, that the size is more apparent than real, and the appearance has been attributed to the relatively short limbs of the people and to the unusual proportion of round heads which one sees everywhere. It may also be due to the shape of the head. But, after all has been said, it remains true that the Japanese head, as related to his body, is unexpectedly large.

Prof. Marsh of Yale University is reported to have said that, on the basis of brain size, the Japanese is the race best fitted to survive in the struggle for existence, or at least in the struggle for pre-eminence.

Statements have been widely circulated to the effect that not only relatively to the body, but even absolutely, the Japanese possess larger brains than the European, but craniological statistics do not verify the assertion. The matter has been somewhat discussed in Japanese magazines of late, to which, through the assistance of a Japanese friend, I am indebted for the following figures. They are given in Japanese measurements, but are, on this account, however, none the less satisfactory for comparative purposes.

According to Dr. Davis, the average European male brain weighs 36,498 momme, and the Australian, 22,413, while the Japanese, according to Dr. Taguchi weighs 36,205. Taking the extremes, the largest English male brain weighs 38,100 momme and the smallest 35,377, whereas the corresponding figures for Japan are 43,919 and 30,304, respectively, showing an astonishing range between extremes. According to Dr. E. Baelz of the Imperial University of Tokyo, the lower classes of Japan have a larger skull circumference than either the middle or upper classes (1.8414, 1.7905, and 1.8051 feet, respectively), and the Ainu (1.8579) exceed the Japanese. From these facts it might almost appear that brain size and civilizational development are in inverse ratio. Were the Japanese brain larger, then, than that of the European, it might plausibly be argued that they are therefore inferior in brain power. This would be in accord with certain of De Quatrefages's investigations. He has shown that negroes born in America have smaller brains, but are intellectually superior to their African brothers. "With them, therefore, intelligence increases, while the cranial capacity diminishes."[V]

Those who trace racial and civilizational nature to brain development cannot gain much consolation from a comparative statistical study of race brains. De Quatrefages's conclusion is repeatedly forced home: "We must confess that there can be no real relation between the dimension of the cranial capacity and social development."[Z] "The development of the intellectual faculties of man is, to a great extent, independent of the capacity of the cranium and the volume of the brain."[AA]

We may conclude at once, then, that Japanese intellectual peculiarities are in no way due to the size of their brains, but depend rather on their social evolution. Yet it will not be amiss to study in detail the various mental peculiarities of the race, real and supposed, and to note their relation to the social order.

In becoming acquainted with the Japanese and Chinese peoples, an Occidental is much impressed with their powers of memory, and this especially in connection with the written language, the far-famed "Chinese Character," or ideograph. My Chinese dictionary contains over 50,000 different characters. The task of learning them is appalling. How the Japanese or Chinese do it is to us a constant wonder. We assume at once their possession of astonishing memories. We argue that, for hundreds of years, each generation has been developing powers of memory through efforts to conquer this cumbersome contrivance for writing, and that, as a consequence for the nations using this system, there is now prodigious ability to remember.

It is my impression, however, that we greatly overrate these powers. In the first place, few Japanese claim any acquaintance with the entire 50,000 characters; only the educated make any pretense of knowing more than a few hundred, and a vast majority even of learned men do not know more than 10,000 characters. Some Japanese newspapers have undertaken to limit themselves in the use of the ideograph. It is said that between four and five thousand characters suffice for all the ordinary purposes of communication. These are, without doubt, fairly well known to the educated classes. But for the masses, there is need that the pronunciation be placed beside each printed character, before it can be read. Furthermore, we must remember that a Japanese youth gives the best years of his life to the bare memorizing of these symbols.[AB]

Were European or American youth to devote to the study of Chinese the same number of hours each day for the same number of years, I doubt if there would be any conspicuous difference in the results. We should not forget also that some Occidentals manifest astonishing facility in memorizing Chinese characters.

In this connection is the important fact that the social order serves to sift out individuals of marked mnemonic powers and bring them into prominence, while those who are relatively deficient are relegated to the background. The educated class is necessarily composed of those who have good powers of memory. All others fail and are rejected. We see and admire those who succeed; of those who fail we know nothing and we even forget that there are such.

In response to my questions Japanese friends have uniformly assured me that they are not accustomed to think of the Japanese as possessed of better memories than the people of the West. They appear surprised that the question should be raised, and are specially surprised at our high estimate of Japanese ability in this direction.

If, however, we inquire about their powers of memory in connection with daily duties and the ordinary acquisition of knowledge and its retention, my own experience of twelve years, chiefly with the middle and lower classes of society, has left the impression that, while some learn easily and remember well, a large number are exceedingly slow. On the whole, I am inclined to believe that, although the Japanese may be said to have good memories, yet it can hardly be maintained that they conspicuously exceed Occidentals in this respect.

In comparing the Occidental with the Oriental, it is to be remembered that there is not among Occidental nations that attention to bare memorizing which is so conspicuous among the less civilized nations. The astonishing feats performed by the transmitters of ancient poems and religious teachings seem to us incredible. Professor Max Müller says that the voluminous Vedas have been handed down for centuries, unchanged, simply from mouth to mouth by the priesthood. Every progressive race, until it has attained a high development of the art of writing, has manifested similar power of memory. Such power is not, however, inherent; that is to say, it is not due to the innate peculiarity of brain structure, but rather to the nature of the social order which demands such expenditure of time and strength for the maintenance of its own higher life. Through the art of writing Occidental peoples have found a cheaper way of retaining their history and of preserving the products of their poets and religious teachers. Even for the transactions of daily life we have resorted to the constant use of pen and notebook and typewriter, by these devices saving time and strength for other things. As a result, our memories are developed in directions different from those of semi-civilized or primitive man. The differences of memory characterizing different races, then, are for the most part due to differences in the social order and to the nature of the civilization, rather than to the intrinsic and inherited structure of the brain itself.

Since memory is the foundation of all mental operations, we have given to it the first place in the present discussion. And that the Japanese have a fair degree of memory argues well for the prospect of high attainment in other directions. With this in mind, we naturally ask whether they show any unusual proficiency or deficiency in the acquisition of foreign languages? In view of her protracted separation from the languages of other peoples, should we not expect marked deficiency in this respect? On the contrary, however, we find that tens of thousands of Japanese students have acquired a fairly good reading knowledge of English, French, and German. Those few who have had good and sufficient teaching, or who have been abroad and lived in Occidental lands, have in addition secured ready conversational use of the various languages. Indeed, some have contended that since the Japanese learn foreign languages more easily than foreigners learn Japanese, they have greater linguistic powers than the foreigner. It should be borne in mind, however, that in such a comparison, not only are the time required and the proficiency; attained to be considered, but also the inherent difficulty of the language studied and the linguistic helps provided the student.

I have come gradually to the conclusion that the Japanese are neither particularly gifted nor particularly deficient in powers of language acquisition. They rank with Occidental peoples in this respect.

To my mind language affords one of the best possible proofs of the general contention of this volume that the characteristics which distinguish the races are social rather than biological. The reason why the languages of the different races differ is not because the brain-types of the races are different, but only because of the isolated social evolution which the races have experienced. Had it been possible for Japan to maintain throughout the ages perfect and continuous social intercourse with the ancestors of the Anglo-Saxon race, while still maintaining biological isolation, i.e., perfect freedom from intermarriage, there is no reason to think that two distinct languages so different as English and Japanese would have arisen. The fact that Japanese children can accurately acquire English, and that English or American children can accurately acquire Japanese, proves conclusively that diversities of language do not rest on brain differences and brain heredity, but exclusively on social differences and social heredity.

If this is true, then the argument can easily be extended to all the features that differentiate the civilizations of different races; for the language of any race is, in a sense, the epitome of the civilization of that race. All its ideas, customs, theologies, philosophies, sciences, mythologies; all its characteristic thoughts, conceptions, ideals; all its distinguishing social features, are represented in its language. Indeed, they enter into it as determining factors, and by means of it are transmitted from age to age. This argument is capable of much extension and illustration.

The charge that the Japanese are a nation of imitators has been repeated so often as to become trite, and the words are usually spoken with disdain. Yet, if the truth were fully told, it would be found that, from many points of view, this quality gives reason rather for congratulation. Surely that nation which can best discriminate and imitate has advantage over nations that are so fixed in their self-sufficiency as to be able neither to see that which is advantageous nor to imitate it. In referring to the imitative powers of the Japanese, then, I do not speak in terms of reproach, but rather in those of commendation. "Monkeyism" is not the sort of imitation that has transformed primitive Japan into the Japan of the early or later feudal ages, nor into the Japan of the twentieth century. Bare imitation, without thought, has been relatively slight in Japan. If it has been known at times, those times have been of short duration.

In his introduction to "The Classic Poetry of the Japanese" Professor Chamberlain has so stated the case for the imitative quality of the people that I quote the following:

"The current impression that the Japanese are a nation of imitators is in the main correct. As they copy us to-day, so did they copy the Chinese and Koreans a millennium and a half ago. Religion, philosophy, laws, administration, written characters, all arts but the very simplest, all science, or at least what then went by that name, everything was imported from the neighboring continent; so much so that of all that we are accustomed to term 'Old Japan' scarce one trait in a hundred is really and properly Japanese. Not only are their silk and lacquer not theirs by right of invention, nor their painting (albeit so often praised by European critics for its originality), nor their porcelain, nor their music, but even the larger part of their language consists of mispronounced Chinese; and from the Chinese they have drawn new names for already existing places, and new titles for their ancient Gods."

While the above cannot be disputed in its direct statements, yet I can but feel that it makes, on the whole, a false impression. Were these same tests applied to any European people, what would be the result? Of what European nation may it be said that its art, or method of writing, or architecture, or science, or language even, is "its own by right of invention"? And when we stop to examine the details of the ancient Japanese civilization which is supposed to have been so, slavishly copied from China and India, we shall find that, though the beginnings were indeed imitated, there were also later developments of purely Japanese creation. In some instances the changes were vital.

In examining the practical arts, while we acknowledge that the beginnings of nearly all came from Korea or China, we must also acknowledge that in many important respects, Japan has developed along her own lines. The art of sword-making, for instance, was undoubtedly imported; but who does not know of the superior quality and beauty of Japanese swords, the Damascus blades of the East? So distinct is this Japanese production that it cannot be mistaken for that of any other nation. It has received the impress of the Japanese social order. Its very shape is due to the habit of carrying the sheath in the "obi" or belt.

If we study the home of the laborer, or the instruments in common use, we shall find proof that much more than imitation has been involved.

Were the Japanese mere imitators, how could we explain their architecture, so different from that of China and Korea? How explain the multiplied original ways in which bamboo and straw are used?

For a still closer view of the matter, let us consider the imported ethical and religious codes of the country. In China the emphasis of Confucianism is laid on the duty of filial piety. In Japan the primary emphasis is on loyalty. This single change transformed the entire system and made the so-called Confucianism of Japan distinct from that of China. In Buddhism, imported from India, we find greater changes than Occidental nations have imposed on their religion imported from Palestine. Indeed, so distinct has Japanese Buddhism become that it is sometimes difficult to trace its connections in China and India. And the Buddhistic sects that have sprung up in Japan are more radically diverse and antagonistic to each other and to primitive Buddhism than the denominations of Christianity are to each other and to primitive Christianity.

In illustration is the most popular of all the Buddhist sects to-day, Shinshu. This has sometimes been called by foreigners "Reformed" Buddhism; and so similar are many of its doctrines to those of Christianity that some have supposed them to have been derived from it, but without the slightest evidence. All its main doctrines and practices were clearly formulated by its founder, Shinrah, six hundred years ago. The regular doctrines of Buddhism that salvation comes only through self-effort and self-victory are rejected, and salvation through the merits of another is taught. "Ta-riki," "another's power," not "Ji-riki," "self-power," is with them the orthodox doctrine. Priests may marry and eat meat, practices utterly abhorrent to the older and more primitive Buddhism. The sacred books are printed in the vernacular, in marked contrast to the customs of the other sects. Women, too, are given a very different place in the social and religious scale and are allowed hopes of attaining salvation that are denied by all the older sects. "Penance, fasting, prescribed diet, pilgrimages, isolation from society, whether as hermits or in the cloister, and generally amulets and charms, are all tabooed by this sect. Monasteries imposing life vows are unknown within its pale. Family life takes the place of monkish seclusion. Devout prayer, purity, earnestness of life, and trust in Buddha himself as the only worker of perfect righteousness, are insisted on. Morality is taught as more important than orthodoxy."[AC] It is amazing how far the Shin sect has broken away from regular Buddhistic doctrine and practice. Who can say that no originality was required to develop such a system, so opposed at vital points to the prevalent Buddhism of the day?

Another sect of purely Japanese origin deserving notice is the "Hokke" or "Nicheren." Its founder, known by the name of Nichiren, was a man of extraordinary independence and religious fervor. Wholly by his original questions and doubts as to the prevailing doctrines and customs of the then dominant sects, he was led to make independent examination into the history and meaning of Buddhistic literature and to arrive at conclusions quite different from those of his contemporaries. Of the truth and importance of his views he was so persuaded that he braved not only fierce denunciations, but prolonged opposition and persecution. He was rejected and cast out by his own people and sect; he was twice banished by the ruling military powers. But he persevered to the end, finally winning thousands of converts to his views. The virulence of the attacks made upon him was due to the virulence with which he attacked what seemed to him the errors and corruption of the prevailing sects. Surely his was no case of servile imitation. His early followers had also to endure opposition and severe persecution.

Glancing at the philosophical ideas brought from China, we find here too a suggestion of the same tendency toward originality. It is true that Dr. Geo. Wm. Knox, in his valuable monograph on "A Japanese Philosopher," makes the statement that, "In acceptance and rejection alike no native originality emerges, nothing beyond a vigorous power of adoption and assimilation. No improvements of the new philosophy were even attempted. Wherein it was defective and indistinct, defective and indistinct it remained. The system was not thought out to its end and independently adopted. Polemics, ontology, ethics, theology, marvels, heroes—all were enthusiastically adopted on faith. It is to be added that the new system was superior to the old, and so much of discrimination was shown."[AD]And somewhat earlier he likewise asserts that "There is not an original and valuable commentary by a Japanese writer. They have been content to brood over the imported works and to accept unquestioningly politics, ethics, and metaphysics." After some examination of these native philosophers, I feel that, although not without some truth, these assertions cannot be strictly maintained. It is doubtless true that no powerful thinker and writer has appeared in Japan that may be compared to the two great philosophers of China, Shushi and Oyomei. The works and the system of the former dominated Japan, for the simple reason that governmental authority forbade the public teaching or advocacy of the other. Nevertheless, not a few Japanese thinkers rejected the teachings and philosophy of Shushi, regardless of consequences. Notable among those rejecters was Kaibara Yekken, whose book "The Great Doubt" was not published until after his death. In it he rejects in emphatic terms the philosophical and metaphysical ideas of Shushi. An article[AE] by Dr. Tetsujiro Inouye, Professor of Philosophy in the Imperial University in Tokyo, on the "Development of Philosophical Ideas in Japan," concludes with these words:

"From this short sketch the reader can clearly see that philosophical considerations began in our country with the study of Shushi and Oyomei. But many of our thinkers did not long remain faithful to that tradition; they soon formed for themselves new conceptions of life and of the world, which, as a rule, are not only more practical, but also more advanced than those of the Chinese."

An important reason for our Western thought, that the Japanese have had no independence in philosophy, is our ignorance of the larger part of Japanese and Chinese literature. Oriental speculation was moving in a direction so diverse from that of the West that we are impressed more with the general similarity that prevails throughout it than with the evidences of individual differences. Greater knowledge would reveal these differences. In our generalized knowledge, we see the uniformity so strongly that we fail to discover the originality.

As a traveler from the West, on reaching some Eastern land, finds it difficult at first to distinguish between the faces of different individuals, his mind being focused on the likeness pervading them all, so the Occidental student of Oriental thought is impressed with the remarkable similarity that pervades the entire Oriental civilization, modes of thought, and philosophy, finding it difficult to discover the differences which distinguish the various Oriental races. In like manner, a beginner in the study of Japanese philosophy hardly gives the Japanese credit for the modifications of Chinese philosophy which they have originated.

In this connection it is well to remember that, more than any Westerner can realize, the Japanese people have been dependent on governmental initiative from time immemorial. They have never had any thought but that of implicit obedience, and this characteristic of the social order has produced its necessary consequences in the present characteristics of the people. Individual initiative and independence have been frowned upon, if not always forcibly repressed, and thus the habit of imitation has been stimulated. The people have been deliberately trained to imitation by their social system. The foreigner is amazed at the sudden transformations that have swept the nation. When the early contact with China opened the eyes of the ruling classes to the fact that China had a system of government that was in many respects better than their own, it was an easy thing to adopt it and make it the basis for their own government. This constituted the epoch-making period in Japanese history known as the Taikwa Reform. It occurred in the seventh century, and consisted of a centralizing policy; under which, probably for the first time in Japanese history, the country was really unified. Critics ascribe it to an imitation of the Chinese system. Imitation it doubtless was; but its significant feature was its imposition by the few rulers on the people; hence its wide prevalence and general acceptance.

Similarly, in our own times, the Occidentalized order now dominant in Japan was adopted, not by the people, but by the rulers, and imposed by them on the people; these had no idea of resisting the new order, but accepted it loyally as the decision of their Emperor, and this spirit of unquestioning obedience to the powers that be is, I am persuaded, one of the causes of the prevalent opinion respecting Japanese imitativeness as well as of the fact itself.

The reputation for imitativeness, together with the quality itself, is due in no small degree, therefore, to the long-continued dominance of the feudal order of society. In a land where the dependence of the inferior on the superior is absolute, the wife on the husband, the children on the parents, the followers on their lord, the will of the superior being ever supreme, individual initiative must be rare, and the quality of imitation must be powerfully stimulated.

XVII
ORIGINALITY—INVENTIVENESS

Originality is the obverse side of imitation. In combating the notion that Japan is a nation of unreflective imitators, I have given numerous examples of originality. Further extensive illustration of this characteristic is, accordingly, unnecessary. One other may be cited, however.

The excellence of Japanese art is admitted by all. Japanese temples and palaces are adorned with mural paintings and pieces of sculpture that command the admiration of Occidental experts. The only question is as to their authors. Are these, properly speaking, Japanese works of art—or Korean or Chinese? That Japan received her artistic stimulus, and much of her artistic ideas and technique, from China is beyond dispute. But did she develop nothing new and independent? This is a question of fact. Japanese art, though Oriental, has a distinctive quality. A magnificent work entitled "Solicited Relics of Japanese Art" is issuing from the press, in which there is a large number of chromo-xylographic and collotype reproductions of the best specimens of ancient Japanese art. Reviewing this work, the *Japan Mail* remarks:

"But why should the only great sculptors that China or Korea ever produced have come to Japan and bequeathed to this country the unique results of their genius? That is the question we have to answer before we accept the doctrine that the noblest masterpieces of ancient Japan were from foreign lands. When anything comparable is found in China or Korea, there will be less difficulty in applying this doctrine of over-sea-influence to the genius that enriched the temples of antique Japan."[AF]

Under the early influence of Buddhism (900-1200 A.D.) Japan fairly bloomed. Those were the days of her glory in architecture, literature, and art. But a blight fell upon her from which she is only now recovering. The causes of this blight will receive attention in a subsequent chapter. Let us note here only one aspect of it, namely, official repression of originality.

Townsend Harris, in his journal, remarks on the way in which the Japanese government has interfered with the originality of the people. "The genius of their government seems to forbid any exercise of ingenuity in producing articles for the gratification of wealth and luxury. Sumptuary laws rigidly enforce the forms, colors, material, and time of changing the dress of all. As to luxury of furniture, the thing is unknown in Japan.... It would be an endless task to attempt to put down all the acts of a Japanese that are regulated by authority."

81

The Tokugawa rule forbade the building of large ships; so that, by the middle of the nineteenth century, the art of ship-building was far behind what it had been two centuries earlier. Government authority exterminated Christianity in the early part of the seventeenth century and freedom of religious belief was forbidden. The same power that put the ban on Christianity forbade the spread of certain condemned systems of Confucianism. Even in the study of Chinese literature and philosophy, therefore, such originality as the classic models stimulated was discouraged by the all-powerful Tokugawa government. The avowed aim and end of the ruling powers of Japan was to keep the nation in its *status quo*. Originality was heresy and treason; progress was impiety. The teaching of Confucius likewise lent its support to this policy. To do exactly as the fathers did is to honor them; to do, or even to think, otherwise is to dishonor them. There have not been wanting men of originality and independence in both China and Japan; but they were not great enough to break over, or break down, the incrusted system in which they lived—the system of blind devotion to the past. This system, that deliberately opposed all invention and originality, has been the great incubus to national progress, in that it has rejected and repressed every tendency to variation. What results might not the country have secured, had Christianity been allowed to do its work in stimulating individual development and in creating the sense of personal responsibility towards God and man!

A curious anomaly still remains in Japan on the subject of liberty in study and belief. Though perfect liberty is the rule, one topic is even yet under official embargo. No one may express public dissent from the authorized version of primitive Japanese history. A few years ago a professor in the Imperial University made an attempt to interpret ancient Japanese myths. His constructions were supposed to threaten the divine descent of the Imperial line, and he was summarily dismissed.

Dr. E. Inouye, Professor of Buddhist Philosophy in the Imperial University, addressing a Teachers' Association of Sendai, delivered a conservative, indirectly anti-foreign speech. He insisted, as reported by a local English correspondent, that the Japanese people "were descended from the gods. In all other countries the sovereign or Emperor was derived from the people, but here the people had the honor of being derived from the Emperor. Other countries had filial piety and loyalty, but no such filial piety and loyalty as exist in Japan. The moral attainments of the people were altogether unique. He informed his audience that though they might adopt foreign ways of doing things, their minds needed no renovating; they were good enough as they were."[AG]

As a result of this position, scholarship and credulity are curiously combined in modern historical production. Implicit confidence seems to be placed in the myths of the primitive era. Tales of the gods are cited as historical events whose date, even, can be fixed with some degree of accuracy. Although writing was unknown in Japan until early in the Christian era, the chronology of the previous six or eight hundred years is accepted on the authority of a single statement in the Kojiki, written 712 years A.D. This statement was reproduced from the memory of a single man, who remembered miraculously the contents of a book written shortly before, but accidentally destroyed by fire. In the authoritative history of Japan, prepared and translated into English at the command of the government for the Columbian Exposition, we find such statements as these:

"From the time that Amaterasu-Omikami made Ninigi-no-mikoto to descend from the heavens and subject to his administrative sway Okini-nushi-no-mikoto and other offspring of the deities in the land, descendants of the divine beings have sat upon the throne, generation after generation in succession."[AH] "Descended in a direct line from the heavenly deities, the Emperor has stood unshaken in his high place through all generations, his prestige and dignity immutable from time immemorial and independent of all the vicissitudes of the world about him."[AI]"Never has there been found a single subject of the realm who sought to impair the Imperial prestige."[AJ] It is true that in a single passage the traditions of the "age of the Deities" are described as "strange and incredible legends," but it is added that, however singular they are, in order to understand the history of the Empire's beginnings, they must be studied. Then follows, without a word of criticism or dissent, the account of the doings of the heavenly deities, in creating Japan and its people, as well as the myriads of gods. There is no break between the age of the gods and the history of men. The first inventions and discoveries, such as those of fire, of mining, and of weaving are ascribed to Amate rasu-Omikami (the Sun Goddess). According to these traditions and the modern histories built upon them, the Japanese race came into existence wholly independently of all other races of men. Such is the authoritative teaching in the schools to-day.

Occidental scholars do not accept these statements or dates. That the Japanese will evince historical and critical ability in the study of their own early history, as soon as the social order will allow it, can hardly be doubted. Those few who even now entertain advanced ideas do not dare to avow them. And this fact throws an interesting light on the way in which the social order, or a despotic government, may thwart for a time the natural course of development. The present apparent credulity of Japanese historical scholarship is due neither to race character nor to superstitions lodged in the inherited race brain, but simply to the social system, which, as yet, demands the inviolability of the Imperial line.

Now that the Japanese have been so largely relieved from the incubus of the older social order, the question rises whether they are showing powers of originality. The answer is not doubtful, for they have already made several important discoveries and inventions. The Murata rifle, with which the army is equipped, is the invention of a Japanese. In 1897 Colonel Arisaka invented several improvements in this same rifle, increasing the velocity and accuracy, and lessening the weight. Still more recently he has invented a rapid-fire field-piece to superintend whose manufacture he has been sent to Europe. Mr. Shimose has invented a smokeless powder, which the government is manufacturing for its own use. Not infrequently there appear in the papers notices of new inventions. I have recently noted the invention of important improvements in the hand loom universally used in Japan, also a "smoke-consumer" which not only abolishes the smoke, but reduces the amount of coal used and consequently the expense. These are but a few of the ever-increasing number of Japanese inventions.

In the, field of original scientific research is the famous bacteriologist, Dr. Kitazato. Less widely known perhaps, but none the less truly original explorers in the field of science, are Messrs. Hirase and Ikeno, whose discoveries of spermatozoids in Ginko and Cycas have no little value for botanists, especially in the development of the theory of certain forms of fertilization. These instances show that the faculty of original thought is not entirely lacking among the Japanese. Under favorable conditions, such as now prevail, there is good reason for holding that the Japanese will take their place among the peoples of the world, not only as skillful imitators and adapters, but also as original contributors to the progress of civilization and of science.

Originality may be shown in imitation as well as in production, and this type of originality the Japanese have displayed in a marked way. They have copied the institutions of no single country. It might even be difficult to say which Western land has had the greatest influence in molding the new social order of Japan. In view of the fact that it is the English language which has been most in favor during the past thirty years, it might be assumed that England and America are the favored models. But no such hasty conclusion can be drawn. The Japanese have certainly taken ideas and teachers from many different sources; and they have changed them frequently, but not thoughtlessly. A writer in *The Far East* brings this points out clearly:

"While Japan remained secluded from other countries, she had no necessity for and scarcely any war vessels, but after the country was opened to the free intercourse of foreign powers—immediately she felt the urgent necessity of naval defense and employed a Dutch officer to construct her navy. In 1871 the Japanese government employed a number of English officers, and almost wholly reconstructed her navy according to the English system. But in the matter of naval education our rulers found the English system altogether unsatisfactory, and adopted the American system for the model of our naval academy. So, in discipline, our naval officers found the German principle much superior to the English, and adopted that in point of discipline. Thus the Japanese navy is not wholly after the English system, or the American, or the French, or the German system. But it has been so constructed as to include the best portions of all the different systems. In the case of the army, we had a system of our own before we began to utilize gunpowder and foreign methods of discipline. Shortly before the present era we reorganized our army by adopting the Dutch system, then the English, then the French, and after the Franco-Prussian war, made an improvement by adopting the German system. But on every occasion of reorganization we retained the most advantageous parts of the old systems and harmonized them with the new one. The result has been the creation of an entirely new system, different from any of those models we have adopted. So in the case of our civil code, we consulted most carefully the laws of many civilized nations, and gathered the cream of all the different codes before we formulated our own suited to the customs of our people. In the revision of our monetary system, our government appointed a number of prominent economists to investigate the characteristics of foreign systems, as to their merits and faults, and also the different circumstances under which various systems present their strength and weakness. The investigation lasted more than two years, which finally culminated in our adoption of the gold in the place of the old silver standard."

This quotation gives an idea of the selective method that has been followed. There has been no slavish or unconscious imitation. On the contrary, there has been a constant conscious effort to follow the best model that the civilized world afforded. Of course, it may be doubted whether in fact they have always chosen the best; but that is a different matter. The Japanese think they have; and what foreigner can say that, under the circumstances and in view of the conditions of the people, they have not? One point is clear, that on the whole the nation has made great progress in recent decades, and that the conduct of the government cannot fail to command the admiration of every impartial student of Oriental lands. This is far from saying that all is perfection. Even the Japanese make no such claim. Nor is this equivalent to an assertion of Japan's equality with the leading lands of the West, although many Japanese are ready to assert this. But I merely say that the leaders of New Japan have revealed a high order of judicious originality in their imitation of foreign nations.

XVIII
INDIRECTNESS—"NOMINALITY"

The Japanese have two words in frequent use which aptly describe certain striking aspects of their civilization. They are "tomawashi ni," "yumei-mujitsu," the first translated literally signifying "roundabout" or "indirect," the second meaning "having the name, but not the reality." Both these aspects of Japanese character are forced on the attention of any who live long in Japan.

Some years ago I had a cow that I wished to sell. Being an American, my natural impulse was to ask a dairyman directly if he did not wish to buy; but that would not be the most Japanese method. I accordingly resorted to the help of a "go-between." This individual, who has a regular name in Japanese, "nakadachi," is indispensable for many purposes. When land was being bought for missionary residences in Kumamoto, there were at times three or even four agents acting between the purchaser and the seller and each received his "orei," "honorable politeness," or, in plain English, commission. In the purchase of two or three acres of land, dealings were carried on with some fifteen or more separate landowners. Three different go-betweens dealt directly with the purchaser, and each of these had his go-between, and in some cases these latter had theirs, before the landowner was reached. A domestic desiring to leave my employ conferred with a go-between, who conferred with his go-between, who conferred with me! In every important consultation a go-between seems essential in Japan. That vexatious delays and misunderstandings are frequent may be assumed.

The system, however, has its advantages. In case of disagreeable matters the go-between can say the disagreeable things in the third person, reducing the unpleasant utterances to a minimum.

I recall the case of two evangelists in the employ of the Kumamoto station. Each secured the other to act as go-between in presenting his own difficulties to me. To an American the natural course would have been for each man to state his own grievances and desires, and secure an immediate settlement.

The characteristic of "roundaboutness" is not, however, confined to Japanese methods of action, but also characterizes their methods of speech. In later chapters on the alleged Japanese impersonality we shall consider the remarkable deficiency of personal pronouns in the language, and the wide use of "honorifics." This substitution of the personal pronouns by honorifics makes possible an indefiniteness of speech that is exceedingly difficult for an Anglo-Saxon to appreciate. Fancy the amount of implication in the statement, "Ikenai koto-we shimashita" which, strictly translated, means "Can't go thing have done." Who has done? you? or he? or I? This can only be inferred, for it is not stated. If a speaker wishes to make his personal allusion blind, he can always do so with the greatest ease and without the slightest degree of grammatical incorrectness. "Caught cold," "better ask," "honorably sorry," "feel hungry," and all the common sentences of daily life are entirely free from that personal definiteness which an Occidental language necessitates. We shall see later that the absence of the personal element from the wording of the sentence does not imply, or prove, its absence from the thought of either the speaker or hearer. The Japanese language abounds in roundabout methods of expression. This is specially true in phrases of courtesy. Instead of saying, "I am glad to see you," the Japanese say, "Well, honorably have come"; instead of, "I am sorry to have troubled you," they say, "Honorable hindrance have done"; instead of "Thank you," the correct expression is, "It is difficult."

In a conversation once with a leading educator, I was maintaining that a wide study of English was not needful for the Japanese youth; that the majority of the boys would never learn enough English to make it of practical use to them in after-life, and that it would be wiser for them to spend the same amount of time on more immediately practical subjects. The reply was that the boys needed to have the drill in English in order to gain clear methods of thought: that the sharp distinctness of the English sentence, with its personal pronouns and tense and number, affords a mental drill which the Japanese can get in no other way; and that even if the boys should never make the slightest after-use of English in reading or conversation, the advantage gained was well worth the time expended. I have since noticed that those men who have spent some time in the study of a foreign language speak very much more clearly in Japanese than those who have not had this training. In the former case, the enunciation is apt to be more distinct, and the sentences rounded into more definite periods. The conversation of the average Japanese tends to ramble on in a never-ending sentence. But a marked change has come over vast numbers of the people during the last three decades. The roundaboutness of to-day is as nothing to that which existed under the old order of society. For the new order rests on radically different ideas; directness of speech and not its opposite is being cultivated, and in absolute contrast to the methods of the feudal era, directness of governmental procedure is well-nigh universal to-day. In trade, too, there has come a straightforwardness that is promising, though not yet triumphant. It is safe to assume that in all respectable stores the normal price is charged; for the custom of fixed prices has been widely adopted. If individuals are known to have the "beating down" habit, special prices are added for their sakes.

A personal experience illustrates the point. My wife and I had priced several lamps, had made note of the most satisfactory, and had gone home without buying. The next day a domestic was sent to secure the one which pleased us best. He was charged more than we had been, and in surprise mentioned the sum which we had authorized him to pay. The shopkeeper explained by saying that he always told us the true price in the beginning, because we never tried to beat him down. In truth, modern industrial conditions have pretty well banished the old-time custom of haggling. A premium is set on straightforwardness in business unknown to the old social order.

Roundaboutness is, however, closely connected with "yumei-mujitsu," the other characteristic mentioned at the beginning of this chapter. This, for the sake of simplicity, I venture to call "nominality." Japanese history is a prolonged illustration of this characteristic. For over a thousand years "yumei-mujitsu" has been a leading feature in governmental life. Although the Emperor has ostensibly been seated on the throne, clothed with absolute power, still he has often reigned only in name.[AK] Even so early as 130 A.D., the two families of Oomi and Omuraji began to exercise despotic authority in the central government, and the feudal system, as thus early established, continued with but few breaks to the middle of the present century. There were also the great families which could alone furnish wives to the Imperial line. These early took possession of the person of the Emperor, and the fathers of the wives often exercised Imperial power. The country was frequently and long disturbed by intense civil wars between these rival families. In turn the Fujiwaras, the Minamotos, and the Tairas held the leading place in the control of the Emperor; they determined the succession and secured frequent abdication in favor of their infant sons, but within these families, in turn, there appeared the influence of the "yumei-mujitsu" characteristic. Lesser men, the retainers of these families, manipulated the family leaders, who were often merely figureheads of the contending families and clans. Emperors were made and unmade at the will of these men behind the scenes, most of whom are quite unknown to fame. The creation of infant Emperors, allowed to bear the Imperial name in their infancy and youth, but compelled to abdicate on reaching manhood, was a common device for maintaining nominal Imperialism with actual impotence.

When military clans began to monopolize Imperial power, the people distinctly recognized the nature of their methods and gave it the name of "Bakufu" or "curtain government," a roundabout expression for military government. There has been a succession of these "curtain governments," the last and most successful being that of the Tokugawa, whose fall in 1867-68 brought the entire system to an end and placed the true Emperor on the throne.

But this "yumei-mujitsu" characteristic of Japanese life has been by no means limited to the national government. Every daimyate was more or less blighted by it; the daimyo, or "Great Name," was in too many cases but a puppet in the hands of his "kerai," or family retainers. These men, who were entirely out of sight, were, in very many cases, the real holders of the power which was supposed to be exercised by the daimyo. The lord was often a "great name" and nothing more. That this state of affairs was always attended with evil results is by no means the contention of these pages. Not infrequently the people were saved by it from the incompetence and ignorance and selfishness of hereditary rulers. Indeed, this system of "yumei-mujitsu" government was one of the devices whereby the inherent evils of hereditary rulers were more or less obviated. It may be questioned, however, whether the device did not in the long run cost more than it gained. Did it not serve to maintain, if not actually to produce, a system of dissimulation and deception which could but injure the national character? It certainly could not stimulate the straightforward frankness and outspoken directness and honesty so essential to the well-being of the human race.

Although "yumei-mujitsu" government is now practically extinct in Japan, yet in the social structure it still survives.

The Japanese family is a maze of "nominality." Full-grown young men and women are adopted as sons and daughters, in order to maintain the family line and name.

A son is not a legal son unless he is so registered, while an illegitimate child is recognized as a true son if so registered. A man may be the legal son of his grandmother, or of his sister, if so registered. Although a family may have no children, it does not die out unless there has been a failure to adopt a son or daughter, and an extinct family may be revived by the legal appointment of someone to take the family name and worship at the family shrine. The family pedigree, therefore, does not describe the actual ancestry, but only the nominal, the fictitious. There is no deception in this. It is a well-recognized custom of Old Japan. Its origin, moreover, is not difficult to explain. Nor is this kind of family peculiar to Japan. It is none the less a capital illustration of the "yumei-mujitsu" characteristic permeating the feudal civilization, and still exerting a powerful influence. Even Christians are not free from "nominalism," as we have frequently found in our missionary work.

A case in mind is of an evangelist employed by our mission station. He was to receive a definite proportion of his salary from the church for which he worked and the rest from the station. On inquiry I learned that he was receiving only that provided by the station, and on questioning him further he said that probably the sum promised by the church was being kept as his monthly contribution to the expenses of the church! Instances of this kind are not infrequent. While in Kyushu I more than once discovered that a body of Christians, whose evangelists we were helping to support proportionately, were actually raising not a cent of their proportion. On inquiry, I would be told that the evangelists themselves contributed out of their salary the sums needed, and that, therefore, the Christians did not need to raise it.

The mission, at one time, adopted the plan of throwing upon the local churches the responsibility of deciding as to the fitness of young men for mission aid in securing a theological education. It was agreed by representatives of the churches and the mission that each candidate should secure the approval of the deacons ofthe church of which he was a member, and that the church should pay a certain proportion of the candidate's school expenses. It was thought that by this method the leading Christians of the young man's acquaintance would become his sponsors, and that they would be unwilling to take this responsibility except for men in whom they had personal confidence, and for whom they would be willing to make personal contributions. In course of time the mission discovered that the plan was not working as expected. The young men could secure the approval of the deacons of their church without any difficulty; and as for the financial aid from the church, that could be very easily arranged for by the student's making a monthly contribution to the church of the sum which the church should contribute toward his expenses. Although this method seems to the average Occidental decidedly deceptive, it seemed to the Japanese perfectly proper. The arrangement, it is needless to state, was not long continued. I am persuaded that the correct explanation of these cases is "yumei-mujitsu."

Not long since express trains were put on between Kobe and Tokyo. One morning at Osaka I planned to take the early express to Kyoto, distant about thirty miles. These are the second and third cities of Japan, and the travel between them is heavy. On applying for a ticket I was refused and told there was no train for Kyoto. But as multitudes were buying tickets, and going out upon the platform, I asked an official what the trouble was, and received the explanation that for this express train no tickets could be sold for less than forty miles; but if I would buy a ticket for the next station beyond Kyoto, it would be all right; I could get off at Kyoto. I was assured that I would be allowed to land and leave the station at Kyoto. This I did then, and have repeatedly done since. The same absurd rule is applied, I am told, between Yokohama and Tokyo.

But our interest in these illustrations is the light they shed on Japanese character. They indicate the intellectual angle from which the people have looked out on life. What is the origin of the characteristic? Is it due to deep-lying race nature, to the quality of the race brain? Even more clearly than in the case of "roundaboutness," it seems to me that "nominality" is due to the nature of the old social order. Feudalism has always exhibited more or less of these same features. To Anglo-Saxons, reared in a land blessed by direct government of the people, by the people, and for the people, such methods were not only needless but obnoxious. Nominal responsibility without real power has been seen to breed numberless evils. We have learned to hate all nominalism, all fiction in government, in business and, above all, in personal character. But this is due to the Anglo-Saxon social order, the product in large measure of centuries of Christian instruction.

Through contact with Westerners and the ideas they stand for, directness and reality are being assimilated and developed by the Japanese. This would be impossible were the characteristic in question due to inherent race nature necessarily bequeathed from generation to generation by intrinsic heredity.

XIX
INTELLECTUALITY

Some writers hold that the Japanese are inherently deficient in the higher mental faculties. They consider mediocre mentality to be an inborn characteristic of Japan and assert that it lies at the root of the civilizational differences distinguishing the East from the West. The puerility of Oriental science in all its departments, the prevalence of superstition even among the cultivated, the lack of historical insight and interpretation of history are adduced as conclusive evidences of this view.

Foreign teachers in Japanese employ have told me that Japanese students, as compared with those of the West, manifest deficient powers of analysis and of generalization. Some even assert that the Japanese have no generalizing ability whatever, their progress in civilization being entirely due to their remarkable power of clever imitation. Mr. W.G. Aston, in ascribing the characteristic features of Japanese literature to the fundamental nature of the race, says they are "hardly capable of high intellectual achievement."[AL]

While we may admit that the Japanese do not seem to have at present the same power of scientific generalization as Occidentals, we naturally ask ourselves whether the difference is due to natal deficiency, or whether it may not be due to difference in early training. We must not forget that the youth who come under the observation of foreign teachers in Japanese schools are already products of the Japanese system of education, home and school, and necessarily are as defective as it is.

In a previous chapter a few instances of recent invention and important scientific discovery were given.

These could not have been made without genuine powers of analysis and generalization. We need not linger to elaborate this point.

Another set of facts throwing light on our problem is the success of so many Japanese students, at home and in foreign lands, in mastering modern thought. Great numbers have come back from Europe and America with diplomas and titles; not a few have taken high rank in their classes. The Japanese student abroad is usually a hard worker, like his brother at home. I doubt if any students in the new or the old world study more hours in a year than do these of Japan. It has often amazed me to learn how much they are required to do. This is one fair sign of intellectuality. The ease too with which young Japan, educated in Occidental schools and introduced to Occidental systems of thought, acquires abstruse speculations, searching analyses, and generalized abstractions proves conclusively Japanese possession of the higher mental faculties, in spite of the long survival in their civilization of primitive puerility and superstitions and the lack of science, properly so called.

Japanese youths, furthermore, have a fluency in public speech decidedly above anything I have met with in the United States. Young men of eighteen or twenty years of age deliver long discourses on religion or history or politics, with an apparent ease that their uncouth appearance would not lead one to expect. In the little school of less than 150 boys in Kumamoto there were more individuals who could talk intelligibly and forcefully on important themes of national policy, the relation of religion and politics, the relation of Japan to the Occident and the Orient, than could be found in either of the two colleges in the United States with which I was connected. I do not say that they could bring forth original ideas on these topics. But they could at least remember what they had heard and read and could reproduce the ideas with amazing fluency.

A recent public meeting in Tokyo in which Christian students of the University spoke to fellow-students on the great problems of religion, revealed a power of no mean order in handling the peculiar difficulties encountered by educated young men. A competent listener, recently graduated from an American university and widely acquainted with American students, declared that those Japanese speakers revealed greater powers of mind and speech than would be found under similar circumstances in the United States.

The fluency with which timid girls pray in public has often surprised me. Once started, they never seem to hesitate for ideas or words. The same girls would hardly be able to utter an intelligible sentence in reply to questions put to them by the pastor or the missionary, so faint would be their voices and so hesitating their manner.

The question as to whether the Japanese have powers of generalization receives some light from a study of the language of the people. An examination of primitive Japanese proves that the race, prior to receiving even the slightest influence from China, had developed highly generalized terms. It is worth while to call attention here to a simple fact which most writers seem to ignore, namely, that all language denotes and indeed rests on generalization. Consider the word "uma," "horse"; this is a name for a whole class of objects, and is therefore the product of a mind that can generalize and express its generalization in a concept which no act of the imagination can picture; the imagination can represent only individuals; the mind that has concepts of classes of things, as, for instance, of horses, houses, men, women, trees, has already a genuine power of generalization. Let me also call attention to such words as "wake," "reason"; "mono," "thing"; "koto," "fact"; "aru," "is"; "oro," "lives"; "aru koto," "is fact," or "existence"; "ugoku koto," "movement"; "omoi," "thought"; this list might be indefinitely extended. Let the reader consider whether these words are not highly generalized; yet these are all pure Japanese words, and reveal the development of the Japanese mind before it was in the least influenced by Chinese thought. Evidently it will not do to assert the entire lack of the power of generalization to the Japanese mind.

Still further evidence proving Japanese possession of the higher mental faculties may be found in the wide prevalence and use of the most highly generalized philosophical terms. Consider for instance, "Ri" and "Ki," "In" and "Yo." No complete translation can be found for them in English; "Ri" and "Ki" may be best translated as the rational and the formative principles in the universe, while "In" and "Yo" signify the active and the passive, the male and the female, the light and the darkness; in a word, the poles of a positive and negative. It is true that these terms are of Chinese origin as well as the thoughts themselves, but they are to-day in universal use in Japan. Similar abstract terms of Buddhistic origin are the possession of the common people.

Of course the possession of these Chinese terms is not offered as evidence of independent generalizing ability. But wide use proves conclusively the possession of the higher mental faculties, for, without such faculties, the above terms would be incomprehensible to the people and would find no place in common speech. We must be careful not to give too much weight to the foreign origin of these terms. Chinese is to Japanese what Latin and Greek are to modern European languages. The fact that a term is of Chinese origin proves nothing as to the nature of the modern Japanese mind. The developing Japanese civilization demanded new terms for her new instruments and increasing concepts. These for over fifteen centuries have been borrowed from, or constructed out of, Chinese in the same way that all our modern scientific terms are constructed out of Latin and Greek. It is doubtful if any of the Chinese terms, even those borrowed bodily, have in Japan the same significance as in China. If this is true, then the originating feature of Japanese power of generalization becomes manifest.

Indeed from this standpoint, the fact that the Japanese have made such extensive use of the Chinese language shows the degree to which the Japanese mind has outgrown its primitive development, demanding new terms for the expression of its expanding life. But mental growth implies energy of acquisition. The adoption of Chinese terms is not a passive but an active process.

Acquisition of generalized terms can only take place with the development of a generalizing mind. Foreign terms may help, but they do not cause that development.

In a study of the question whether or not the Japanese possess independent powers of analysis and generalization, we must ever remember the unique character of the social environment to which they have been subjected. Always more or less of an isolated nation, they have been twice or thrice suddenly confronted with a civilization much superior to that which they in their isolation had developed. Under such circumstances, adoption and modification of ideas and language as well as of methods and machinery were the most rational and natural courses.

The explanation usually given for the puerilities of Oriental science, history, and religion has been short and simple, namely, the inherent nature of the Oriental races, as if this were the final fact, needing and admitting no further explanation. That the Orient has not developed history or science is doubtless true, but the correct explanation of this fact is, in my opinion, that the educational method of the entire Orient has rested on mechanical memorization; during the formative period of the mind the exclusive effort of education has been to develop a memory which acts by arbitrary or fanciful connections and relations. A Japanese boy of Old Japan, for instance, began his education at from seven to eight years of age and spent three or four years in memorizing the thousands of Chinese hieroglyphic characters contained in the Shisho and Gokyo, nine of the Chinese classics. This completed, his teacher would begin to explain to him the meaning of the characters and sentences. The entire educational effort was to develop the powers of observing and memorizing accidental, superficial, or even purely artificial relations. This double faculty of observing trifling and irrelevant details, and of remembering them, became phenomenally and abnormally developed.

Recent works on the psychology of education, however, have made plain how an excessive development of a child's lower mental faculties may arrest its latergrowth in all the higher departments of its intellectual nature; the development of a mechanical memory is well known as a serious obstacle to the higher activities of reason. Now Japanese education for centuries, like Chinese, has developed such memory. It trained the lower and ignored the higher. Much of the Japanese education of to-day, although it includes mathematics, science, and history, is based on the mechanical memory method. The Orient is thus a mammoth illustration of the effects of over-development of the mechanical memory, and the consequent arrest of the development of the remaining powers of the mind.

Encumbered by this educational ideal and system, how could the ancient Chinese and Japanese men of education make a critical study of history, or develop any science worthy of the name? The childish physics and astronomy, the brutal therapeutics and the magical and superstitious religions of the Orient, are a necessary consequence of its educational system, not of its inherent lack of the higher mental powers.

If Japanese children brought up from infancy in American homes, and sent to American schools from kindergarten days onward, should still manifest marked deficiencies in powers of analysis and generalization, as compared with American children, we should then be compelled to conclude that this difference is due to diverse natal psychic endowment. Generalizations as to the inherent intellectual deficiencies of the Oriental are based on observations of individuals already developed in the Oriental civilization, whose psychic defects they accordingly necessarily inherit through the laws of social heredity. Such observations have no relevancy to our main problem. We freely admit that Oriental civilization manifests striking deficiencies of development of the higher mental faculties, although it is not nearly so great as many assert; but we contend that these deficiencies are due to something else than the inherent psychic nature of the Oriental individual. Innumerable causes have combined to produce the Oriental social order and to determine its slow development. These cannot be stated in a sentence, nor in a paragraph.

In the final analysis, however, the causes which produce the characteristic features of Japanese social order are the real sources of the differentiating intellectual traits now characterizing the Japanese. Introduce a new social heredity,—a new system of education,—one which relegates a mechanical memory to the background,—one which exalts powers of rational observation of the profound causal relations of the phenomena of nature, and which sets a premium on such observation, analysis, and generalization, and the results will show the inherent psychic nature of the Oriental to be not different from that of the Occidental.

XX
PHILOSOPHICAL ABILITY

We are now prepared to consider whether or not the Japanese have philosophical ability. The average educated Japanese believe such to be the case. The rapidity and ease with which the upper classes have abandoned their superstitious faiths is commonly attributed by themselves to the philosophical nature of their minds. Similarly the rapid spread of so-called rationalism and Unitarian thought and Higher Criticism among once earnest Christians, during the past decade, they themselves ascribe to their interest in philosophical questions, and to their ability in handling philosophical problems.

Foreigners, on the other hand, usually deny them the possession of philosophical ability.

Dr. Peery, in his volume entitled "The Gist of Japan," says: "By nature, I think, they are more inclined to be practical than speculative. Abstract theological ideas have little charm for them. There is a large element in Japan that simulates a taste for philosophical study. Philosophy and metaphysics are regarded by them as the profoundest of all branches of learning, and in order to be thought learned they profess great interest in these studies. Not only are the highly metaphysical philosophies of the East studied, but the various systems of the West are looked into likewise. Many of the people are capable of appreciating these philosophies, too; but they do it for a purpose." Other writers make the same general charge of philosophical incompetence. One or two quotations from Dr. Knox's writings were given on this subject, under the head of Imitation.[AM]

What, then, are the facts? Do the Japanese excel in philosophy, or are they conspicuously deficient? In either case, is the characteristic due to essential race nature or to some other cause?

We must first distinguish between interest in philosophical problems and ability in constructing original philosophical systems. In this distinction is to be found the reconciliation of many conflicting views. Many who argue for Japanese philosophical ability are impressed with the interest they show in metaphysical problems, while those who deny them this ability are impressed with the dependence of Japanese on Chinese philosophy.

The discussions of the previous chapter as to the nature of Japanese education and its tendency to develop the lower at the expense of the higher mental faculties, have prepared us not to expect any particularly brilliant history of Japanese philosophy. Such is indeed the case. Primitive Japanese cosmology does not differ in any important respect from the primitive cosmology of other races. The number of those in Old Japan who took a living interest in distinctly metaphysical problems is indisputably small. While we admit them to have manifested some independence and even originality, as Professor Inouye urges,[AN] yet it can hardly be maintained that they struck out any conspicuously original philosophical systems. There is no distinctively Japanese philosophy.

These facts, however, should not blind us to the distinction between latent ability in philosophical thought and the manifestation of that ability. The old social order, with its defective education, its habit of servile intellectual dependence on ancestors, and its social and legal condemnation of independent originality, particularly in the realm of thought, was a mighty incubus on speculative philosophy. Furthermore, crude science and distorted history could not provide the requisite material from which to construct a philosophical interpretation of the universe that would appeal to the modern Occidental.

In spite, however, of social and educational hindrances, the Japanese have given ample evidence of interest in metaphysical problems and of more or less ability in their solution. Religious constructions of the future life, conceptions as to the relations of gods and men and the universe, are in fact results of the metaphysical operations of the mind. Primitive Japan was not without these. As she developed in civilization and came in contact with Chinese and Hindu metaphysical thought, she acquired their characteristic systems. Buddhist first, and later Confucian, metaphysics dominated the thought of her educated men. In view of the highly metaphysical character of Buddhist doctrines and the interest they have produced at least among the better trained priests, the assertion that the Japanese have no ability in metaphysics cannot be maintained.

At one period in the history of Buddhism in Japan, prolonged public discussions were all the fashion. Priests traveled from temple to temple to engage in public debate. The ablest debater was the abbot, and he had to be ready to face any opponent who might appear. If a stranger won, the abbot yielded his place and his living to the victor. Many an interesting story is told of those times, and of the crowds that would gather to hear the debates. But our point is that this incident in the national life shows the appreciation of the people for philosophical questions. And although that particular fashion has long since passed away, the national interest in discussions and arguments still exists. No monks of the West ever enjoyed hair-splitting arguments more than do many of the Japanese. They are as adept at mental refinements and logical juggling as any people of the West, though possibly the Hindus excel them.

If it be said that Confucianism was not only non-metaphysical, but uniquely practical, and for this reason found wide acceptance in Japan, the reply must be first that, professing to be non-metaphysical, it nevertheless had a real metaphysical system of thought in the background to which it ever appealed for authority, a system, be it noted, more in accord with modern science and philosophy than Buddhist metaphysics; and secondly, although Confucianism became the bulwark of the state and the accepted faith of the samurai, it was limited to them. The vast majority of the nation clung to their primitive Buddhistic cosmology. That Confucianism rested on a clearly implied and more or less clearly expressed metaphysical foundation may be seen in the quotations from the writings of Muro Kyuso which are given in chapter xxiv. We should note that the revolt of the educated classes of Japan from Buddhism three hundred years ago, and their general adoption of Confucian doctrine, was partly in the interests of religion and partly in the interests of metaphysics. In both respects the progressive part of the nation had become dissatisfied with Buddhism. The revolt proves not lack of religious or metaphysical interest and insight, but rather the reverse.

Not a little of the teaching of Shushi (1130-1200 A.D.) and of Oyomei (1472-1528 A.D.), Chinese philosophical expounders of Confucianism, is metaphysical. The doctrine of the former was widely studied and was the orthodox doctrine in Japan for more than two centuries, all other doctrine and philosophy being forbidden by the state. It is true that the central interest in this philosophical instruction was the ethical. It was felt that the entire ethical system rested on the acceptance of a particular metaphysical system. But so far from detracting from our argument this statement rather adds. For in what land has not the prime interest in metaphysics been ethical? A study of the history of philosophy shows clearly that philosophy and metaphysics arose out of religious and ethical problems, and have ever maintained their hold on thinking men, because of their mutually vital relations. In Japan it has not been otherwise. If anyone doubts this he should read the Japanese philosophers—in the original, if possible; if not, then in such translations and extracts as Dr. Knox has given us in his "A Japanese Philosopher," and Mr. Aston in his "Japanese Literature." The ethical interest is primary, and the metaphysical interest is secondary,[10] to be sure, but not to be denied.

Occidental philosophy has found many earnest and capable Japanese students. The Imperial University has a strong corps of philosophical instructors. Occidental metaphysical thought, both materialistic and idealistic, has found many congenial minds. Indeed, it is not rash to say that in the thought of New Japan the distinguishing Oriental metaphysical conceptions of the universe have been entirely displaced by those of the West. Christians, in particular, have entirely abandoned the old polytheistic, pantheistic, and fatalistic metaphysics and have adopted thoroughgoing monotheism.

Ability to understand and sufficient interest to study through philosophical and metaphysical systems of foreign lands indicate a mental development of no slight order, whatever may be the ability, or lack of it, in making original contributions to the subject. That educated Japanese have shown real ability in the former sense can hardly be doubted by those who have read the writings of such men as Goro Takahashi, ex-president Hiroyuki Kato, Prof. Yujiro Motora, Prof. Rikizo Nakashima, or Dr. Tetsujiro Inouye. The philosophical brightness of many of Japan's foreign as well as home-trained scholars argues well for the philosophical ability of the nation.

A recent conversation with a young Japanese gives point to what has just been said. The young man suddenly appeared at my study door, and, with unusually brief salutations, said that he wished me to talk to him about religion. In answer to questions he explained that he had been one of my pupils ten years ago in the Kumamoto Boys' School; that he had been baptized as a Christian at that time, but had become cold and filled with doubts; that he had been studying ever since, having at one time given considerable attention to the Zen sect of Buddhism; but that he had found no satisfaction there. He accordingly wished to study Christianity more carefully. For three hours we talked, he asking questions about the Christian conception of God, of the universe, of man, of sin, of evolution, of Christ, of salvation, of the object of life, of God's purpose in creation, of the origin and nature of the Bible. Toward the latter part of our conversation, referring to one idea expressed, he said, "That is about what Hegel held, is it not?" As he spoke he opened his knapsack, which I then saw to be full of books, and drew out an English translation of Hegel's "Philosophy of History"; he had evidently read it carefully, making his notes in Japanese on the margin. I asked him if he had read it through. "Yes," he replied, "three times." He also incidentally informed me that he had thought of entering our mission theological training class during the previous winter, but that he was then in the midst of the study of the philosophy of Kant, and had accordingly decided to defer entering until the autumn. How thoroughly he had mastered these, the most profound and abstruse metaphysicians that the West can boast, I cannot state. But this at least is clear; his interest in them was real and lasting. And in his conversation he showed keen appreciation of philosophical problems. It is to be noted also that he was a self-taught philosopher—for he had attended no school since he studied elementary English, ten years before, while a lad of less than twenty.

As a sample of the kind of men I not infrequently meet, let me cite the case of a young business man who once called on me in the hotel at Imabari, popularly called "the little philosopher." He wished to talk about the problem of the future life and to ask my personal belief in the matter. He said that he believed in God and in Jesus as His unique son and revealer, but that he found great difficulty in believing in the continued life of the soul after death. His difficulty arose from the problems of the nature of future thinking; shall we continue to think in terms of sense perception, such as time, space, form, color, pleasure, and pain? If not, how can we think at all? And can we then remember our present life? If we do, then the future life will not be essentially different from this, *i.e.*, we must still have physical senses, and continue to live in an essentially physical world. Here was a set of objections to the doctrine of the future life that I have never heard as much as mentioned by any Occidental youth. Though without doubt not original with him, yet he must have had in some degree both philosophical ability and interest in order to appreciate their force and to seek their solution.

In conversation not long since with a Buddhist priest of the Tendai sect, after responding to his request for a criticism of Buddhism, I asked him for a similarly frank criticism of Christianity. To my surprise, he said that while Christianity was far ahead of Buddhism in its practical parts and in its power to mold character, it was deficient in philosophical insight and interest. This led to a prolonged conversation on Buddhistic philosophy, in which he explained the doctrines of the "Ku-ge-chu," and the "Usa and Musa." Without attempting to explain them here, I may say that the first is amazingly like Hegel's "absolute nothing," with its thesis, antithesis, and synthesis, and the second a psychological distinction between volitional and spontaneous emotions.

In discussing Japanese philosophical ability, a point often forgotten is the rarity of philosophical ability or even interest in the West. But a small proportion of college students have the slightest interest in philosophical or metaphysical problems. The majority do not understand what the distinctive metaphysical problems are. In my experience it is easier to enter into a conversation with an educated man in Japan on a philosophical question than with an American. If interest in philosophical and metaphysical questions in the West is rare, original ability in their investigation is still rarer.

We conclude, then, that in regard to philosophical ability the Japanese have no marked racial characteristic differentiating them from other races. Although they have not developed a distinctive national philosophy, this is not due to inherent philosophical incompetence. Nor, on the other hand, is the relatively wide interest now manifest in philosophical problems attributable to the inherent philosophical ability of the race. So far as Japan is either behind or in advance of other races, in this respect, it is due to her social order and social inheritance, and particularly to the nature, methods, and aims of the educational system, but not to her intrinsic psychic inheritance.

XXI
IMAGINATION

In no respect, perhaps, have the Japanese been more sweepingly criticised by foreigners than in regard to their powers of imagination and idealism. Unqualified generalizations not only assert the entire lack of these powers, but they consider this lack to be the distinguishing inherent mental characteristic of the race. The Japanese are called "prosaic," "matter-of-fact," "practical," "unimaginative."

Mr. Walter Dening, describing Japanese mental characteristics, says:

"Neither their past history nor their prevailing tastes show any tendency to idealism. They are lovers of the practical and the real; neither the fancies of Goethe nor the reveries of Hegel are to their liking. Our poetry and our philosophy and the mind that appreciates them are alike the results of a network of subtle influences to which the Japanese are comparative strangers. It is maintained by some, and we think justly, that the lack of idealism in the

Japanese mind renders the life of even the most cultivated a mechanical, humdrum affair when compared with that of Westerners. The Japanese cannot understand why our controversialists should wax so fervent over psychological, ethical, religious, and philosophical questions, failing to perceive that this fervency is the result of the intense interest taken in such subjects. The charms that the cultured Western mind finds in the world of fancy and romance, in questions themselves, irrespective of their practical bearings, is for the most part unintelligible to the Japanese."[AP]

Mr. Percival Lowell expends an entire chapter in his "Soul of the Far East," in showing how important imagination is as a factor in art, religion, science, and civilization generally, and how strikingly deficient Japanese are in this faculty. "The Far Orientals," he argues, "ought to be a particularly unimaginative set of people. Such is precisely what they are. Their lack of imagination is a well-recognized fact."[AQ]

Mr. Aston, characterizing Japanese literature, says:

"A feature which strikingly distinguishes the Japanese poetic muse from that of Western nations is a certain lack of imaginative power. The Japanese are slow to endow inanimate objects with life. Shelley's 'Cloud,' for example, contains enough matter of this kind for many volumes of Japanese verse. Such lines as:

'From   my   wings   are   shaken
The   dews   that   waken
The   sweet   buds   every   one,
When   rocked   to   rest
On   their   mother's   breast
As she dances about the sun,'

would appear to them ridiculously overcharged with metaphor, if not absolutely unintelligible."[AR]

On the other hand, some writers have called attention to the contrary element of Japanese mental nature. Prof. Ladd, for instance, maintains that the characteristic mental trait of the Japanese is their sentimentality. He has shown how their lives are permeated with and regulated by sentiment. Ancestral worship, patriotism, Imperial apotheosis, friendship, are fashioned by idealizing sentiment. In our chapters on the emotional elements of Japanese character we have considered how widespread and powerful these ideals and sentiments have been and still are.

Writers who compare the Chinese with the Japanese remark the practical business nature of the former and the impractical, visionary nature of the latter.

For a proper estimate of our problem we should clearly distinguish between the various forms of imagination. It reveals itself not merely in art and literature, in fantastic conception, in personification and metaphor, but in every important department of human life. It is the tap-root of progress, as Mr. Lowell well points out. It pictures an ideal life in advance of the actual, which ideal becomes the object of effort. The forms of imagination may, therefore, be classified according to the sphere of life in which it appears. In addition to the poetic fancy and the idealism of art and literature generally, we must distinguish the work of imagination in the æsthetic, in the moral, in the religious, in the scientific, and in the political life. The manifestation of the imaginative faculty in art and in literature is only one part of the æsthetic imagination.

In studying Japanese æsthetic characteristics, we noted how unbalanced was the development of their æsthetic sense. This proposition of unbalanced development applies with equal force to the imaginative faculty as a whole. Conspicuously lacking in certain directions, it is as conspicuously prominent in others. Rules of etiquette are the products of the æsthetic imagination, and in what land has etiquette been more developed than in feudal Japan? Japanese imagination has been particularly active in the political world. The passionate loyalty of retainers to their lord, of samurai to their daimyo, of all to their "kuni," or clan, in ancient times, and now, of the people to their Emperor, are the results of a vivid political idealizing imagination. Imperial apotheosis is a combination of the political and religious imagination. And in what land has the apotheosizing imagination been more active than in Japan? Ambition and self-conceit are likewise dependent on an active imaginative faculty.

There can be no doubt the writers quoted above have drawn attention to some salient features of Japanese art. In the literature of the past, the people have not manifested that high literary imagination that we discover in the best literature of many other nations.

This fact, however, will not justify the sweeping generalizations based upon it. Judging from the pre-Elizabethan literature, who would have expected the brilliancy of the Elizabethan period? Similarly in regard to the Victorian period of English literature. Because the Japanese have failed in the past to produce literature equal to the best of Western lands, we are not justified in asserting that she never will and that she is inherently deficient in literary imagination. In regard to certain forms of light fancy, all admit that Japanese poems are unsurpassed by those of other lands. Japanese amative poetry is noted for its delicate fancies and plays on words exceedingly difficult, if not impossible, of translation, or even of expression, to one unacquainted with the language.

The deficiencies of Japanese literature, therefore, are not such as to warrant the conclusion that they both mark and make a fundamental difference in the race mind. For such differences as exist are capable of a sociological explanation.

The prosaic matter-of-factness of the Japanese mind has been so widely emphasized that we need not dwell upon it here. There is, however, serious danger of over-emphasis, a danger into which all writers fall who make it the ground for sweeping condemnatory criticism.

They are right in ascribing to the average Japanese a large amount of unimaginative matter-of-factness, but they are equally wrong in unqualified dogmatic generalizations. They base their inductions on insufficient facts, a habit to which foreigners are peculiarly liable, through ignorance of the language and also of the inner thoughts and life of the people.

The prosaic nature of the Japanese has not impressed me so much as the visionary tendency of the people, and their idealism. The Japanese themselves count this idealism a national characteristic. They say that they are theorizers, and numberless experiences confirm this view.

They project great undertakings; they scheme; they discuss contingencies; they make enormous plans; all with an air of seriousness and yet with a nonchalance which shows a semi-conscious sense of the unreality of their proposals. In regard to Korea and China and Formosa, they have hatched political and business schemes innumerable. The kaleidoscopic character of Japanese politics is in part due to the rapid succession of visionary schemes. One idea reigns for a season, only to be displaced by another, causing constant readjustment of political parties. Frequent attacks on government foreign policy depend for their force on lordly ideas as to the part Japan should play in international relations. Writing about the recent discussions in the public press over the question of introducing foreign capital into Japan, one contributor to the *Far East* remarks that "It has been treated more from a theoretical than from a practical standpoint.... This seems to me to arise from a peculiar trait of Japanese mind which is prone to dwell solely on the theoretical side until the march of events compels a sudden leap toward the practical." This visionary faculty of the Japanese is especially conspicuous in the daily press. Editorials on foreign affairs and on the relations of Japan to the world are full of it.

I venture to jot down a few illustrations of impractical idealism out of my personal knowledge. An evangelist in the employ of the Kumamoto station exemplified this visionary trait in a marked degree. Nervous in the extreme, he was constantly having new ideas. For some reason his attention was turned to the subject of opium and the evils China was suffering from the drug, forced on her by England. Forthwith he came to me for books on the subject; he wished to become fully informed, and then he proposed to go to China and preach on the subject. For a few weeks he was full of his enterprise. It seemed to him that if he were only allowed the opportunity he could convince the Chinese of their error, and the English of their crime. One of his plans was to go to England and expostulate with them on their un-Christian dealings with China. A few weeks later his attention was turned to the wrongs inflicted on the poor on account of their ignorance about law and their inability to get legal assistance. This idea held him longer than the previous.

95

He desired to study law and become a public pleader in order to defend the poor against unjust men of wealth. In his theological ideas he was likewise extreme and changeable; swinging from positive and most emphatic belief to extreme doubt, and later back again. In his periods of triumphant faith it seemed to him that he could teach the world; and his expositions of truth were extremely interesting. He proposed to formulate a new theology that would dissolve forever the difficulties of the old theology. In his doubts, too, he was no less interesting and assertive. His hold on practical matters was exceedingly slender. His salary, though considerably larger than that of most of the evangelists, was never sufficient. He would spend lavishly at the beginning of the month so long as he had the money, and then would pinch himself or else fall into debt.

Mr. ——, the head of the Kumamoto Boys' School during the period of its fierce struggles and final collapse, whom I have already referred to as the Hero-Principal,[AS] is another example of this impractical high-strung visionariness. No sooner had he reached Kumamoto, than there opened before our enchanted eyes the vision of this little insignificant school blooming out into a great university. True, there had been some of this bombast before his arrival; but it took on new and gorgeous form under his master hand. The airs that he put on, displaying his (fraudulent) Ph.D., and talking about his schemes, are simply amusing to contemplate from this distance. His studies in the philosophy of religion had so clarified his mind that he was going to reform both Christianity and Buddhism. His sermons of florid eloquence and vociferous power, never less than an hour in length, were as marked in ambitious thoughts as in pulpit mannerisms. He threw a spell over all who came in contact with him. He overawed them by his vehemence and tremendous earnestness and insistence on perfect obedience to his masterful will. In one of his climactic sermons, after charging missionaries with teaching dangerous errors, he said that while some were urging that the need of the times was to "his back to Luther," and others were saying, that we must "his back to Christ" (these English words being brought into his Japanese sermon), they were both wrong; we must "hie back to God"; and he prophesied a reformation in religion, beginning there in Kumamoto, in that school, which would be far and away more important in the history of the world than was the Lutheran Reformation.

The recent history of Christianity in Japan supplies many striking instances of visionary plans and visionary enthusiasts. The confident expectation entertained during the eighties of Christianizing the nation before the close of the century was such a vision. Another, arising a few years later, was the importance of returning all foreign missionaries to their native lands and of intrusting the entire evangelistic work to native Christians, and committing to them the administration of the immense sums thus set free. For it was assumed by these brilliant Utopians that the amount of money expended in supporting missionaries would be available for aggressive work should the missionaries be withdrawn, and that the Christians in foreign lands would continue to pour in their contributions for the evangelization of Japan.

Still another instance of utopian idealism is the vision that Japan will give birth to that perfect religion, meeting the demands of both heart and head, for which the world waits. In January, 1900, Prof. T. Inouye, of the Imperial University, after showing quite at length, and to his own satisfaction, the inadequacy of all existing religions to meet the ethical and religious situation in Japan, maintained this ambitious view.

Some Japanese Christians are declaring the need of Japonicized Christianity. "Did not the Greeks transform Christianity before they accepted it? And did not the Romans, and finally the Germans, do the same? Before Japan will or can accept the religion of Christ, it must be Japonicized." So they argue; "and who so fit to do it as we?" lies in the background of their thought.

Many a Christian pastor and evangelist, although not sharing the ambition of Prof. Inouye, nevertheless glows with the confident expectation that Japonicized Christianity will be its most perfect type. "No one need wonder if Japan should be destined to present to the world the best type of Christianity that has yet appeared in history," writes an exponent of this view, at one time a Christian pastor. In this connection the reader may recall what was said in chapter xiv. on Japanese Ambition and Conceit, qualities depending on the power of seeing visions. We note, in passing, the optimistic spirit of New Japan. This is in part due, no doubt, to ignorance of the problems that lie athwart their future progress, but it is also due to the vivid imaginative faculty which pictures for them the glories of the coming decades when they shall lead not only the Orient, but also the Occident, in every line of civilization, material and spiritual, moral and religious. A dull, unimaginative, prosaic nature cannot be exuberantly optimistic. It is evident that writers who proclaim the unimaginative matter-of-factness of the Japanese as universal and absolute, have failed to see a large side of Japanese inner life.

Mr. Percival Lowell states that the root of all the peculiarities of Oriental peoples is their marked lack of imagination. This is the faculty that "may in a certain sense be said to be the creator of the world." The lack of this faculty, according to Mr. Lowell, is the root of the Japanese lack of originality and invention; it gives the whole Oriental civilization its characteristic features. He cites a few words to prove the essentially prosaic character of the Japanese mind, such as "up-down" for "pass" (which word, by the way, is his own invention, and reveals his ignorance of the language), "the being (so) is difficult," in place of "thank you." "A lack of any fanciful ideas," he says, "is one of the most salient traits of all Far Eastern peoples, if indeed a sad dearth can properly be called salient. Indirectly, their want of imagination betrays itself in their everyday sayings and doings, and more directly in every branch of thought." I note, in passing, that Mr. Lowell does not distinguish between fancy and imagination. Though allied faculties, they are distinct. Mr. Lowell's extreme estimate of the prosaic nature of the Japanese mind I cannot share. Many letters received from Japanese friends refute this view by their fanciful expressions. The Japanese language, too, has many fanciful terms. Why "pass" is any more imaginative than "up-down," to accept Mr. Lowell's etymology, or "the being (so) is difficult" than "thank you," I do not see. To me the reverse proposition would seem the truer. And are not "breaking-horns" for "on purpose," and "breaking-bones" for "with great difficulty," distinctly imaginative terms, more imaginative than the English? In the place of our English term "sun," the Japanese have several alternative terms in common use, such as "*hi*," "day," "*Nichirin*," "day-ball," "*Ten-to Sama*," "the god of heaven's light;" and for "moon," it has "*tsuki*," "month," "*getsu-rin*," "month ball." The names given to her men-of-war also indicate a fanciful nature. The torpedo destroyers are named "Dragon-fly," "Full Moon," "The Moon in the Cloud," "Seabeach," "Dawn of Day," "Clustering Clouds," "Break of Day," "Ripples," "Evening Mist," "Dragon's Lamp," "Falcon," "Magpie," "White-naped Crane," and "White Hawk." Surely, it cannot be maintained that the Japanese are utterly lacking in fancy.

Distinguishing between fancy as "the power of forming pleasing, graceful, whimsical, or odd mental images, or of combining them with little regard to rational processes of construction," and imagination, in its more philosophical use, as "the act of constructive intellect in grouping the materials of knowledge or thought into new, original, and rational systems," we assert without fear of successful contradiction, that the Japanese race is not without either of these important mental faculties.

In addition to the preceding illustrations of visionary and fanciful traits, let the reader reflect on the significance of the comic and of caricature in art. Japanese*Netsuke* (tiny carvings of exquisite skill representing comical men, women, and children) are famous the world over. Surely, the fancy is the most conspicuous mental characteristic revealed in this branch of Japanese art. In Japanese poetry "a vast number of conceits, more or less pretty," are to be found, likewise manifesting the fancy of both the authors who wrote and the people who were pleased with and preserved their writings.[A] The so-called "impersonal habit of the Japanese mind," with a corresponding "lack of personification of abstract qualities," doubtless prevents Japanese literature from rising to the poetic heights attained by Western nations. But this lack does not prove the Japanese mind incapable of such flights. As describing the actual characteristics of the literature of the past the assertion of "a lack of imaginative power" is doubtless fairly correct. But the inherent nature of the Japanese mind cannot be inferred from the deficiencies of its past literature, without first examining the relation between its characteristic features and the nature of the social order and the social inheritance.

Are the Japanese conspicuously deficient in imagination, in the sense of the definition given above? The constructive imagination is the creator of civilization. Not only art and literature, but, as already noted, science, philosophy, politics, and even the practical arts and prosaic farming are impossible without it. It is the tap-root of invention, of discovery, of originality.

It is needless to repeat what has been said in previous chapters[AU] on Japanese imitation, invention, discovery, and originality. Yet, in consideration of the facts there given, are we justified in counting the Japanese so conspicuously deficient in constructive, imagination as to warrant the assertion that such a lack is the fundamental characteristic of the race psychic nature?

As an extreme case, look for a moment at their imitativeness. Although imitation is considered a proof of deficient originality, and thus of imagination, yet reflection shows that this depends on the nature of the imitation. Japanese imitation has not been, except possibly for short periods, of that slavish nature which excludes the work of the imagination. Indeed, the impulse to imitation rests on the imagination. But for this faculty picturing the state of bliss or power secured in consequence of adopting this or that feature of an alien civilization, the desire to imitate could not arise. In view, moreover, of the selective nature of Japanese imitation, we are further warranted in ascribing to the people no insignificant development of the imagination.

In illustration, consider Japan's educational system. Established no doubt on Occidental models, it is nevertheless a distinctly Japanese institution. Its buildings are as characteristically Japonicized Occidental school buildings as are its methods of instruction. Japanese railroads and steamers, likewise constructed in Japan, are similarly Japonicized— adapted to the needs and conditions of the people. To our eyes this of course signifies no improvement, but assuredly, without such modification, our Western railroads and steamers would be white elephants on their hands, expensive and difficult of operation.

What now is the sociological interpretation of the foregoing facts? How are the fanciful, visionary, and idealistic characteristics, on the one hand, and, on the other, the prosaic, matter-of-fact, and relatively unimaginative characteristics, related to the social order?

It is not difficult to account for the presence of accentuated visionariness in Japan. Indeed, this quality is conspicuous among the descendants of the military and literary classes; and this fact furnishes us the clew. "From time immemorial," to use a phrase common on the lips of Japanese historians, up to the present era, the samurai as a class were quite separated from the practical world; they were comfortably supported by their liege lords; entirely relieved from the necessity of toiling for their daily bread, they busied themselves not only with war and physical training, but with literary accomplishments, that required no less strenuous mental exertions.

Furthermore, in a class thus freed from daily toil, there was sure to arise a refined system of etiquette and of rank distinctions. Even a few centuries of life would, under such conditions, develop highly nervous individuals in large numbers, hypersensitive in many directions. These men, by the very development of their nervous constitutions, would become the social if not the practical leaders of their class; high-spirited, and with domineering ideas and scheming ambitions, they would set the fashion to all their less nervously developed fellows. Freed from the exacting conditions of a practical life, they would inevitably fly off on tangents more or less impractical, visionary.

If, therefore, this trait is more marked in Japanese character than in that of many other nations, it may be easily traced to the social order that has ruled this land "from time immemorial." More than any other of her mental characteristics, impractical visionariness may be traced to the development of the nervous organization at the expense of the muscular. This characteristic accordingly may be said to be more inherently a race characteristic than many others that have been mentioned. Yet we should remember that the samurai constitute but a small proportion of the people. According to recent statistics (1895) the entire class to-day numbers but 2,050,000, while the common people number over 40,000,000. It is, furthermore, to be remembered that not all the descendants of the samurai are thus nervously organized. Large numbers have a splendid physical endowment, with no trace of abnormal nervous development. While the old feudal order, with its constant carrying of swords, and the giving of honor to the most impetuous, naturally tended to push the most high-strung individuals into the forefront and to set them up as models for the imitation of the young, the social order now regnant in Japan faces in the other direction. Such visionary men are increasingly relegated to the rear. Their approach to insanity is recognized and condemned. Even this trait of character, therefore, which seems to be rooted in brain and nerve structure is, nevertheless, more subject to the prevailing social order than would at first seem possible.

Its rise we have seen was due to that order, and the setting aside of these characteristics as ideals at least, and thus the bringing into prominence of more normal and healthy ideals, is due to the coming in of a new order.

Japanese prosaic matter-of-factness may similarly be shown to have intimate relations to the nature of the social order. Oppressive military feudalism, keeping the vast majority of the people in practical bondage, physical, intellectual, and spiritual, would necessarily render their lives and thoughts narrow in range and spiritless in nature. Such a system crushes out hope. From sunrise to sunset, "*nembyaku nenju*," "for a hundred years and through all the year," the humdrum duties of daily life were the only psychic stimuli of the absolutely uneducated masses. Without ambition, without self-respect, without education or any stimulus for the higher mental life, what possible manifestation of the higher powers of the mind could be expected? Should some "sport" appear by chance, it could not long escape the sword of domineering samurai. Even though originally possessing some degree of imagination, cringing fear of military masters, with the continuous elimination by ruthless slaughter of the more idealizing, less submissive, and more self-assertive individuals of the non-military classes, would finally produce a dull, imitative, unimaginative, and matter-of-fact class such as we find in the hereditary laboring and merchant classes.

Furthermore, Japanese civilization, like that of the entire Orient, with its highly communalized social order, is an expression of passive submission to superior authority. Although an incomplete characterization, there is still much truth in saying that the Orient is an expression of Fate, the Occident of Freedom. We have seen that a better contrasted characterization is found in the terms communal and individual. The Orient has known nothing of individualism. It has not valued the individual nor sought his elevation and freedom. In every way, on the contrary, it has repressed and opposed him. The high development of the individual culminating in powerful personality has been an exceptional occurrence, due to special circumstances. A communal social order, often repressing and invariably failing to evoke the higher human faculties, must express its real nature in the language, literature, and customs of the people. Thus in our chapter on the Æsthetic Characteristics of the Japanese[AV] we saw how the higher forms of literature were dependent on the development of manhood and on a realization of his nature. A communal social order despising, or at least ignoring the individual, cannot produce the highest forms of literature or art, because it does not possess the highest forms of psychic development. Take from Western life all that rests on or springs from the principles of individual worth, freedom, and immortality, and how much of value or sublimity will remain? The absence from Japanese literature and language of the higher forms of fancy, metaphor, and personification on the one hand, and, on the other, the presence of widespread prosaic matter-of-factness, are thus intimately related to the communal nature of Japan's long dominant social order.

Similarly, in regard to the constructive imagination, whose conspicuous lack in Japan is universally asserted by foreign critics, we reply first that the assertion is an exaggeration, and secondly, that so far as it is fact, it is intimately related to the social order. In our discussions concerning Japanese Intellectuality and Philosophical Ability,[AW] we saw how intimate a relation exists between the social order, particularly as expressed in its educational system, and the development of the higher mental faculties. Now a moment's reflection will show how the constructive imagination, belonging as it does to the higher faculties, was suppressed by the system of mechanical and superficial education required by the social order. Religion apotheosized ancestral knowledge and customs, thus effectively condemning all conscious use of this faculty. So far as it was used, it was under the guise of reviving old knowledge or of expounding it more completely.

This, however, has been the experience of every race in certain stages of its development. Such periods have been conspicuously deficient in powerful literature, progressive science, penetrating philosophy, or developing political life. When a nation has once entered such a social order it becomes stagnant, its further development is arrested. The activity of the higher faculties of the mind are in abeyance, but not destroyed. It needs the electric shock of contact and conflict with foreign races to startle the race out of its fatal repose and start it on new lines of progress by demanding, on pain of death, or at least of racial subordination, the introduction of new elements into its social order by a renewed exercise of the constructive imagination. For without such action of the constructive imagination a radical and voluntary modification of the dominant social order is impossible.

Old Japan experienced this electric shock and New Japan is the result. She is thus a living witness to the inaccuracy of those sweeping generalizations as to her inherent deficiency of constructive imagination.

It is by no means our contention that Japanese imagination is now as widely and profoundly exercised as that of the leading Western nations. We merely contend that the exercise of this mental faculty is intimately related to the nature of the whole social order; that under certain circumstances this important faculty may be so suppressed as to give the impression to superficial observers of entire absence, and that with a new environment necessitating a new social order, this faculty may again be brought into activity.

The inevitable conclusion of the above line of thought is that the activity and the manifestation of the higher faculties is so intimately related to the nature of the social order as to prevent our attributing any particular mental characteristics to a race as its inherent and unchangeable nature. The psychic characteristics of a race at any given time are the product of the inherited social order. To transform those characteristics changes in the social order, introduced either from without, or through individuals within the race, are alone needful. This completes our specific study of the intellectual characteristics of the Japanese. It may seem, as it undoubtedly is, quite fragmentary. But we have purposely omitted all reference to those characteristics which the Japanese admittedly have in common with other races. We have attempted the consideration of only the more outstanding characteristics by which they seem to be differentiated from other races. We have attempted to show that in so far as they are different, the difference is due not to inherent psychic nature transmitted by organic heredity, but to the nature of the social order, transmitted by social heredity.

XXII
MORAL IDEALS

Even a slight study of Japanese history suffices to show that the faculty of moral discrimination was highly developed in certain directions. In what land have the ideal and practice of loyalty been higher? The heroes most lauded by the Japanese to-day are those who have proved their loyalty by the sacrifice of their lives. When Masashige Kusunoki waged a hopeless war on behalf of one branch of the then divided dynasty, and finally preferred to die by his own hand rather than endure the sight of a victorious rebel, he is considered to have exhibited the highest possible evidence of devoted loyalty. One often hears his name in the sermons of Christian preachers as a model worthy of all honor. The patriots of the period immediately preceding the Meiji era, known as the "Kinnoka," some of whom lost their lives because of their devotion to the cause of their then impotent Emperor, are accorded the highest honor the nation can give.

The teachings of the Japanese concerning the relations that should exist between parents, and children, and, in multitudes of instances, their actual conduct also, can hardly be excelled. We can assert that they have a keen moral faculty, however further study may compel us to pronounce its development and manifestations to be unbalanced.

Better, however, than generalizations as to the ethical ideals of Japan, past and present, are actual quotations from her moral teachers. The following passages are taken from "A Japanese Philosopher," by Dr. Geo. W. Knox, the larger part of the volume consisting of a translation of one of the works of Muro Kyuso—who lived from 1658 to 1734. It was during his life that the famous forty-seven ronin performed their exploit, and

Kyu-so gave them the name by which they are still remembered, Gi-shi, the "Righteous Samurai." The purpose of the work is the defense of the Confucian faith and practice, as interpreted by Tei-shu, the philosopher of China whom Japan delighted to honor. It discusses among other things the fundamental principles of ethics, politics, and religion. Dr. Knox has done all earnest Western students of Japanese ethical and religious ideas an inestimable service in the production of this work in English.

"The 'Way' of Heaven and Earth is the 'Way' of Gyo and Shun [semi-mythical rulers of ancient China idealized by Confucius]; the 'Way' of Gyo and Shun is the 'Way' of Confucius and Mencius, and the 'Way' of Confucius and Mencius is the 'Way' of Tei-Shu. Forsaking Tei-Shu, we cannot find Confucius and Mencius; forsaking Confucius and Mencius, we cannot find Gyo and Shun; and forsaking Gyo and Shun, we cannot find the 'Way' of Heaven and Earth. Do not trust implicitly an aged scholar; but this I know, and therefore I speak. If I say that which is false, may I be instantly punished by Heaven and Earth."[AX]

"Recently I was astounded at the words of a philosopher: 'The "Way" comes not from Heaven,' he said, 'it was invented by the sages. Nor is it in accord with nature; it is a mere matter of æsthetics and ornament. Of the five relations, only the conjugal is natural, while loyalty, filial obedience, and the rest were invented by the sages, and have been maintained by their authority ever since.' Surely, among all heresies from ancient days until now, none has been so monstrous as this."[AY]

"Kujuro, a lad of fifteen years, quarreled with a neighbor's son over a game of go, lost his self-control, and before he could be seized, drew his sword and cut the boy down. While the wounded boy was under the surgeon's care, Kujuro was in custody, but he showed no fear, and his words and acts were calm beyond his years. After some days the boy died, and Kujuro was condemned to hara-kiri. The officers in charge gave him a farewell feast the night before he died. He calmly wrote to his mother, took ceremonious farewell of his keeper and all in the house, and then said to the guests: 'I regret to leave you all, and should like to stay and talk till daybreak; but I must not be sleepy when I commit hara-kiri to-morrow, so I'll go to bed at once. Do you stay at your ease and drink the wine.' So he went to his room and fell asleep, all being filled with admiration as they heard him snore. On the morrow he rose early, bathed and dressed himself with care, made all his preparations with perfect calmness, and then, quiet and composed, killed himself. No old, trained, self-possessed samurai could have excelled him. No one who saw it could speak of it for years without tears.... I have told you this that Kujuro may be remembered. It would be shameful were it to be forgotten that so young a boy performed such a deed."[AZ]

"We are not to cease obeying for the sake of study, nor must we establish the laws before we begin to obey. In obedience we are to establish its Tightness and wrongness."[BA]

"We learn loyalty and obedience as we are loyal and obedient. To-day I know yesterday's short-comings, and to-morrow I shall know to-day's.... In our occupations we learn whether conduct conforms to right and so advance in the truth by practice."[BB]

"Besides a few works on history, like the Sankyo Ega Monogatari, which record facts, there are no books worth reading in our literature. For the most part they are sweet stories of the Buddhas, of which one soon wearies. But the evil is traditional, long-continued, and beyond remedy. And other books are full of lust, not even to be mentioned, like the Genji Monogatari, which should never be shown to a woman or a young man. Such books lead to vice. Our nobles call the Genji Monogatari a national treasure, why, I do not know, unless it is that they are intoxicated with its style. That is like plucking the spring blossom unmindful of the autumn's fruit. The book is full of adulteries from beginning to end. Seeing the right, ourselves should become good, seeing the wrong, we should reprove ourselves. The Genji Monogatari, Chokonka, and Seishoki are of a class, vile, mean, comparable to the books of the sages as charcoal to ice, as the stench of decay to the perfume of flowers."[BC]

"To the samurai, first of all is righteousness; next life, then silver and gold. These last are of value, but some put them in the place of righteousness. But to the samurai even life is as dirt compared to righteousness. Until the middle part of the middle ages customs were comparatively pure, though not really righteous. Corruption has come only during this period of government by the samurai. A maid servant in China was made ill with astonishment when she saw her mistress, soroban (abacus) in hand, arguing prices and values. So was it once with the samurai. They knew nothing of trade, were economical and content."[BD]

"Even in the days of my youth, young folks never mentioned the price of anything; and their faces reddened if the talk was of women. Their joy was in talk of battles and plans for war. And they studied how parents and lords should be obeyed, and the duty of samurai. But nowadays the young men talk of loss and gain, of dancing girls and harlots and gross pleasures. It is a complete change from fifty or sixty years ago.... Said Aochi to his son: 'There is such a thing as trade. See that you know nothing of it. In trade the profit should always go to the other side.... To be proud of buying high-priced articles cheap is the good fortune of merchants, but should be unknown to samurai. Let it not be even so much as mentioned.... Samurai must have a care of their words, and are not to speak of avarice, cowardice, or lust.'"[BE]

A point of considerable interest to the student of Japanese ethical ideals is the fact that the laws of Old Japan combined legal and moral maxims. Loyalty andmorality were conceived as inseparable. Ieyasu (abdicated in 1605, and died in 1616), the founder of the Tokugawa Shogunate, left a body of laws to his successors as his last will, in accordance with which they should rule the land. These laws were not made public, but were kept strictly for the guidance of the rulers. They are known as the Testament or "Honorable Will" of Ieyasu, and consist of one hundred rules. It will serve our purpose here to quote some of those that refer to the moral ideal.

"No one is to act simply for the gratification of his own desires, but he is to strive to do what may be opposed to his desires, i.e., to exercise self-control, in order that everyone may be ready for whatever he may be called upon by his superiors to do."

"The aged, whether widowers or widows, and orphans, and persons without relations, every one should assist with kindness and liberality; for justice to these four is the root of good government."

"Respect the gods [or God], keep the heart pure, and be diligent in business during the whole life."

"When I was young I determined to fight and punish all my own and my ancestors' enemies, and I did punish them; but afterwards, by deep consideration, I found that the way of heaven was to help the people, and not to punish them. Let my successors follow out this policy, or they are not of my line. In this lies the strength of the nation."

"To insure the Empire peace, the foundation must be laid in the ways of holiness and religion, and if men think they can be educated, and will not remember this, it is as if a man were to go to a forest to catch fish, or thought he could draw water out of fire. They must follow the ways of holiness."

"Japan is the country of the gods [or God—'Shinkoku']. Therefore, we have among us Confucianism, Buddhism, and Shintoism, and other sects. If we leave our gods [or God] it is like refusing the wages of our master and taking them from another."

"In regard to dancing women, prostitutes, brothels, night work, and all other improper employments, all these are like caterpillars or locusts in the country. Good men and writers in all times have written against them."

"It is said that the Mikado, looking down on his people, loves them as a mother does her children. The same may be said of me and my government. This benevolence of mind is called Jin. This Jin may be said to consist of five parts; these are humanity, integrity, courtesy, wisdom, and truth. My mode of government is according to the way of heaven. This I have done to show that I am impartial, and am not assisting my own relatives and friends only."[BF]

These quotations are perhaps sufficient, though one more from a recent writer has a peculiar interest of its own, from the fact that the purpose of the book from which the quotation is taken was the destruction of the tendencies toward approval of Western thought. It was published in 1857. The writer, Junzo Ohashi, felt himself to be a witness for truth and righteousness, and, in the spirit of the doctrine he professed, sealed his faith with a martyr's suffering and death, dying (in August, 1868) from the effect of repeated examination by torture for a supposed crime, innocence of which he maintained to the end.

It is interesting to note that two of his granddaughters, "with the physics and astronomy of the West, have accepted its religion."

"The West knows not the 'Ri'[BG] of the virtues of the heart which are in all men unchangeably the same. Nor does it know that the body is the organ of the virtues, however careful its analysis of the body may be. The adherents of the Western Philosophy indeed study carefully the outward appearances, but they have no right to steal the honored name of natural philosophy. As when 'Ki' is destroyed, 'Ri' too disappears, so, with their analysis of 'Ki,' they destroy 'Ri,' and thus this learning brings benevolence and righteousness and loyalty and truth to naught. Among the Westerners who from of old have studied details minutely, I have not heard of one who was zealous for the Great Way, for benevolence, righteousness, loyalty, and truth, and who opposed the absurdities of the Lord of Heaven [God].'[BH] 'Let then the child make its parent, Heaven; the retainer, his lord; the wife, her husband; and let each give up life for righteousness. Thus will each serve Heaven. But if we exalt Heaven above parent or lord, we shall come to think that we can serve it though they be disobeyed, and like wolf or tiger shall rejoice to kill them. To such fearful end does the Western learning lead."[BI]

The foregoing quotations reveal the exalted nature of the ideals held by at least some of the leaders of ethical thought in Japan. Taken as a whole, the moral ideals characterizing the Japanese during their entire historical period have been conspicuously communal. The feudal structure of society has determined the peculiar character of the moral ideal. Loyalty took first rank in the moral scale; the subordination of the inferior to the superior has come next, including unquestioning obedience of children to parents, and of wife to husband. The virtues of a military people have been praised and often gloriously exemplified. The possession of these various ideals and their attainment in such high degree have given the nation its cohesiveness. They make the people a unit. The feudal training under local daimyos was fitting the people for the larger life among the nations of the world on which they are now entering. Especially is their sense of loyalty, as exhibited toward the Emperor, serving them well in this period of transition from Oriental to Occidental social ideals.

Let us now examine some defective moral standards and observe their origin in the social order. Take, for instance, the ideal of truthfulness. Every Occidental remarks on the untruthfulness of the Japanese. Lies are told without the slightest apparent compunction; and when confronted with the charge of lying, the culprit often seems to feel little sense of guilt. This trait of character was noted repeatedly by the early negotiators with Japan. Townsend Harris and Sir Rutherford Alcock made frequent mention of it. When we inquire as to the moral ideal and actual instruction concerning truthfulness, we are amazed to find how inadequate it was. The inadequacy of the teaching, however, was not the primal cause of the characteristic. There is a far deeper explanation, yet very simple, namely, the nature of the social order. The old social order was feudal, and not industrial or commercial. History shows that industrial and commercial nations develop the virtue of truthfulness far in advance of military nations. For these virtues are essential to them; without them they could not long continue to prosper.

So in regard to all the aspects of business morality, it must be admitted that, from the Occidental standpoint, Old Japan was very deficient. But it must also be stated that new ideals are rapidly forming. Buying and selling with a view to making profit, though not unknown in Old Japan, was carried on by a despised section of the community. Compared with the present, the commercial community of feudal times was mean and small. Let us note somewhat in detail the attitude of the samurai toward the trader in olden times, and the ideals they reveal.

The pursuit of business was considered necessarily degrading, for he who handled money was supposed to be covetous. The taking of profit was thought to be ignoble, if not deceitful. They who condescended to such an occupation were accordingly despised and condemned to the lowest place in the social scale. These ideas doubtless helped to make business degrading; traders were doubtless sordid and covetous and deceitful. In the presence of the samurai they were required to take the most abject postures. In addressing him, they must never stand, but must touch the ground with their foreheads; while talking with him they must remain with their hands on the ground. Even the children of samurai always assumed the lordly attitude toward tradesmen. The sons of tradesmen might not venture into a quarrel with the sons of samurai, for the armed children of the samurai were at liberty to cut down and kill the children of the despicable merchant, should they insult or even oppose them.

All this, however, has passed away. Commerce is now honored; trade and manufacture are recognized not only as laudable, but as the only hope of Japan for the future. The new social order is industrial and commercial. The entire body of the former samurai, now no longer maintaining their distinctive name, are engaged in some form of business. Japan is to-day a nation of traders and farmers. Accompanying the changes in the social order, new standards as to honesty and business integrity are being formulated and enforced.[BI]

XXIII
MORAL IDEALS

(*Continued*)

An Occidental is invariably filled with astonishment on learning that a human being, as such, had no value in Old Japan. The explanation lies chiefly in the fact that the social order did not rest on the inherent worth of the individual. As in all primitive lands and times, the individual was as nothing compared to the family and the tribe. As time went on, this principle took the form of the supreme worth of the higher classes in society. Hence arose the liberty allowed the samurai of cutting down, in cold blood, a beggar, a merchant, or a farmer on the slightest provocation, or simply for the purpose of testing his sword.

Japanese social and religious philosophy had not yet discovered that the individual is of infinite worth in himself, apart from all considerations of his rank in society. As we have seen, the absence of this idea from Japanese civilization resulted in various momentous consequences, of which the frequency of murder and suicide is but one.

Another, and this constitutes one of the most striking differences between the moral ideals of the East and the West, is the low estimate put upon the inherent nature and value of woman, by which was determined her social position and the moral relations of the sexes. Japan seems to have suffered somewhat in this respect from her acceptance of Hindu philosophy. For there seems to be considerable unanimity among historians that in primitive times in Japan there prevailed a much larger liberty, and consequently a much higher regard, forwoman than in later ages after Buddhism became powerful. With regard, however, to that earlier period of over a thousand years ago, it is of little use to speculate. I cannot escape the feeling, however, that the condition of woman then has been unconsciously idealized, in order to make a better showing in comparison with the customs of Western lands. Be that as it may, the notions and ideals presented by Buddhism in regard to woman are clear, and clearly degrading. She is the source of temptation and sin; she is essentially inferior to man in every respect. Before she may hope to enter Nirvana she must be born again as man. How widely these extreme views of woman have found acceptance in Japan, I am not in a position to state. It is my impression, however, that they never received as full acceptance here as in India. Nevertheless, as has already been shown,[BK] the ideals of what a woman should do and be make it clear that her social position for centuries has been relatively low; as wife she is a domestic rather than a helpmeet. The "three obediences," to parents, to husband, to son, set forth the ideal, although, without doubt, the strict application of the third, obedience to one's son after he becomes the head of the household, is relatively rare.

What especially strikes the notice of the Occidental is the slight amount of social intercourse that prevails to-day between men and women. Whenever women enter into the social pleasures of men, they do so as professional singers and dancers, they being mere girls and unmarried young women; this social intercourse is all but invariably accompanied with wine-drinking, even if it does not proceed to further licentiousness. The statement that woman is man's plaything has been often heard in Japan. Confucian no less than Buddhistic ethics must bear the responsibility for putting and keeping woman on so low a level. Concubinage, possibly introduced from China, was certainly sanctioned by the Chinese classics.

The Lei-ki allows an Emperor to have in addition to the Empress three consorts, nine maids of high rank, and twenty-seven maids of lower rank, all of whom rank as wives, and, beside these, eighty-one other females called concubines. Concubinage and polygamy, being thus sanctioned by the classics, became an established custom in Japan.

The explanation for this ideal and practice is not far to seek. It rests in the communal character of the social order. The family was the social unit of Japan. No individual member was of worth except the legal head and representative, the father. A striking proof of the correctness of this explanation is the fact that even the son is obeyed by the father in case he has become "in kio,"[BL] that is, has abdicated; the son then becomes the authoritative head. The ideals regarding woman then were not unique; they were part of the social order, and were determined by the principle of "communalism" unregulated by the principle of "individualism." Ideals respecting man and woman were equally affected. So long as man is not valued as a human being, but solely according to his accidental position in society, woman must be regarded in the same way. She is valued first as a begetter of offspring, second as a domestic. And when such conceptions prevail as to her nature and function in society, defective ideals as to morality in the narrower sense of this term, leading to and justifying concubinage, easy divorce, and general loose morality are necessary consequences.

But this moral or immoral ideal is by no means peculiar to Japan. The peculiarity of Japan and the entire Orient is that the social order that fostered it lasted so long, before forces arose to modify it. But, as will be shown later,[BM] the great problem of human evolution, after securing the advantages of "communalism," and the solidification of the nation, is that of introducing the principle of individualism into the social order. In the Orient the principle of communalism gained such headway as effectually to prevent the introduction of this new principle. There is, in my opinion, no probability that Japan, while maintaining her isolation, would ever have succeeded in making any radical change in her social order; her communalism was too absolute. She needed the introduction of a new stimulus from without. It was providential that this stimulus came from the Anglo-Saxon race, with its pronounced principle of "individualism" wrought out so completely in social order, in literature, and in government. Had Russia or Turkey been the leading influences in starting Japan on her new career, it is more than doubtful whether she would have secured the principles needful for her healthful moral development.

Justice to the actual ideals and life of Old Japan forbids me to leave, without further remark, what was said above regarding the ideals of morality in the narrower significance of this word. Injunctions that women should be absolutely chaste were frequent and stringent. Nothing more could be asked in the line of explicit teaching on this theme. And, furthermore, I am persuaded, after considerable inquiry, that in Old Japan in the interior towns and villages, away from the center of luxury and out of the beaten courses of travel, there was purity of moral life that has hardly been excelled anywhere. I have repeatedly been assured that if a youth of either sex were known to have transgressed the law of chastity, he or she would at once be ostracised; and that such transgressions were, consequently, exceedingly rare. It is certainly a fact that in the vast majority of the interior towns there have never, until recent times, been licensed houses of prostitution. Of late there has been a marked increase of dancing and singing girls, of whom it is commonly said that they are but "secret prostitutes." These may to-day be found in almost every town and village, wherever indeed there is a hotel. Public as well as secret prostitution has enormously increased during the last thirty or forty years.[BN]

Thanks to Mr. Murphy's consecrated energy, the appalling legalized and hopeless slavery under which these two classes of girls exist is at last coming to light. He has shown, by several test cases, that although the national laws are good to look at they are powerless because set aside by local police regulations over which the courts are powerless! In September, 1900, however, in large part due no doubt to the facts made public by him, and backed up by the public press, and such leaders of Japan's progressive elements as Shimada Sabur, the police regulations were modified, and with amazing results. Whereas, previous to that date, the average monthly suicides throughout the land among the public prostitutes were between forty and fifty, during the two months of September and October there were none! In that same period, out of about five thousand prostitutes in the city of Tokyo, 492 had fled from their brothels and declared their intentions of abandoning the "shameful business," as the Japanese laws call it, and in consequence a prominent brothel had been compelled to stop the business! We are only in the first flush of this new reform as these lines are written, so cannot tell what end the whole movement will reach. But the conscience of the nation is beginning to waken on this matter and we are confident it will never tolerate the old slavery of the past, enforced as it was by local laws, local courts, so that girls were always kept in debt, and when they fled were seized and forced back to the brothels in order to pay their debts!

But in contrast to the undoubted ideal of Old Japan in regard to the chastity of women, must be set the equally undoubted fact that the sages have very little to say on the subject of chastity for men. Indeed there is no word in the Japanese language corresponding to our term "chastity" which may be applied equally to men and women. In his volume entitled "Kokoro," Mr. Hearn charges the missionaries with the assertion that there is no word for chastity in Japanese. "This," he says, "is true in the same sense only that we might say that there is no word for chastity in the English language, because such words as honor, virtue, purity, chastity have been adopted into English from other languages."[80] I doubt if any missionary has made such a statement. His further assertion, that "the word most commonly used applies to both sexes," would have more force, if Mr. Hearn had stated what the word is. His English definition of the term has not enabled me to find the Japanese equivalent, although I have discussed this question with several Japanese. It is their uniform confession that the Japanese language is defective in its terminology on this topic, the word with which one may exhort a woman to be chaste being inapplicable to a man. The assertion of the missionaries has nothing whatever to do with the question as to whether the terms used are pure Japanese or imported Chino-Japanese; nor has it any reference to the fact that the actual language is deficient in abstract terms. It is simply that the term applicable to a woman is not applicable to a man. And this in turn proves sharp contrasts between the ideals regarding the moral duties of men and of women.

An interesting point in the Japanese moral ideal is the fact that the principle of filial obedience was carried to such extremes that even prostitution of virtue at the command of the parents, or for the support of the parents, was not only permitted but, under special conditions, was highly praised. Modern prostitution is rendered possible chiefly through the action of this perverted principle. Although the sale of daughters for immoral purposes is theoretically illegal, yet, in fact, it is of frequent occurrence.

Although concubinage was not directly taught by Confucius, yet it was never forbidden by him, and the leaders and rulers of the land have lent the custom the authority and justification of their example. As we have already seen, the now ruling Emperor has several concubines, and all of his children are the offspring of these concubines. In Old Japan, therefore, there were two separate ideals of morality for the two sexes.

The question may be raised how a social order which required such fidelity on the part of the woman could permit such looseness on the part of the man, whether married or not. How could the same social order produce two moral ideals? The answer is to be found in several facts. First, there is the inherent desire of each husband to be the sole possessor of his wife's affections. As the stronger of the two, he would bring destruction on an unfaithful wife and also on any who dared invade his home. Although the woman doubtless has the same desire to be the sole possessor of her husband's affection, she has not the same power, either to injure a rival or to punish her faithless husband. Furthermore, licentiousness in women has a much more visibly disastrous effect on her procreative functions than equal licentiousness in man. This, too, would serve to beget and maintain different ethical standards for the two sexes. Finally, and perhaps no less effective than the two preceding, is the fact that the general social consciousness held different conceptions in regard to the social positions of man and woman. The one was the owner of the family, the lord and master; to him belonged the freedom to do as he chose. The other was a variety of property, not free in any sense to please herself, but to do only as her lord and master required.

An illustration of the first reason given above came to my knowledge not long since. Rev. John T. Gulick saw in Kanagawa, in 1862, a man going through the streets carrying the bloody heads of a man and a woman which he declared to be those of his wife and her seducer, whom he had caught and killed in the act of adultery. This act of the husband's was in perfect accord with the practices and ideals of the time, and not seldom figures in the romances of Old Japan.

The new Civil Code adopted in 1898 furnishes an authoritative statement of many of the moral ideals of New Japan. For the following summary I am indebted to the *Japan Mail*.[BP] In regard to marriage it is noteworthy that the "prohibited degrees of relationship are the same as those in England"—including the deceased wife's sister. "The minimum age for legal marriage is seventeen in the case of a man and fifteen in the case of a woman, and marriage takes effect on notification to the registrar, being thus a purely civil contract. As to divorce, it is provided that the husband and wife may effect it by mutual consent, and its legal recognition takes the form of an entry by the registrar, no reference being necessary to the judicial authorities. Where mutual consent is not obtained, however, an action for divorce must be brought, and here it appears that the rights of the woman do not receive the same recognition as those of the man. Thus, although adultery committed by the wife constitutes a valid ground of divorce, we do not find that adultery on the husband's part furnishes a plea to the wife. Ill-treatment or gross insult, such as renders living together impracticable, or desertion, constitutes a reason for divorce from the wife's point of view." The English reviewer here adds that "since no treatment can be worse nor any insult grosser than open inconstancy on the part of a husband, it is conceivable that a judge might consider that such conduct renders living together impracticable. But in the presence of an explicit provision with regard to the wife's adultery and in the absence of any such provision with regard to the husband's, we doubt whether any court of law would exercise discretion in favor of the woman." The gross "insult of inconstancy" on the part of the husband is a plea that has never yet been recognized by Japanese society. The reviewer goes on to say: "One cannot help wishing that the peculiar code of morality observed by husbands in this country had received some condemnation at the hands of the framers of the new Code. It is further laid down that a 'person who is judicially divorced or punished because of adultery cannot contract a marriage with the other party to the adultery.' If that extended to the husband it would be an excellent provision, well calculated to correct one of the worst social abuses of this country. Unfortunately, as we have seen, it applies apparently to the case of the wife only." The provision for divorce by "mutual consent" is striking and ominous. It makes divorce a matter of entirely private arrangement, unless one of the parties objects. In a land where women are so docile, is it likely that the wife would refuse to consent to divorce when her lord and master requests or commands her to leave his home? "There are not many women in Japan who could refuse to become a party to the 'mutual consent' arrangement if they were convinced that they had lost their husband's affection and that he could not live comfortably with them." It would appear that nothing whatever is said by the Code with reference to concubinage, either allowing or forbidding it. Presumably a man may have but one legitimate wife, and children by concubines must be registered as illegitimate. Nothing, however, on this point seems to be stated, although provision is made for the public acknowledgment of illegitimate children. "Thus, a father can acknowledge a natural child, making what is called a 'shoshi,' and if, subsequent to acknowledgment, the father and mother marry, the 'shoshi,' acquires the status of a legitimate child, such status reckoning back, apparently to the time of birth." Evidently, this provision rests on the implication that the mother is an unmarried woman—presumably a concubine.

Recent statistics throw a rather lurid light on these provisions of the Code. The Imperial Cabinet for some years past has published in French and Japanese a résumé of national statistics. Those bearing on marriage and divorce, in the volume published in 1897, may well be given at this point.

	MARRI AGES	DIV ORCES	LEGITI MATE BIRTHS	ILLEGITI MATE
890	325,141	109,08 8	1,079,121	66,253

891	325,651	112,411	1,033,653	64,122
892	349,489	133,498	1,134,665	72,369
893	358,398	116,775	1,105,119	73,677
894	361,319	114,436	1,132,897	76,407
895	365,633	110,838	1,166,254	80,168
897	395,207	124,075	1,335,125	89,996[BQ]

These authoritative statistics show how divorce is a regular part of the Japanese family system, one out of three marriages proving abortive.

Morally Japan's weak spot is the relation of the sexes, both before and after marriage. Strict monogamy, with the equality of duties of husband and wife, is the remedy for the disease.

This slight sketch of the provision of the new Code as it bears on the purity of the home, and on the development of noble manhood and womanhood, shows that the Code is very defective. It practically recognizes and legalizes the present corrupt practices of society, and makes no effort to establish higher ideals. Whether anything more should be expected of a Code drawn up under the present circumstances is, of course, an open question. But the Code reveals the astonishingly low condition of the moral standards for the home, one of the vital weaknesses of New Japan. The defectiveness of the new Code in regard to the matters just considered must be argued, however, not from the failure to embody Occidental moral standards, but rather from the failure to recognize the actual nature of the social order of New Japan. While the Code recognizes the principle of individualism and individual rights and worth in all other matters, in regard to the home, the most important social unit in the body politic, the Code legalizes and perpetuates the old pre-Meiji standards. Individualism in the general social order demands its consistent recognition in every part.

We cannot conclude our discussion of Japanese ideas as to woman, and the consequent results to morality, without referring to the great changes which are to-day taking place. Although the new Civil Code has not done all that we could ask, we would not ignore what it has secured. Says Prof. Gubbins in the excellent introduction to his translation of the Codes:

"In no respect has modern progress in Japan made greater strides than in the improvement of the position of woman. Though she still labors under certain disabilities, a woman can now become a head of a family, and exercise authority as such; she can inherit and own property and manage it herself; she can exercise parental authority; if single, or a widow, she can adopt; she is one of the parties to adoption effected by her husband, and her consent, in addition to that of her husband, is necessary to the adoption of her child by another person; she can act as guardian, or curator, and she has a voice in family councils." In all these points the Code marks a great advance, and reveals by contrast the legally helpless condition of woman prior to 1898. But in certain respects practice is preceding theory. We would call special attention to the exalted position and honor publicly accorded to the Empress. On more than one historic occasion she has appeared at the Emperor's side, a thing unknown in Old Japan. The Imperial Silver Wedding (1892) was a great event, unprecedented in the annals of the Orient. Commemorative postage stamps were struck off which were first used on the auspicious day.

The wedding of the Prince Imperial (in May, 1900) was also an event of unique importance in Japanese social and moral history. Never before, in the 2600 years claimed by her historians, has an heir to the throne been honored by a public wedding. The ceremony was prepared *de novo* for the occasion and the pledges were mutual. In the reception that followed, the Imperial bride stood beside her Imperial husband. On this occasion, too, commemorative postage stamps were issued and first used on the auspicious day; the entire land was brilliantly decorated with flags and lanterns. Countless congratulatory meetings were held throughout the country and thousands of gifts, letters, and telegraphic messages expressed the joy and good will of the people.

But the chief significance of these events is the new and exalted position accorded to woman and to marriage by the highest personages of the land. It is said by some that the ruling Emperor will be the last to have concubines. However that may be, woman has already attained a rank and marriage an honor unknown in any former age in Japan, and still quite unknown in any Oriental land save Japan.

A serious study of Japanese morality should not fail to notice the respective parts taken by Buddhism and Confucianism. The contrast is so marked. While Confucianism devoted its energies to the inculcation of proper conduct, to morality as contrasted to religion, Buddhism devoted its energies to the development of a cultus, paying little attention to morality. A recent Japanese critic of Buddhism remarks that "though Buddhism has a name in the world for the excellence of its ethical system, yet there exists no treatise in Japanese which sets forth the distinctive features of Buddhist ethics." Buddhist literature is chiefly occupied with mythology, metaphysics, and eschatology, ethical precepts being interwoven incidentally. The critic just quoted states that the pressing need of the times is that Buddhist ethics should be disentangled from Buddhist mythology. The great moralists of Japan have been Confucianists. Distinctively Japanese morality has derived its impulse from Confucian classics. A new spirit, however, is abroad among the Buddhist priesthood. Their preaching is increasingly ethical. The common people are saying that the sermons heard in certain temples are identical with those of Christians. How widely this imitation of Christian preaching has spread I cannot say; but that Christianity has in any degree been imitated is significant, both ethically and sociologically.

Buddhism is not alone, however, in imitating Christianity. A few years ago Dr. D.C. Greene attended the preaching services of a modern Shinto sect, the "Ten-Ri-Kyo," the Heaven-Reason-Teaching, and was surprised to hear almost literal quotations from the "Sermon on the Mount"; the source of the sentiment and doctrine was not stated and very likely was not known to the speaker. Dr. Greene, who has given this sect considerable study, is satisfied that the insistence of its teachers on moral conduct is general and genuine. When I visited their headquarters, not far from Nara, in 1895, and inquired of one of the priests as to the chief points of importance in their teaching, I was told that the necessity of leading an honorable and correct life was most emphasized. There are reasons for thinking that the Kurozumi sect of Shintoism, with its emphasis on morality, is considerably indebted to Christianity both for its origin and its doctrine.

It is evident that Christianity is having an influence in Japan, far beyond the ranks of its professed believers. It is proving a stimulus to the older faiths, stirring them up to an earnestness in moral teaching that they never knew in the olden times. It is interesting to note that this widespread emphasis on ethical truth comes at a time when morality is suffering a wide collapse.

An important point for the sociological student of Japanese moral ideals is the fact that her moralists have directed their attention chiefly to the conduct of the rulers. The ideal of conduct as stated by them is for a samurai. If any action is praised, it is said that it becomes a samurai; if condemned, it is on the ground that it is not becoming to a samurai. Anything wrong or vulgar is said to be what you might expect of the common man. All the terms of the higher morality, such as righteousness, duty, benevolence, are expounded from the standpoint of a samurai, that is, from the standpoint of loyalty. The forty-seven ronin were pronounced "righteous samurai" because they avenged the death of their lord, even though in doing so they committed deeds that, by themselves, would have been condemned. Japanese history and literature proclaim the same ideal. They are exclusively concerned with the deeds of the higher class, the court and the samurai. The actual condition of the common people in ancient times is a matter not easily determined. The morality of the common people was more a matter of unreasoning custom than of theory and instruction. But these facts are susceptible of interpretation if we remember that the interest of the historian and the moralist was not in humanity, as such, but in the external features of the social order. Their gaze was on the favored few, on the nobility, the court, and the samurai.

In closing our discussion of Japanese moral ideals it may not be amiss to append the Imperial Edict concerning the moral education of the youth of Japan, issued by the Emperor November 31, 1890. This is supposed to be the distilled essence of Shinto and Confucian teaching. It is to-day the only authoritative teaching on morality given in the public schools. It is read with more reverence than is accorded to the Bible in England or America. It is considered both holy and inspired.

IMPERIAL EDICT ON MORAL EDUCATION

"We consider that the Founder of Our Empire and the ancestors of Our Imperial House placed the foundation of the country on a grand and permanent basis, and established their authority on the principles of profound humanity and benevolence.

"That Our subjects have throughout ages deserved well of the state by their loyalty and piety, and by their harmonious co-operation, is in accordance with the essential character of Our nation; and on these very same principles Our education has been founded.

"You, Our subjects, be therefore filial to your parents; be affectionate to your brothers; be harmonious as husbands and wives; and be faithful to your friends; conduct yourselves with propriety and carefulness; extend generosity and benevolence toward your neighbors; attend to your studies and follow your pursuits; cultivate your intellects and elevate your morals; advance public benefits and promote social interests; be always found in the good observance of the laws and constitution of the land; display your personal courage and public spirit for the sake of the country whenever required; and thus support the Imperial prerogative, which is coexistent with the Heavens and the Earth.

"Such conduct on your part will not only strengthen the character of Our good and loyal subjects, but conduce also to the maintenance of the fame of your worthy forefathers.

"This is the instruction bequeathed by Our ancestors and to be followed by Our subjects; for it is the truth which has guided and guides them in their own affairs and their dealings toward aliens.

"We hope, therefore, that We and Our subjects will regard these sacred precepts with one and the same heart in order to attain the same ends."

XXIV
MORAL PRACTICE

One noticeable characteristic of the Japanese is the publicity of the life of the individual. He seems to feel no need for privacy. Houses are so constructed that privacy is practically impossible. The slight paper shoji and fusuma between the small rooms serve only partially to shut out peering eyes; they afford no protection from listening ears. Moreover, these homes of the middle and lower classes open upon public streets, and a passer-by may see much of what is done within. Even the desire for privacy seems lacking. The publicity of the private (?) baths and sanitary conveniences which the Occidental puts entirely out of sight has already been noted.

I once passed through a village and was not a little amazed to see two or three bathtubs on the public road, each occupied by one or more persons; nor were the occupants children alone, but men and women also. Calling at the home of a gentleman in Kyushu with whom I had some business, and gaining no notice at the front entrance, I went around to the side of the house only to discover the lady of the place taking her bath with her children, in a tub quite out of doors, while a manservant chopped wood but a few paces distant.

The natural indifference of the Japanese to the exposure of the unclothed body is an interesting fact. In the West such indifference is rightly considered immodest. In Japan, however, immodesty consists entirely in the intention of the heart and does not arise from the accident of the moment or the need of the occasion. With a fellow missionary, I went some years since to some famous hot springs at the foot of Mount Ase, the smoking crater of Kyushu. The spot itself is most charming, situated in the center of an old crater, said to be the largest in the world. Wearied with a long walk, we were glad to find that one of the public bath tubs or tanks, some fifteen by thirty feet in size, in a bath house separate from other houses, was quite unoccupied; and on inquiry we were told that bathers were few at that hour of the day, so that we might go in without fear of disturbance. It seems that in such places the tiers of boxes for the clothing on either side of the door, are reserved for men and women respectively. Ignorant of this custom, we deposited our clothing in the boxes on the left hand, and as quickly as we could accommodate ourselves to the heat of the water, we got into the great tank. We were scarcely in, when a company of six or eight men and women entered the bath house; they at once perceived our blunder, but without the slightest hesitation, the women as well as the men went over to the men's side and proceeded to undress and get into the tank with us, betraying no consciousness that aught was amiss. So far as I could see there was not the slightest self-consciousness in the entire proceeding. In the tank, too, though it is customary for women to occupy the left side, on this occasion they mingled freely with the men. I suppose it is impossible in England or America to conceive of such a state of unconsciousness. Yet it seems to be universal in Japan. It is doubtless explained by the custom, practiced from infancy, not only of public bathing, but also of living together so unreservedly. The heat of the summer and the nature of Japanese clothing, so easily thrown off, has accustomed them to the greater or less exposure of the person. All these customs have prevented the development of a sense of modesty corresponding to that which has developed in the West. Whether this familiarity of the sexes is conducive to purity of life or not, is a totally different question, on which I do not here enter.

In this connection I can do no better than quote from a popular, and in many respects deservedly popular, writer on Japan. Says Mr. Hearn, "There is little privacy of any sort in Japan. Among the people, indeed, what we term privacy in the Occident does not exist. There are only walls of paper dividing the lives of men; there are only sliding screens instead of doors; there are neither locks nor bolts to be used by day; and whenever the weather permits, the fronts and perhaps even the sides of the houses are literally removed, and its interior widely opened to the air, the light, and the public gaze. Within a hotel or even a common dwelling house, nobody knocks before entering your room; there is nothing to knock at except a shoji or a fusuma, which cannot be knocked at without being broken. And in this world of paper walls and sunshine, nobody is afraid or ashamed of fellow-man or fellow-woman. Whatever is done is done after a fashion in public. Your personal habits, your idiosyncrasies (if you have any), your foibles, your likes and dislikes, your loves and your hates must be known to everybody. Neither vices nor virtues can be hidden; there is absolutely nowhere to hide them.... There has never been, for the common millions at least, even the idea of living unobserved." The Japanese language has no term for "privacy," nor is it easy to convey the idea to one who does not know the English word. They lack the term and the clear idea because they lack the practice.

These facts prove conclusively that the Japanese individual is still a gregarious being, and this fact throws light on the moral life of the people. It follows of necessity that the individual will conform somewhat more closely to the moral standards of the community, than a man living in a strong segregarious community.

The converse of this principle is that in a community whose individuals are largely segregarious, enjoying privacy, and thus liberty of action, variations from the moral standards will be frequent and positive transgressions not uncommon. In the one case, where "communalism" reigns, moral action is, so to speak, automatic; it requires no particular assertion of the individual will to do right; conformity to the standard is spontaneous. In the latter case, however, where "individualism" is the leading characteristic of the community, the acceptance of the moral standards usually requires a definite act of the individual will.

The history of Japan is a capital illustration of this principle. The recent increase of immorality and crime is universally admitted. The usual explanation is that in olden times every slight offense was punished with death; the criminal class was thus continuously exterminated. Nowadays a robber can ply his trade continuously, though interrupted by frequent intervals of imprisonment. In former times, once caught, he never could steal again, except in the land of the shades. While this explanation has some force, it does not cover the ground. A better explanation for the modern increase of lawlessness is the change in the social order itself. The new order gives each man wider liberty of individual action. He is free to choose his trade and his home. Formerly these were determined for him by the accident of his birth. His freedom is greater and so, too, are his temptations.

Furthermore, the standards of conduct themselves have been changing. Certain acts which would have brought praise and honor if committed fifty years ago, such, for instance, as "kataki uchi," revenge, would to-day soon land one behind prison doors. In a word, "individualism" is beginning to work powerfully on conduct; it has not yet gained the ascendancy attained in the West; it is nevertheless abroad in the land. The young are especially influenced by it. Taking advantage of the liberty it grants, many forms of immorality seem to be on the increase. So far as I can gather by inquiry, there has been a great collapse not only in honesty, but also in the matter of sexual morality. It will hardly do to say dogmatically that the national standards of morality have been lowered, but it is beyond question that the power of the community to enforce those standards has suddenly come to naught by reason of the changing social order. Western thought and practice as to the structure of society and the freedom of the individual have been emphasized; Spencer and Mill and Huxley have been widely read by the educated classes.[BR]

Furthermore, freedom and ease of travel, and liberty to change one's residence at will, and thus the ability to escape unpleasant restraints, have not a little to do with this collapse in morality. Tens of thousands of students in the higher schools are away from their homes and are entirely without the steadying support that home gives. Then, too, there is a wealth among the common people that was, never known in earlier times. Formerly the possession of means was limited to a relatively small number of families. To-day we see general prosperity, and a consequent tendency to luxury that was unknown in any former period.

To be specific, let us note that in feudal times there were some 270 daimyo living in the utmost luxury. About 1,500,000 samurai were dependent on them as retainers, while 30,000,000 people supported these sons of luxury. In 1863 the farmers of Japan raised 30,000,000 koku of rice, and paid 22,000,000 of it to the government as taxes. Taxed at the same rate to-day the farmers would have to pay 280,000,000 yen, whereas the actual payment made by them is only 38,000,000 yen. "The farmer's manner of life has radically changed. He is now prosperous and comfortable, wearing silk where formerly he could scarcely afford cotton, and eating rice almost daily, whereas formerly he scarcely knew its taste."[BS]

It is stated by the *Japan Mail* that whereas but "one person out of ten was able thirty years ago to afford rice, the nine being content to live from year's end to year's end on barley alone or barley mixed with a modicum of rice, six persons to-day out of ten count it a hardship if they cannot sit down to a square meal of rice daily.... Rice is no longer a luxury to the mass of the people, but has become a necessity."

Financially, then, the farming and middle classes are incomparably better off to-day than in olden times. The amount of ready money which a man can earn has not a little to do with his morality. If his uprightness depends entirely or chiefly on his lack of opportunity to do wrong, he will be a moral man so long as he is desperately poor or under strict control. But give him the chance to earn ready cash, together with the freedom to live where he chooses, and to spend his income as he pleases, and he is sure to develop various forms of immorality.

I have made a large number of inquiries in regard to the increase or decrease of concubinage during the present era. Statistics on this subject are not to be had, for concubines are not registered as such nor yet as wives. If a concubine lives in the home of the man, she is registered as a domestic, and her children should be registered as hers, although I am told that they are very often illegally registered as his. If she lives in her own home, the concubine still retains the name and registry of her own parents. The government takes no notice of concubinage, and publishes no statistics in regard to it. The children of concubines who live with their own parents are, I am told, usually registered as the children of the mother's father; otherwise they are registered as illegitimate; statistics, therefore, furnish no clew as to the increase or decrease or amount of concubinage and illegitimacy, most important questions in Japanese sociology. But my informants are unanimous in the assertion that there has been a marked increase of concubinage during recent years. The simple and uniform explanation given is that multitudes of merchants and officials, and even of farmers, can afford to maintain them to-day who formerly were unable to do so. The older ideals on this subject were such as to allow of concubinage to the extent of one's financial ability.

During the year 1898 the newspapers and leading writers of Japan carried on a vigorous discussion concerning concubinage. The *Yorozu Choho* published an inventory of 493 men maintaining separate establishments for their concubines, giving not only the names and the business of the men, but also the character of the women chosen to be concubines. Of these 493 men, 9 are ministers of state and ex-ministers; 15 are peers or members of House of Peers; 7 are barristers; 3 are learned doctors; the rest are nearly all business men. The women were, previous to concubinage, Dancing girls, 183; Servants, 69; Prostitutes, 17; "Ordinary young girls," 91; Adopted daughters, 15; Widows, 7; Performers, 7; Miscellaneous, 104. In this discussion it has been generally admitted that concubinage has increased in modern times, and the cause attributed is "general looseness of morals." Some of the leading writers maintain that the concubinage of former times was largely confined to those who took concubines to insure the maintenance of the family line; and also that the taking of dancing girls was unknown in olden times.

It is interesting to note in this connection that some of those who defend the practice of concubinage appeal to the example of the Old Testament, saying that what was good enough for the race that gave to Christians the greater part of their Bible is good enough for the Japanese. Another point in the discussion interesting to the Occidental is the repeated assertion that there is no real difference between the East and the West in point of practice; the only difference is that whereas in the East all is open and above board, in the West extra-marital relations are condemned by popular opinion, and are therefore concealed.[BT] A few writers publicly defend concubinage; most, however, condemn it vigorously, even though making no profession of Christian faith. Of the latter class is Mr. Fukuzawa, one of Japan's leaders of public opinion. In his most trenchant attack, he asserts that if Japan is to progress in civilization she must abandon her system of concubinage. That new standards in regard to marital relations are arising in Japan is clear; but they have as yet little force; there is no consensus of opinion to give them force. He who transgresses them is still recognized as in good standing in the community.

Similarly, with respect to business honesty, it is the opinion of all with whom I have conversed on the subject that there has been a great decline in the honesty of the common people. In feudal days thefts and petty dishonesty were practically unknown. To-day these are exceedingly common. Foreign merchants complain that it is impossible to trust Japanese to carry out verbal or written promises, when the conditions of the market change to their disadvantage. It is accordingly charged that the Japanese have no sense of honor in business matters.

The *Kokumin Shinbun* (People's News) has recently discussed the question of Japanese commercial morality, with the following results: It says, first, that goods delivered are not up to sample; secondly, that engagements as to time are not kept; thirdly, that business men have no adequate appreciation of the permanent interests of business; fourthly, that they are without ability to work in common; and fifthly, that they do not get to know either their customers or themselves.[BU]

"The Japanese consul at Tientsin recently reported to the Government that the Chinese have begun to regard Japanese manufactures with serious distrust. Merchandise received from Japan, they allege, does not correspond with samples, and packing is, in almost all cases, miserably unsubstantial. The consul expresses the deepest regret that Japanese merchants are disposed to break their faith without regard to honor."[BV]

In this connection it may not be amiss to revert to illustrations that have come within my own experience. I have already cited instances of the apparent duplicity to which deacons and candidates for the ministry stoop. I do not believe that either the deacons or the candidates had the slightest thought that they were doing anything dishonorable. Nor do I for a moment suppose that the President and the Trustees of the Doshisha at all realized the gravity of the moral aspect of the course they took in diverting the Doshisha from its original purposes. They seemed to think that money, once given to the Doshisha, might be used without regard to the wishes of the donors. I cannot help wondering how much of their thought on this subject is due to the custom prevalent in Japan ever since the establishment of Buddhist temples and monasteries, of considering property once given as irrevocable, so that the individuals who gave it or their heirs, have no further interest or right in the property. Large donations in Japan have, from time immemorial, been given thus absolutely; the giver assumed that the receiver would use it aright; specific directions were not added as to the purposes of the gift. American benefactors of the Doshisha have given under the standards prevailing in the West. The receivers in Japan have accepted these gifts under the standards prevailing in the East. Is not this in part the cause of the friction that has arisen in recent years over the administration of funds and lands and houses held by Japanese for mission purposes?

In this connection, however, I should not fail to refer to the fact that the Christians of the Kumiai churches,[BW] in their annual meeting (1898), took strong grounds as to the mismanagement of the Doshisha by the trustees. The action of the latter in repealing the clause of the constitution which declared the six articles of the constitution forever unchangeable, and then of striking out the word "Christian" in regard to the nature of the moral education to be given in all departments of the institution, was characterized as "fu-ho," that is to say, unlawful, unrighteous, or immoral. Resolutions were also passed demanding that the trustees should either restore the expunged words or else resign and give place to men who would restore them and carry out the will of the donors. This act on the part of a large majority of the delegates of the churches shows that a standard of business morality is arising in Japan that promises well for the future.

Before leaving this question, it is important for us to consider how widely in lands which have long been both Christian and commercial, the standards of truthfulness and business morality are transgressed. I for one do not feel disposed to condemn Japanese failure very severely, when I think of the failure in Western lands. Then, again, when we stop to think of it, is it not a pretty fine line that we draw between legitimate and illegitimate profits? What a relative distinction this is! Even the Westerner finds difficulty in discovering and observing it, especially so when the man with whom he is dealing happens to be ignorant of the real value of the goods in question. Let us not be too severe, then, in condemning the Japanese, even though we must judge them to be deficient in ideals and conduct. The explanation for the present state of Japan in regard to business morality is neither far to seek nor hard to find. It has nothing whatever to do with brain structure or inherent race character, but is wholly a matter of changing social order. Feudal communalism has given way to individualistic commercialism. The results are inevitable. Japan has suddenly entered upon that social order where the individuals of the nation are thrown upon their own choice for character and life as they have been at no previous time. Old men, as well as young, are thrown off their feet by the new temptations into which they fall.

One of the strongest arguments in my mind for the necessity of a rapid introduction into Japan of the Gospel of Christ, is to be built on this fact. An individualistic social order demands an individualizing religion. So far as I know, the older religions, with the lofty moral teachings which one may freely admit them to have, make no determined or even distinct effort to secure the activity of the individual will in the adoption of moral ideals. The place both of "conversion" and of the public avowal of one's "faith" in the establishment of individual character, and the peculiar fitness of a religion having such characteristics to a social order in which "individualism" is the dominant principle, have not yet been widely recognized by writers on sociology. These practices of the Protestant churches are, nevertheless, of inestimable value in the upbuilding both of the individual and of society. And Japan needs these elements at the earliest possible date in order to supplement the new order of society which is being established. Without them it is a question whether in the long run this new order may not prove a step downward rather than upward.

This completes our detailed study of Japanese moral characteristics as revealed alike in their ideals and their practices. Let us now seek for some general statement of the facts and conclusions thus far reached. It has become clear that Japanese moralists have placed

114

the emphasis of their ethical thinking on loyalty; subordinated to this has been filial piety. These two principles have been the pivotal points of Japanese ethics. All other virtues flowed out of them, and were intimately dependent upon them. These virtues are especially fitted to upbuild and to maintain the feudal order of society. They are essentially communal virtues. The first group, depending on and growing out of loyalty, was concerned with the maintenance of the larger communal unity, formerly the tribe, and now the nation. The virtues connected with the second principle—filial piety—were concerned with the maintenance of the smaller unit of society— the family. Righteousness and duty, of which much was made by Japanese moralists, consisted in the observance of these two ideals.

The morality of individualism was largely wanting. From this lack sprang the main defects of the moral ideal and of the actual practice. The chief sins of Old Japan—and, as a matter of fact, of all the heathen world, as graphically depicted by Mr. Dennis in his great work on "Christian Missions and Social Progress"—were sins of omission and commission against the individual. The rights of inferiors practically received no consideration at the hands of the moralists. In the Japanese conception of righteousness and duty, the rights and value of the individual, as such, whatever his social standing or sex, were not included.

One class of defects in the Japanese moral ideal arose out of the feudal order itself, namely, its scorn of trade. Trade had no vital relation to the communal unity; hence it found and developed no moral sanctions for its guidance. The West conceives of business deceit as concerned not only with the integrity of the community, but also with the rights of the individual. The moral ideals and sanctions for business honesty are therefore doubly strong with us. The old order of Japan was in no way dependent for its integrity on business honor and honesty, and, as we have seen, individuals, as such, were not thought to have inherent rights. Under such conditions, it is difficult to conceive how universal moral ideals and sanctions for business relations could be developed and maintained.

One further point demands attention. We naturally ask what the grounds were on which the ethical ideals were commonly supposed to have authority. So far as my knowledge goes, this question received almost no consideration by the ordinary person, and but little from the moralist. Old Japan was not accustomed to ask "Why?" It accepted everything on the authority of the teacher, as children do, and as all primitive peoples do. There was little or no thought as to the source of the moral ideals or as to the nature or the function of the social sanctions. If, as in a few instances, the questions were raised as to their authority, the reply ordinarily would be that they had derived their teachings from ancient times. And, if the matter were pressed, it would be argued that the most ancient times were nearer the beginning of men, and, therefore, nearer to Heaven, which decreed that all the duties and customs of men; in the final resort, therefore, authority would be attributed to Heaven. But such a questioner was rare. Moral law was unhesitatingly accepted on the authority of the teacher, and no uncomfortable questions were asked. It is easy to see that both of the pivotal moral ideals, *i.e.*, loyalty and filial piety, would support this unquestioning habit of mind, for to ask questions as to authority is the beginning both of disloyalty to the master and of irreverence to the parents and ancestors.

The whole social order, being one of authority, unquestioned and absolute, moral standards were accepted on the ipse dixit of great teachers.

In closing, we revert to our ever-recurring question: Are the moral characteristics wherein the Japanese differ from other races inherent and necessary, as are their physiological characteristics, or are they incidental and transient, liable to transformation? Light has been thrown on this problem by every illustration adduced. We have seen in detail that every characteristically Japanese moral trait is due to the nature of her past social order, and is changing With that order. Racial moral traits, therefore, are not due to inherent nature, to essential character, to brain structure, nor are they transmitted from father to son by the mere fact of physical generation. On the contrary, the distinguishing ethical characteristics of races, as seen in their ethical ideals and their moral conduct, are determined by the dominant social order, and vary with it. Ethical characteristics are transmitted by association, transmission is therefore not limited to the relation of parents and children. The bearing of this fact on the problem of the moral transformation of races could be easily shown.

XXV

ARE THE JAPANESE RELIGIOUS?

Said Prof. Pfleiderer to the writer in the winter of 1897: "I am sorry to know that the Japanese are deficient in religious nature." In an elaborate article entitled, "Wanted, a Religion," a missionary describes the three so-called religions of Japan, Buddhism, Confucianism, and Shintoism, and shows to his satisfaction that none of these has the essential characteristics of religion.

Mr. Percival Lowell has said that "Sense may not be vital to religion, but incense is."[BX] In my judgment, this is the essence of nonsense, and is fitted to incense a man's sense.

The impression that the Japanese people are not religious is due to various facts. The first is that for about three hundred years the intelligence of the nation has been dominated by Confucian thought, which rejects active belief in supra-human beings. When asked by his pupils as to the gods, Confucius is reported to have said that men should respect them, but should have nothing to do with them. The tendency of Confucian ethics, accordingly, is to leave the gods severely alone, although their existence is not absolutely denied. When Confucianism became popular in Japan, the educated part of the nation broke away from Buddhism, which, for nearly a thousand years, had been universally dominant. To them Buddhism seemed superstitious in the extreme. It was not uncommon for them to criticise it severely. Muro Kyu-so,[BY] speaking of the immorality that was so common in the native literature, says: "Long has Buddhism made Japan to think of nothing as important except the worship of Buddha.

So it is that evil customs prevail, and there is no one who does not find pleasure in lust.... Take out the lust and Buddhism from that book, and the scenery and emotions are well described.... Had he learned in the 'Way' of the sages, he had not fallen into Buddhism."[BZ] The tendency of all persons trained in Confucian classics was toward thoroughgoing skepticism as to divine beings and their relation to this world. For this reason, beyond doubt, has Western agnosticism found so easy an entrance into Japan. This ready acceptance of Western agnosticism is a second fact that has tended to give the West the impression referred to above. Complete indifference to religion is characteristic of the educated classes of to-day. Japanese and foreigners, Christians and non-Christians, alike, unite in this opinion. The impression usually conveyed by this statement, however, is that agnosticism is a new thing in Japan. In point of fact, the old agnosticism is merely re-enforced by the support it receives from the agnosticism of the West.

The Occidental impression of Japanese irreligious race nature is further strengthened by the frequent assertion of it by writers, some of whom at least are neither partial nor ignorant. Prof. Basil H. Chamberlain, for instance, repeatedly makes the assertion or necessitates the inference. Speaking of pilgrimages, he remarks that the Japanese "take their religion lightly." Discussing the general question of religion, he speaks of the Japanese as "essentially undevotional," but he guards against the inference that they are therefore specially immoral. Yet, in the same paragraph, he adds, "Though they pray little and make light of supernatural dogma, the religion of the family binds them down in truly social bonds." Percival Lowell also, as we have seen, makes light of Japanese religion.

This conclusion of foreigner observers is rendered the more convincing to the average reader when he learns that such an influential man as Mr. Fukuzawa declares that "religion is like tea," it serves a social end, and nothing more; and that Mr. Hiroyuki Kato, until recently president of the Imperial University, and later Minister of Education, states that "Religion depends on fear." Marquis Ito, Japan's most illustrious statesman, is reported to have said: "I regard religion itself as quite unnecessary for a nation's life; science is far above superstition, and what is religion—Buddhism or Christianity—but superstition, and therefore a possible source of weakness to a nation? I do not regret the tendency to free thought and atheism, which is almost universal in Japan, because I do not regard it as a source of danger to the community."[CA]

If leaders of national thought have such conceptions as to the nature and origin of religion, is it strange that the rank and file of educated people should have little regard for it, or that foreigners generally should believe the Japanese race to be essentially non-religious?

But before we accept this conclusion, various considerations demand our notice. Although the conception of religion held by the eminent Japanese gentlemen just quoted is not accepted by the writer as correct, yet, even on their own definitions, a study of Japanese superstitions and religious ceremonies would easily prove the people as a whole to be exceedingly religious. Never had a nation so many gods. It has been indeed "the country of the gods." Their temples and shrines have been innumerable. Priests have abounded and worshipers swarmed. For worship, however indiscriminate and thoughtless, is evidence of religious nature.

Furthermore, utterances like those quoted above in regard to the nature and function of religion, are frequently on the lips of Westerners also, multitudes of whom have exceedingly shallow conceptions of the real nature of religion or the part it plays in the development of society and of the individual. But we do not pronounce the West irreligious because of such utterances. We must not judge the religious many by the irreligious few.

Again, are they competent judges who say the Japanese are non-religious? Can a man who scorns religion himself, who at least reveals no appreciation of its real nature by his own heart experience, judge fairly of the religious nature of the people? Still further, the religious phenomena of a people may change from age to age. In asking, then, whether a people is religious by nature, we must study its entire religious history, and not merely a single period of it. The life of modern Japan has been rudely shocked by the sudden accession of much new intellectual light. The contents of religion depends on the intellect; sudden and widespread accession of knowledge always discredits the older forms of religious expression. An undeveloped religion, still bound up with polytheistic symbolism, with its charms and mementoes, inevitably suffers severely at the hands of exact modern science. For the educated minority, especially, the inevitable reaction is to complete skepticism, to apparent irreligion. For the time being, religion itself may appear to have been discredited. In an advancing age, prophets of religious dissolution are abundant. Such prophecies, with reference to Christianity, have been frequent, and are not unheard even now. Particular beliefs and practices of religion have indeed changed and passed away, even in Christianity. But the essentially religious nature of man has re-asserted itself in every case, and the outward expressions of that nature have thereby only become freer from elements of error and superstition. Exactly this is taking place in Japan to-day. The apparent irreligion of to-day is the groundwork of the purer religion of to-morrow.

If the Japanese are emotional and sentimental, we should expect them to be, perhaps more than most peoples, religious. This expectation is not disappointed by a study of their history. However imperfect as a religion we must pronounce original Shinto to have been, consisting of little more than a cultus and a theogony, yet even with this alone the Japanese should be pronounced a religious people. The universality of the respect and adoration, not to say love, bestowed throughout the ages of history on the "Kami" (the multitudinous Gods of Shintoism), is a standing witness to the depth of the religious feeling in the Japanese heart. True, it is associated with the sentiments of love of ancestors and country, with filial piety and loyalty; but these, so far from lowering the religion, make it more truly religious?

Unending lines of pilgrims, visiting noted Shinto temples and climbing sacred mountain peaks, arrest the attention of every thoughtful student of Japan. These pilgrims are numbered by the hundreds of thousands every year. The visitors to the great shrine at Kizuki of Izumo number about 250,000 annually. "The more prosperous the season, the larger the number of pilgrims. It rarely falls below two hundred thousand." In his "Occult Japan," Mr. Lowell has given us an interesting account of the "pilgrim clubs," The largest known to him numbered about twelve thousand men, but he thinks they average from one hundred to about five hundred persons each. The number of yearly visitors to the Shinto shrines at Ise is estimated at half a million, and ten thousand pilgrims climb Mt. Fuji every summer. The number of pilgrims to Kompira, in Shikoku, is incredibly large; according to the count taken during the first half of 1898, the first ever taken, the average for six months was 2500 each day; at this rate the number for the year is nearly 900,000. The highest for a single day was over 12,000. These figures were given me by the chief official of this district. The highest mountain in Shikoku, Ishidzuchi San, some six thousand feet in height, is said to be ascended by ten thousand pilgrims each summer. These pilgrims eat little or nothing at

117

hotels, depending rather on what they carry until they return from their arduous three days' climb; nor do they take any prolonged rest until they are on the homeward way. The reason for this is that the climb is supposed to be a test of the heart; if the pilgrim fail to reach the summit, the inference is that he is at fault, and that the god does not favor him. They who offer their prayers from the summit are supposed to be assured of having them answered.

But beside these greater pilgranages to mountain summits and national shrines, innumerable lesser ones are made. Each district has a more or less extended circuit of its own. In Shikoku there is a round known as the "Hachi-Ju-hakka sho mairi," or "The Pilgrimage to the 88 Places," supposed to be the round once made by Kobo Daishi (A.D. 774-834), the founder of the Shinton sect of Buddhism. The number of pilgrims who make this round is exceedingly large, since it is a favorite circuit for the people not only of Shikoku, but also of central and western Japan. Many of the pilgrims wear on the back, just below the neck, a pair of curious miniature "waraji" or straw sandals, because Kobo Daishi carried a real pair along with him on his journey. I never go to Ishite Temple (just out of Matsuyama), one of the eighty-eight places of the circuit, without seeing some of these pilgrims. But this must suffice. The pilgrim habit of the Japanese is a strong proof of widespread religious enthusiasm, and throws much light on the religious nature of the people. There seems to be reason for thinking that the custom existed in Japan even before the introduction of Buddhism. If this is correct, it bears powerful testimony to the inherently religious nature of the Japanese race.

The charge has been made that these pilgrimages are mere pleasure excursions. Mr. Lowell says, facetiously, that "They are peripatetic picnic parties, faintly flavored with piety; just a sufficient suspicion of it to render them acceptable to the easy-going gods." Beneath this light alliterative style, which delights the literary reader, do we find the truth? To me it seems like a slur on the pilgrims, evidently due to Mr. Lowell's idea that a genuine religious feeling must be gloomy and solemn. Joy may seem to him incompatible with heartfelt religion and aspiration. That these pilgrims lack the religious aspiration characteristic of highly developed Christians of the West, is, of course, true; but that they have a certain type of religious aspiration is equally indisputable. They have definite and strong ideas as to the advantage of prayer at the various shrines; they confidently believe that their welfare, both in this world and the next, will be vitally affected by such pilgrimages and such a faithful worship. It is customary for pilgrims, who make extended journeys, to carry what may be called a passbook, in which seals are placed by the officials of each shrine. This is evidence to friends and to the pilgrim himself, in after years, of the reality of his long and tedious pilgrimage. Beggars before these shrines are apt to display these passbooks as an evidence of their worthiness and need. For many a pilgrim supports himself, during his pilgrimage, entirely by begging.

Pilgrims also buy from each shrine of note some charm, "o mamori," "honorable preserver," and "o fuda," "honorable ticket," which to them are exceedingly precious. There is hardly a house in Japan but has some, often many, of these charms, either nailed on the front door or placed on the god-shelf. I have seen a score nailed one above another. In some cases the year-names are still legible, and show considerable age. The sale of charms is a source of no little revenue to the temples, in some cases amounting to thousands of yen annually. We may smile at the ignorance and superstition which these facts reveal, but, as I already remarked, these are external features, the material expression or clothing, so to speak, of the inner life. Their particular form is due to deficient intellectual development. I do not defend them; I merely maintain that their existence shows conclusively the possession by the people at large of a real religious emotion and purpose. If so, they, are not to be sneered at, although the mood of the average pilgrim may be cheerful, and the ordinary pilgrimage may have the aspect of a "peripatetic picnic, faintly flavored with piety." The outside observer, such as the foreigner of necessity is, is quick to detect the picnic quality, but he cannot so easily discern the religious significance or the inner thoughts and emotions of the pilgrims. The former is discernible at a glance, without knowledge of the Japanese language or sympathy with the religious heart; the latter can be discovered only by him who intimately understands the people, their language and their religion.

If religion were necessarily gloomy, festivals and merry-making would be valid proof of Japanese religious deficiency. But such is not the case. Primitive religions, like primitive people, are artless and simple in religious joy as in all the aspects of their life. Developed races increasingly discover the seriousness of living, and become correspondingly reflective, if not positively gloomy. Religion shares this transformation. But those religions in which salvation is a prominent idea, and whose nature is such as to satisfy at once the head and the heart, restore joyousness as a necessary consequence. While certain aspects of Christianity certainly have a gloomy look,—which its critics are much disposed to exaggerate, and then to condemn,—yet Christianity at heart is a religion of profound joy, and this feature shows itself in such universal festivals as Christmas and Easter. Even though the Japanese popular religious life showed itself exclusively in festivals and on occasions of joy, therefore, that would not prove them to be inherently lacking in religious nature.

But there is another set of phenomena, even more impressive to the candid and sympathetic student. It is the presence in every home of the "Butsu-dan," or Buddha shelf, and the "Kami-dana," or God shelf. The former is Buddhist, and the latter Shinto. Exclusive Shintoists, who are rare, have the latter alone. Where both are found, the "I-hai," ancestral memorial tablets, are placed on the "Butsu-dan"; otherwise they are placed on the "Kami-dana." The Kami-dana are always quite simple, as are all Shinto charms and utensils. The Butsu-dan are usually elaborate and beautiful, and sometimes large and costly. The universality of these tokens of family religion, and the constant and loving care bestowed upon them, are striking testimony to the universality of the religion in Japan. The pathos of life is often revealed by the faithful devotion of the mother to these silent representatives of divine beings and departed ancestors or children. I have no hesitation in saying that, so far as external appearances go, the average home in Japan is far more religious than the average home in enlightened England or America, especially when compared with such as have no family worship. There may be a genuine religious life in these Western homes, but it does not appear to the casual visitor. Yet no casual visitor can enter a Japanese home, without seeing at once the evidences of some sort, at least, of religious life.

It is impossible for me to believe, as many assert, that all is mere custom and hollow form, without any kernel of meaning or sincerity. Customs may outlast beliefs for a time, and this is particularly the case with religious customs; for the form is so often taken to involve the very essence of the reality. But customs which have lost all significance, and all belief, inevitably dwindle and fade away, even if not suddenly rejected; they remain them; they leave their trace indeed, but so faintly that only the student of primitive customs can detect them and recognize their original nature and purpose. The Butsu-dan and Kami-dana do not belong to this order of beliefs. The average home of Japan would feel itself desecrated were these to be forcibly removed. The piety of the home centers, in large measure, about these expressions of the religious heart. Their practical universality is a significant witness to the possession by the people at large of a religious nature.

If it is fair to argue that the Christian religion has a vital hold on the Western peoples because of the cathedrals and churches to be found throughout the length and breadth of Christendom, a similar argument applies to Japan and the hold of the religions of this land upon its people. For over a thousand years the external manifestations of religion in architecture have been elaborate. Temples of enormous size, comparing not unfavorably with the cathedrals of Europe as regards the cost of erection, are to be found in all parts of the land. Immense temple bells of bronze, colossal statues of Buddha, and lesser ones of saints and worthies innumerable, bear witness to the lavish use of wealth in the expression of religious devotion. It is sometimes said that Buddhism is moribund in Japan. It is seriously asserted that its temples are falling into decay. This is no more true of the temples of Buddhism in Japan, than of the cathedrals Of Christendom. Local causes greatly affect the prosperity of the various temples. Some are falling into decay, but others are being repaired, and new ones are being built. No one can have visited any shrine of note without observing the large number of signboards along either side of the main approach, on which are written the sums contributed for the building or repairing of the temple. These gifts are often munificent, single gifts sometimes reaching the sum of a thousand yen; I have noticed a few exceeding this amount. The total number of these temples and shrines throughout the country is amazing. According to government statistics, in 1894 the Buddhist temples numbered 71,831; and the Shinto temples and shrines which have received official registration reached the vast number of 190,803. The largest temple in Japan, costing several million dollars, the Nishihongwanji in Kyoto, has been built during the past decade. Considering the general poverty of the nation, the proportion of gifts made for the erection and maintenance of these temples and shrines is a striking testimony to the reality of some sort of religious zeal. That it rests entirely on form and meaningless rites, is incredible.

XXVI
SOME RELIGIOUS PHENOMENA

Without doubt, many traits are attributed to the Japanese by the casual observer or captious critic, through lack of ability to read between the lines. We have already seen how the stoical element of Japanese character serves to conceal from the sociologist the emotional nature of the people. If a Japanese conceals his ordinary emotions, much more does he refrain from public exhibition of his deeper religious aspirations. Although he may feel profoundly, his face and manner seldom reveal it. When torn with grief over the loss of a parent or son, he will tell you of his loss with smiles, if not with actual laughter. "The Japanese smile" has betrayed the solemn foreigner into many an error of individual and racial character interpretation. Particularly frequent have been such errors in matters of religion.

Although the light and joyous, "smiling" aspect of Japanese religious life is prominent, the careful observer will come incidentally and unexpectedly on many signs of an opposite nature, if he mingle intimately with the people. Japan has its sorrows and its tragedies, no less than other lands. These have their part in determining religious phenomena.

The student who takes his stand at a popular shrine and watches the worshipers come and go will be rewarded by the growing conviction that, although many are manifestly ceremonialists, others are clearly subjects of profound feeling. See that mother leading her toddling child to the image of Binzuru, the god of healing, and teaching it to rub the eyes and face of the god and then its own eyes and face. See that pilgrim before a bare shrine repeating in rapt devotion the prayer he has known from his childhood, and in virtue of which he has already received numberless blessings. Behold that leper pleading with merciful Kwannon of the thousand hands to heal his disease. Hear that pitiful wail of a score of fox-possessed victims for deliverance from their oppressor. Watch that tearful maiden performing the hundred circuits of the temple while she prays for a specific blessing for herself or some loved one. Observe that merchant solemnly worshiping the god of the sea, with offering of rice and wine. Count those hundreds of votive pictures, thanksgiving remembrances of the sick who have been healed, in answer, as they firmly believe, to their prayers to the god of this particular shrine. These are not imaginary cases. The writer has seen these and scores more like them. Here is a serious side to Japanese religious life easily overlooked by a casual or unsympathetic observer.

In addition to these simpler religious phenomena, we find in Japan, as in other lands, the practice of ecstatic union with the deity. In Shinto it is called "Kami-oroshi," the bringing down of the gods. It is doubtless some form of hypnotic trance, yet the popular interpretation of the phenomenon is that of divine possession.

Among Buddhists, the practice of ecstasy takes a different form. The aim is to attain absolute vacuity of mind and thus complete union with the Absolute. When attained, the soul becomes conscious of blissful superiority to all the concerns of this mundane life, a foretaste of the Nirvana awaiting those who shall attain to Buddhahood. The actual attainment of this experience is practically limited to the priesthood, who alone have the time and freedom from the cares of the world needful for its practice. For it is induced only by long and profound "meditation." Especially is this experience the desire of the Zen sect, which makes it a leading aim, taking its name "zen" (to sit) from this practice. To sit in religious abstraction is the height of religious bliss.

The practical business man of the West may perhaps find some difficulty in seeing anything particularly religious in ecstasy or mental vacuity. But if I mistake not, this religious phenomenon of the Orient does not differ in essence from the mystical religious experience so common in the middle and subsequent ages in Europe, and represented to-day by mystical Christians. Indeed, some of the finest religious souls of Western lands have been mystics. Mystic Christianity finds ready acceptance with certain of the Japanese.

The critical reader may perhaps admit, in view of the facts thus far presented, that the ignorant millions have some degree of religious feeling and yet, in view of the apparently irreligious life of the educated, he may still feel that the religious nature of the race is essentially shallow. He may feel that as soon as a Japanese is lifted out of the superstitious beliefs of the past, he is freed from all religious ideas and aspirations. I admit at once that there seems to be some ground for such an assertion. Yet as I study the character of the samurai of the Tokugawa period, who alone may be called the irreligious of the olden times, I see good reasons for holding that, though rejecting Buddhism, they were religious at heart. They developed little or no religious ceremonial to replace that of Buddhism, yet there were indications that the religious life still remained. Intellectual and moral growth rendered it impossible for earnest and honest men to accept the old religious expressions. They revolted from religious forms, rather than from religion, and the revolt resulted not in deeper superstitions and a poorer life, but in a life richer in thought and noble endeavor. Muro Kyu-so, the "Japanese Philosopher" to whom we have referred more than once, rejected Buddhism, as we have already seen. The high quality of his moral teachings we have also noticed. Yet he had no idea that he was "religious." Those who reject Buddhism often use the term "Shukyo-kusai," "stinking religion." For them religion is synonymous with corrupt and superstitious Buddhism. To have told Muro that he was religious would doubtless have offended him, but a few quotations should satisfy anyone that at heart he was religious in the best sense of the term.

"Consider all of you. Whence is fortune? From Heaven. Even the world says, Fortune is in Heaven. So then there is no resource save prayer to Heaven. Let us then ask: what does Heaven hate, and what does Heaven love? It loves benevolence and hates malevolence. It loves truth and hates untruth.... That which in Heaven begets all things, in man is called love. So doubt not that Heaven loves benevolence and hates its opposite. So too is it with truth. For countless ages sun and moon and stars constantly revolve and we make calendars without mistake. Nothing is more certain. It is the very truth of the universe.... I have noticed prayers for good luck, brought year by year from famous temples and hills, decorating the entrances to the homes of famous samurai. But none the less they have been killed or punished, or their line has been destroyed and house extinguished. Or at least to many, shame and disgrace have come. They have not learned fortune, but foolishly depend on prayers and charms. Confucius said: 'When punished by Heaven there is no place for prayer.' Women of course follow the temples and trust in charms, but not so should men. Alas! Now all are astray, those who should be teachers, the samurai and those higher still" (pp. 63-5). "Sin is the source of pain and righteousness of happiness. This is the settled law. The teaching of the sages and the conduct of superior men is determined by principles and the result is left to Heaven. Still, we do not obey in the hope of happiness, nor do we forbear to sin from fear. Not with this meaning did Confucius and Mencius teach that happiness is in virtue and pain in sin. But the 'way' is the law of man. It is said, 'The way of Heaven blesses virtue and curses sin.' That is intended for the ignorant multitude. Yet it is not like the Buddhist 'hoben' (pious device), for it is the determined truth" (p. 66). "Heaven is forever and is not to be understood at once, like the promises of men. Shortsighted men consider its ways and decide that there is no reward for virtue or vice. So they doubt when the good are virtuous and fear not when the wicked sin. They do not know that there is no victory against Heaven when it decrees" (p. 67). "Reason comes from Heaven, and is in men.... The philosopher knows the truth as the drinker knows the taste of *saké* and the abstainer the taste of sweets. How shall he forget it? How shall he fall into error? Lying down, getting up, moving, resting, all is well. In peace, in trouble, in death, in joy, in sorrow, all is well. Never for a moment will he leave this 'way.' This is to know it in ourselves" (p. 71).

One day, five or six students remained after the lecture to ask Kyu-so about his view as to the gods, stating their own dissatisfaction with the fantastic interpretations given to the term "Shinto" by the native scholars. Making some quotations from the Chinese classics, he went on to say for himself:

"I cannot accept that which is popularly called Shinto.... I do not profess to understand the profound reason of the deities, but in outline this is my idea: The Doctrine of the Mean speaks of the 'virtue of the Gods' and Shu-shi explains this word 'virtue' to mean the 'heart and its revelation.' Its meaning is thus stated in the Saden: 'God is pure intelligence and justice.' Now all know that God is just, but do not know that he is intelligent. But there is no such intelligence elsewhere as God's. Man hears by the ear and where the ear is not he hears not ...; man sees with his eyes, and where they are not he sees not ...; with his heart man thinks and the swiftest thought takes time. But God uses neither ear nor eye, nor does he pass over in thought. Directly he feels, and directly does he respond.... Is not this the divinity of Heaven and Earth? So the Doctrine of the Mean says: 'Looked for it cannot be seen, listened to it cannot be heard. It enters into all things. There is nothing without it.' ... 'Everywhere, everywhere, on the right and on the left.' This is the revealing of God, the truth not to be concealed. Think not that God is distant, but seek him in the heart, for the heart is the House of God. Where there is no obstacle of lust, there is communion of one spirit with the God of Heaven and Earth.... And now for the application. Examine yourselves, make the truth of the heart the foundation, increase in learning and at last you will attain. Then will you know the truth of what I speak" (pp. 50-52).

In the above passage Dr. Knox has translated the term "Shin," the Chinese ideograph for the Japanese word "Kami," by the English singular, God. This lends to the passage a fullness of monotheistic expression which the original hardly, if at all, justifies. The originals are indefinite as to number and might with equal truth be translated "gods," as Dr. Knox suggests himself in a footnote.

These and similar passages are of great interest to the student of Japanese religious development. They should be made much of by Christian preachers and missionaries. Such writers and thinkers as Muro evidently was might not improperly be called the pre-Christian Christians of Japan. They prepared the way for the coming of more light on these subjects. Japanese Christian apologists should collect such utterances from her wise men of old, and by them lead the nation to an appreciation of the truths which they suggest and for which they so fitly prepare the way. Scattered as they now are, and seldom read by the people, they lie as precious gems imbedded in the hills, or as seed safely stored. They can bear no harvest till they are sown in the soil and allowed to spring up and grow.

The more I have pondered the implications of these and similar passages, the more clear has it become that their authors were essentially religious men. Their revolt from "religion" did not spring from an irreligious motive, but from a deeper religious insight than was prevalent among Buddhist believers. The irrational and often immoral nature of many of the current religious expressions and ceremonials and beliefs became obnoxious to the thinking classes, and were accordingly rejected. The essence of religion, however, was not rejected. They tore off the accumulated husks of externalism, but kept intact the real kernel of religion.

The case for the religious nature of modern, educated Japan is not so simple. Irreligious it certainly appears. Yet it, too, is not so irreligious as perhaps the Occidental thinks. Though immoral, a Japanese may still be a filial son and a loyal subject, characteristics which have religious value in Japan, Old and New. It would not be difficult to prove that many a modern Japanese writer who proclaims his rejection of religion—calling all religion but superstition and ceremony—is nevertheless a religious man at heart. The religions he knows are too superstitious and senseless to satisfy the demands of his intellectually developed religious nature. He does not recognize that his rejection of what he calls "religion" is a real manifestation of his religious nature rather than the reverse.

The widespread irreligious phenomena of New Japan are, therefore, not difficult of explanation, when viewed in the light of two thousand years of Japanese religious history. They cannot be attributed to a deficient racial endowment of religious nature. They are a part of nineteenth-century life by no means limited to Japan. If the Anglo-Saxon race is not to be pronounced inherently irreligious, despite the fact that irreligious phenomena and individuals are in constant evidence the world over, neither can New Japan be pronounced irreligious for the same reason. The irreligion now so rampant is a recent phenomenon in Japan. It may not immediately pass away, but it must eventually. Religion freed from superstition and ceremonialism, resting in reality, identifying moral and scientific with religious truth, is already finding hearty support from many of Japan's educated men. If appeal is made under the right conditions, the Japanese manifest no lack of a genuine religious nature. That they seem to be deficient in the sense of reverence is held by some to be proof presumptive of a deficient religious nature. A few illustrations will make clear what the critic means and will guide us to an interpretation of the phenomena. Occidentals are accustomed to consider a religious service as a time of solemn quiet, for we feel ourselves in a special sense in the presence of God; His majesty and glory are realities to the believing worshiper. But much occurs during a Christian service in Japanese churches which would seem to indicate a lack of this feeling. It is by no means uncommon for little children to run about without restraint during the service, for mothers to nurse their infants, and for adults to converse with each other in an undertone, though not so low but that the sound of the conversation may be heard by all. I know a deacon occupying a front mat in church who spends a large part of service time during the first two sabbaths of each month in making out the receipts of the monthly contributions and distributing them among the members. His apparent supposition is that he disturbs no one (and it is amazing how undisturbed the rest of the congregation is), but also that he is in no way interfering with the solemnity or value of the service. The freedom, too, with which individuals come and go during the service is in marked contrast to our custom. From our standpoint, there is lack of reverence.

I recently attended a young men's meeting at which the places for each were assigned by written quotations, from the Bible, one-half of which was given to the individual and the other half placed at the seat. One quotation so used was the text, "The birds of the air have nests, but the Son of Man hath not where to lay his head." It would hardly seem as if earnest Christians could have made such use of this text. Some months ago at a social gathering held in connection with the annual meeting of the churches of Shikoku, one of the comic performances consisted in the effort on the part of three old men to sing through to the end without a break-down the song which to us is so sacred, "Rock of Ages, cleft for me." Only one man succeeded, the others going through a course of quavers and breaks which was exceedingly laughable, but absolutely irreverent. The lack of reverence which has sometimes characterized the social side of the Christmas services in Japan has been the source of frequent regret to the missionaries. In a social gathering of earnest young Christians recently, a game demanding forfeits was played; these consisted of the recitation of familiar texts from the Bible. There certainly seems to be a lack of the sense of the fitness of things.

But the question is, are these practices due to an inherent deficiency of reverence, arising from the character of the Japanese nature, or are they due rather to the religious history of the past and the conditions of the present? That the latter seems to me the correct view I need hardly state. The fact that the Japanese are an emotional people renders it probable, a priori, that under suitable conditions they would be especially subject to the emotion of reverence. And when we look at their history, and observe the actual reverence paid by the multitudes to the rulers, and by the superstitious worshipers to the "Kami" and "Hotoke," it becomes evident that the apparent irreverence in the Christian churches must be due to peculiar conditions. Reverence is a subtle feeling; it depends on the nature of the ideas that possess the mind and heart. From the very nature of the case, Japanese Christians cannot have the same set of associations clustering around the church, the service, the Bible, or any of the Christian institutions, as the Occidental who has been reared from childhood among them, and who has derived his spiritual nourishment from them. All the wealth of nineteen centuries of experience has tended to give our services and our churches special religious value in our eyes. The average Christian in Japan and in any heathen land cannot have this fringe of ideas and subtle feelings so essential to a profound feeling of reverence. But as the significance of the Christian conception of God, endowed with glory and honor, majesty and might, is increasingly realized, and as it is found that the spirit of reverence is one that needs cultivation in worship, and especially as it is found that the spirit of reverence is important to high spiritual life and vitalizing spiritual power, more and more will that spirit be manifested by Japanese Christians. But its possession or its lack is due not to the inherent character of the people, but rather to the character of the ideas which possess them. In taking now a brief glance at the nature and history of the three religions of Japan it seems desirable to quote freely from the writings of recognized authorities on the subject.

/#

"*Shinto*, which means literally 'the way of the Gods,' is the name given to the mythology and vague ancestor-and nature-worship which preceded the introduction of Buddhism into Japan—Shinto, so often spoken of as a religion, is hardly entitled to that name. It has no set of dogmas, no sacred book, no moral code. The absence of a moral code is accounted for in the writings of modern native commentators by the innate perfection of Japanese humanity, which obviates the necessity for such outward props.... It is necessary, however, to distinguish three periods in the existence of Shinto. During the first of these—roughly speaking, down to A.D. 550—the Japanese had no notion of religion as a separate institution. To pay homage to the gods, that is, to the departed ancestors of the Imperial family, and to the names of other great men, was a usage springing from the same soil as that which produced passive obedience to, and worship of, the living Mikado. Besides this, there were prayers to the wind-gods, to the god of fire, to the god of pestilence, to the goddess of food, and to deities presiding over the sauce-pan, the caldron, the gate, and the kitchen. There were also purifications for wrongdoing.... But there was not even a shadowy idea of any code of morals, or any systematization of the simple notions of the people concerning things unseen. There was neither heaven nor hell—only a kind of neutral-tinted Hades. Some of the gods were good and some were bad; nor was the line between men and gods at all clearly drawn."

The second period of Shinto began with the introduction of Buddhism into Japan, in which period Shinto became absorbed into Buddhism through the doctrine that the Shinto deities were ancient incarnations of Buddhas. In this period Shinto retained no distinctive feature. "Only at court and at a few great shrines, such as those of Ise and Idzumo, was a knowledge of Shinto in its native simplicity kept up; and it is doubtful whether changes did not creep in with the lapse of ages. Most Shinto temples throughout the country were served by Buddhist priests, who introduced the architectural ornaments and the ceremonial of their own religion. Thus was formed the Ryobu Shinto—a mixed religion founded on a compromise between the old creed and the new, and hence the tolerant ideas on theological subjects of most of the middle-lower classes, who worship indifferently at the shrines of either faith."

The third period began about 1700. It was introduced by the scholarly study of history. "Soon the movement became religious and political—above all, patriotic.... The Shogunate was frowned on, because it had supplanted the autocracy of the heaven-descended Mikados. Buddhism and Confucianism were sneered at because of their foreign origin. The great scholars Mabuchi (1697-1769), Motoori (1730-1801), and Hirata (1776-1843) devoted themselves to a religious propaganda—if that can be called a religion which sets out from the principle that the only two things needful are to follow one's natural impulses and to obey the Mikado. This order triumphed for a moment in the revolution of 1868." It became for a few months the state religion, but soon lost its status.[CB]

Buddhism came to Japan from Korea *via* China in 552 A.D. It was already a thousand years old and had, before it reached Japan, broken up into numerous sects and subsects differing widely from each other and from the original teaching of Sakya Muni. After two centuries of propagandism it conquered the land and absorbed the religious life of the people, though Shinto was never entirely suppressed. "All education was for centuries in Buddhist hands; Buddhism introduced art, and medicine, molded the folklore of the country, created its dramatic poetry, deeply influenced politics and every sphere of social and intellectual activity. In a word, Buddhism was the teacher under whose instruction the Japanese nation grew up. As a nation they are now grossly forgetful of this fact. Ask an educated Japanese a question about Buddhism, and ten to one he will smile in your face. A hundred to one that he knows nothing about the subject and glories in his nescience." "The complicated metaphysics of Buddhism have awakened no interest in the Japanese nation. Another fact, curious but true, is that these people have never been at the trouble to translate the Buddhist canon into their own language. The priests use a Chinese version, and the laity no version at all, though ... they would seem to have been given to searching the Scriptures a few hundred years ago. The Buddhist religion was disestablished and disendowed during the years 1871-74, a step taken in consequence of the temporary ascendency of Shinto." Although Confucianism took a strong hold on the people in the early part of the seventeenth century, yet its influence was limited to the educated and ruling classes. The vast multitude still remained Shinto-Buddhists.

As for doctrine, philosophic Buddhism with its dogmas of salvation through intellectual enlightenment, by means of self-perfecting, with its goal of absorption into Nirvana, has doubtless been the belief and aim of the few. But such Buddhism was too deep for the multitudes. "By the aid of hoben, or pious devices, the priesthood has played into the hands of popular superstition. Here, as elsewhere, there have been evolved charms, amulets, pilgrimages, and gorgeous temple services, in which the people worship not only the Buddha, who was himself an agnostic, but his disciple, and even such abstractions as Amida, which are mistaken for actual divine personages."[CC] The deities of Shinto have been more or less confused with those of popular Buddhism; in some cases, inextricably so.

Confucianism, as known in Japan, was the elaborated doctrine of Confucius. "He confined himself to practical details of morals and government, and took submission to parents and political rulers as the corner stone of his system. The result is a set of moral truths—some would say truisms—of a very narrow scope, and of dry ceremonial observances, political rather than personal." "Originally introduced into Japan early in the Christian era, along with other products of Chinese civilization, the Confucian philosophy lay dormant during the middle ages, the period of the supremacy of Buddhism. It awoke with a start in the early part of the seventeenth century when Iccasu, the great warrior, ruler, and patron of learning, caused the Confucian classics to be printed in Japan for the first time. During the two hundred and fifty years that followed, the intellect of the country was molded by Confucian ideas. Confucius himself had, it is true, labored for the establishment of a centralized monarchy. But his main doctrine of unquestioning submission to rulers and parents fitted in perfectly with the feudal ideas of Old Japan; and the conviction of the paramount importance of such subordination lingers on, an element of stability, in spite of the recent social cataclysm which has involved Japanese Confucianism, properly so-called, in the ruin of all other Japanese institutions."[CD]

Christianity was first brought to Japan by Francis Xavier, who landed in Kagoshima in 1549. His zeal knew no bounds and his results were amazing. "The converts were drawn from all classes alike. Noblemen, Buddhist priests, men of learning, embraced the faith with the same alacrity as did the poor and ignorant.... One hundred and thirty-eight European missionaries" were then on the field. "Until the breaking out of the persecution of 1596 the work of evangelization proceeded apace. The converts numbered ten thousand yearly, though all were fully aware of the risk to which they exposed themselves by embracing the Catholic faith." "At the beginning of the seventeenth century, the Japanese Christians numbered about one million, the fruit of half a century of apostolic labor accomplished in the midst of comparative peace. Another half-century of persecution was about to ruin this flourishing church, to cut off its pastors, more than two hundred of whom suffered martyrdom, and to leave its laity without the offices of religion.... The edicts ordering these measures remained in force for over two centuries." Tens of thousands of Christians preferred death to perjury. It was supposed that Christianity was entirely exterminated by the fearful and prolonged persecutions. Yet in the vicinity of Nagasaki over four thousand Christians were discovered in 1867, who were again subject to persecution until the pressure of foreign lands secured religious toleration in Japan.

Protestant Christianity came to Japan with the beginning of the new era, and has been preached with much zeal and moderate success. For a time it seemed destined to sweep the land even more astonishingly than did Romanism in the sixteenth century. But in 1888 an anti-foreign reaction began in every department of Japanese life and thought which has put a decided check on the progress of Christian missions.

This must suffice for our historical review of the religious life of the Japanese. Were we to forget Japan's long and repeated isolations, and also to ignore fluctuations of belief and of other religious phenomena in other lands, we might say, as many do, that the

125

Japanese have inherently shallow and changeable religious convictions. But remembering these facts, and recalling the persecutions of Buddhists by each other, of Christianity by the state, and knowing to-day many earnest, self-sacrificing and persistent Christians, I am convinced that such a judgment is mistaken. There are other and sufficient reasons to account for this appearance of changeableness in religion.

I close this chapter with a single observation on the religious history just outlined. Bearing in mind the great changes that have come over Japanese religious thinking and forms of religion I ask if religious phenomena are the expressions of the race nature, as some maintain, and if this nature is inherent and unchangeable, how are such profound changes to be accounted for? If the religious character of the Japanese people is inherent, how is it conceivable that they should so easily adopt foreign religions, even to the exclusion of their own native religion, as did those who became Buddhist or Confucian or Christian? I conclude from these facts, and they are paralleled in the history of many other peoples, that even religious characteristics are not dependent on biological, but are wholly dependent on social evolution. It seems to me capable of the clearest proof that the religious phenomena of any age are dependent on the general development of the intellect, on the ruling ideas, and on the entire conditions of the civilization of the age rather than on brain structure or essential race nature.

XXVII
SOME RELIGIOUS CONCEPTIONS

The conceptions of the common people in regard to deity are chaotic. They believe in local spirits who are to be worshiped; some of these are of human origin, and some antedate all human life. The gods of the Shinto pantheon are "yaoyorodzu" in number, eight thousand myriads; yet in their "norito," or prayer rituals, reference is made not only to the "yaoyorodzu" who live in the air, but also to the "yaoyorodzu" who live on earth, and even to the "yaoyorodzu" who live beneath the earth. If we add these together there must be at least twenty-four thousand myriads of gods. These of course include sun, moon, stars, and all the forces of nature, as well as the spirits of men. Popular Buddhism accepts the gods of Shinto and brings in many more, worshiping not only the Buddha and his immediate "rakan," disciples, five hundred in number, but numberless abstractions of ideal qualities, such as the varieties of Kwannon (Avelokitesvara, gods and goddesses of mercy), Amida (Amitabha, the ideal of boundless light), Jizo (Kshitigarbha, the helper of those in trouble, lost children, and pregnant women), Emma O (Yama-raja, ruler of Buddhist hells), Fudo (Achala, the "immovable," "unchangeable"), and many others. Popular Buddhism also worships every man dead or living who has become a "hotoke," that is, has attained Buddhahood and has entered Nirvana. The gods of Japan are innumerable in theory and multitudinous in practice. Not only are there gods of goodness but also gods of lust and of evil, to whom robbers and harlots may pray for success and blessing.

In the Japanese pantheon there is no supreme god, such, for instance, as the Roman Jupiter, or the Greek Chronos, nor is there a thoroughgoing divine hierarchy.

According to the common view (although there is no definite thought about it), the idea seems to be that the universe with its laws and nature were already existent before the gods appeared on the scene; they created specific places, such as Japan, out of already existing material. Neither in Shinto nor in popular Buddhism is the conception formed of a primal fount of all being with its nature and laws. In this respect Japanese thought is like all primitive religious thought. There is no word in the Japanese language corresponding to the English term "God." The nearest approach to it are the Confucian terms "Jo-tei," "Supreme Emperor," "Ten," "Heaven," and "Ten-tei," "Heavenly Emperor"; but all of these terms are Chinese, they are therefore of late appearance in Japan, and represent rather conceptions of educated and Confucian classes than the ideas of the masses. These terms approach closely to the idea of monotheism; but though the doctrine may be discovered lying implicit in these words and ideas it was never developed. Whether "Heaven" was to be conceived as a person, or merely as fate, was not clearly thought out; some expressions point in one direction while others point in the other.

I may here call attention to a significant fact in the history of recent Christian work in Japan. Although the serious-minded Japanese is first attracted to Christianity by the character of its ethical thought—so much resembling, also so much surpassing that of Confucius, it is none the less true that monotheism is another powerful source of attraction. I have been repeatedly told by Christians that the first religious satisfaction they ever experienced was upon their discovery of monotheism. How it affected Dr. Neesima, readers of his life cannot have overlooked. He is a type of multitudes. In the earlier days of Christian work many felt that they had become Christians upon rejection of polytheism and acceptance of monotheism. And in truth they were so far forth Christian, although they knew little of Christ, and felt little need of His help as a personal Saviour. The weakness of the Church in recent years is due in part, I doubt not, to the acceptance into its membership of numbers who were, properly speaking, monotheistic, but not in the complete sense of the term Christian. Their discovery later that more was needed than the intellectual acceptance of monotheism ere they could be considered, or even be, truly "Christian," has led many such "believers" to abandon their relations with the Church. This, while on many accounts to be regretted, was nevertheless inevitable. The bare acceptance of the monotheistic idea does not secure that transformation of heart and produce that warmth of living faith which are essential elements in the altruistic life demanded of the Christian.

Nor is it difficult to understand why monotheism has proved such an attraction to the Japanese when we consider that through it they first recognized a unity in the universe and even in their own lives. Nature, and human nature took on an intelligibility which they never had had under the older philosophy. History likewise was seen to have a meaning and an order, to say nothing of a purpose, which the non-Christian faiths did not themselves see and could not give to their devotees. Furthermore the monotheistic idea furnished a satisfactory background and explanation for the exact sciences. If there is but one God, who is the fount and cause of all being, it is easy to see why the truths of science should be universal and absolute, rather than local and diverse, as they would be were they subject to the jurisdiction of various local deities. The universality of nature's laws was inconceivable under polytheism. Monotheism thus found a ready access to many minds. Polytheism pure and simple is the belief of no educated Japanese to-day. He is a monist of some kind or other. Philosophic Buddhism always was monistic, but not monotheistic. Thinking Confucianists were also monistic. But neither philosophic Buddhism nor Confucianism emphasized their monistic elements; they did not realize the importance to popular thought of monistic conceptions. But possessing these ideas, and being now in contact with aggressive Christian monotheism, they are beginning to emphasize this truth.

As Japan has had no adequate conception of God, her conception of man has been of necessity defective. Indeed, the cause of her inadequate conception of God is due in large measure to her inadequate conception of man, which we have seen to be a necessary consequence of the primitive communal order. Since, however, we have already given considerable attention to Japan's inadequate conception of man, we need do no more than refer to it in this connection.

Corresponding to her imperfect doctrines of God and of man is her doctrine of sin. That the Japanese sense of sin is slight is a fact generally admitted. This is the universal experience of the missionary. Many Japanese with whom I have conversed seem to have no consciousness of it whatever. Indeed, it is a difficult matter to speak of to the Japanese, not only because of the etiquette involved, but for the deeper reason of the deficiency of the language. There exists no term in Japanese which corresponds to the Christian word "sin." To tell a man he is a sinner without stopping to explain what one means would be an insult, for he is not conscious of having broken any of the laws of the land. Yet too much stress must not be laid on this argument from the language, for the Buddhistic vocabulary furnishes a number of terms which refer to the crime of transgressing not the laws of the land, but those of Buddha.

In Shinto, sin is little, if anything, more than physical impurity. Although Buddhism brought a higher conception of religion for the initiated few, it gave no help to the ignorant multitudes, rather it riveted their superstitions upon them. It spoke of law indeed, and lust and sin; and of dreadful punishments for sin; but when it explained sin it made its nature too shallow, being merely the result of mental confusion; salvation, then, became simply intellectual enlightenment; it also made the consequences of sin too remote and the escape from them too easy. The doctrine of "Don," suddenness of salvation, the many external and entirely formal rites, short pilgrimages to famous shrines, the visiting of some neighboring temple having miniature models of all the other efficacious shrines throughout the land, the wearing of charms, the buying of "o fuda," and even the single utterance of certain magic prayers, were taught to be quite enough for the salvation of the common man from the worst of sins. Where release is so easily obtained, the estimate of the heinousness of sin is correspondingly slight. How different was the consciousness of sin and the conception of its nature developed by the Jewish worship with its system of sin offerings! Life for life. Whatever we may think of the efficacy of offering an animal as an expiation for sin, it certainly contributed far more toward deepening the sense of sin than the rites in common practice among the Buddhists. So far as I know, human or animal sacrifice has never been known in Japan.

In response to the not unlikely criticism that sacrifice is the result of profound sense of sin and not its cause, I reply that it is both. The profound sense is the experience of the few at the beginning; the practice educates the multitudes and begets that feeling in the nation.

Ceremonial purification is an old rite in Japan. In this connection we naturally think of the "Chozu-bachi" which may be found before every Shinto shrine, containing the "holy water" with which to rinse the mouth and wash the hands. Pilgrims and worshipers invariably make use of this water, wiping their hands on the towels provided for the purpose by the faithful. To our eyes, few customs in Japan are more conducive to the spread of impurity and infectious disease than this rite of ceremonial purification. No better means could be devised for the wide dissemination of the skin diseases which are so common. The reformed religion of New Japan—whether Buddhist, Shinto, or Christian—could do few better services for the people at large than by entering on a crusade against this religious rite. It could and should preach the doctrine that sin and defilement of the hearts are not removed by such an easy method as the rite implies and the masses believe. If retained as a symbol, the purification rite should at least be reformed as a practice.

Whether the use of purificatory water is to be traced to the sense of moral or spiritual sin is doubtful to my mind; in view of the general nature of primitive Shinto. The interpretation given the system by W.E. Griffis, in his volume on the "Religions of Japan," is suggestive, but in view of all the facts does not seem conclusive. "One of the most remarkable features of Shinto" he writes, "was the emphasis laid on cleanliness. Pollution was calamity, defilement was sin, and physical purity at least was holiness. Everything that could in any way soil the body or clothing was looked upon with abhorrence and detestation."[CE] The number of specifications given in this connection is worthy of careful perusal. But it is a strange nemesis of history that the sense of physical pollution should develop a religious rite fitted to become the very means for the dissemination of physical pollution and disease.

Japanese personal cleanliness is often connected in the descriptions of foreigners with ceremonial purification, but the facts are much exaggerated. In contrast to nearly if not quite all non-Christian peoples, the Japanese are certainly astonishingly cleanly in their habits. But it is wholly unnecessary to exaggerate the facts. The "tatami," or straw-mats, an inch or more in thickness, give to the room an appearance of cleanliness which usually belies the truth. The multitudes of fleas that infest the normal Japanese home are convincing proof of the real state of the "tatami." There are those who declare that a Japanese crowd has the least offensive odor of any people in the world. One writer goes so far as to state that not only is there no unpleasant odor whatever, but that there is even a pleasant intimation of lavender about their exhalations. This exactly contradicts my experience. Not to mention the offensive oil with which all women anoint their hair to give it luster and stiffness, the Japanese habit of wearing heavy cotton wadded clothing, with little or no underwear, produces the inevitable result in the atmosphere of any closed room. In cold weather I always find it necessary to throw open all the doors and windows of my study or parlor, after Bible classes of students or even after the visits of cultured and well-to-do guests. That the

Japanese bathe so frequently is certainly an interesting fact and a valuable feature of their civilization; it indicates no little degree of cleanliness; but for that, their clothing would become even more disagreeable than it is, and the evil effect upon themselves of wearing soiled garments would be much greater. In point of fact, their frequent baths do not wholly remove the need of change in clothing. To a Japanese the size of the weekly wash of a foreigner seems extravagant.

As to the frequent bathing, its cleanliness is exaggerated by Western thought, for instead of supplying fresh water for each person, the Japanese public baths consist usually of a large tank used by multitudes in common. Clean water is allowed for the face, but the main tank is supplied with clean hot water only once each day. In Kumamoto, schoolgirls living with us invariably asked permission to go to the bath early in the day that they might have the first use of the water. They said that by night it was so foul they could not bear to use it. Each hotel has its own private bath for guests; this is usually heated in the afternoon, and the guests take their baths from four o'clock on until midnight, the waiting girls of the hotel using it last. My only experience with public baths has been mentioned already. At first glance the conditions were reassuring, for a large stream of hot water was running in constantly, and the water in the tank itself was quite transparent. But on entering I was surprised, not to say horrified, to see floating along the margin of the tank and on the bottom of it suggestive proofs of previous bathers. On inquiry I learned that the tank was never washed out, nor the water entirely discharged at a single time; the natural overflow along the edge of the tank being considered sufficient. In the interest of accuracy it is desirable to add that New Japan is making progress in the matter of public baths. In some of the larger cities, I am told, provision is sometimes made for entirely fresh water for each bather in separate bathrooms.

In view of these facts—as unpleasant to mention as they are essential to a faithful description of the habits of the people—it is clear that the "horror of physical impurity" has not been, and is not now, so great as some would have us believe. Whatever may have been the condition in ancient times, it would be difficult to believe that the rite of ceremonial purification could arise out of the present practices and habits of thought. One may venture the inquiry whether the custom of using the "purificatory water" may not have been introduced from abroad.

But whatever be the present thought of the people, on the general subject of sin, it may be shown to be due to the prevailing system of ideas, moral and religious, rather than to the inherent racial character. In an interesting article by Mr. G. Takahashi on the "Past, Present, and Future of Christianity in Japan" I find the statement that the preaching of the monks who came to Japan in the sixteenth century was of such a nature as to produce a very deep consciousness of sin among the converts. "The Christians or martyrs repeatedly cried out 'we miserable sinners,' 'Christ died for us,' etc., as their letters abundantly prove. It was because of this that their consciences were aroused by the burning words of Christ, and kept awake by means of contrition and confession." Among modern Christians the sense of sin is much more clear and pronounced than among the unconverted. Individual instances of extreme consciousness of sin are not unknown, especially under the earlier Protestant preaching. If the Christians of the last decade have less sense of sin, it is due to the changed character of recent preaching, in consequence of the changed conception of Christianity widely accepted in Protestant lands. Who will undertake to say that Christians in New England of the nineteenth century have the same oppressive sense of sin that was customary in the sixteenth, seventeenth, and eighteenth centuries? The sense of sin is due more to the character of the dominant religious ideas of the age than to brain structure or to race nature. I cannot agree with Mr. Takahashi that "To be religious one needs a Semitic tinge of mind." It is not a question of mind, of race nature, but of dominant ideas.

In this connection I may refer to an incident that came under my notice some years ago. A young man applied for membership in the Kumamoto Church, who at one time had been a student in one of my Bible classes. I had not known that he had received any special help from his study with me, until I heard his statement as to how he had discovered his need of a Saviour, and had found that need satisfied in Christ. In his statement before the examining committee of the church, he said that when he first read the thirteenth chapter of

129

1 Corinthians, he was so impressed with its beauty as a poem that he wrote it out entire on one of the fusuma (light paper doors) of his room, and each morning, as he arose, he read it. This practice continued several weeks. Then, as we continued our study of the Bible, we took up the third chapter of John, and when he came to the sixteenth verse, he was so impressed with its statement that he wrote that beside the poem from Corinthians, and read them together. Gradually this daily reading, together with the occasional sermons and other Christian addresses which he heard at the Boys' School, led him to desire to secure for himself the love described by Paul, and to know more vitally the love of God described by John. It occurred to him, that, to secure these ends, he should pray. Upon doing so he said that, for the first time in his life, his unworthiness and his really sinful nature overwhelmed him. This was, of course, but the beginning of his Christian life. He began then to search the Scriptures in earnest, and with increasing delight. It was not long before he wished to make public confession of his faith, and thus identify himself with the Christian community. This brief account of the way in which this young man was brought to Christ illustrates a good many points, but that for which I have cited it is the testimony it bears to the fact that under similar circumstances the human heart undergoes very much the same religious experience, whatever be the race or nationality of the individual.

In regard to the future life, Shinto has little specific doctrine. It certainly implies the continued existence of the soul after death, as its ancestral worship shows, but its conception as to the future state is left vague in the extreme. Confucius purposely declined to teach anything on this point, and, in part, for this reason, it has been maintained that Confucianism cannot properly be called a religion. Buddhism brought to Japan an elaborate system of eschatological ideas, and so far as the common people of Japan have any conception of the future life, it may be attributed to Buddhistic teachings. Into their nature I need not inquire at any length. According to popular Buddhism, the future world, or more properly speaking, worlds (for there are ten of them, into any one of which a soul may be born either immediately or in the course of its future transmigrations), does not differ in any vital way from the present world. It is a world of material blessings or woes; the successive stages or worlds are graded one above the other in fantastic ways. Salvation consists in passing to higher grades of life, the final or perfect stage being paradise, which, once attained, can never be lost. Transmigration is universal, the period of life in each world being determined by the merits and demerits of the individual soul.

Here we must consider two widely used terms "ingwa" and "mei." The first of these is Buddhistic and the other Confucianistic; though differing much in origin and meaning, yet in the end they amount to much the same thing. "Ingwa" is the law of cause and effect. According to the Buddhistic teaching, however, the "in," or cause, is in one world, while the "gwa," or effect, is in the other. The suffering, for instance, or any misfortune that overtakes one in this present life, is the "gwa" or effect of what was done in the previous, and is thus inevitable. The individual is working off in this life the "gwa" of his last life, and he is also working up the "in" of the next He is thus in a kind of vise. His present is absolutely determined for him by his past, and in turn is irrevocably fixing his future. Such is the Buddhistic "wheel of the law." The common explanation of misfortune, sickness, or disease, or any calamity, is that it is the result of "ingwa," and that there is, therefore, no help for it. The paralyzing nature of this conception on the development of character, or on activity of any kind, is apparent not only theoretically but actually. As an escape from the inexorable fatality of this scheme of thought, the Buddhist faith of the common people has resorted to magic. Magic prayers, consisting of a few mystic syllables of whose meaning the worshiper may be quite ignorant, are the means for overcoming the inexorableness of "ingwa," both for this life and the next. "Namu Amida Butsu," "Namu Myo Ho Ren Ge Kyo," "Namu Hen Jo Kongo," are the most common of such magic formulæ. These prayers are heard on the lips of tens of thousands of pious pilgrims, not only at the temples, but as they pass along the highways. It is believed that each repetition secures its reward. Popular Buddhism's appeal to magic was not only winked at by philosophical Buddhism, but it was encouraged. Magic was justified by religious philosophy, and many a "hoben," "pious device," for saving the ignorant was invented by the priesthood. It will be apparent that while Buddhism has in certain respects a vigorous system of punishment for sin, yet its method of relief is such that the common people can gain only the most shallow and superficial views of salvation. Buddhism has not served to deepen the sense of responsibility, nor helped to build up character. That the more serious-minded thinkers of the nation have, as a rule, rejected Buddhism is not strange.

One point of great interest for us is the fact that this eschatological and soteriological system was imported, and is not the spontaneous product of Japan. The wide range of national religious characteristics thus clearly traceable to Buddhistic influence shows beyond doubt how large a part of a nation's character is due to the system of thought that for one reason or another prevails, rather than to the essential race character.

The other term mentioned above, "mei," literally means "command" or "decree"; but while the English terms definitely imply a real being who decides, decrees, and commands, the term "mei" is indeterminate on this point. It is frequently joined to the word "Ten," or Heaven; "Ten-mei," Heaven's decree, seeming to imply a personality in the background of the thought. Yet, as I have already pointed out, it is only implied; in actual usage it means the fate decreed by Heaven; that is, fated fate, or absolute fate. The Chinese and the Japanese alike failed to inquire minutely as to the implication of the deepest conceptions of their philosophy. But "mei" is commonly used entirely unconnected with "Ten," and in this case its best translation into English is probably "fate." In this sense it is often used. Unlike Buddhism, however, Confucianism provided no way of escape from "mei" except moral conduct. One of its important points of superiority was its freedom from appeal to magic in any form, and its reliance on sincerity of heart and correctness of conduct.

Few foreigners have failed to comment on the universal use by the Japanese of the phrase "Shikataga nai," "it can't be helped." The ready resignation to "fate," as they deem it, even in little things about the home and in the daily life, is astonishing to Occidentals. Where we hold ourselves and each other to sharp personal responsibility, the sense of subjection to fate often leads them to condone mistakes with the phrase "Shikataga nai."

But this characteristic is not peculiar to Japan. China and India are likewise marked by it. During the famines in India, it was frequently remarked how the Hindus would settle down to starve in their huts in submission to fate, where Westerners would have been doing something by force, fighting even the decrees of heaven, if needful. But it is important to note that this characteristic in Japan is undergoing rapid change. The spirit of absolute submission, so characteristic of the common people of Old Japan, is passing away and self-assertion is taking its place. Education and developing intelligence are driving out the fear of fate. Had our estimate of the Japanese race character been based wholly on the history of Old Japan, it might have been easy to conclude that the spirit of submission to rulers and to fate was a national characteristic due to racial nature; but every added year of New Japan shows how erroneous that view would have been. Thus we see again that the characteristics of Japan, Old and New, are not due to race nature, but to the prevailing civilization in the broadest sense of the term. The religious characteristics of a people depend primarily on the dominant religious ideas, not on the inherent religious nature.

XXVIII
SOME RELIGIOUS PRACTICES

Among the truly religious sentiments of the Japanese are those of loyalty and filial piety. Having already given them considerable attention, we need not delay long upon them here. The point to be emphasized is that these two principles are exalted into powerful religious sentiments, which have permeated and dominated the entire life of the nation. Not only were they at the root of courage, of fidelity, of obedience, and of all the special virtues of Old Japan, but they were also at the root of the larger part of her religion. These emotions, sentiments, and beliefs have built 190,000 Shinto shrines. Loyalty to the daimyo was the vital part of the religion of the past, as loyalty to the Emperor is the vital part of the popular religion of to-day. Next to loyalty came filial piety; it not only built the cemeteries, but also maintained god-shelves and family ancestral worship throughout the centuries. One of the first questions which many an inquirer about Christianity has put to me is as to the way we treat our parents living and dead, and the tombs and memories of our ancestors.

These two religious sentiments of loyalty and filial piety were essential elements of primitive Shinto. The imported religions, particularly Confucianism and Christianity, served to strengthen them. In view of the indubitable religious nature of these two sentiments it is difficult to see how anyone can deny the name of religion to the religions that inculcate them, Shinto and Confucianism. It shows how defective is the current conception of the real nature of religion.

Despite the reality of these religious, sentiments, however, many things are done in Japan quite opposed to them. Of course this is so. These violations spring from irreligion, and irreligion is found in every land. Furthermore, many things done in the name of loyalty and piety seem to us Westerners exceedingly whimsical and illogical. Deeds which to us seem disloyal and unfilial receive no rebuke. Filial piety often seems to us more active toward the dead than toward the living.

Closely connected with loyalty and filial piety, and in part their expression, is one further religious sentiment, namely, gratitude. In his chapter in "Kokoro" "About Ancestor-Worship," Mr. Hearn makes some pertinent remarks as to the nature of Shinto. "Foremost among the moral sentiments of Shinto is that of loving gratitude to the past." This he attributes to the fact that "To Japanese thought the dead are not less real than the living. They take part in the daily life of the people, sharing the humblest sorrows and the humblest joys ... and they are universally thought of as finding pleasure in the offerings made to them or the honors conferred upon them." There is much truth in these statements, though I by no means share the opinion that in connection with the Japanese belief in the dead there "have been evolved moral sentiments wholly unknown to Western civilization," or that their "loving gratitude to the past" is "a sentiment having no real correspondence in our own emotional life." Mr. Hearn may be presumed to be speaking for himself in these matters; but he certainly does not correctly represent the thought or the feelings of the circle of life known to me. The feeling of gratitude of Western peoples is as real and as strong as that of the Japanese, though it does not find expression in the worship of the dead. That the Japanese are profuse in their expressions of gratitude to the past and to the powers that be is beyond dispute. It crops out in sermons and public speeches, as well as in the numberless temples to national heroes.

But it is a matter of surprise to note how often there is apparent ingratitude toward living benefactors. Some years ago I heard a conversation between some young men who had enjoyed special opportunities of travel and of study abroad by the liberality of American gentlemen.

It appeared that the young men considered that instead of receiving any special favors, they were conferring them on their benefactors by allowing the latter to help such brilliant youth as they, whose subsequent careers in Japan would preserve to posterity the names of their benefactors. I have had some experience in the line of giving assistance to aspiring students, in certain cases helping them for years; a few have given evidence of real gratitude; but a large proportion have seemed singularly deficient in this grace. It is my impression that relatively few of the scores of students who have received a large proportion of their expenses from the mission, while pursuing their studies, have felt that they were thereby under any special debt of gratitude. An experience that a missionary had with a class to which he had been teaching the Bible in English for about a year is illustrative. At the close of the school year they invited him to a dinner where they made some very pleasant speeches, and bade each other farewell for the summer. The teacher was much gratified with the result of the year's work, feeling naturally that these boys were his firm friends. But the following September when he returned, not only did the class not care to resume their studies with him, but they appeared to desire to have nothing whatever to do with him. On the street many of them would not even recognize him. Other similar cases come to mind, and it should be remembered that missionaries give such instruction freely and always at the request of the recipient. In the case cited the teacher came to the conclusion that the elaborate dinner and fine farewell speeches were considered by the young men as a full discharge of all debts of gratitude and a full compensation for services. This, however, is to be said: the city itself was at that time the seat of a determined antagonism to Christianity and, of course, to the Christian missionary; and this fact may in part, but not wholly, account for the appearance of ingratitude.

The Japanese pride themselves on their gratitude. It is, however, limited in its scope. It is vigorous toward the dead and toward the Emperor, but as a grace of daily life it is not conspicuous.

Few achievements of the Japanese have been more remarkable than the suppression of certain religious phenomena. Any complete statement of the religious characteristics of the Japanese fifty years ago would have included most revolting and immoral practices under the guise of religion. Until suppressed by the government in the early years of Meiji there were in many parts of Japan phallic shrines of considerable popularity, at which, on festivals at least, sexual immorality seemed to be an essential part of the worship. At Uji, not far from Kyoto, the capital of the Empire, for a thousand years and more, and the center of Buddhism, there was a shrine of great repute and popularity. Thither resorted the multitudes for bacchanalian purposes. Under the auspices of the Goddess Hashihime and the God Sumiyoshi, free rein was given to lust. Since the beginning of the new régime such revels have been forbidden and apparently stopped; the phallic symbols themselves are no longer visible, although it is asserted by the keeper of the shrine that they are still there, concealed in the boxes on the pedestals formerly occupied by the symbols. When I visited the place some years since with a fellow missionary we were told that multitudes still come there to pray to the deities; those seeking divorce pray to the female deity, while those seeking a favorable marriage pray to the male deity; on asking as to the proportion of the worshipers, we were told that there are about ten of the former to one of the latter, a significant indication of the unhappiness of many a home. Prof. Edmund Buckley has made a special study of the subject of phallic worship in Japan; in his thesis on the topic he gives a list of thirteen places where these symbols of phallic worship might be seen a few years since. It is significant that at Uji, not a stone's throw from the phallic shrine, is a temple to the God Agata, whose special function is the cure of venereal diseases.

But though phallic worship and its accompanying immorality have been extirpated, immorality in connection with religion is still rampant in certain quarters. Not far from the great temples at Ise, the center of Shintoism and the goal for half a million pilgrims yearly, are large and prosperous brothels patronized by and existing for the sake of the pilgrims. A still more popular resort for pilgrims is that at Kompira, whither, as we have seen, some 900,000 come each year; here the best hotels, and presumably the others also, are provided with prostitutes who also serve as waiting girls; on the arrival of a guest he is customarily asked whether or not the use of a prostitute shall be included in his hotel bill. It seems strange, indeed, that the government should take such pains to suppress phallicism, and allow such immorality to go on under the eaves of the greatest national shrines; for these shrines are not private affairs; the government takes possession of the gifts, and pays the regular salaries of the attending priests. It would appear from its success in the extermination of distinctly phallic worship that the government could put a stop to all public prostitution in connection with religion if it cared to do so.

One point of interest in connection with the above facts is that the old religions, however much of force, beauty, and truth we may concede to them, have never made warfare against these obscene forms of worship, nor against the notorious immorality of their devotees. Whatever may be said of the profound philosophy of life involved in phallic worship, for many hundreds of years it has been a source of outrageous immorality. Nevertheless, there has never been any continued and effective effort on the part of the higher types of religion to exterminate the lower. But Japan is not peculiar in this respect. India is even now amazingly immoral in certain forms of her worship.

Another point of interest in this connection is that the change of the nation in its attitude to this form of religion was due largely, probably wholly, to contact with the nations of the West. The uprooting of phallic worship was due, not to a moral reformation, but to a political ambition. It was carried out, not in deference to public opinion, but wholly by government command, though without doubt the nobler opinion of the land approved of the government action. But even this nobler public sentiment was aroused by the Occidental stimulus. The success of the effort must be attributed not a little to the age-long national custom of submitting absolutely to governmental initiative and command.

Another point of interest is that, in consequence of official pressure, the religious character of a large number of the people seems to have undergone a radical change. The ordinary traveler in Japan would not suspect that phallicism had ever been a prominent feature of Japanese religious life. Only an inquisitive seeker can now find the slightest evidences of this once popular cult. Here we have an apparent change in the character of a people sudden and complete, induced almost wholly by external causes. It shows that the previous characteristic was not so deeply rooted in the physical or spiritual nature of the race as many would have us believe. Can we escape the conclusion that national characteristics are due much more to the circle of dominant ideas and actual practices, than to the inherent race nature?

The way in which phallicism has been suppressed during the present era raises the general question of religious liberty in Japan. In this respect, no less than in many others, a change has taken place so great as to amount to a revolution. During two hundred and fifty years Christianity was strictly forbidden on pain of extreme penalties. In 1872 the edict against Christianity was removed, free preaching was allowed, and for a time it seemed as if the whole nation would become Christian in a few decades; even non-Christians urged that Christianity be made the state religion. What an amazing volte-face! Religious liberty is now guaranteed by the constitution promulgated in 1888. There are those who assert that until Christianity invaded Japan, religious freedom was perfect; persecutions were unknown. This is a mistake. When Buddhism came to Japan, admission was first sought from the authorities, and for a time was refused. When various sects arose, persecutions were severe. We have seen how belief in Christianity was forbidden under pain of death for more than two hundred and fifty years. Under this edict, many thousand Japanese Christians and over two hundred European missionaries were put to death. Yet, on the whole, it may be said that Old Japan enjoyed no little religious freedom. Indeed, the same man might worship freely at all the shrines and temples in the land. To this day multitudes have never asked themselves whether they are Shinto or Buddhist or Confucianist. The reason for this religious eclecticism was the fractional character of the old religions; they supplemented each other. There was no collision between them in doctrine or in morals. The religious freedom was, therefore, not one of principle but of indifference. As Rome was tolerant of all religions which made no exclusive claims, but fiercely persecuted Christianity, so Japan was tolerant of the two religions that found their way into her territory because they made no claims of exclusiveness. But a religion that demanded the giving up of rivals was feared and forbidden.

New Japan, however, following Anglo-Saxon example, has definitely adopted religious freedom as a principle. First tacitly allowed after the abolition of the edict against Christianity in 1872, it was later publicly guaranteed by the constitution promulgated in 1888. Since that date there has been perfect religious liberty for the individual.

Yet this statement must be carefully guarded. If we may judge from some recent decrees of the Educational Department, it would appear that a large and powerful section of the nation is still ignorant of the real nature and significance of "religious liberty." Under the plea of maintaining secular education, the Educational Department has forbidden informal and private Christian teaching, even in private schools. An adequate statement of the present struggle for complete religious liberty would occupy many pages. We note but one important point.

In the very act of forbidding religious instruction in all schools the Educational Department is virtually establishing a brand-new religion for Japan, a religion based on the Imperial Educational Edict.[CF] The essentially religious nature of the attitude taken by the government toward this Edict has become increasingly clear in late years. In the summer of 1898 one who has had special opportunities of information told me that Mr. Kinoshita, a high official in the Educational Department, suggested the ceremonial worship of the Emperor's picture and edict by all the schools, for the reason that he saw the need of cultivating the religious spirit of reverence together with the need for having religious sanctions for the moral law. He felt convinced that a national school system without any such sanctions would be helpless in teaching morality to the pupils. His suggestion was adopted by the Educational Department and has been enforced.

In this attitude toward the religious character of entirely private schools, the government is materially abridging the religious liberty of the people. It is abridging their liberty of carrying belief into action in one important respect, that, namely, of giving a Christian education. It virtually insists on the acceptance of that form of religion which apotheosizes the Emperor, and finds the sanctions for morality in his edict; it excludes from the schools every other form of religion. It should, of course, be said that this attitude is maintained not only toward Christian schools, but theoretically also toward all religious schools. It, however, operates more severely on Christian schools than upon others, because Christians are the only ones who establish high-grade schools for secular education under religious influences.

It is evident, therefore, that in the matter of religious liberty the present attitude of the government is paradoxical, granting in one breath, what, in an important respect, it denies in the next. But throughout all these changes and by means of them we see more and more clearly that even religious tolerance is a matter of the prevailing social ideas and of the dominant social order, rather than of inherent race character. By a single transformation of the social order, Japan passed from a state of perfect religious intolerance to one just the reverse, so far as individual belief was concerned.

Taking a comprehensive review of our study thus far, we see that the forms of Japanese religious life have been determined by the history, rather than by any inherent racial character of the people. Although they had a religion prior to the coming of any external influence, yet they have proved ready disciples of the religions of other lands. The religion of India, its esoteric, and especially its exoteric forms, has found wide acceptance and long-continued popularity. The higher life of the nation readily took on in later times the religious characteristics of the Chinese, predominantly ethical, it is true, and only slightly religious as to forms of worship. When Roman Catholic Christianity came to Japan in the sixteenth century, it, too, found ready acceptance. It is true that it presented a view of the nature of religion not very different from that held by Buddhism in many respects, yet in others there was a marked divergence, as for instance, in the doctrine of God, of individual sin, and of the nature and method of salvation. The Japanese have thus shown themselves ready assimilators of all these diverse systems of religious expression. Just at present a new presentation of Christianity is being made to the Japanese; some are urging upon them the acceptance of the Roman Catholic form of it; others are urging the Greek; and still others are presenting the Protestant point of view. Each of these groups of missionaries seems to be reaping good harvests. Speaking from my own experience, I may say, that many of the Japanese show as great an appreciation of the essence of the religious life, and find the ideas and ideals, doctrines and ceremonies, of Christianity as fitted to their heart's deepest needs, as do any in the most enlightened parts of Christendom. It is true that the Christian system is so opposed to the Buddhistic and Shinto, and in some respects to the Confucian, that it is an exceedingly difficult matter at the beginning to give the Buddhist or Shintoist any idea of what Christianity is. Yet the difficulty arises not from the structure of the brain, nor from the inherent race character, but solely from the diversity of hitherto prevailing systems of thought. When once the passage from the one system of thought to the other has been effected, and the significance of the Christian system and life has been appreciated,—in other words, when the Japanese Buddhist or Shintoist or Confucianist has become a Christian,—he is as truly a Christian and as faithful as is the Englishman or American.

Of course I do not mean to say that he looks at every doctrine and at every ceremony in exactly the same way as an Englishman or American. But I do say that the different point of view is due to the differing social and religious history of the past and the differing surroundings of the present, rather than to inherent racial character or brain structure. The Japanese are human beings before they are Japanese.

For these reasons have I absolute confidence in the final acceptance of Christianity by the Japanese. There is no race characteristic in true Christianity that bars the way. Furthermore, the very growth of the Japanese in recent years, intellectually and in the reorganization of the social order, points to their final acceptance of Christianity and renders it necessary. The old religious forms are not satisfying the religious needs of to-day. And if history proves anything, it proves that only the religion of Jesus can do this permanently. Religion is a matter of humanity, not of nationality. It is for this reason that the world over, religions, though of so many forms, are still so much alike. And it is because the religion of Jesus is pre-eminently the religion of humanity and has not a trace of exclusive nationality about it, that it is the true religion, and is fitted to satisfy the deepest religious wants of the most highly developed as well as the least developed man of any and every race and nation. In proportion as man develops, he grows out of his narrow surroundings, both physical and mental and even moral; he enters a larger and larger world. The religious expressions of his nature in the local provincial and even national stages of his life cannot satisfy his larger potential life. Only the religion of humanity can do this. And this is the religion of Jesus. The white light of religion, no less than that of scientific truth, has no local or national coloring. Perfect truth is universal, eternal, unchangeable. Occidental or Oriental colorations are in reality defects, discolorations.

XXIX
SOME PRINCIPLES OF NATIONAL EVOLUTION

And now, having studied somewhat in detail various distinctive Japanese characteristics, it is important that we gain an insight into the general principles which govern the development of unified, national life. These principles render Japanese history luminous.

Let us first fix our attention on the fact that every step in the progress of mankind has been from smaller to larger communities. In other words, human progress has been through the increasing extension of the communal principle. The primitive segregative man, if there ever really was such a being, hardly deserves to be called man. Social qualities he had very slight, if at all; his altruistic actions and emotions were of the lowest and feeblest type. His life was so self-centered—we may not call it selfish, for he was not conscious of his self-centeredness—that he was quite sufficient to himself except for short periods of time. It was a matter of relative indifference to him whether his kinsmen survived or perished. His life was in only the slightest degree involved in theirs. The first step of progress for him depended on the development of some form of communal life. The primary problem of the social evolution of man was that of taking the wild, self-centered, self-sufficient man, and of teaching him to move in line with his fellow-men. And this problem confronted not only mankind at the beginning, but it has also been the great problem of each successive stage. After the individual has been taught to live with, to work with and for, and to love, his immediate kinsmen (in other words to merge his individual interests in those of the family, and to count the family interests of more importance than his own), the next step was to induce the family to look beyond its little world and be willing to work with and for neighboring families. When, after ages of conflict, this step was in a measure secured and the family-tribe was fairly formed, this group in turn must be taught to take into its view a still larger group, the tribal nation. Throughout the ages the constant problem has been the development of larger and larger communal groups. This general process has been very aptly called by Mr. Bagehot the taming process. The selfward thoughts and ambitions of the individual man have been thus far driven more and more into the background of fact, if not of consciousness. The individual has been brought into vital and organic relations with ever-increasing multitudes of his fellow-men. It is, therefore, pre-eminently a process of social or associational development. It not only develops social relations in an ever-increasing scale, but also social qualities and ideals and desires.

Now this taming, this socializing process, has been successful because it has had back of it, always enforcing it, the law of the survival of the strongest. What countless millions of men must have perished in the first step! They consisted of the less fit; of those who would not, or did not, learn soon enough the secret of existence through permanent family union. And what countless millions of families must have perished because they did not discover the way, or were too independent, to unite with kindred families in order to fight a common foe or develop a common food supply. And still later, what countless tribes must have

136

perished before the secret of tribal federation was widely accepted! In each case the problem has been to secure the subordination of the interests of the smaller and local community to those of the larger community. Death to self and life to the larger interest was often the condition of existence at all. How slow men always have been and still are to learn this great lesson of history!

The method whereby this taming process has been carried on has been through the formation of increasingly comprehensive and rigid customs and ideas. Through the development and continued existence of a common language, series of common customs, and sets of common ideas, unity was secured for the community; these, indeed, are the means whereby a group is transformed into a community. As the smaller community gave way to the larger, so the local languages, customs, and ideas had to break up and become so far modified as to form a new bond of unity. Until this unity was secured the new community was necessarily weak; the group easily broke up into its old constituent elements. We here gain a glimpse into one reason why the development of large composite communities, uniting and for the most part doing away with smaller ones, was so difficult and slow.

The process of absorption of smaller groups and their unification into larger ones, when carried out completely in any land, tends to arrest all further growth, not simply because there is no further room for expansion by the absorption of other divergent tribes, but also because the "cake of custom" is apt to become so hard, the uniformity enforced on all the individuals is liable to become so binding, that fruitful variation from within is effectually cut off. The evolution of relatively isolated or segregated groups necessarily produces variety; and the process whereby these divergent types of life and thought and organization are gradually brought together into one large community provides wide elements of variation, in the selection and general adoption of which the evolution of the whole community may be secured. But let the divergent elements of the lesser groups once be entirely absorbed by the composite community and let the "cake of custom" become so rigid that every individual who varies from it is branded as a heretic and a traitor, and the progressive evolution of that community must cease.

The great problem, therefore, which then confronts man and seems to threaten all further progress is, how to break the bondage of custom so as to secure local or individual variations. This can be done only through some form of individualism. The individual must be free to think and act as experience or fancy may suggest, without fear of being branded as a traitor, or at least he must have the courage to do so in spite of such fears. And to produce an effect on the community he must also be more or less protected in his idiosyncrasies by popular toleration.

He must be allowed to live and work out his theories, proving whether they are valuable or not. But since individualism is just what all previous communal development has been most assiduous in crushing out, how is the rise of individualism possible, or even desirable? If the first and continued development of man depended on the attainment and the maintenance of the communal principle, we may be sure that his further progress will not consist in the reversal of that principle. If, therfore, individualism must be developed, it must manifestly be of a variety which does not conflict with or abrogate communalism. Only as the individualistic includes the communal principle will it be a source of strength; otherwise it can only be a source of weakness to the community. But is not this an impossible condition to satisfy? Certainly, before the event, it would seem to be so. The rarity with which this step in human evolution has been taken would seem to show that it is far more difficult to accomplish than any of the previous steps. To give it a name we may call it communo-individualism. What this variety of individualism is, how this forward step was first actually taken, and how it is maintained and extended to-day, we shall consider in a later chapter. In the present place its importance for us is twofold. First we must realize the logical difficulty of the step—its apparently self-contradictory nature. And secondly we need to see that fully developed and continuously progressive national life is impossible without it. The development of a nation under the communal principle may advance far, even to the attainment of a relatively high grade of civilization. But the fully centralized and completely self-conscious nation cannot come into existence except on the basis of this last step of communo-individualism. The growth of nationalism proper, and the high development of civilization through the rise of the sciences and the arts based upon individualism, all await the dawn of the era of which communo-individualism is the leading, though at first unrecognized, characteristic.

This individualistic development of the communal principle is its intensive development; it is the focalizing and centralizing of the consciousness of the national unity in each individual member. The extensive process of communal enlargement must ever be accompanied by the intensive establishment in the individual of the communal ideal, the objective by the subjective, the physical by the psychical, if the accidental association for individual profit is to develop into the permanent association for the national as well as the individual life. The intensive or subjective development of the communal principle does, as a matter of fact, take place in all growing communities, but it is largely unconscious. Not until the final stages of national development does it become a self-conscious process, deserving the distinctive name I have given it here, communo-individualism.[CG]

The point just made is, however, only one aspect of a more general fact, too, of cardinal importance for the sociologist and the student of human evolution. It is that, throughout the entire period of the expansion of the community, there has been an equally profound, although wholly unconscious, development of the individual. This fact seems to have largely escaped the notice of all but the most recent thinkers and writers on the general topic of human and social evolution. The fact and the importance of the communal life have been so manifest that, in important senses, the individual has been almost, if not wholly, dropped out of sight. The individual has been conceived to have been from the very beginning of social evolution fully endowed with mind, ideas, and brains, and to be perfectly regardless of all other human beings. The development of the community has accordingly been conceived to be a progressive taming and subduing of this wild, self-centered, primitive man; a process of eliminating his individualistic instincts. So far as the individual is concerned, it has been conceived to be chiefly a negative process; a process of destroying his individual desires and plans and passions. Man's natural state has been supposed to be that of absolute selfishness. Only the hard necessity of natural law succeeded in forcing him to curb his natural selfish desires and to unite with his fellows. Only on these terms could he maintain even an existence. Those who have not accepted these terms have been exterminated. Communal life in all its forms, from the family upward to the most unified and developed nation, is thus conceived as a continued limiting of the individual—a necessity, indeed, to his existence, but none the less a limitation.

I am unable to take this view, which at best is a one-sided statement. It appears to me capable of demonstration, that communal and individual development proceed pari passu; that every gain in the communal life is a gain to the individual and vice versa. They are complementary, not contradictory processes. Neither can exist, in any proper sense, apart from the other; and the degree of the development of the one is a sure index of the degree of the development of the other. So important is this matter that we must pause to give it further consideration.

Consider, first, man in his earliest stage of development. A relatively segregarious animal; with a few ideas about the nuts and fruits and roots on which he lives; with a little knowledge as to where to find them; the subject of constant fear lest a stronger man may suddenly appear to seize and carry off his wife and food; possessing possibly a few articulate sounds answering to words; such probably was primitive man. He must have been little removed from the ape. His "self," his mind, was so small and so empty of content that we could hardly recognize him as a man, should we stumble on him in the forest.

Look next upon him after he has become a family-man. Living in the group, his life enlarges; his existence broadens; his ideas multiply; his vocabulary increases with his ideas and experiences; he begins to share the life and thinking and interests and joys and sorrows of others; their ideas and experiences become his, to his enormous advantage. What he now is throws into the shade of night what he used to be. So far from being the loser by his acceptance of even this limited communal life, he is a gainer in every way. He begins to know what love is, and hate; what joy is, and sorrow; what kindness is, and cruelty; what altruism is, and selfishness. Thus, not only in ideas and language, in industry and property, but also in emotions, in character, in morality, in religion, in the knowledge of self, and even in opportunity for selfishness, he is the gainer. In just the degree that communal life is developed is the life of the individuals that compose it extended both subjectively and objectively. Human psychogenesis takes place in the communal stage of his life. Human association is its chief external cause.

It matters not at what successive stage of man's developing life we may choose to look at him, the depth and height and breadth, in a word, the fullness and vigor and character of the inner and private life of the individual, will depend directly on the nature and development of the communal life. As the community expands, taking in new families or tribes or nations, reaching out to new regions, learning new industries, developing new ideas of man, of nature, of the gods, of duty, inventing new industries, discovering new truths, and developing a new language, all these fresh acquirements of the community become the possession of its individual members. In the growing complexity of society the individual unit, it is true, is increasingly lost among the millions of his fellow-units, yet all these successive steps serve to render his life the larger and richer. His horizon is no longer the little family group in which he was born; he now looks out over large and populous regions and feels the thrill of his growing life as he realizes the unity and community of his life and interests with those of his fellow-countrymen. His language is increasingly enriched; it serves to shape all his thinking and thus even the structure of his mind. His knowledge reaches far beyond his own experience; it includes not only that of the few persons whom he knows directly, but also that of unnumbered millions, remote in time and space. He increasingly discovers, though he never has analyzed, and is perhaps wholly unable to analyze, the discovery that he is not a thing among things; his life has a universal aspect. He lives more and more the universal life, subjecting the demands of the once domineering present to decisions of a cool judgment that looks back into the past and carefully weighs the interests of the future, temporal and eternal. Every advance made by the community is thus stored up to the credit of its individual members. So far, then, from the development of the communal principle consisting of and coming about through a limitation of the individual, it is exactly the reverse. Only as the individual develops are communal unity and progress possible. And on the other hand, only where the communal principle has reached its highest development, both extensively and intensively, do we find the most highly developed personality. The one is a necessary condition of the other. The deepest, blackest selfishness, even, can only come into existence where the communal principle has reached its highest development.

The preceding statement, however, is not equivalent to saying that when communalism and individualism arose in human consciousness they were both accepted as equally important. The reverse seems always to have been the case. As soon as the two principles are distinguished in thought, the communal is at once ranked as the higher, and the individual principle is scorned if not actually rejected. And the reason for this is manifest. From earliest times the constant foe which the community has had to fight and exterminate has been the wanton, selfish individual. Individualism of this type was the spontaneous contrast to the communal life, and was ever manifesting itself. No age or race has been without it, nor ignorant of it. As soon as the two principles became clearly contrasted in thought, therefore, because of his actual experience, man could conceive of individualism only as the antithesis to communalism; it was felt that the two were mutually destructive. It inevitably followed that communalism as a principle was accepted and individualism condemned. In their minds not only social order, but existence itself, was at stake. And they were right. Egoistic individualism is necessarily atomistic. No society can long maintain its life as a unified and peaceful society, when such a principle has been widely accepted by its members. The social ills of this and of every age largely arise from the presence of this type of men, who hold this principle of life.

If, therefore, after a fair degree of national unity has been attained, the higher stages of national evolution depend on the higher development of individualism, and if the only kind of individualism of which men can conceive is the egoistic, it becomes evident that further progress must cease. Stagnation, or degeneration, must follow. This is what has happened to nearly all the great nations and races of the world. They progressed well up to a

139

certain point. Then they halted or fell back. The only possible condition under which a new lease of progressive life could be secured by them was a new variety of individualism, which would unite the opposite and apparently contradictory poles of communalism and egoism, namely, communo-individualism. Inconceivable though it be to those men and nations who have not experienced this type of life, it is nevertheless a fact, and a mighty factor in human and in national evolution. In its light we are able to see that the communal life itself has not reached its fullest development until the individualistic principle has been not only recognized in thought, but exalted, both in theory and in fact, to its true and coordinate position beside the communal principle. Only then does the nation become fully and completely organized. Only then does the national organism contain within itself the means for an endless, because a self-sustained, life.

It is important to guard against a misunderstanding of the principles just enunciated which may easily arise. In saying that the development of the individual has proceeded pari passu with that of the community, that every gain by the community has contributed directly to the development of the individual, I do not say that the communal profits are at once distributed among all the members of the group, or that the distribution is at all equal. Indeed, such is far from the case. Some few individuals seem to appropriate a large and unfair proportion of the communal bank account. So far as a people live a simple and relatively undifferentiated life, all sharing in much the same kind of pursuits, and enjoying much the same grade of life,—such as prevailed in a large measure in the earlier times, and decreasingly as society has become industrial,—and so far also as the new acquirements of thought are transformed into practical life and common language, all the members of the community share these acquirements in fairly equal measure. So far, however, as the communal profits consist of more or less abstract ideas, embodied in religious and philosophic thought, and stored away in books and literature accessible only to scholars, they are distributed very unequally. The more highly developed and consequently differentiated the society, the more difficult does distribution become. The very structure of the highly differentiated communal organism forbids the equal distribution of these goods. The literary and ruling minority have exclusive access to the treasures. The industrial majority are more and more rigidly excluded from them. Thus, although it is strictly true that every advance in the communal principle accrues to the benefit of the individual, it is not true that such advance necessarily accrues to the benefit of every individual, or equally to all individuals. In its lowest stages, developing communalism lifts all its individual members to about the same level of mental and moral acquirement. In its middle stages it develops all individuals to a certain degree, and certain individuals to a high degree. In its highest stages it develops among all its members a uniformly high grade of personal worth and acquirement.

Now the great problem on whose solution depends the possibility of continued communal evolution is, from this view-point, the problem of distributing the gains of the community to all its members more and more equally. It is the problem of giving to each human unit all the best and truest thought and character, all the highest and noblest ideals and motives, which the most advanced individuals have secured. If we stop to inquire minutely and analytically just what is the nature of the greatest attainments made by the community, we discover that it is not the possession of wealth in land or gold, it is not the accident of social rank, it is not any incident of temporal happiness or physical ease of life. It consists, on the contrary, in the discovery of the real nature of man. He is no mere animal, living in the realm of things and pleasures, limited by the now and the here. He is a person, a rational being. His thoughts and desires can only be expressed in terms of infinity. Nothing short of the infinite can satisfy either his reason or his heart Though living in nature and dependent on it, he is above it, and may and should understand it and rule it. His thoughts embrace all time and all being. In a very real sense he lives an infinite and eternal life, even here in this passing world.

The discovery of this set of facts, slowly emerging into consciousness, is the culmination of all past history, and the beginning of all man's higher life. It is the turning point in the history of the human race. Every onward step in man's preceding life, whereby he has united to form higher and higher groups, has been leading onward and upward to the

140

development of strong personality, to the development of individuals competent to make this great discovery. But this is not enough.

The next step is to discover the fact, *and to believe it*, that this infinite life is the potential possession of every member of the community; that the bank account which the community has been storing up for ages is for the use not only of a favored few, but also of the masses. That since every man is a man, he has an infinite and an eternal life and value, which no accident of birth, or poverty, can annul. Each man needs to discover himself. The great problem, then, which confronts progressive communal evolution is to take this enlarged definition of the individual and scatter it broadcast over the land, persuading all men to accept and believe it both for themselves and for others. This definition must be carried in full confidence to the lowest, meanest, most ignorant man that lives in the community, and by its help this down-most man must be shown his birthright, and in the light of it he must be raised to actual manhood. He must "come to himself"; only so can he qualify for his heritage.

After a nation, therefore, has secured a large degree of unity, of the confederated tribal type, the step which must be taken, before it can proceed to more complete nationalization even, is, first, the discovery of personality as the real and essential characteristic of men, and secondly the discovery that high-grade personality may and can and must be developed in all the members of the community. In proportion as the members of the community become conscious persons, fully self-conscious and self-regulating, fully imbued with the idea and the spirit of true personality, of communo-individualism, in that proportion will the community be unified and centralized, as well as capable of the most complex and differentiated internal structure. The strength of such a nation will be indefinitely greater than that of any other less personalized and so less communalized nation.

XXX

ARE THE JAPANESE IMPERSONAL?

Few phases of the Japanese character have proved so fascinating to the philosophical writer on Japan as that of the personality of this Far Eastern people. From the writings of Sir Rutherford Alcock, the first resident English minister in Japan, down to the last publication that has come under my eye, all have something to say on this topic. One writer, Mr. Percival Lowell, has devoted an entire volume to it under the title of "The Soul of the Far East," in which he endeavors to establish the position that the entire civilization of the Orient, in its institutions, such as the family and the state, in the structure of its language, in its conceptions of nature, in its art, in its religion, and finally in its inherent mental nature, is essentially *impersonal.* One of the prominent and long resident missionaries in Japan once delivered a course of lectures on the influence of pantheism in the Orient, in which he contended, among other things, that the lack of personal pronouns and other phenomena of Japanese life and religion are due to the presence and power in this land of pantheistic philosophy preventing the development of personality.

The more I have examined these writings and their fundamental assumptions, the more manifest have ambiguities and contradictions in the use of terms become. I have become also increasingly impressed with the failure of advocates of Japanese "impersonality" to appreciate the real nature of the phenomena they seek to explain. They have not comprehended the nature or the course of social evolution, nor have they discovered the mutual relation existing between the social order and personality. The arguments advanced for the "impersonal" view are more or less plausible, and this method of interpreting the Orient appeals for authority to respectable philosophical writers. No less a philosopher than Hegel is committed to this interpretation. The importance of this subject, not only for a correct understanding of Japan, but also of the relation existing between individual, social, and religious evolution, requires us to give it careful attention. We shall make our way most easily into this difficult discussion by considering some prevalent misconceptions and defective arguments. I may here express my indebtedness to the author of "The Soul of the Far East" for the stimulus received from his brilliant volume, differ though I do from his main thesis. We begin this study with a few quotations from Mr. Lowell's now classic work.

141

"Capability to evolve anything is not one of the marked characteristics of the Far East. Indeed, the tendency to spontaneous variation, Nature's mode of making experiments, would seem there to have been an enterprising faculty that was early exhausted. Sleepy, no doubt, from having got up betimes with the dawn, these inhabitants of the land of the morning began to look upon their day as already far spent before they had reached its noon. They grew old young, and have remained much the same age ever since. What they were centuries ago, that at bottom they are to-day. Take away the European influences of the past twenty years, and each man might almost be his own great-grandfather. In race character, he is yet essentially the same. The traits that distinguished these peoples in the past have been gradually extinguishing them ever since. Of these traits, stagnating influences upon their career, perhaps the most important is the great quality of "impersonality."[CGa] "The peoples inhabiting it [the northern hemisphere] grow steadily more personal as we go West. So unmistakable is this gradation that we are almost tempted to ascribe it to cosmical rather than to human causes.... The sense of self grows more intense as we follow the wake of the setting sun, and fades steadily as we advance into the dawn. America, Europe, the Levant, India, Japan, each is less personal than the one before. We stand at the nearer end of the scale, the Far Orientals at the other. If with us the 'I' seems to be the very essence of the soul, then the soul of the Far East may be said to be 'Impersonality.'"[CH]

Following the argument through the volume we see that individual physical force and aggressiveness, deficiency of politeness, and selfishness are, according to this line of thought, essential elements of personality. The opposite set of qualities constitutes the essence of impersonality. "The average Far Oriental, indeed, talks as much to no purpose as his Western cousin, only in his chit-chat politeness takes the place of personalities. With him, self is suppressed, and an ever-present regard for others is substituted in its stead. A lack of personality is, as we have seen, the occasion of this courtesy; it is also its cause.... Considered a priori, the connection between the two is not far to seek. Impersonality, by lessening the interest in one's self, induces one to take an interest in others. Introspection tends to make a man a solitary animal, the absence of it a social one. The more impersonal the people, the more will the community supplant the individual in the popular estimation.... Then, as the social desires develop, politeness, being the means of their enjoyment, develops also."[CI]

Let us take a look at some definitions:

"Individuality, personality, and the sense of self, are only three aspects of the same thing. They are so many various views of the soul, according as we regard it from an intrinsic, an altruistic, or an egoistic standpoint.... By individuality we mean that bundle of ideas, thoughts, and day-dreams which constitute our separate identity, and by virtue of which we feel each one of us at home within himself.... Consciousness is the necessary attribute of mental action. Not only is it the sole way we have of knowing mind; without it there would be no mind to know. Not to be conscious of one's self is, mentally speaking, not to be. This complex entity, this little cosmos of a world, the 'I,' has for its very law of existence, self-consciousness, while personality is the effect it produces upon the consciousness of others."[CJ]

The more we study the above definitions, the more baffling they become. Try as I may, I have not been able to fit them, not only to the facts of my own experience, which may not be strange, but I cannot reconcile them even to each other. There seem to me inherent ambiguities and self-contradictions lurking beneath their scientific splendor. Individuality is stated to be "that bundle of ideas, thoughts, and day-dreams which constitute our separate identity." This seems plain and straightforward, but is it really so? Consciousness is stated to be not only "the necessary attribute of mental action" (to which exception might be taken on the ground of abundant proof of unconscious mental action), but it is also considered to be the very cause of mind itself. Not only by consciousness do we know mind, but the consciousness itself constitutes the mind; "without it there would be no mind to know." "Not to be conscious of one's self is not to be." Do we then cease to be, when we sleep? or when absorbed in thought or action? And do we become new-created when we awake? What is the bond of connection that binds into one the successive consciousnesses of the successive days? Does not that "bundle of ideas" become broken into as many wholly independent fragments as there are intervals between our sleepings? Or rather is not each fragment a whole in itself, and is not the idea of self-continuity from day to day and from week to week a self-delusion? How can it be otherwise if consciousness constitutes existence? For after the consciousness has ceased and "the bundle of ideas," which constitutes the individuality of that day, has therefore gone absolutely out of existence, it is impossible that the old bundle shall be resurrected by a new consciousness. Only a new bundle can be the product of a new consciousness. Evidently there is trouble somewhere. But let us pass on.

"The 'I' has for its very law of existence self-consciousness." Is not "self-consciousness" here identified with "consciousness" in the preceding sentence? The very existence of the mind, the "I," is ascribed to each in turn. Is there, then, no difference between consciousness and self-consciousness? Finally, personality is stated to be "the effect it [the "I"] produces on the self-consciousness of others." I confess I gain no clear idea from this statement. But whatever else it may mean, this is clear, that personality is not a quality or characteristic of the "I," but only some effect which the "I" produces on the consciousness of another. Is it a quality, then, of the other person? And does impersonality mean the lack of such an effect? But does not this introduce us to new confusion? When a human being is wholly absorbed in an altruistic act, for instance, wholly forgetful of self, he is, according to a preceding paragraph, quite impersonal; yet, according to the definition before us, he cannot be impersonal, for he is producing most lively effects on the consciousness of the poor human being he is befriending; in his altruistic deed he is strongly personal, yet not he, for personality does not belong to the person acting, but somehow to the person affected. How strange that the personality of a person is not his own characteristic but another's!

But still more confusing is the definition when we recall that if the benevolent man is wholly unconscious of self, and is thinking only of the one whom he is helping, then he himself is no longer existing. But in that case how can he help the poor man or even continue to think of him? Perfect altruism is self-annihilation! Knowledge of itself by the mind is that which constitutes it! But enough. It has become clear that these terms have not been used consistently, nor are the definitions such as to command the assent of any careful psychologist or philosopher. What the writer means to say is, I judge, that the measure of a man's personality is the amount of impression he makes on his fellows. For the whole drift of his argument is that both the physical and mental aggressiveness of the Occidental is far greater than that of the Oriental; this characteristic, he asserts, is due to the deficient development of personality in the Orient, and this deficient development he calls "impersonality." If those writers who describe the Orient as "impersonal" fail in their definition of the term "personal," their failure to define "impersonal" is even more striking. They use the term as if it were so well known as to need no definition; yet their usage ascribes to it contrary conceptions. As a rule they conceive of "impersonality" as a deficiency of development; yet, when they attempt to describe its nature, they speak of it as self-suppression. A clear statement of this latter point may be found in a passage already quoted: "Politeness takes the place of personalities. With him [the Oriental], self is suppressed, and an ever-present regard for others is substituted." "Impersonality, by lessening the interest in one's self, induces one to take interest in others." In this statement it will be noted the "*self is suppressed.*" Does "impersonality" then follow personality, as a matter of historical development? It would so appear from this and kindred passages. But if this is true, then Japan is *more* instead of less developed than the Occident. Yet this is exactly the reverse of that for which this school of thought contends.

Let us now examine some concrete illustrations adduced by those who advocate Japanese impersonality. They may be arranged in two classes: those that are due wholly to invention, and those that are doubtless facts, but that may be better accounted for by some other theory than that of "impersonality."

Mr. Lowell makes amusing material out of the two children's festivals, known by the Japanese as "Sekku," occurring on March 3 and June 5 (old calendar). Because the first of these is exclusively for the girls and the second is exclusively for the boys, Mr. Lowell concludes that they are general birthdays, in spite of the fact which he seems to know that the ages are not reckoned from these days. He calls them "the great impersonal birthdays"; for, according to his supposition, all the girls celebrate their birthdays on the third day of the third moon and all the boys celebrate theirs on the fifth day of the fifth moon, regardless of the actual days on which they may have been born. With regard to this understanding of the significance of the festival, I have asked a large number of Japanese, not one of whom had ever heard of such an idea. Each one has insisted that individual birthdays are celebrated regardless of these general festivals; the ages of children are never computed from these festivals; they have nothing whatever to do with the ages of the children.[CK]

The report of the discussions of the Japanese Society of Comparative Religion contains quite a minute statement of all the facts known as to these festivals, much too long in this connection, but among them there is not the slightest reference to the birthday feature attributed to them by Mr. Lowell.[CL]

Mr. Lowell likewise invents another fact in support of his theory by his interpretation of the Japanese method of computing ages. Speaking of the advent of an infant into the home he says, that "from the moment he makes his appearance he is spoken of as a year old, and this same age he continues to be considered in most simple cases of calculation, till the beginning of the next calendar year. When that epoch of general rejoicing arrives, he is credited with another year himself. So is everybody else. New Year's day is a common birthday for the community, a sort of impersonal anniversary for his whole world." Now this is a very entertaining conceit, but it will hardly pass muster as a serious argument with one who has any real understanding of Japanese ideas on the subject. The simple fact is that the Japanese does not ordinarily tell you how old the child is, but only in how many year periods he has lived. Though born December 31, on January 1 he has undoubtedly lived in two different year periods. This method of counting, however, is not confined to the counting of ages, but it characterizes all their counting. If you ask a man how many days before a certain festival near at hand he will say ten where we would say but nine. In other words, in counting periods the Japanese count all, including both the first and the last, whereas we omit the first. This as a custom is an interesting psychological problem, but it has not the remotest connection with "personality" or "impersonality." Furthermore, the Japanese have another method of signifying the age of a child which corresponds exactly to ours. You have but to ask what is the "full" age of a child to receive a statement which satisfies our ideas of the problem. The idea of calling New Year's day a great "impersonal" birthday because forsooth all the members of the community and the nation then enter on a new year period, and of using that as an argument for the "impersonality" of the whole race, is as interesting as it is inconclusive.

Much is made of the fact that Japanese art has paid its chief attention to nature and to animals, and but little to man. This proves, it is argued, that the Japanese artist and people are "impersonal"—that they are not self-conscious, for their gaze is directed outward, toward "impersonal" nature; had they been an aggressive personal people, a people conscious of self, their art would have depicted man. The cogency of this logic seems questionable to me. Art is necessarily objective, whether it depicts nature or man; the gaze is always and necessarily outward, even when it is depicting the human form. In our consideration of the æsthetic elements of Japanese character[CM] we gave reasons for the Japanese love of natural beauty and for their relatively slight attention to the human form. If the reasons there given were correct, the fact that Japanese art is concerned chiefly with nature has nothing whatever to do with the "impersonality" of the people. If "impersonality" is essentially altruistic, if it consists of self-suppression and interest in others, then it is difficult to see how art that depicts the form even of human beings can escape the charge of being "impersonal" except when the artist is depicting himself. If, again, supreme interest in objective "impersonal" nature proves the lack of "personality," should we not argue that the West is supremely "impersonal" because of its extraordinary interest in nature and in the natural and physical sciences? Are naturalists and scientists "impersonal," and are philosophers and psychologists "personal" in nature? If it be argued that art which depicts the human emotions is properly speaking subjective, and therefore a proof of developed personality, will it be maintained that Japan is devoid of such art? How about the pictures and the statues of warriors? How about the passionate features of the Ni-o, the placid faces of the Buddhas and other religious imagery? Are there not here the most powerful representations possible of human emotions, both active and passive? But even so, is not the gaze of the artist still *outward* on others, *i.e.*, is he not altruistic; and, therefore, "impersonal," according to this method of thought and use of terms? Are European artists who revel in landscape and animal scenes deficient in "personal" development, and are those who devote their lives to painting nude women particularly developed in "personality"? Truly, a defective terminology and a distorted conception of what "personality" is, land one in most contradictory positions.

Those who urge the "impersonality" of the Orient make much of the Japanese idea of the "family," with the attendant customs. The fact that marriage is arranged for by the parents, and that the two individuals most concerned have practically no voice in the matter, proves conclusively, they argue, that the latter have little "personality." Here again all turns on the definition of this important word. If by "personality" is meant consciousness of one's self as an independent individual, then I do not see what relation the two subjects have. If, however, it means the willingness of the subjects of marriage to forego their own desires and choices; because indeed they do not have any of their own, then the facts will not bear out the argument. These writers skillfully choose certain facts out of the family customs whereby to illustrate and enforce this theory, but they entirely omit others having a significant bearing upon it. Take, for instance, the fact that one-third of the marriages end in divorce. What does this show? It shows that one-third of the individuals in each marriage are so dissatisfied with the arrangements made by the parents that they reject them and assert their own choice and decision. According to the argument for "impersonality" in marriage, these recalcitrant, unsubmissive individuals have a great amount of "personality," that is, consciousness of self; and this consciousness of self produces a great effect on the other party to the marriage; and the effect on the other party (in the vast majority of the cases women), that is to say, the effect of the divorce on the consciousness of the women, constitutes the personality of the men! The marriage customs cited, therefore, do not prove the point, for no account is taken of the multitudinous cases in which one party or the other utterly refuses to carry out the arrangements of the parents. Many a girl declines from the beginning the proposals of the parents. These cases are by no means few. Only a few days before writing the present lines a waiting girl in a hotel requested me to find her a place of service in some foreign family. On inquiry she told me how her parents wished her to marry into a certain family; but that she could not endure the thought and had run away from home. One of the facts which strike a missionary, as he becomes acquainted with the people, is the frequency of the cases of running away from home. Girls run away, probably not as frequently as boys, yet very often. Are we to believe that these are individuals who have an excessive amount of "personality"? If so, then the development of "personality" in Japan is far more than the advocates of its "impersonality" recognize or would allow us to believe. Mr. Lowell devotes three pages to a beautiful and truthful description of the experience known in the West as "falling in love." Turning his attention to the Orient, because of the fact that marriages are arranged for by the families concerned, he argues that: "No such blissful infatuation falls to the lot of the Far Oriental. He never is the dupe of his own desire, the willing victim of his self-delusion. He is never tempted to reveal himself, and by thus revealing, realize.... For she is not his love; she is only his wife; and what is left of a romance when the romance is left out?" Although there is an element of truth in this, yet it is useless as a support for the theory of Japanese "impersonality." For it is not a fact that the Japanese do not fall in love; it is a well-known experience to them. It is inconceivable how anyone at all acquainted with either Japanese life or literature could make such an assertion. The passionate love of a man and a woman for each other, so strong that in multitudes of cases the two prefer a common death to a life apart, is a not uncommon event in Japan. Frequently we read in the daily papers of a case of mutual suicide for love. This is sufficiently common to have received a specific name "joshi."[CN]

So far as the argument for "impersonality" is concerned this illustration from the asserted lack of love is useless, for it is one of those manufactured for the occasion by imaginative and resourceful advocates of "impersonality."

But I do not mean to say that "falling in love" plays the same important part in the life and development of the youth in Japan that it does in the West. It is usually utterly ignored, so far as parental planning for marriage is concerned. Love is not recognized as a proper basis for the contraction of marriage, and is accordingly frowned upon. It is deemed a sign of mental and moral weakness for a man to fall in love. Under these conditions it is not at all strange that "falling in love" is not so common an experience as in the West. Furthermore, this profound experience is not utilized as it is in the West as a refining and elevating influence in the life of a young man or woman. In a land where "falling in love" is regarded as an immoral thing, a breaking out of uncontrollable animal passion, it is not strange that it should not be glorified by moralists or sanctified by religion. There are few experiences in the West so ennobling as the love that a young man and a young woman bear to each other during the days of their engagement and lasting onward throughout the years of their lengthening married life. The West has found the secret of making use of this period in the lives of the young to elevate and purify them of which the East knows little.

But there are still other and sadder consequences following from the attitude of the Japanese to the question of "falling in love." It can hardly be doubted that the vast number of divorces is due to the defective method of betrothal, a method which disregards the free choice of the parties most concerned. The system of divorce is, we may say, the device of society for remedying the inherent defects of the betrothal system. It treats both the man and the woman as though they were not persons but unfeeling machines. Personality, for a while submissive, soon asserts its liberty, in case the married parties prove uncongenial, and demands the right of divorce. Divorce is thus the device of thwarted personality. But in addition to this evil, there is that of concubinage or virtual polygamy, which is often the result of "falling in love." And then, there is the resort of hopelessly thwarted personality known in the West as well as in the East, murder and suicide, and oftentimes even double suicide, referred to above. The marriage customs of the Orient are such that hopeless love, though mutual, is far more frequent than in the West, and the death of lovers in each other's arms, after having together taken the fatal draught, is not rare. The number of suicides due to hopeless love in 1894 was 407, and the number of murders for the same cause was 94. Here is a total of over five hundred deaths in a single year, very largely due to the defective marriage system. Do not these phenomena refute assertions to the effect that the Japanese are so impersonal as not to know what it is to "fall in love"? If the question of the personality of the Japanese is to be settled by the phenomena of family life and the strength of the sexual emotion, would we not have to pronounce them possessed of strongly developed personality?

XXXI
THE JAPANESE NOT IMPERSONAL

We must now face the far more difficult task of presenting a positive statement in regard to the problem of personality in the Orient. We need to discover just what is or should be meant by the terms "personality" and "impersonality." We must also analyze this Oriental civilization and discover its elementary factors, in order that we may see what it is that has given the impression to so many students that the Orient is "impersonal." In doing this, although our aim is constructive, we shall attain our end with greater ease if we rise to positive results through further criticism of defective views. We naturally begin with definitions.

"Individuality" is defined by the Standard Dictionary as "the state or quality of being individual; separate or distinct existence." "Individual" is defined as "Anything that cannot be divided or separated into parts without losing identity.... A single person, animal, or thing." "Personality" is defined as "That which constitutes a person; conscious, separate existence as an intelligent and voluntary being." "Person" is defined as "Any being having life, intelligence, will, and separate individual existence." On these various definitions the following observations seem pertinent.

"Individuality" has reference only to the distinctions existing between different objects, persons, or things. The term draws attention to the fact of distinctness and difference and not to the qualities which make the difference, and least of all to the consciousness of identity by virtue of which "we feel each one of us at home within himself."

146

"Personality" properly has reference only to that which constitutes a person. As contrasted with an animal a person has not only life, but also a highly developed and self-conscious intelligence, feeling, and will; these involve moral relations toward other persons and religious relations toward God.

Consciousness is not attendant on every act of the person, much less is self-consciousness, although both are always potential and more or less implicit. A person is often so absorbed in thought or act as to be wholly unconscious of his thinking or acting; the consciousness is, so to speak, submerged for the time being. Self-consciousness implies considerable progress in reflection on one's own states of mind, and in the attainment of the consciousness of one's own individuality. It is the result of introspection. Self-consciousness, however, does not constitute one's identity; it merely recognizes it.

The foundation for a correct conception of the term "personality" rests on the conception of the term "soul" or "spirit." In my judgment, each human being is to be conceived as being a separate "soul," endowed by its very nature with definite capacities or qualities or attributes which we describe as mental, emotional, and volitional, having powers of consciousness more or less developed according to the social evolution of the race, the age of the individual, his individual environment, and depending also on the amount of education he may have received. The possession of a soul endowed with these qualities constitutes a person; their possession in marked measure constitutes developed personality, and in defective measure, undeveloped personality.

The unique character of a "person" is that he combines perfect separateness with the possibility and more or less of the actuality of perfect universality. A "person" is in a true sense a universal, an infinite being. He is thus through the constitution of his psychic nature a thinking, feeling, and willing being. Through his intellect and in proportion to his knowledge he becomes united with the whole objective universe; through his feelings he may become united in sympathy and love with all sentient creation, and even with God himself, the center and source of all being; through his active will he is increasingly creator of his environment. Man is thus in a true sense creating the conditions which make him to be what he is. Thus in no figurative sense, but literally and actually, man is in the process of creating himself. He is realizing the latent and hitherto unsuspected potentialities of his nature. He is creating a world in which to express himself; and this he does by expressing himself. In proportion as man advances, making explicit what is implicit in his inner nature, is he said to grow in personality. A man thus both possesses personality and grows in personality. He could not grow in it did he not already actually possess it. In such growth both elements of his being, the individual and the universal, develop simultaneously. A person of inferior personal development is at once less individual and less universal. This is a matter, however, not of endowment but of development. We thus distinguish between the original personal endowment, which we may call intrinsic or inherent personality, and the various forms in which this personality has manifested and expressed itself, which we may call extrinsic or acquired personality. Inherent personality is that which differentiates man from animal. It constitutes the original involution which explains and even necessitates man's entire evolution. There may be, nay, must be, varying degrees of expression of the inherent personality, just as there may be and must be varying degrees of consciousness of personality. These depend on the degree of evolution attained by the race and by the individuals of the race.

It is no part of our plan to justify this conception of the nature of personality, or to defend these brief summary statements as to its inherent nature. It is enough if we have gained a clear idea of this conception on which the present chapter, and indeed this entire work, rests. In discussing the question as to personality in the Orient, it is important for us ever to bear in mind the distinctions between the inherent endowment that constitutes personal beings, the explicit and external expression of that endowment, and the possession of the consciousness of that endowment. For these are three things quite distinct, though intimately related.

The term "impersonality" demands special attention, being the most misused and abused term of all. The first and natural signification of the word is the mere negation of personality; as a stone, for instance, is strictly "impersonal." This is the meaning given by the dictionaries. But in this sense, of course, it is inapplicable to human beings. What, then, is the meaning when applied to them? When Mr. Lowell says, "If with us [of the West] the 'I' seems to be of the very essence of the soul, then the soul of the Far East may be said to be 'impersonal,'" what does he mean? He certainly does not mean that the Chinese and Japanese and Hindus have no emotional or volitional characteristics, that they are strictly "impersonal"; nor does he mean that the Oriental has less development of powers of thinking, willing, feeling, or of introspective meditation. The whole argument shows that he means that *their sense of the individuality or separateness of the Ego is so slight that it is practically ignored; and this not by their civilization alone, but by each individual himself.* The supreme consciousness of the individual is not of himself, but of his family or race; or if he is an intensely religious man, his consciousness is concerned with his essential identity with the Absolute and Ultimate Being, rather than with his own separate self. In other words, the term "impersonal" is made to do duty for the non-existent negative of "individual." "Impersonal" is thus equivalent to "universal" and personal to "individual." To change the phraseology, the term "impersonal" is used to signify a state of mind in which the separateness or individuality of the individual ego is not fully recognized or appreciated even by the individual himself. The prominent element of the individual's consciousness is the unity or the universalism, rather than the multiplicity or individualism.

Mr. Lowell in effect says this in his closing chapter entitled "Imagination." His thesis seems to be that the universal mind, of which, each individual receives a fragment, becomes increasingly differentiated as the race mind evolves. In proportion as the evolution has progressed does the individual realize his individuality—his separateness; this individualization, this differentiation of the individual mind is, in his view, the measure as well as the cause of the higher civilization. The lack of such individualization he calls "impersonality"; in such a mind the dominant thought is not of the separateness between, but of the unity that binds together, himself and the universal mind.

If the above is a correct statement of the conception of those who emphasize the "impersonality" of the Orient, then there are two things concerning it which may be said at once. First, the idea is a perfectly clear and intelligible one, the proposition is definite and tangible. But why do they not so express it? The terms "personality" and "individuality" are used synonymously; while "impersonal" is considered the equivalent of the negative of individual, un-individual—a word which has not yet been and probably never will be used. But the negation of individual is universal; "impersonal," therefore, according to the usage of these writers, becomes equivalent to universal.

But, secondly, even after the use of terms has become thus understood, and we are no longer confused over the words, having arrived at the idea they are intended to convey, the idea itself is fundamentally erroneous. I freely admit that there is an interesting truth of which these writers have got a glimpse and to which they are striving to give expression, but apparently they have not understood the real nature of this truth and consequently they are fundamentally wrong in calling the Far East "impersonal," even in their sense of the word. They are furthermore in error, in ascribing this "impersonal" characteristic of the Japanese to their inherent race nature, If they are right, the problem is fundamentally one of biological evolution.

In contrast to this view, it is here contended, first, that the feature they are describing is not such as they describe it; second, that it is not properly called "impersonality"; third, that it is not a matter of inherent race nature, of brain structure, or of mind differentiation, but wholly a matter of social evolution; and, fourth, that if there is such a trait as they describe, it is not due to a deficiently developed but on the contrary to a superlatively developed personality, which might better be called super-personality. To state the position here advocated in a nutshell, it is maintained that the asserted "impersonality" of the Japanese is the result of the communalistic nature of the social order which has prevailed down to the most recent times; it has put its stamp on every feature of the national and individual life, not omitting the language, the philosophy, the religion, or even the inmost thoughts of the people. This dominance of the communalistic type of social order has doubtless had an effect on the physical and psychic, including the brain, development of the people. These physical and psychical developments, however, are not the cause, but the product, of the social order. They are, furthermore, of no superlative import, since they offer no insuperable obstacle to the introduction of a social order radically different from that of past millenniums.

Before proceeding to elaborate and illustrate this general position, it seems desirable to introduce two further definitions.

Communalism and individualism are the two terms used throughout this work to describe two contrasted types of social order.

By communalism I mean that order of society, whether family, tribal, or national, in which the idea and the importance of the community are more or less clearly recognized, and in which this idea has become the constructive principle of the social order, and where at the same time the individual is practically ignored and crushed.

By individualism I mean that later order of society in which the worth of the individual has been recognized and emphasized, to the extent of radically modifying the communalism, securing a liberty for individual act and thought and initiative, of which the old order had no conception, and which it would have considered both dangerous and immoral. Individualism is not that atomic social order in which the idea of the communal unity has been rejected, and each separate human being regarded as the only unit. Such a society could hardly be called an order, even by courtesy. Individualism is that developed stage of communalism, wherein the advantages of close communal unity have been retained, and wherein, at the same time, the idea and practice of the worth of the individual and the importance of giving him liberty of thought and action have been added. Great changes in the internal structure, of society follow, but the communial unity or idea is neither lost nor injured. In taking up our various illustrations regarding personality in Japan, three points demand our attention; what are the facts? are they due to, and do they prove, the asserted "impersonality" of the people? and are the facts sufficiently accounted for by the communal theory of the Japanese social order?

Let us begin, then, with the illustration of which advocates of "impersonality" make so much, Japanese politeness. As to the reality of the fact, it is hardly necessary that I present extended proof. Japanese politeness is proverbial. It is carried into the minutest acts of daily life; the holding of the hands, the method of entering a room, the sucking in of the breath on specific occasions, the arrangement of the hair, the relative places of honor in a sitting-room, the method of handing guests refreshments, the exchange of friendly gifts—every detail of social life is rigidly dominated by etiquette. Not only acts, but the language of personal address as well, is governed by ideas of politeness which have fundamentally affected the structure of the language, by preventing the development of personal pronouns.

Now what is the cause of this characteristic of the Japanese? It is commonly attributed by writers of the impersonal school to the "impersonality" of the Oriental mind. "Impersonality" is not only the occasion, it is the cause of the politeness of the Japanese people. "Self is suppressed, and an ever-present regard for others is substituted in its stead." "Impersonality, by lessening the interest in one's self, induces one to take interest in others."[CO] Politeness is, in these passages, attributed to the impersonal nature of the Japanese mind. The following quotations show that this characteristic is conceived of as inherent in race and mind structure, not in the social order, as is here maintained. "The nation grew up to man's estate, keeping the mind of its child-hood."[CP] "In race characteristics, he is yet essentially the same.... Of these traits ... perhaps the most important is the great quality of impersonality."[CQ] "The peoples inhabiting it [the earth's temperate zone] grow steadily more personal as we go West. So unmistakable is this gradation that one is almost tempted to ascribe it to cosmical rather than human causes.... The essence of the soul of the Far East may be said to be impersonality."[CR]

In his chapter on "Imagination," Mr. Lowell seeks to explain the cause of the "impersonality" of the Orient. He attributes it to their marked lack of the faculty of "imagination"—the faculty of forming new and original ideas. Lacking this faculty, there has been relatively little stimulus to growth, and hence no possibility of differentiation and thus of individualization.

If politeness were due to the "impersonal" nature of the race mind, it would be impossible to account for the rise and decline of Japanese etiquette, for it should have existed from the beginning, and continued through all time, nor could we account for the gross impoliteness that is often met with in recent years. The Japanese themselves deplore the changes that have taken place. They testify that the older forms of politeness were an integral element of the feudal system and were too often a thin veneer of manner by no means expressive of heart interest. None can be so absolutely rude as they who are masters of the forms of politeness, but have not the kindly heart. The theory of "impersonality" does not satisfactorily account for the old-time politeness of Japan.

The explanation here offered for the development and decline of politeness is that they are due to the nature of the social order. Thoroughgoing feudalism long maintained, with its social ranks and free use of the sword, of necessity develops minute unwritten rules of etiquette; without the universal observance of these customs, life would be unbearable and precarious, and society itself would be impossible. Minute etiquette is the lubricant of a feudal social order. The rise and fall of Japan's phenomenal system of feudal etiquette is synchronous with that of her feudal system, to which it is due rather than to the asserted "impersonality" of the race mind.

The impersonal theory is amazingly blind to adverse phenomena. Such a one is the marked sensitiveness of the middle and upper classes to the least slight or insult. The gradations of social rank are scrupulously observed, not only on formal occasions, but also in the homes at informal and social gatherings. Failure to show the proper attention, or the use of language having an insufficient number of honorific particles and forms, would be instantly interpreted as a personal slight, if not an insult.[CS]

Now if profuse courtesy is a proof of "impersonality," as its advocates argue, what does morbid sensitiveness prove but highly developed personality? But then arises the difficulty of understanding how the same individuals can be both profusely polite and morbidly sensitive at one and the same time? Instead of inferring "impersonality" from the fact of politeness, from the two facts of sensitiveness and politeness we may more logically infer a considerable degree of personality. Yet I would not lay much stress on this argument, for oftentimes (or is it always true?) the weaker and more insignificant the person, the greater the sensitiveness. Extreme sensitiveness is as natural and necessary a product of a highly developed feudalism as is politeness, and neither is particularly due to the high or the low development of personality.

Similarly with respect to the question of altruism, which is practically identified with politeness by expounders of Oriental "impersonality." They make this term (altruism) the virtual equivalent of "impersonality"—interest in others rather than in self, an interest due, according to their view, to a lack of differentiation of the individual minds; the individuals, though separate, still retain the universalism of the original mind-stuff. This use of the term altruism makes it a very different thing from the quality or characteristic which in the West is described by this term.

But granting that this word is used with a legitimate meaning, we ask, is altruism in this sense an inherent quality of the Japanese race? Let the reader glance back to our discussion of the possession by the Japanese of sympathy, and the humane feelings.[CT] We saw there marked proofs of their lack. The cruelty of the old social order was such as we can hardly realize. Altruism that expresses itself only in polite forms, and does not strive to alleviate the suffering of fellow-men, can have very little of that sense, which this theory requires. So much as to the fact. Then as to the theory. If this alleged altruism were inherent in the mental structure, it ought to be a universal characteristic of the Japanese; it should be all-pervasive and permanent. It should show itself toward the foreigner as well as toward the native. But such is far from the case. Few foreigners have received a hearty welcome from the people at large. They are suspected and hated; as little room as possible is made for them. The less of their presence and advice, the better. So far as there is any interest in them, it is on the ground of utility, and not of inherent good will because of a feeling of aboriginal unity. Of course there are many exceptions to these statements, especially among the Christians. But such is the attitude of the people as a whole, especially of the middle and upper classes toward the foreigners.

If we turn our attention to the opposite phase of Japanese character, namely their selfishness, their self-assertiveness, and their aggressiveness, whether as a nation or as individuals, and consider at the same time the recent rise of this spirit, we are again impressed both with the narrow range of facts to which the advocates of "impersonality" call our attention, and also with the utter insufficiency of their theory to account for the facts they overlook. According to the theory of altruism and "impersonality," these are characteristics of undeveloped races and individuals, while the reverse characteristics, those of selfishness and self-assertiveness, are the products of a later and higher development, marks of strong personality. But neither selfishness nor individual aggressiveness is a necessary element of developed "personality." If it were, children who have never been trained by cultivated mothers, but have been allowed to have their own way regardless of the rights or desires of others, are more highly developed in "personality" than the adult who has, through a long life of self-discipline and religious devotion, become regardless of his selfish interests and solicitous only for the welfare of others. If the high development of altruism is equivalent to the development of "impersonality," then those in the West who are renowned for humanity and benevolence are "impersonal," while robbers and murderers and all who are regardless of the welfare of others are possessed of the most highly developed "personality." And it also follows that highly developed altruistic benefactors of mankind are such, after all, because they are *undeveloped*,—their minds are relatively undifferentiated,— hence their fellow-feeling and kindly acts. There is a story of some learned wit who met a half-drunken boor; the latter plunged ahead, remarking, "I never get out of the way of a fool"; to which the quick reply came, "I always do." According to this argument based on self-assertive aggressiveness, the boor was the man possessed of a strong personality, while the gentleman was relatively "impersonal." If pure selfishness and aggressiveness are the measure of personality, then are not many of the carnivorous animals endowed with a very high degree of "personality"?

The truth is, a comprehensive and at the same time correct contrast between the East and the West cannot be stated in terms of personality and impersonality. They fail not only to take in all the facts, but they fail to explain even the facts they take in. Such a contrast of the East and the West can be stated only in the terms of communalism and individualism. As we have already seen,[CLI] every nation has to pass through the communal stage, in order to become a nation at all. The families and tribes of which it is composed need to become consolidated in order to survive in the struggle for existence with surrounding families, tribes, and nations. In this stage the individual is of necessity sunk out of sight in the demands of the community. This secures indeed a species of altruism, but of a relatively low order. It is communal altruism which nature compels on pain of extermination. This, however, is very different from the altruism of a high religious experience and conscious ethical devotion. This latter is volitional, the product of character. This altruism can arise chiefly in a social order where individualism to a large extent has gained sway. It is this variety of altruism that characterizes the West, so far as the West is altruistic. But on the other hand, in a social order in which individualism has full swing, the extreme of egoistic selfishness can also find opportunity for development. It is accordingly in the West that extreme selfishness, the most odious of sins, is seen at its best, or rather its worst.

So again we see that selfish aggressiveness and an exalted consciousness of one's individuality or separateness are not necessary marks of developed personality, nor their opposite the marks of undeveloped personality—so-called "impersonality." On the contrary, the reverse statement would probably come nearer the truth. He who is intensely conscious of the great unities of nature and of human nature, of the oneness that unites individuals to the nation and to the race, and who lives a corresponding life of goodness and kindness, is by far the more developed personality. But the manifestations of personality will vary much with the nature of the social order. This may change with astonishing rapidity. Such a change has come over the social order of the Japanese nation during the past thirty years, radically modifying its so-called impersonal features. Their primitive docility, their politeness, their marriage customs, their universal adoption of Chinese thoughts, language, and literature, and now, in recent times, their rejection of the Chinese philosophy and science, their assertiveness in Korea and China and their aggressive attitude toward the whole world—all these multitudinous changes and complete reversals of ideals and customs, point to the fact that the former characteristics of their civilization were not "impersonal," but communal, and that they rested on social development rather than on inherent nature or on deficient mental differentiation.

A common illustration of Japanese "impersonality," depending for its force wholly on invention, is the deficiency of the Japanese language in personal pronouns and its surplus of honorifics. At first thought this argument strikes one as very strong, as absolutely invincible indeed. Surely, if there is a real lack of personal pronouns, is not that proof positive that the people using the language, nay, the authors of the language, must of necessity be deficient in the sense of personality? And if the verbs in large numbers are impersonal, does not that clinch the matter? But further consideration of the argument and its illustrations gradually shows its weakness. At present I must confess that the argument seems to me utterly fallacious, and for the sufficient reason that the personal element is introduced, if not always explicitly yet at least implicitly, in almost every sentence uttered. The method of its expression, it is true, is quite different from that adopted by Western languages, but it is none the less there. It is usually accomplished by means of the titles, "honorific" particles, and honorific verbs and nouns. "Honorable shoes" can't by any stretch of the imagination mean shoes that belong to me; every Japanese would at once think "your shoes"; his attention is not distracted by the term "honorable" as is that of the foreigner; the honor is largely overlooked by the native in the personal element implied. The greater the familiarity with the language the more clear it becomes that the impressions of "impersonality" are due to the ignorance of the foreigner rather than to the real "impersonal" character of the Japanese thought or mind. In the Japanese methods of linguistic expression, politeness and personality are indeed, inextricably interwoven; but they are not at all confused. The distinctions of person and the consciousness of self in the Japanese *thought* are as clear and distinct as they are in the English thought. In the Japanese *sentence*, however, the politeness and the personality cannot be clearly separated. On that account, however, there is no more reason for denying one element than the other.

So far from the deficiency of personal pronouns being a proof of Japanese "impersonality," *i.e.*, of lack of consciousness of self, this very deficiency may, with even more plausibility, be used to establish the opposite view. Child psychology has established the fact that an early phenomenon of child mental development is the emphasis laid on "meum" and "tuum," mine and yours. The child is a thoroughgoing individualist in feelings, conceptions, and language. The first personal pronoun is ever on his lips and in his thought. Only as culture arises and he is trained to see how disagreeable in others is excessive emphasis on the first person, does he learn to moderate his own excessive egoistic tendency. Is it not a fact that the studied evasion of first personal pronouns by cultured people in the West is due to their developed consciousness of self? Is it possible for one who has no consciousness of self to conceive as impolite the excessive use of egoistic forms of speech? From this point of view we might argue that, because of the deficiency of her personal pronouns, the Japanese nation has advanced far beyond any other nation in the process of self-consciousness. But this too would be an error. Nevertheless, so far from saying that the lack of personal pronouns is a proof of the "impersonality" of the Japanese, I think we may fairly use it as a disproof of the proposition.

The argument for the inherent impersonality of the Japanese mind because of the relative lack of personal pronouns is still further undermined by the discovery, not only of many substitutes, but also of several words bearing the strong impress of the conception of self. There are said to be three hundred words which may be used as personal pronouns— "Boku," "servant," is a common term for "I," and "kimi," "Lord," for "you"; these words are freely used by the student class. Officials often use "Konata," "here," and "Anata," "there," for the first and second persons. "Omaye," "honorably in front," is used both condescendingly and honorifically; "you whom I condescend to allow in my presence," and "you who confer on me the honor of entering your presence." The derivation of the most common word for I, "Watakushi," is unknown, but, in addition to its pronominal use, it has the meaning of "private." It has become a true personal pronoun and is freely used by all classes.

In addition to the three hundred words which may be used as personal pronouns the Japanese language possesses an indefinite number of ways for delicately suggesting the personal element without its express utterance. This is done either by subtle praise, which can then only refer to the person addressed or by more or less bald self-depreciation, which can then only refer to the first person. "Go kanai," "honorable within the house," can only mean, according to Japanese etiquette, "your wife," or "your family," while "gu-sai," "foolish wife," can only mean "my wife." "Gufu," "foolish father," "tonji," "swinish child," and numberless other depreciatory terms such as "somatsu na mono," "coarse thing," and "tsumaranu mono," "worthless thing," according to the genius of the language can only refer to the first person, while all appreciative and polite terms can only refer to the person addressed. The terms, "foolish," "swinish," etc., have lost their literal sense and mean now no more than "my," while the polite forms mean "yours." To translate these terms, "my foolish wife," "my swinish son," is incorrect, because it twice translates the same word. In such cases the Japanese *thought* is best expressed by using the possessive pronoun and omitting the derogative adjective altogether. Japanese indirect methods for the expression of the personal relation are thus numberless and subtile. May it not be plausibly argued since the European has only a few blunt pronouns wherewith to state this idea while the Japanese has both numberless pronouns and many other delicate ways of conveying the same idea, that the latter is far in advance of the European in the development of personality? I do not use this argument, but as an argument it seems to me much more plausible than that which infers from the paucity of true pronouns the absence, or at least the deficiency, of personality.

Furthermore, Japanese possesses several words for self. "Onore," "one's self," and "Ware," "I or myself," are pure Japanese, while "Ji" (the Chinese pronunciation for "onore"), "ga," "self," and "shi" (the Chinese pronunciation of "watakushi," meaning private) are Sinico-Japanese words, that is, Chinese derived words. These Sinico-Japanese terms are in universal use in compound words, and are as truly Japanese as many Latin, Greek and Norman-derived words are real English. "Ji-bun," "one's self"; "jiman," "self-satisfaction"; "ji-fu," "self-assertion"; "jinin," "self-responsibility"; "ji-bo ji-ki," "self-destruction, self-abandonment"; "ji-go ji-toku," "self-act, self-reward"—always in a bad sense; "ga-yoku," "selfish desire"; "ga-shin," "selfish heart"; "ga oru," "self-mastery"; "muga," "unselfish"; "shi-shin shi-yoku," "private or self-heart, private or self-desire," that is, selfishness; "shi-ai shi-shin," "private-or self-love, private-or-self heart," *i.e.*, selfishness—these and countless other compound words involving the conception of self, can hardly be explained by the "impersonal," "altruistic" theory of Japanese race mind and language. In truth, if this theory is unable to explain the facts it recognizes, much less can it account for those it ignores.

To interpret correctly the phenomena we are considering, we must ask ourselves how personal pronouns have arisen in other languages. Did the primitive Occidental man produce them outright from the moment that he discovered himself? Far from it. There are abundant reasons for believing that every personal pronoun is a degenerate or, if you prefer, a developed noun. Pronouns are among the latest products of language, and, in the sphere of language, are akin to algebraic symbols in the sphere of mathematics or to a machine in the sphere of labor. A pronoun, whether personal, demonstrative, or relative, is a wonderful linguistic invention, enabling the speaker to carry on long trains of unbroken thought. Its invention was no more connected with the sense of self, than was the invention of any labor-saving device. The Japanese language is even more defective for lack of relative pronouns than it is for lack of personal pronouns. Shall we argue from this that the Japanese people have no sense of relation? Of course personal pronouns could not arise without or before the sense of self, but the problem is whether the sense of self could arise without or exist before that particular linguistic device, the personal pronoun? On this problem the Japanese language and civilization throw conclusive light.

The fact is that the ancestors of the Anglo-Saxon and Japanese peoples parted company so long ago that in the course of their respective linguistic evolutions, not only have all common terms been completely eliminated, but even common methods of expression. The so-called Indo-European races hit upon one method of sentence structure, a method in which pronouns took an important part and the personal pronoun was needed to express the personal element, while the Japanese hit upon another method which required little use of pronouns and which was able to express the personal element wholly without the personal pronoun. The sentence structure of the two languages is thus radically different.

Now the long prevalent feudal social order has left its stamp on the Japanese language no less than on every other feature of Japanese civilization. Many of the quasi personal pronouns are manifestly of feudal parentage. Under the new civilization and in contact with foreign peoples who can hardly utter a sentence without a personal pronoun, the majority of the old quasi personal pronouns are dropping out of use, while those in continued use are fast rising to the position of full-fledged personal pronouns. This, however, is not due to the development of self-consciousness on the part of the people, but only to the development of the language in the direction of complete and concise expression of thought. It would be rash to say that the feudal social order accounts for the lack of pronouns, personal or others, from the Japanese language, but it is safe to maintain that the feudal order, with its many gradations of social rank, minute etiquette, and refined and highly developed personal sensitiveness would adopt and foster an impersonal and honorific method of personal allusion. Even though we may not be able to explain the rise of the non-pronominal method of sentence structure, it is enough if we see that this is a problem in the evolution of language, and that Japanese pronominal deficiency is not to be attributed to lack of consciousness of self, much less to the inherent "impersonality" of the Japanese mind.

An interesting fact ignored by advocates of the "impersonal" theory is the Japanese inability of conceiving nationality apart from personality. Not only is the Emperor conceived as the living symbol of Japanese nationality, but he is its embodiment and substance. The Japanese race is popularly represented to be the offspring of the royal house. Sovereignty resides completely and absolutely in him. Authority to-day is acknowledged only in those who have it from him. Popular rights are granted the people by him, and exist because of his will alone. A single act of his could in theory abrogate the constitution promulgated in 1889 and all the popular rights enjoyed to-day by the nation. The Emperor of Japan could appropriate, without in the least shocking the most patriotic Japanese, the long-famous saying of Louis XIV., "L'état, c'est moi." Mr. H. Kato, ex-president of the Imperial University, in a recent work entitled the "Evolution of Morality and Law" says this in just so many words: "Patriotism in this country means loyalty to the throne. To the Japanese, the Emperor and the country are the same. The Emperor of Japan, without the slightest exaggeration, can say, 'L'état, c'est moi.' The Japanese believe that all their happiness is bound up with the Imperial line and have no respect for any system of morality or law that fails to take cognizance of this fact."

Mr. Yamaguchi, professor of history in the Peeresses' School and lecturer in the Imperial Military College, thus writes in the *Far East*: "The sovereign power of the State cannot be dissociated from the Imperial Throne. It lasts forever along with the Imperial line of succession, unbroken for ages eternal. If the Imperial House cease to exist, the Empire falls." "According to our ideas the monarch reigns over and governs the country in his own right.... Our Emperor possesses real sovereignty and also exercises it. He is quite different from other rulers, who possess but a partial sovereignty." This is to-day the universally accepted belief in Japan. It shows clearly that national unity and sovereignty are not conceived in Japan apart from personality.

One more point demands our attention before bringing this chapter to a close. If "impersonality" were an inherent characteristic of Japanese race nature, would it be possible for strong personalities to arise?

Mr. Lowell has described in telling way a very common experience. "About certain people," he says, "there exists a subtle something which leaves its impress indelibly upon the consciousness of all who come in contact with them. This something is a power, but a power of so indefinable a description that we beg definition by calling it simply the personality of the man.... On the other hand, there are people who have no effect upon us whatever. They come and they go with a like indifference.... And we say that the difference is due to the personality or the want of personality of the man."[CV] The first thing to which I would call attention is the fact that "personality" is here used in its true sense. It has no exclusive reference to consciousness of self, nor does it signify the effect of self-consciousness on the consciousness of another. It here has reference to those inherent qualities of thinking and feeling and willing which we have seen to be the essence of personality. These qualities, possessed in a marked way or degree, make strong personalities. Their relative lack constitutes weak personality. Bare consciousness of self is a minor evidence of personality and may be developed to a morbid degree in a person who has a weak personality.

In the second place this distinction between weak and strong personalities is as true of the Japanese as of the Occidental. There have been many commanding persons in Japanese history; they have been the heroes of the land. There are such to-day. The most commanding personality of recent times was, I suppose, Takamori Saigo, whose very name is an inspiration to tens of thousands of the choicest youth of the nation. Joseph Neesima was such a personality. The transparency of his purpose, the simplicity of his personal aim, his unflinching courage, fixedness of belief, lofty plans, and far-reaching ambitions for his people, impressed all who came into contact with him. No one mingles much with the Japanese, freely speaking with them in their own language, but perceives here and there men of "strong personality" in the sense of the above-quoted passage. Now it seems to me that if "impersonality" in the corresponding sense were a race characteristic, due to the nature of their psychic being, then the occurrence of so many commanding personalities in Japan would be inexplicable. Heroes and widespread hero-worship[CW] could hardly arise were there no commanding personalities. The feudal order lent itself without doubt to the development of such a spirit. But the feudal order could hardly have arisen or even maintained itself for centuries without commanding personalities, much less could it have created them. The whole feudal order was built on an exalted oligarchy. It was an order which emphasized persons, not principles; the law of the land was not the will of the multitudes, but of a few select persons. While, therefore, it is beyond dispute that the old social order was communal in type, and so did not give freedom to the individual, nor tend to develop strong personality among the masses, it is also true that it did develop men of commanding personality among the rulers. Those who from youth were in the hereditary line of rule, sons of Shoguns, daimyos, and samurai, were forced by the very communalism of the social order to an exceptional personal development. They shot far ahead of the common man. Feudalism is favorable to the development of personality in the favored few, while it represses that of the masses. Individualism, on the contrary, giving liberty of thought and act, with all that these imply, is favorable to the development of the personality of all.

In view of the discussions of this chapter, is it not evident that advocates of the "impersonal" theory of Japanese mind and civilization not only ignore many important elements of the civilization they attempt to interpret, but also base their interpretation on a mistaken conception of personality? We may not, however, leave the discussion at this point, for important considerations still demand our attention if we would probe this problem of personality to its core.

XXXII
IS BUDDHISM IMPERSONAL?

Advocates of Japanese "impersonality" call attention to the phenomena of self-suppression in religion. It seems strange, however, that they who present this argument fail to see how "self-suppression" undermines their main contention. If "self-suppression" be actually attained, it can only be by a people advanced so far as to have passed through and beyond the "personal" stage of existence. "Self-suppression" cannot be a characteristic of a primitive people, a people that has not yet reached the stage of consciousness of self. If the alleged "impersonality" of the Orient is that of a primitive people that has not yet reached the stage of self-consciousness, then it cannot have the characteristic of "self-suppression." If, on the other hand, it is the "impersonality" of "self-suppression," then it is radically different from that of a primitive people. Advocates of "impersonality" present both conceptions, quite unconscious apparently that they are mutually exclusive. If either conception is true, the other is false.

Furthermore, if self-suppression is a marked characteristic of Japanese politeness and altruism (as it undoubtedly is when these qualities are real expressions of the heart and of the general character), it is a still more characteristic feature of the higher religious life of the people, which certainly does not tend to "impersonality." The ascription of esoteric Buddhism to the common people by advocates of the "impersonal" theory is quite a mistake, and the argument for the "impersonality" of the race on this ground is without foundation, for the masses of the people are grossly polytheistic, wholly unable to understand Buddhistic metaphysics, or to conceive of the nebulous, impersonal Absolute of Buddhism. Now if consciousness of the unity of nature, and especially of the unity of the individual soul with the Absolute, were a characteristic of undeveloped, that is, of undifferentiated mind, then all primitive peoples should display it in a superlative degree. It should show itself in every phase of their life. The more primitive the people, the more divine their life—because the less differentiated from the original divine mind! Such are the requirements of this theory. But what are the facts? The primitive undeveloped mind is relatively unconscious of self; it is wholly objective; it is childlike; it does not even know that there is self to suppress. Primitive religion is purely objective. Implicit, in primitive religion without doubt, is the fact of a unity between God and man, but the primitive man has not discovered this implication of his religious thinking. This is the state of mind of a large majority of Japanese.

Yet this is by no means true of all. No nation, with such a continuous history as Japan has had, would fail to develop a class capable of considerable introspection. In Japan introspection received early and powerful impetus from the religion of Buddha. It came with a philosophy of life based on prolonged and profound introspection. It commanded each man who would know more than the symbols, who desired, like Buddha, to attain the great enlightenment and thus become a Tathagata, a Blessed one, a Buddha, an Enlightened one, to know and conquer himself. The emphasis laid by thoughtful Buddhism on the need of self-knowledge, in order to self-suppression, is well recognized by all careful students. Advocates of Oriental "impersonality" are not one whit behind others in recognizing it. In this connection we can hardly do better than quote a few of Mr. Lowell's happy descriptions of the teaching of philosophic Buddhism.

"This life, it says, is but a chain of sorrows.... These desires that urge us on are really causes of all our woe. We think they are ourselves. We are mistaken. They are all illusion.... This personality, this sense of self, is a cruel deception.... Realize once the true soul behind it, devoid of attributes ... an invisible part of the great impersonal soul of nature, then ... will you have found happiness in the blissful quiescence of Nirvana" [p. 186]. "In desire alone lies all the ill. Quench the desire, and the deeds [sins of the flesh] will die of inanition. Get rid, then, said Buddha, of these passions, these strivings, for the sake of self. As a man becomes conscious that he himself is something distinct from his body, so if he reflect and ponder, he will come to see that in like manner, his appetites, ambitions, hopes, are really extrinsic to the spirit proper.... Behind desire, behind even the will, lies the soul, the same for all men, one with the soul of the universe. When he has once realized this eternal truth, the man has entered Nirvana.... It [Nirvana] is simply the recognition of the eternal oneness of the two [the individual and the universal soul]" [p. 189].

Accepting this description of philosophic Buddhism as fairly accurate, it is plain that the attainment of this consciousness of the unity of the individual self with the universal is the result, according to Buddha, and also according to the advocates of "impersonality," of a highly developed consciousness of self. It is not a simple state of undifferentiated mind, but a complex and derivative one—absolutely incomprehensible to a primitive people. The means for this suppression of self *depends entirely on the development of the consciousness of self.* The self is the means for casting out the self, and it is done by that introspection which ultimately leads to the realization of the unity. If, then, Japanese Buddhism seeks to suppress the self, this very effort is the most conclusive proof we could demand of the possession by this people of a highly developed consciousness of self.

It is one of the boasts of Buddhism that a man's saviour is himself; no other helper, human or divine, can aught for him. Those who reject Christianity in Christian lands are quite apt to praise Buddhism for this rejection of all external help. They urge that by the very nature of the case salvation is no external thing; each one must work out his own salvation. It cannot be given by another. Salvation through an external Christ who lived 1900 years ago is an impossibility. Such a criticism of Christianity shows real misunderstanding of the

Christian doctrine and method of salvation. Yet the point to which attention is here directed is not the correctness or incorrectness of these characterizations of Christianity, but rather to the fact that "ji-riki," salvation through self-exertion, which is the boast of Buddhism, is but another proof of the essentially self-conscious character of Buddhism. It aims at Nirvana, it is true, at self-suppression, but it depends on the attainment of clear self-consciousness in the first place, and then on prolonged self-exertion for the attainment of that end. In proportion as Buddhism is esoteric is it self-conscious.

Such being the nature of Buddhism, we naturally ask whether or not it is calculated to develop strongly personalized men and women. If consciousness of self is the main element of personality, we must pronounce Buddhism a highly personal rather than impersonal religion, as is commonly stated. But a religion of the Buddhistic type, which casts contempt on the self, and seeks its annihilation as the only means of salvation, has ever tended to destroy personality; it has made men hermits and pessimists; it has drawn them out of the great current of active life, and thus has severed them from their fellow-men. But a prime condition of developed personalities is largeness and intensity of life, and constant intercourse with mankind. Personality is developed in the society of persons, not in the company of trees and stones. Buddhism, which runs either to gross and superstitious polytheism on its popular side or to pessimistic introspection on its philosophical side, may possibly, by a stretch of the term, be called "impersonal" in the sense that it does not help in the production of strong, rounded personality among its votaries, but not in the sense that it does not produce self-consciousness. Buddhism, therefore, cannot be accurately described in terms of personality or impersonality.

We would do well in this connection to ponder the fact that although Buddhism in its higher forms does certainly develop consciousness of self, it does not attribute to that self any worth. In consequence of this, it never has modified, and however long it might be allowed to run its course, never could modify, the general social order in the direction of individualism. This is one reason why the whole Orient has maintained to modern times its communal nature, in spite of its high development in so many ways, even in introspection and self-consciousness.

This failure of Buddhism is all the more striking when we stop to consider how easy and, to us, natural an inference it would have been to pass from the perception of the essential unity between the separate self and the universal soul, to the assertion of the supreme worth of that separate soul because of the fact of that unity. But Buddhism never seems to have made that inference. Its compassion on animals and even insects depended on its doctrine of the transmigration of souls, not on its doctrine of universal soul unity. Its mercy was shown to animals in certain whimsical ways, but the universal lack of sympathy for suffering man, man who could suffer the most exquisite pains, exposed the shallowness of its solicitude about destroying life. The whole influence of Buddhism on the social order was not conducive to the development of personality in the Orient. The so-called impersonal influence of Buddhism upon the Eastern peoples, then, is not due to its failure to recognize the separateness of the human self, on the one hand, nor to its emphasis on the universal unity subsisting between the separate finite self and the infinite soul, on the other; but only on its failure to see the infinite worth of the individual; and in consequence of this failure, its inability to modify the general social order by the introduction of individualism.

The asserted "impersonal" characteristic of Buddhism and of the Orient, therefore, I am not willing to call "impersonality"; for it is a very defective description, a real misnomer. I think no single term can truly describe the characteristic under consideration. As regards the general social order, the so-called impersonal characteristic is its communal nature; as regards the popular religious thought, whether of Shintoism or Buddhism, its so-called impersonality is its simple, artless objectivity; as regards philosophic Buddhism its so-called impersonality is its morbid introspective self-consciousness, leading to the desire and effort to annihilate the separateness of the self. These are different characteristics and cannot be described by any single term. So far as there are in Japan genuine altruism, real suppression of selfish desires, and real possession of kindly feelings for others and desires to help them, and so far as these qualities arise through a sense of the essential unity of the human race and of the unity of the human with the divine soul, this is not "impersonality"—but a form of highly developed personality—not infra-personality, but true personality.

We have noted that although esoteric Buddhism developed a highly accentuated consciousness of self, it attributed no value to that self. This failure will not appear strange if we consider the historical reasons for it. Indeed, the failure was inevitable. Neither the social order nor the method of introspective thought suggested it. Both served, on the contrary, absolutely to preclude the idea.

When introspective thought began in India the social order was already far beyond the undifferentiated communal life of the tribal stage. Castes were universal and fixed. The warp and woof of daily life and of thought were filled with the distinctions of castes and ranks. Man's worth was conceived to be not in himself, but in his rank or caste. The actual life of the people, therefore, did not furnish to speculative thought the slightest suggestion of the worth of man as man. It was a positive hindrance to the rise of such an idea.

Equally opposed to the rise of this idea was the method of that introspective thought which discovered the fact of the self. It was a method of abstraction; it denied as part of the real self everything that could be thought of as separate; every changing phase or expression of the self could not be the real self, it was argued, because, if a part of the real self, how could it sometimes be and again not be? Feeling cannot be a part of the real self, for sometimes I feel and sometimes I do not. Any particular desire cannot be a part of my real self, for sometimes I have it and sometimes I do not. A similar argument was applied to every objective thing. In the famous "Questions of King Melinda," the argument as to the real chariot is expanded at length; the wheels are not the chariot; the spokes are not the chariot; the seat is not the chariot; the tongue is not the chariot; the axle is not the chariot; and so, taking up each individual part of the chariot, the assertion is made that it is not the chariot. But if the chariot is not in any of its parts, then they are not essential parts of the chariot. So of the soul—the self; it does not consist of its various qualities or attributes or powers; hence they are not essential elements of the self. The real self exists apart from them.

Now is it not evident that such a method of introspection deprives the conception of self of all possible value? It is nothing but a bare intellectual abstraction. To say that this self is a part of the universal self is no relief,—brings no possible worth to the separate self,—for the conception of the universal soul has been arrived at by a similar process of thought. It, too, is nothing but a bare abstraction, deprived of all qualities and attributes and powers. I can see no distinction between the absolute universal soul of Brahmanism and Buddhism, and the Absolute Nothing of Hegel.[CX]

Both are the farthest possible abstraction that the mind can make. The Absolute Soul of Buddhism, the Atman of Brahmanism, and Hegel's Nothing are the farthest possible remove from the Christian's conception of God. The former is the utter emptiness of being; the latter the perfect fullness of being and completeness of quality. The finite emptiness receives and can receive no richness of life or increase in value by its consciousness of unity with the infinite emptiness; whereas the finite limited soul receives in the Christian view an infinite wealth and value by reason of the consciousness of its unity with the divine infinite fullness. The usual method of stating the difference between the Christian conception of God and the Hindu conception of the root of all being is that the one is personal and the other impersonal. But these terms are inadequate. Rather say the one is perfectly personal and the other perfectly abstract. Impersonality, even in its strictest meaning, i.e., without "conscious separate existence as an intelligent and voluntary being," only partially expresses the conception of Buddhism. The full conception rejects not only personality, but also every other quality; the ultimate and the absolute of Buddhism—we may not even call it being—is the absolutely abstract.

With regard, then, to the conception of the separate self and of the supreme self, the Buddhistic view may be called "impersonal," not in the sense that it lacks the consciousness of a separate self; not in the sense that it emphasizes the universal unity—nay, the identity of all the separate abstract selves and the infinite abstract self; but in the sense that all the qualities and characteristics of human beings, such as consciousness, thought, emotion, volition, and even being itself, are rejected as unreal. The view is certainly "impersonal," but it is much more. My objection to the description of Buddhism as "impersonal," then, is not because the word is too strong, but because it is too weak; it does not sufficiently characterize its real nature. It is as much below materialism, as materialism is below monotheism. Such a scheme of thought concerning the universe necessarily reacts on those whom it possesses, to destroy what sense they may have of the value of human personality; that which we hold to be man's glory is broken into fragments and thrown away.

But this does not constitute the whole of the difficulty. This method of introspective thought necessarily resulted in the doctrine of Illusion. Nothing is what it seems to be. The reality of the chariot is other than it appears. So too with the self and everything we see or think. The ignoant are perfectly under the spell of the illusion and cannot escape it. The deluded mind creates for itself the world of being, with all its woes and evils. The great enlightenment is the discovery of this fact and the power it gives to escape the illusion and to see that the world is nothing but illusion. To see that the illusion is an illusion destroys it as such. It is then no longer an illusion, but only a passing shadow. We cannot now stop to see how pessimism, the doctrine of self-salvation, and the nature of that salvation through contemplation and asceticism and withdrawal from active life, all inevitably follow from such a course of thought. That which here needs emphasis is that all this thinking renders it still more impossible to think of the self as having any intrinsic worth. On-the contrary, the self is the source of evil, of illusion. The great aim of Buddhism is necessarily to get rid of the self, with all its illusions and pains and disappointments.

Is it now clear why Buddhism failed to reach the idea of the worth of the individual self? It was due to the nature of the social order, and the nature of its introspective and speculative thinking. Lacking, therefore, the conception of individual worth, we see clearly why it failed, even after centuries of opportunity, to secure individualism in the social order and a general development of personality either as an idea or as a fact among any of the peoples to which it has gone. It is not only a fact of history, but we have seen that it could not have been otherwise. The very nature of its conception of self and, in consequence, the nature of its conception of salvation absolutely prohibited it.[CY]

We have thus far confined our view entirely to philosophic Buddhism. It is important, therefore, to state again that very few of the Japanese people outside of the priesthood have any such ideas with regard to the abstract nature of the individual, of the absolute self, and of their mutual relations as I have just described. These ideas are a part of esoteric Buddhism, the secret truth, which is an essential part of the great enlightenment, but far too profound for the vulgar multitudes. The vast majority, even of the priesthood, I am told, do not get far enough to be taught these views. The sweep of such conceptions, therefore, is very limited. That they are held, however, by the leaders, that they are the views of the most learned expounders and the most advanced students of Buddhism serves to explain why Buddhism has never been, and can never become, a power in reorganizing society in the direction of individualism.

Popular Buddhism contains many elements alien to philosophic Buddhism. For a full study of the subject of this chapter we need to ask whether popular Buddhism tended to produce "impersonality," and if so, in what sense. The doctrine of "ingwa,"[CZ] with its consequences on character, demands fresh attention at this point. According to this doctrine every event of this life, even the minutest, is the result of one's conduct in a previous life, and is unalterably fixed by inflexible law. "Ingwa" is the crude idea of fate held by all primitive peoples, stated in somewhat philosophic and scientific form. It became a central element in the thought of Oriental peoples. Each man is born into his caste and class by a law over which neither he nor his parents have any control, and for which they are without responsibility. The misfortunes of life, and the good fortunes as well, come by the same impartial, inflexible laws. By this system of thought moral responsibility is practically removed from the individual's shoulders. This doctrine is held in Japan far more widely than the philosophic doctrine of the self, and is correspondingly baleful.

This system of thought, when applied to the details of life, means that individual choice and will, and their effect in determining both external life and internal character have been practically lost sight of. As a sociological fact the origin of this conception is not difficult to understand. The primitive freedom of the individual in the early communal order of the tribe became increasingly restricted with the multiplication and development of the Hindu peoples; each class of society became increasingly specialized. Finally the individual had no choice whatever left him, because of the extreme rigidity of the communal order. As a matter of fact, the individual choice and will was allowed no play whatever in any important matter. Good sense saw that where no freedom is, there moral responsibility cannot be. All one's life is predetermined by the powers that be. Thus we again see how vital a relation the social order bears to the innermost thinking and belief of a people.

Still further. Once let the idea be firmly grounded in an individual that he has no freedom of belief, of choice, or of act, and in the vast majority of cases, as a matter of fact, he will have none. "As a man thinketh in his heart, so is he." "According to your faith be it unto you." This doctrine of individual freedom is one of those that cannot be forced on a man who does not choose to believe it. In a true sense, it is my belief that I am free that makes me free. As Prof. James well says, the doctrine of the freedom of the will cannot be rammed down any man's intellectual throat, for that very act would abridge his real freedom. Man's real freedom is proved by his freedom to reject even the doctrine of his freedom. But so long as he rejects it, his freedom is only potential. Because of his belief in his bondage he is in bondage. Now this doctrine of fate has been the warp and woof of the thinking of the bulk of the Japanese people in their efforts to explain all the vicissitudes of life. Not only, therefore, has it failed to stimulate the volitional element of the psychic nature, but in the psychology of the Orient little if any attention has been given to this faculty. Oriental psychology practically knows nothing of personality because it has failed to note one of its central elements, the freedom of the will. The individual, therefore, has not been appealed to to exercise his free moralchoice, one of the highest prerogatives of his nature. Moral responsibility has not been laid on his individual shoulders. A method of moral appeal fitted to develop the deepest element of his personality has thus been precluded.

It thus resulted that although philosophic Buddhism developed a high degree of self-consciousness, yet because it failed to discover personal freedom it did not deliver popular Buddhism from its grinding doctrine of fate, rather it fastened this incubus of social progress more firmly upon it. Philosophic and popular Buddhism alike thus threw athwart the course of human and social evolution the tremendous obstacle of fatalism, which the Orient has never discovered a way either to surmount or evade. Buddhism teaches the impotence of the individual will; it destroys the sense of moral responsibility; it thus fails to understand the real nature of man, his glory and power and even his divinity, which the West sums up in the term personality. In this sense, then, the influence of Buddhism and the condition of the Orient may be called "impersonal," but it is the impersonality of a defective religious psychology, and of communalism in the social order. Whether it is right to call this feature of Japan "impersonality," I leave with the reader to judge.

We draw this chapter to a close with a renewed conception of the inadequacy of the "impersonal" theory to explain Japanese religious and social phenomena. Further considerations, however, still merit attention ere we leave this subject.

XXXIII
TRACES OF PERSONALITY IN SHINTOISM, BUDDHISM, AND CONFUCIANISM

Regret as we sometimes must the illogicalness of the human mind, yet it is a providential characteristic of our as yet defective nature; for thanks to it few men or nations carry out to their complete logical results erroneous opinions and metaphysical speculations. Common sense in Japan has served more or less as an antidote for Buddhistic poison. The blighting curse of logical Buddhism has been considerably relieved by various circumstances. Let us now consider some of the ways in which the personality-destroying characteristics of Buddhism have been lessened by other ideas and influences.

First of all there is the distinction, so often noted, between esoteric and popular Buddhism. Esoteric Buddhism was content to allow popular Buddhism a place and even to invent ways for the salvation of the ignorant multitudes who could not see the real nature of the self. Resort was had to the use of magic prayers and symbols and idols. These were bad enough, but they did not bear so hard on the development of personality as did esoteric Buddhism.

The doctrine of the transmigration of the soul was likewise a relief from the pressure of philosophic Buddhism, for, according to this doctrine, the individual soul continues to live its separate life, to maintain its independent identity through infinite ages, while passing through the ten worlds of existence, from nethermost hell to highest heaven; and the particular world into which it is born after each death is determined by the moral character of its life in the immediately preceding stage. By this doctrine, then, a practical appeal is made to the common man to exert his will, to assert his personality, and so far forth it was calculated to undo a part of the mischief done by the paralyzing doctrine of fate and illusion.

But a more important relief from the blight of Buddhistic doctrine was afforded by its own practice. At the very time that it declared the worthlessness of the self and the impotence of the will, it declared that salvation can come only from the self, by the most determined exercise of the will. What more convincing evidence of powerful, though distorted, wills could be asked than that furnished by Oriental asceticism? Nothing in the West exceeds it. As an *idea*, then, Buddhism interfered with the development of the conception of personality; but by its *practice* it helped powerfully to develop it as a fact in certain phases of activity. The stoicism of the Japanese is one phase of developed personality. It shows the presence of a powerful, disciplined will keeping the body in control, so that it gives no sign of the thoughts and emotions going on in the mind, however fierce they may be.

That in Japan, however, which has interfered most powerfully with the spread and dominance of Buddhism has been the practical and prosaic Confucian ethics. Apparently, Confucius never speculated. Metaphysics and introspection alike had no charm for him. He was concerned with conduct. His developed doctrine demanded of all men obedience to the law of the five relations. In spite, therefore, of the fact that he said nothing about individuality and personality, his system laid real emphasis on personality and demanded its continuous activity. In all of his teachings the idea of personality in the full and proper sense of this word is always implicit, and sometimes is quite distinct.

The many strong and noble characters which glorify the feudal era are the product of Japonicized Confucianism, "Bushido," and bear powerful witness to its practical emphasis on personality. The loyalty, filial piety, courage, rectitude, honor, self-control, and suicide which it taught, defective though we must pronounce them from certain points of view, were yet very lofty and noble, and depended for their realization on the development of personality.

Advocates of the "impersonal" interpretation of the Orient have much to say about pantheism. They assert the difficulty of conveying to the Oriental mind the idea of the personality of the Supreme Being. Although some form of pantheism is doubtless the belief of the learned, the evidence that a personal conception of deity is widespread among the people seems so manifest that I need hardly do more than call attention to it. This belief has helped to neutralize the paralyzing tendency of Buddhist fatalistic pantheism.

Shinto is personal from first to last. Every one of its myriads of gods is a personal being, many of them deified men.

The most popular are the souls of men who became famous for some particularly noble, brave, or admirable deed. Hero-worship is nothing if not personal. Furthermore, in its doctrine of "San-shin-ittai," "three gods, one body," it curiously suggests the doctrine of the Trinity.

Popular Buddhism holds an equally personal conception of deity. The objects of its worship are personifications of various qualities. "Kwannon," the goddess of mercy; "Jizo," the guardian of travelers and children; "Emma O," "King of Hell," who punishes sinners; "Fudo Sama," "The Immovable One," are all personifications of the various attributes of deity and are worshiped as separate gods, each being represented by a uniform type of idol. It is a curious fact that Buddhism, which started out with such a lofty rejection of deity, finally fell to the worship of idols, whereas Shinto, which is peculiarly the worship of personality, has never stooped to its representation in wood or stone.

Confucianism, however, surpasses all in its intimations of the personality of the Supreme Being. Although it never formulated this doctrine in a single term, nor definitely stated it as a tenet of religion, yet the entire ethical and religious thinking of the classically educated Japanese is shot through with the idea. Consider the Chinese expression "Jo-Tei," which the Christians of Japan freely use for God; it means literally "Supreme Emperor," and refers to the supreme ruler of the universe; he is here conceived in the form of a human ruler having of course human, that is to say, personal, attributes. A phrase often heard on the lips of the Japanese is:

"Aoide Ten ni hajizu; fushite Chi ni hajizu."

"Without self-reproach, whether looking up to Heaven, or down to Earth."

This phrase has reference to the consciousness of one's life and conduct, such that he is neither ashamed to look up in the face of Heaven nor to look about him in the presence of man. Paul expressed this same idea when he wrote "having a conscience void of offense to God and to man." Or take another phrase:

"Ten-mo kwaikwai so ni shite morasazu."

"Heaven's net is broad as earth; and though its meshes are large, none can escape it." This is constantly used to illustrate the certainty that Heaven punishes the wicked.

"Ten ni kuchi ari; kabe ni mimi ari."

"Heaven has a mouth and even the wall has ears," signifies that all one does is known to the ruler of heaven and earth. Another still more striking saying ascribing knowledge to Heaven is the "Yoshin no Shichi," "the four knowings of Yoshin." This sage was a Chinaman of the second century A.D. Approached with a large bribe and urged to accept it with the assurance that no one would know it, he replied, "Heaven knows it; Earth knows it; you know it; and I know it. How say you that none will know it?" This famous saying condemning bribery is well known in Japan. The references to "Heaven" as knowing, seeing, doing, sympathizing, willing, and always identifying the activity of "Heaven" with the noblest and loftiest ideals of man, are frequent in Chinese and Japanese literature. The personality of God is thus a doctrine clearly foreshadowed in the Orient. It is one of those great truths of religion which the Orient has already received, but which in a large measure lies dormant because of its incomplete expression. The advent of the fully expressed teaching of this truth, freed from all vagueness and ambiguity, is a capital illustration of the way in which Christianity comes to Japan to fulfill rather than to destroy; it brings that fructifying element that stirs the older and more or less imperfectly expressed truths into new life, and gives them adequate modes of expression. But the point to which I am here calling attention is the fact that the idea of the personality of the Supreme Being is not so utterly alien to Oriental thought as some would have us think. Even though there is no single word with which conveniently to translate the term, the idea is perfectly distinct to any Japanese to whom its meaning is explained.

The statement is widely made that because the Japanese language has no term for "personality" the people are lacking in the idea; that consequently they have difficulty in grasping it even when presented to them, and that as a further consequence they are not to be criticised for their hesitancy in accepting the doctrine of the "Personality of God." It must be admitted that if "personality" is to be defined in the various ambiguous and contradictory ways in which we have seen it defined by advocates of Oriental "impersonality" much can be said in defense of their hesitancy. Indeed, no thinking Christian of the Occident for a moment accepts it. But if "personality" is defined in the way here presented, which I judge to be the usage of thoughtful Christendom, then their hesitancy cannot be so defended. It is doubtless true that there is in Japanese no single word corresponding to our term "personality." But that is likewise true of multitudes of other terms. The only significance of this fact is that Oriental philosophy has not followed in exactly the same lines as the Occidental. As a matter of fact I have not found the idea of personality to be a difficult one to convey to the Japanese, if clear definitions are used. The Japanese language has, as we have seen, many words referring to the individuality, to the self of manhood; it merely lacks the general abstract term, "personality." This is, however, in keeping with the general characteristics of the language. Abstract terms are, compared with English, relatively rare. Yet with the new civilization they are being coined and introduced. Furthermore, the English term "personality" is readily used by the great majority of educated Christians just as they use such words as "life," "power," "success," "patriotism," and "Christianity."

In the summer of 1898, with the Rev. C.A. Clark I was invited to speak on the "Outlines of Christianity" in a school for Buddhist priests. At the close of our thirty-minute addresses, a young man arose and spoke for fifty minutes, outlining the Buddhist system of thought; his address consisted of an exposition of the law of cause and effect; he also stated some of the reasons why the Christian conception of God and the universe seemed to him utterly unsatisfactory; the objections raised were those now current in Japan—such, for example, as that if God really were the creator of the universe, why are some men rich and some poor, some high-born and some low-born. He also asked the question who made God? In a two-minute reply I stated that his objections showed that he did not understand the Christian's position; and I asked in turn what was the origin of the law of cause and effect. The following day the chief priest, the head of the school and its most highly educated instructor, dined with us. We of course talked of the various aspects of Christian and Buddhist doctrine. Finally he asked me how I would answer the question as to who created God, and as to the origin of the law of cause and effect. I explained as clearly as I could the Christian view of God, in his personality and as being the original and only source of all existence, whether of physical or of human nature. He seemed to drink it all in and expressed his satisfaction at the close in the words, "Taihen ni man zoku shimashita," "That is exceedingly satisfactory"; these words he repeated several times. This is not my first personal proof of the fact that the idea of personality is not alien or incomprehensible to the Orient, nor even to a Buddhist priest, steeped in Buddhist speculation, provided the idea is clearly stated.

Before bringing to a close this discussion of the problem of personality in Japan, it would seem desirable to trace the history of the development of Japanese personality. In view of all that has now been said, and not forgetting what was said as to the principles of National Evolution,[DA] this may be done in a paragraph.

The amalgamation of tribes, the development of large clans, and finally the establishment of the nation, with world-wide relations, has reacted on the individual members of the people, giving them larger and richer lives. This constitutes one important element of personal development. The subordination of individual will to that of the group, the desire and effort to live for the advantage, not of the individual self, but of the group, whether family, tribe, clan, nation, or the world, is not a limitation of personality. On the contrary, it is its expansion and development. Shinto and Japonicized Confucianism contributed powerful motives to this subordination, and thus to this personal development. These were attended, however, by serious limitations in that they confined their attention to the upper and ruling classes. The development of personality was thus extremely limited. Buddhism contributed to the development of Japanese personality in so far as it taught Japanese the marvels revealed by introspection and self-victory. Its contribution, however, was seriously hampered by defects already sufficiently emphasized. Japan has developed personality to a high degree in a few and to a relatively low degree in the many. The problem confronting New Japan is the development of a high degree of personality among the masses. This is to be accomplished by the introduction of an individualistic social order.

One further topic demands our attention in closing. What is the nature of personal heredity? Is it biological and inherent, or, like all the characteristics of the Japanese people thus far studied, is personality transmitted by social heredity? Distinguishing between intrinsic or inherent personality,[DB] which constitutes the original endowment differentiating man from animal, and extrinsic or acquired personality, which consists of the various forms in which the inherent personality has manifested itself in the different races of men and the different ages of "history, it is safe to say that the latter is transmitted according to the laws of association or social heredity. Intrinsic personality can be inherited only by lineal offspring, passing from father to son. Extrinsic personality may fail to be inherited by lineal descendants and may be inherited by others than lineal descendants. It is transmitted and determined by social inheritance. Yet it is through personality that the individual may break away from the dominant currents of the social order, and become thus the means for the transformation of that order. The secret of social progress lies in personality. In proportion as the social order is fitted, accordingly, widely to develop high-grade personality,[DC] is its own progress rapid and safe.

Does acquired personality react on intrinsic personality? This is the problem of "the inheritance of acquired characteristics." Into this problem I do not enter further than to note that in so far as newly developed personal traits produce transformations of body and brain transmittable from parent to offspring by the bare fact of parentage, in that degree does acquired pass over into intrinsic personality and thereby become intrinsic. In regard to the degree in which acquired has passed over into intrinsic personality, thus differentiating the leading races of mankind, we contend that it is practically non-existent. The phenomena of personality characterizing the chief races of men are due, not to intrinsic, but to acquired personality; in other words they are the products of the respective social orders and are transmitted from generation to generation by social rather than by biological heredity.

XXXIV
THE BUDDHIST WORLD-VIEW

Fully to comprehend the genius and history of Japan and her social order, we need to gain a still more thorough insight into the various conceptions of the universe that have influenced the people. What have been their views as to the nature of the ultimate reality lying behind all phenomena? What as to the relation of mankind to that Ultimate Reality? And what has been the relation of these world-views to the social order? To prepare the way for our final answer to these questions, we confine ourselves in this chapter to a study of the inner nature of the Buddhist world-view.

Since the Buddhist conception of the Ultimate Reality and of the universe is one of the three important types of world-views dominating the human mind, a type too that is hardly known in Western lands, in order to set it forth in terms intelligible to the Occidental and the Christian, it will be necessary in expounding it to contrast it with the two remaining types; namely, the Greek and the Christian. As already pointed out, according to the Buddhistic conception, the Ultimate is a thoroughgoing Abstraction. All the elements of personality are denied. It is perfectly passionless, perfectly thoughtless, and perfectly motionless. It has neither feeling, idea, nor will. As a consequence, the phenomena of the universe are wholly unrelated to it; all that is, is only illusion; it has no reality of being. Human beings who think the world real, and who think even themselves real, are under the spell. This illusion is the great misery and source of pain. Salvation is the discovery of the illusion; and this discovery is the victory over it; for no one fears the lion's skin, however much he may fear the lion. This discovery secures the dropping back from the little, limited, individual self-line, into the infinite passionless, thoughtless, and motionless existence of the absolute being, Nirvana.

The Ancient Greek and not a little modern thought, conceived of the Ultimate as a thorough-going intellectualism. One aspect of personality was perceived and emphasized. God was conceived as a thinker, as one who contemplates the universe. He does not create matter, nor force, nor does he rule them. They are eternal and real, and subject to fate. God simply observes. He is absolute reason. The Greek view is thus essentially dualistic. Sin, from the Greek point of view, is merely ignorance, and salvation the attainment of knowledge.

In vital and vitalizing contrast to both the Buddhist and Greek conceptions is the Judæo-Christian. To the Christian the Ultimate is a thoroughgoing personality. To him the central element in God is will, guided by reason and controlled by love and righteousness. God creates and rules everything. There is nothing that is not wholly subject to him. There is no dualism for the Christian, nor any illusion. Sin is an act of human will, not an illusion nor a failure of intellect. Salvation is the correction of the will, which comes about through a "new birth."

The elemental difference, then, between these three conceptions of the Ultimate is that in Buddhism the effort to rationalize and ethicize the universe of experience is abandoned as a hopeless task; the world entirely and completely resists the rational and ethical process. The universe is pronounced completely irrational and non-moral. Change is branded as illusion. There is no room for progress in philosophic, thoroughgoing Buddhism.

In the Greek view the universe is subject in part to the rationalizing process; but only in part. The effort at ethicization is entirely futile. The Greek view, equally with the Buddhistic, is at a loss to understand change. It does not brand it as unreal, but change produced by man is branded as a departure from nature. Greeks and Hindus alike have no philosophy of history. In the Christian view the universe is completely subject to the rational and ethical process. God is creator of all that is and it is necessarily good. God is an active will and He is, therefore, still in the process of creating; hence change, evolution, is justified and understood. History is rational and has a philosophy. Evolution and revelation have their place at the very heart of the universe. Hence it is that science, philosophy, and history, in a word a high-grade civilization, finds its intellectual justification, its foundation, its primary postulates, its possibility, only in a land permeated with the Christian idea of God.

In the Buddhistic conception God is an abstract vacuity; in the Greek, a static intellect; in the Christian, a dynamic will. As is the conception of God, so is the conception and character of man. The two are so intimately interdependent that it is useless at this time to discuss which is the cause and which the result. They are doubtless the two aspects of the same movement of thought. The following differences are necessary characteristics of the three religions:

The Buddhist seeks salvation through the attainment of vacuity—Nirvana—in order to escape from the world in which he says there is no reason and no morality. The Greek seeks salvation through the activity of the intellect; all that is needful to salvation is knowledge of the truth. The Christian seeks salvation through the activity of the will; this is secured through the new birth. The Buddhist leaves each man to save himself from his illusion by the discovery that it is an illusion. The Greek relies on intellectual education, on philosophy—the Christian recreates the will. The Buddhist and Greek gods make no effort to help the lost man. The Christian God is dominated by love; He is therefore a missionary God, sending even His only begotten Son to reconcile and win the world of sinning, willful children back to Himself.

In Buddhism salvation is won only by the few and after ages of toil and ceaseless re-births. In the Greek plan only the philosopher who comes to full understanding can attain salvation. In the Christian plan salvation is for all, for all are sons of God, in fact, and may through Christ become so in consciousness. In the Buddhistic plan the hopeless masses resort to magic and keep on with their idolatry and countless gross superstitions. In the Greek plan the hopeless resort to the "mysteries" for the attainment of salvation. In the Christian plan there are no hopeless masses, for all may gain the regenerated will and become conscious sons of God.

The Buddhist mind gave up all effort to grasp or even to understand reality. The Greek mind thought it could arrive at reality through the intellect. But two thousand years of philosophic study and evolution drove philosophy into the absurd positions of absolute subjective idealism on the one hand and sensationalism and absolute materialism on the other. The Christian mind lays emphasis on the will and accordingly is alone able to reach reality, a reality justifiable alike to the reason and to the heart. For will is the creative faculty in man as well as in God. As God through His will creates reality, so man through his will first comes to know reality. Mere intellect can never pass over from thought to being. Being can be known as a reality only through the will.

In consequence of the above-stated methods of thought, the Buddhist was of necessity a pessimist; the Greek only less so; while the Jew and the Christian could alone be thoroughgoing optimists. The Buddhist ever asserts the is-not; the Greek, the is; while the Jew and Christian demand the ought-to be, as the supreme thing. Hence flows the perennial life of the Christian civilization.

Those races and civilizations whose highest and deepest conception of the ultimate is that of mere reason, no less than those races and civilizations whose highest and deepest conception of reality is that of an abstract emptiness, must be landed in an unreal world, must arrive at irrational results, for they have not taken into account the most vital element of thought and life. Such races and civilizations cannot rise to the highest levels of which man is capable; they must of necessity give way to those races and that civilization which build on larger and more complete foundations, which worship Will, Human and Divine, and seek for its larger development both in self and in all mankind.

But I must not pause to trace the contrasts further. Enough has been said to show the source of Occidental belief in the infinite worth of man. In almost diametrical contrast to the Buddhist conception, according to the Christian view, man is a real being, living in a real world, involved in a real intellectual problem, fighting a real battle, on whose issue hang momentous, nay, infinite results. So great is man's value, not only to himself, but also to God, his Father, that the Father himself suffers with him in his sin, and for him, to save him from his sin. The question will be asked how widely the Buddhistic interpretation of the universe has spread in Japan. The doctrine of illusion became pretty general. We may doubt, however, whether the rationale of the philosophy was very generally understood. One Sutra, read by all Japanese sects, is taught to all who would become acquainted with the essentials of Buddhist doctrine. It is so short that I give it in full.[DD]

THE SMALLER-PRAGNA-PARAMITA-HRIDYA-SUTRA

"Adoration to the Omniscient. The venerable Bodhisattva Avalokitesvara performing his study in the deep Pragna-paramita [perfection of Wisdom] thought thus: There are the five Skandhas, and these he considered as by their nature empty [phenomenal]. O Sariputra, he said, form here is emptiness, and emptiness indeed is form. Emptiness is not different from form, and form is not different from emptiness. What is form that is emptiness, what is emptiness that is form. The same applies to perception, name, conception, and knowledge.

"Here, O Sariputra, all things have the character of emptiness; they have no beginning, no end, they are faultless and not faultless, they are not imperfect and not perfect. Therefore, O Sariputra, in this emptiness there is no form, no perception, no name, no concepts, no knowledge. No eye, ear, nose, tongue, body, mind. No form, sound, smell, taste, touch, objects.... There is no knowledge, no ignorance, no destruction of knowledge, no destruction of ignorance, etc., there is no decay and death, no destruction of decay and death; there are not the four truths, viz., that there is pain, the origin of pain, stopping of pain, and the path to it. There is no knowledge, no obtaining of Nirvana.

"A man who has approached the Pragna-paramita of the Bodhisattva dwells enveloped in consciousness. But when the envelop of consciousness has been annihilated, then he becomes free of all fear, beyond the reach of change, enjoying final Nirvana. All Buddhas of the past, present, and future, after approaching the Pragna-paramita, have awakened to the highest perfect knowledge.

"Therefore one ought to know the great verse of the Pragna-paramita, the verse of the great wisdom, the unsurpassed verse, the peerless verse, which appeases all pain; it is truth because it is not false; the verse proclaimed in the Pragna-paramita: 'O wisdom, gone, gone, gone, to the other shore, landed at the other shore, Shava.'

"Thus ends the heart of the Pragna-paramita."

A study of this condensed and widely read Buddhist Sutra will convince anyone that the ultimate conceptions of the universe and of the final reality, are as described above. However popular Buddhism might differ from this, it would be the belief of the thoughtless masses, to whom the rational and ethical problems are of no significance or concern, and who contribute nothing to the development of thought or of the social order. Those nobler and more earnestly inquiring souls whose energy and spiritual longing might have been used for the benefit of the masses, were shunted off on a side track that led only into the desert of atomistic individualism, abandonment of society, ecstatic contemplation, and absolute pessimism. The Buddhist theory of the universe and method of thought denied all intelligible reality, and necessitated the conclusion that the universe of experience is neither rational nor ethical. The common beliefs of the unreflective and uninitiated masses in the ultimate rationality and morality of the universe were felt to have no foundation either in religion or philosophy and were accordingly pronounced mere illusions.

XXXV
COMMUNAL AND INDIVIDUAL ELEMENTS IN THE EVOLUTION OF JAPANESE RELIGIOUS LIFE

Our study of Japanese religion and religious life thus far has been almost, if not exclusively, from the individualistic standpoint. An adequate statement, however, cannot be made from this standpoint alone, for religion through its mighty sanctions exerts a powerful influence on the entire communal life. Indeed, the leading characteristic of primitive religions is their communal nature. The science of religion shows how late in human history is the rise of individualistic religions.

In the present chapter we propose to study Japanese religious history from the communal standpoint. This will lead us to study her present religious problem and the nature of the religion required to solve it.

The real nature of the religious life of Japan has been and still is predominantly communal. Individualism has had a place, but, as we have repeatedly seen, only a minor place in forming the nation. From the communo-individualistic standpoint, in the study of Japan's religious and social evolution, not only can we see clearly that the three religions of Japan are real religions, but we can also understand the nature of the relations of these three religions to each other and the reasons why they have had such relations. Japanese religious history and its main phenomena become luminous in the light of communo-individualistic social principles.

Shinto, the primitive religion of Japan, corresponded well with the needs of primitive times, when the development of strong communal life was the prime problem and necessity. It furnished the religious sanctions for the social order in its customs of worshiping not only the gods, but also the Emperor and ancestors. It gave the highest possible justification of the national social order in its deification of the supreme ruler. Shinto was so completely communal in its nature that the individual aspect of religion was utterly ignored. It developed no specific moral code, no eschatological and soteriological systems, no comprehensive view of nature or of the gods. These deficiencies, however, are no proofs that it was not a religion in the proper sense of the term. The real question is, did it furnish any supra-mundane, supra-legal, supra-communal sanctions both for the conduct of the individual in his social relations and for the fact and the right of the social order? Of this there can be no doubt. Those who deny it the name of a religion do so because they judge religion only from the point of view of a highly developed individualistic religion.

In view of this undoubted fact, it is a strange commentary on the failure of Shinto leaders to realize the real function of the faith they profess that they have sought and obtained from the government the right to be considered and classified no longer as a religion, but only as a society for preserving the memories and shrines of the ancestors of the race. Thus has modern Shinto, so far as it is organized and has a mouth with which to speak, following the abdicating proclivities of the ancient social order, excommunicated itself from its religious heritage, aspiring to be nothing more than a gate-keeper of cemeteries.

The sources of the power of the Shinto sanctions lies in the nature of its conception of the universe. Although it attempted no interpretation of the universe as a whole, it conceived of the origin of the country and people of Japan as due to the direct creative energy of the gods. Japan was accordingly conceived as a divine land and the people a divine people. The Emperor was thought to have descended in direct line from the gods and thus to be a visible representative of the gods to the people, and to possess divine power and authority with which to rule the people. Whenever Japanese came into contact with foreign peoples, it was natural to consider them outside of the divine providence, aliens, whose presence in the divine land was more or less of a pollution. This world-view was well calculated to develop a spirit of submissive obedience and loyal adherence to the hereditary rulers of the land, and of fierce antagonism to foreigners. This view constituted the moral foundation for the social order, the intellectual framework within which the state developed. Paternal feudalism was the natural, if not the necessary, accompaniment of this world-view. Even to this day the scholars of the land see no other ground on which to found Imperial authority, no other basis for ethics and religion, than the divine descent of the Emperor.[D]

The Shinto world-view, conceiving of men as direct offspring of the gods, has in it potentially the doctrine of the divine nature of all men, and their consequent infinite worth. Shinto never developed this truth, however. It did not discover the momentous implications of its view. Failing to discover them, it failed to introduce into the social order that moral inspiration, that social leaven which would have gradually produced the individualistic social order.

No attempt has been made either in ancient or modern times to square this Shinto world-view with advancing knowledge of the world, particularly with the modern scientific conception of the universe. Anthropology, ethnology, and the doctrine of evolution both cosmic and human, are all destructive of the primitive Shinto world-view. It would not be difficult to show, however, that in this world-view exists a profound element of truth. The Shinto world-conception needs to be expanded to take the universe and all races of men into its view; and to see that Japan is not alone the object of divine solicitude, but that all races likewise owe their origin to that same divine power, and that even though the Emperor is not more directly the offspring of the gods than are all men, yet in the providence of Him who ruleth the affairs of men, the Emperor is in fact the visible representative of authority and power for the people over whom he reigns. With this expansion and the consequences that flow from it, the world-view that has cradled Old Japan will come into accord with the scientific Christian world-view, and become fitted to be the foundation for the new and individualistic social order, now arising in Japan, granting full liberty of thought and action, knowing that only so can truth come out of error, and assured that truth is the only ground of permanent welfare.

Throughout the centuries including the present era of Meiji, it is the Shinto religion that has provided and that still provides religious sanctions for the social order—even for the new social order that has come in from the West. It is the belief of the people in the divine descent of the Emperor, and his consequent divine right, that to-day unifies the nation and causes it to accept so readily the new social order; desired by him, they raise no questions, make no opposition, even though in some respects it brings them trouble and anxiety.

Our study of Buddhism has brought to light its extremely individualistic nature, and its lack of asocial ideal. Its world-view we have sufficiently examined in the preceding chapter. We are told that when Buddhism came to Japan it made little headway until it adopted the Shinto deities into its theogony. What does this mean? That only on condition of accepting the Shinto sanctions for the communal order of society was it able to commend itself to the people at large. And Buddhism had no difficulty in fulfilling this condition, because it had no ideal order of society to present and no religious sanctions for any kind of social order; in this respect Buddhism had no ground for conflict with Shinto. Shinto had the field to itself; and Buddhism was perfectly at liberty to adopt, or at least to allow, any social order that might present itself. Furthermore, by its doctrines of incarnation and transmigration, according to which noble souls might appear and reappear in different worlds and different lands, Buddhism could identify Shinto deities with its own deities of Hindu origin, asserting their pre-incarnation. Having accepted the Shinto deities, ideals, and sanctions for the social order, Buddhism became not only tolerable to the people, but also exceedingly popular.

The Shinto-Buddhistic was in truth a new religion, each of the old religions supplying an essential element.

One real reason, beside its accommodation to Shintoism, why Buddhism was so popular was that it brought an indispensable element into the national life. For the first time emphasis began to be laid on the individual. Introspection and deliberate meditation were brought into play. Arts demanding individual skill were fostered. A gorgeous ritual, elaborate architecture, complex religious organism, letters and literature, all gave play to individual activity and development whether in manual, in mental, or in æsthetic lines. The hitherto cramped and primitive life of the Japanese responded to these appeals and opportunities with profound joy. The upper classes especially felt themselves growing in richness and fullness of life. They felt the stimulus in many directions. The reason, then, why Buddhism flourished so mightily, and at the same time caused the nation to bloom, was because it helped develop the individual. The reason, on the other hand, why it failed to carry the nation on from its first bloom into full fruitage was because it failed to develop individualism in the social order. Its religious individualism was, as we have seen, in reality defective. It was abstract and one-sided. It did not discover the whole of the individual. It did not know anything of personality, either human or divine. It accordingly could not recognize the individual's worth, but only his separateness and his weakness. It taught an abstract impoverished idea of self, and made, as the whole aim of the salvation it offered, the final annihilation of all separateness of this individual self. We can now see that its individualism was essentially defective in that it poured contempt on the self, and that if its individualizing salvation were consistently carried out, it was not only no help to the social order, but a positive injury to it. Its individualism was of a nature which could not become an integral part of any social order.

This character led to another inevitable difficulty. Although Buddhism ostensibly adopted Shinto deities and the Shinto sanctions for the social order, it could not wholeheartedly accept the sanctions nor take the deities into full and legitimate partnership. It found no place in its circle of doctrine to teach the important tenets of Shintoism. It left them to survive or perish as chance would have it. In proportion as Buddhism absorbed the life and love of the people, Shinto fell into decay and with it its sanctions. Then came the centuries of civil war during which Imperial power and authority sank to a minimum, and Japan's ignominy and disorder reached their maximum. What the land now needed was the re-introduction, first, of social order, even though it must be by the hand of a dictator, and second, the development of religious sanctions for the order that should be established. The first was secured by those three great generals of Japan, Oda Nobunaga, the Taiko Hideyoshi, and Tokugawa Ieyasu. "The first conceived the idea of centralizing all the authority of the state in a single person; the second, who has been called the Napoleon of Japan, actually put the idea into practice," but died before consolidating his work; the third, by his unsurpassed skill as a diplomat and administrator, carried the idea completely out, arranging the details of the new order so that, without special military genius or power on the part of his successors, the order maintained itself for 250 years.

Yet it is doubtful if this long maintenance of the social order introduced by Ieyasu would have been possible had he not found ready to hand a system of essentially religious sanctions for the social order he had established by force. Confucianism had lain for a thousand years a dormant germ, receiving some study from learned men, but having no special relation to the education of the day or to the political problems that became each century more pressing. In the Confucian doctrines of loyalty to ruler and piety to parents, a doctrine sanctioned by Heaven and by the customs of all the ancients, Ieyasu, with the insight of a master mind, found just the sanctions he desired. He had the Confucian classics printed—it is said for the first time in Japan—"and the whole intellect of the country became molded by Confucian ideas." The classics, edited with diacritical marks for Japanese students, "formed the chief vehicle of every boy's education." These were interpreted by learned Chinese commentators. The intelligence of the land drank of this stream as the European mind refreshed itself with the classic waters of the Renaissance. The Japanese were weary of Buddhistic puerilities and transcendental doctrines that led nowhere. They demanded sanctions for the moral life and the social order; in response to this need Buddhism gave them Nirvana—absolute mental and moral vacuity. Confucianism gave them principles whose working and whose results they could see and understand. Its sanctions appealed both to the imagination and to the reason, antiquity and learning and piety being all in their favor. The sanctions were also seen to be wholly independent of puerile superstitions and foolish fears. The Confucian ideals and sanctions, moreover, coincided with the essential elements of the old Shinto world-view and sanctions. In a true sense, the doctrines of Confucius were but the elaborated and succinctly stated implications of their primitive faith. Confucianism, therefore, swept the land. *It was* accepted as the groundwork and authority for the most flourishing feudal order the world has ever seen. Japan bloomed again.[DF]

This difference, however, is to be noted between the Shinto ideal social order and the Confucian, or rather that development of Confucian ethics and civics which arose during the Tokugawa Shogunate; Shinto appears to have been, properly speaking, nationalistic, while feudal Confucianism was tribal. Although in Confucian theory the supreme loyalty may have been due the Emperor, in point of fact it was shown to the local daimyo. Confucian ethics was communal and might easily have turned in the direction of national communalism; it would then have coincided completely with Shinto in this respect. But for various reasons it did not so turn, but developed an intensely local, a tribal communalism, and pushed loyalty to the Emperor as a vital reality entirely into the background. This was one of the defects of feudal Confucianism which finally led to its own overthrow. Shinto, as we have seen, had long been pushed aside by Buddhism and was practically forgotten by the people. The zeal for Confucian doctrine brought, therefore, no immediate revival to the Shinto cultus, although it did revive the essential elements of the old communal religion. We might say that the old religion was revived under a new name; having a new name and a new body, the real and vital connection between the two was not recognized. We thus discern how the religious history of Japan was not a series of cataclysms or of disconnected leaps in the dark, but an orderly development, one step naturally following the next, as the sun follows the dawn. The different stages of Japan's religious progress have received different names, because due to specific stimuli brought from abroad; the religious life itself, however, has been a continuous development.

Another difference between Shinto and Confucianism as it existed in Japan should not escape our attention, namely, in regard to their respective world-views. Shinto was confessedly a religion; it frankly believed in gods, whom it worshiped and on whose help it relied. Confucianism, or to use the Japanese name, Bushido, was confessedly agnostic. It did not assume to understand the universe, as Buddhism assumed. Nor did it admit the practical existence of gods or their power in this world, as Shinto believed. It maintained that, "if only the heart follows the way of truth, the gods will protect one even though he does not pray." It laid stress on practical moralities, regardless of their philosophical presumptions, into which it would not probe. When pressed it would ascribe all to "Heaven," and, as we have seen, it had many implications that would lead the inquiring mind to a belief in the personal nature of "Heaven." Had it developed these implications, Bushido would have become a genuine religion. It was indeed a system of ethics touched with emotion, it was religious, but it failed to become the religion it might have become because it insisted on its agnosticism and refused to worship the highest and best it knew.

It is interesting to observe that the ideals and sanctions of Confucianism produced effects which proved its ruin. They did this in two ways; first, by developing the prolonged peace necessary for a high grade of scholarship which, turning its attention to ancient history, discovered that the Shogunate was assuming powers not in accord with the primitive practice nor in accord with the theory of the divine descent of the Imperial house. Imperialistic patriots arose, whose aim was to overthrow the Shogunate and restore the Emperor. They felt that, doing this, they were right; that is to say, they became inspired by the Shinto sanctions for a national life. They thus discovered the defect of the disjointed feudal system sanctioned by feudal Confucianism. The second cause of its undoing grew out of the first. The scholarship which led the patriots against the usurper in political life led them also against all foreign innovations such as Buddhism and Confucianism, which they scorned as modern and anti-imperial. The Shinto cultus thus received a powerful revival. With the overthrow of the Shogunate in 1868 Confucianism naturally went with it, and for a time Shinto was the state religion. But its poverty in every line, except the communal sanctions, caused it in a short time to lose its place.

The two causes just assigned for the fall of Bushido, however, could hardly have wrought its ruin had it been more than a utilitarian and agnostic system of morality, calculated to maintain the social ascendency of a small fraction of the nation. As a religion, Bushido would have secured a conservative power enabling it to survive, by adapting itself to a changed social order. As it was, Bushido was snuffed out by a single breath of the breeze that began to blow from foreign lands. As an ethical system it has conferred a blessing on Japan that should never be forgotten. But its identification with a class and a clan social order rendered it too narrow for the national and international life into which the nation was forced by circumstances beyond its control, and its agnostic utilitarianism did not provide it with sufficient moral power to cope with the problems of the new individualistic age that had suddenly burst upon it. In all Japan there remains to the present day only one of those old Confucian schools with its temple to Confucius. All the rest have fallen into ruins or have been used for other purposes, while the gold-covered statues of the once deified teacher have been sold to curio-dealers or for their bullion value. In the worship of Confucius, Bushido almost became a religion, but it worshiped the teacher instead of the Creator, maintaining its agnosticism as to the Creator, as to "Heaven," to the end, and thus lapsed from the path of religious evolution.

This brings us down to modern times—into the seventies. Already in the sixties Japan had discovered herself in a totally new environment. She found that foreign nations had made great progress in every direction since she shut them out two hundred and fifty years before. She discovered her helplessness, she discovered, too, that the social order of Western peoples was totally distinct from hers. These discoveries served to break down all the remaining sanctions for her particular type of social order—Confucianistic feudalism. The whole nation was eager to know the political systems of the West. So long as the Shinto ideal of nationalism was not interfered with, the nation was free to adopt any new social order. Japan's political and commercial intercourse being with England and America, the social order of the Anglo-Saxon had the greatest influence on the Japanese mind. Japan accordingly has become predominantly Anglo-Saxon in its social ideas. Much has been made of the fact that the new social order has come in so easily; that the people have gained rights without fighting for them; and this has been attributed to the peculiarity of Japanese human nature. This is an error. The real reason for the ease with which the individualistic Anglo-Saxon social order has been introduced has been the collapse of the sanctions for the Confucian order. No one had any ground of duty on which to stand and fight. The national mind was open to any newcomer that might have appeared. I am referring, of course, to the thinking classes. All the rest, accustomed to submissive obedience, never thought of any other course than to accept the will of superiors.

Furthermore, the new social order in one important respect fell in with and helped to re-establish the old Shinto ideal, that, namely, of nationalism. In the treaty negotiations, the West would deal with no intermediaries, only with the responsible national head. Western ideals, too, demanded a strong national unity. In this respect, then, the foreign ideals and foreign social order were powerful influences in building up the new patriotism, in re-enforcing the old Shinto social sanctions.

Thus has Japan come to the parting of the ways. What Japan needs to-day is a religion satisfying the intellect as to its world-view, and thus justifying the sanctions it holds out. These must be neither exclusively communal, like those of Shinto, nor exclusively individual, like those of Buddhism. While maintaining at their full value the sanctions for the social life, it must add thereto the sanctions for the individual. It must not look upon the individual as a being whose salvation depends on his being isolated from, taken out of the community, as Buddhism did and does, nor yet as a mere fraction of the community, as Confucianism did, but as a complete, imperishable unit of infinite worth, necessarily living a double life, partly inseparable from the social order and partly superior to it. This religion must provide not only sanctions, but ideals, for a perfect social order in which, while the most complex organization of society shall be possible, the freedom and the high development of the individual's personality shall also be secured.

The fulfillment of such conditions would at first thought seem to be impossible. How can a religion give sanctions which at the very time that they authorize the fullest development and organization of society, apparently making society its chief end, also assume the fullest liberty and development of the individual, making him and his salvation its chief end? Are not these ends incompatible? What has been said already along this general line of thought has prepared us to see that they are not. The great, though unconscious, need of the ages, and the unconscious effort of all religious evolution has been the development of just such a religion. As the "cake" of social custom was at first the great need for, and afterwards the great obstacle in the way of, social evolution, so the sanctions of a communal religion were at first the great need for, and afterwards the great obstacle in the way of, religious evolution and of personal development. Through its sanctions religion is the most powerful of all the factors of the higher human evolution, either helping it onward or holding it back.

Has, then, any religion secured such a dual development as we have just seen to be necessary? As a matter of fact, one and only one has done so, Christianity. This religion clearly attains and maintains the apparently impossible combination of individualism and communalism by the nature of its conception of the method of individual salvation. Its communalism is guaranteed by, because it rests on, its individualism. At the very moment that it pronounces the individual of inestimable worth,—a son of God,—it commands him to show that sonship by loving all God's other sons, and by serving them to the extent of self-sacrifice, and of death if need be. Its communalism is thus inseparable from its individualism and its individualism from its communalism.

Christian individualism embraces and includes thoroughgoing communalism. True and full Christians are the most devoted patriots. As the acorn sends forth far-reaching; roots into the soil for moisture and nourishment, and a mighty trunk and spreading branches upward for air and sunlight, so the seed of Christian life develops in two directions, individualism as the root and communalism as the beautiful tree. They are not contradictory, but supplementary principles. While his own final gain is a real aim of the individual, it is only a part of his aim; he also desires and labors for the gain of all; and even the individual gain, he well knows, can be secured only through the communal principle, through service to his fellow-men. His own welfare, whether temporal or eternal, is inseparably bound up with that of his fellows.

The Christian religion finds the sanctions for any and every social order that history knows, in the fact that all physical and social laws and organisms are part of the divine plan. Because any particular social order is the association of imperfect men and women, it must be more or less imperfect. But the Christian, even while he is seeking to reform the social order and to bring it up to his ideal, must be loyal to it. And for this loyalty to fellow-men and to God, the highest conceivable sanctions are held out, namely, an endless and infinite life of conscious, joyous fellowship with souls made perfect in the Kingdom of God, and with God himself.

A comprehensive study, therefore, of the real nature and the true function of religion in relation to man's development, whether individual or communal, shows that Christianity fulfills the conditions. A comparative study would show that, of all the existing religions, Christianity alone does this. It alone combines in perfect proportion the individual and the communal elements, and the requisite sanctions.

An expansion of communal religion is taking place in modern times. The community now arising is international in scope, interracial and universal in character. Cultivated men and women the world around are beginning to talk of national rights and national duties. Europe is thought to be justified in suppressing the slave trade and its accompanying horrors in Africa, and condemned for not preventing the Turk from carrying on his wholesale slaughter of innocent Armenians. The Spaniard is despised and condemned for his prolonged inhumanities in Cuba and the Philippines, and the American is approved in warring for humanity and justified in interfering with Spain's sovereignty. The conscience of the world is beginning to discover that no nation, though sovereign, has an absolute right over its people. Right is only measured by righteousness. International righteousness, duty and rights, regardless of military power, are coming to the forefront of the thinking of advanced nations.

Looked at closely, and studied in its implications, what is this but a developing form of communal religion? No nation is conceived as existing apart; each exists as but one fraction of the world-wide community; in its relations it has both rights and duties. Does this not mean that appeal has been made from the communal sanctions of might to the supra-communal sanctions of right? We do not simply ask what do other nations think of this or that national act, but what is right, in view of the whole order of the nature which has brought man into being and set him in families and nations. In other words, national rights and duties are felt to flow from the supra-mundane source, God the Creator of heaven and earth and all that in them is. The sanctions for national rights and duties are religious sanctions and rest on a religious world-view.

Now the point, of interest for us is the fact that Japan has entered into this universal community and is feeling the sanctions of this universal communal religion. The international rights and duties of Japan are a theme of frequent discourse and conversation. Japan stoutly maintained that the war with China was a "gi-sen," a righteous war, waged

172

primarily for the sake of Korea. Many a Japanese waxes indignant over the cruelty of the Turk, the savage barbarity of the Spaniard, and the impotence and supineness of England and Europe. I have already spoken of the young man who became so indignant at England's compelling China to take Indian opium, that he proposed to go to England to preach an anti-opium crusade. Japan is beginning to enter into the larger communal life of the world, although, of course, she has as yet little perception of its varied implications.

Many a student of New Japan perceives that she is abandoning her old religious conceptions, and that many moral and social evils are entering the land, who yet does not see that the wide acceptance of some new religion by the people is important for the maintenance of the nation. Some earnest Japanese thinkers are beginning to realize that religion is, indeed, needful to steady the national life, but they fail to see that Christianity alone fulfills the condition. Many are saying that a religion scientifically constructed must be manufactured especially for Japan.

The reason why individualistic religion takes such an important part in the higher evolution of man is, in a word, because the religious sanctions are so much more powerful than all others, either legal or social. For the legal sanctions are chiefly negative; they are also partial and uncertain, and easily evaded by the selfish individual. The social sanctions, too, are often far from just or impartial or wise. Furthermore, the rise of individualism in the social order secures privacy for the individual, and so far forth removes him from the restraints and stimuli of the social sanctions. It is the religious sanctions alone that follow the man in every waking moment. Not one of all his acts escapes the eye of the religious judgment. He is his own judge, and he cannot escape bearing witness against himself.

Now, it is manifest that where superior beings and man's relation to these and the corresponding religious sanctions are defectively conceived, as, for instance, quite apart either from the individual or the communal life, they are valueless to the higher evolution of man and have little interest for the student of social evolution. In proportion, however, as man advances in intellectual grasp of religious truths and in susceptibility to the moral ideas and religious sanctions they provide, conceiving of morality and religion as inseparable parts of the same system, the more powerfully does religion enter into and promote man's higher evolution. An individualistic social order demands the religious sanctions more imperatively than a communal social order; for, in proportion as it is individualistic, the social order is weak in compelling, through the legal and social sanctions alone, the communal or altruistic activity of the individual. Altruistic spirit and action, however, are essential to the maintenance even of that individualistic order. The more highly society develops, therefore, the more religious must each member of the society become.

The same truth may be stated from another standpoint. The higher man develops, the more impatient he becomes with illogical reasonings and defective conceptions; he thus becomes increasingly skeptical in regard to current traditional religions with their crude, primitive ideas; he is accordingly increasingly freed from the restraints they impose. But unless he finds some new religious sanctions for the communal life, for social conduct, and for the individual life,—ideals and sanctions that command his assent and direct his life,—he will drop back into a thoroughgoing atomic, individualistic, selfish life, which can be only a hindrance to the higher development both of society and of the individual. In order that men advancing in intellectual ability may remain useful members of society, they must remain subject to those ideals and sanctions which will actually secure social conduct. While disregarding the chaff of primitive religious superstitions and ceremonials man must retain the wheat; he must feel the force of the religious spirit in a deeper and profounder, because more personal way than did his ancestors. Increasing intellectual power and knowledge must be balanced by increasing individual experience of the religious motives and spirit. This is the reason why each advancing age should study afresh the whole religious problem, and state in the terms of its own experience the prominent and permanent religious truths of all the ages and the sanctions that flow from them. Hence it is that a religion only traditional and ceremonial is quite unfitted for a developing life.

Japan is no exception to the general laws of human evolution. As her intellectual abilities increase, the forms of her old religious life will become increasingly unacceptable to the people at large. If, in rejecting the obsolete forms of religious thought, she rejects religion and its sanctions altogether, atomistic individualism can be the only result, and with it wide moral corruption will eat out the vitality of the national life.

That Christianity alone, of all the religions of the world, fulfills the conditions will not need many words to prove. As a matter of fact Christianity alone has succeeded in surviving the criticism of the nineteenth century. In Christendom, all religions but Christianity have perished. This is a mere matter of fact. As for the reason, Christianity alone gives complete intellectually satisfactory sanctions for both the communal and the individualistic principles of social progress. Christianity, as we have sufficiently shown, has both principles not unrelated to each other, but vitally interrelated. For these reasons it is safe to maintain not only that Japan needs to find a new religion, but that the religion must be Christianity in substance, whatever be the name given it.

The Japanese have been described as essentially irreligious in nature. We have seen how defective such a description is. But have we not now traced one root ofthis seeming characteristic of New Japan? The old religious conceptions have been largely outgrown by the educated. They have come to the conclusion that the old religious forms constitute the whole of religion, and that consequently they are unworthy of attention. The spirit of New Japan is indifferent to religion; but this is not due to an inherently non-religious or irreligious nature, but to the empty externalism and shallow puerilities of the only religions they know. How can they be zealous for them or recognize any authority in them? Those few Japanese who have come within the influence of the larger conception of religion brought to Japan by Christianity are showing a religious zeal and power supporting the contention that the generally asserted lack of a religious nature is only apparent and temporary. Preaching the right set of ideas, those which appeal to the national sense of communal needs, by supplying the demand for sanctions for the social order; ideas which appeal to intellects molded by modern thought, by supplying such an intellectual understanding of the universe as justifies the various supra-communal sanctions; and ideas which appeal to the heart, by supplying the personal demand of each individual for a larger life, for intercourse with the Father of all Spirits and for strength for the prolonged battle of life—preach these and kindred ideas, and the Japanese will again become as conspicuously a religious people as they were when Buddhism came to Japan a thousand years ago.[DG]

But if the real nature of a full and perfect religion is to save not only the individual, providing sanctions for his conduct, but also to justify the social order, and to provide sanctions that shall secure its maintenance, any religion which fails to have both characteristics can hardly claim the name universal. We have seen that Buddhism lacks one of these elements. In my judgment it is not properly universal. So long as it exists in or goes to a land already provided with other religions securing the social order, it may continue to thrive. But, on the one hand, it can never become the exclusive religion of any land for it cannot do without and therefore it cannot depose the other religions; and, on the other hand, it must give way before the stronger religion which has both the individual and communal elements combined. Buddhism, therefore, lacks a vital characteristic of a universal religion. It may better be called a non-local, or an international religion. We now see another reason why Buddhism, although found in many Oriental lands, has never annihilated any of the pre-existing religions, but has only added one more to the many varieties already existing. It is so in Thibet, in China, in Burmah, and in Japan. And in India, its home, it has utterly died out.

Many of the efforts made by students of comparative religion to classify the various religions, seem to the writer defective through lack of the perception that social and religious evolution are vitally connected. From this point of view, the classification of religions as communal, individual, and communo-individual, would seem to be the best.

XXXVI
WHAT ARE THE ESSENTIAL CHARACTERISTICS OF THE ORIENT?

We have now passed in rather detailed review the emotional, æsthetic, intellectual, moral, and religious characteristics of the Japanese race. We have, furthermore, given considerable attention to the problem of personality. We have tried to understand the relation of each characteristic to the Japanese feudal system and social order.

The reader will perhaps feel some dissatisfaction with the results of this study. "Are there, then," he may say, "no distinctive Japanese psychical characteristics by which this Eastern race is radically differentiated from those of the Occident?" "Are there no peculiar features of an Oriental, mental and moral, which infallibly and always distinguish him from an Occidental?" The reply to this question given in the preceding chapters of this work is negative. For the sake, however, of the reader who may not yet be thoroughly satisfied, it may be well to examine this problem a little further, analyzing some of the current characterizations of the Orient.

That Oriental and Occidental peoples are each possessed of certain unique psychic characteristics, sharply and completely differentiating them from each other, is the opinion of scientific sociologists as well as of more popular writers. An Occidental entering the Orient is well-nigh overwhelmed with amusement and surprise at the antipodal characteristics of the two civilizations. Every visible expression of Oriental civilization, every mode of thought, art, architecture; conceptions of God, man, and nature; pronunciation and structure of the language—all seem utterly different from their corresponding elements in the West. Furthermore, as he visits one Oriental country after another, although he discovers differences between Japanese, Koreans, Chinese, and Hindus, yet he is impressed with a strange, a baffling similarity.

The tourist naturally concludes that the unity characterizing the Orient is fundamental; that Oriental civilization is due to Oriental race brain, and Occidental civilization is due to Occidental race brain.

This impression and this conclusion of the tourist are not, however, limited to him. The "old resident" in the East becomes increasingly convinced with every added year that an Oriental is a different kind of human being from a Westerner. As he becomes accustomed to the externals of the Oriental civilization, he forgets its comical aspects, he even comes to appreciate many of its conveniences. But in proportion as he becomes familiar with its languages, its modes of thought and feeling, its business methods, its politics, its literature, its amusements, does he increasingly realize the gulf set between an Oriental and an Occidental. The inner life of the spirit of an Oriental would be utterly inane, spiritless to the average Occidental. The "old resident" accordingly knows from long experience what the tourist only guesses from a hasty glance, that the characteristic differences distinguishing the peoples of the East and the West are racial and ineradicable. An Oriental is an Oriental, and that is the ultimate, only thoroughgoing explanation of his nature.

The conception of the tourist and the "old resident" crops up in nearly every article and book touching on Far Eastern peoples. Whatever the point of remark or criticism, if it strikes the writer as different from the custom of Occidentals, it is laid to the account of Orientalism.

This conception, however, of distinguishing Oriental characteristics, is not confined to popular writers and unscientific persons. Even professed and eminent sociologists advocate it. Prof. Le Bon, in his sophistic volume on the "Psychology of Peoples," advocates it strenuously. A few quotations from this interesting work may not be out of place.

"The object of this work is to describe the psychological characteristics which constitute the soul of races, and to show how the history of a people and its civilization is determined by these characteristics."[DH] "The point that has remained most clearly fixed in mind, after long journeys through the most varied countries, is that each people possesses a mental constitution as unaltering as its anatomical characteristics, a constitution which is the source of its sentiments, thoughts, institutions, beliefs, and arts."[DI]

"The life of a people, its institutions, beliefs, and arts, are but the visible expression of its invisible soul. For a people to transform its institutions, beliefs, and arts it must first transform its soul."[DJ]

"Each race possesses a constitution as unvarying as its anatomical constitution. There seems to be no doubt that the former corresponds to a certain special structure of the brain."[DK]

"A negro or a Japanese may easily take a university degree or become a lawyer; the sort of varnish he thus acquires is, however, quite superficial and has no influence on his mental constitution. What no education can give him, because they are created by heredity alone, are the forms of thought, the logic, and above all the character of the Western man."[DL]

"Cross-breeding constitutes the only infallible means at our disposal of transforming in a fundamental manner the character of a people, heredity being the only force powerful enough to contend with heredity. Cross-breeding allows of the creation of a new race, possessing new physical and psychological characteristics."[DM]

Such, then, being the opinion of travelers, residents, and professional sociologists, it is not to be lightly rejected. Nor has it been lightly rejected by the writer. For years he agreed with this view, but repeated study of the problem has convinced him of the fallacy of both the conception and the argument, and has brought him to the position maintained in this work.

The characteristics differentiating Occidental and

Oriental peoples and civilizations are undoubtedly great. But they are differences of social evolution and rest on social, not on biological heredity. Anatomical differences are natal, racial, and necessary. Not so with social characteristics and differences. These are acquired by each individual chiefly after birth, and depend on social environment which determines the education from infancy upward. Furthermore, an entire nation or race, if subjected to the right social environment, may profoundly transform its institutions, beliefs, and arts, which in turn transform what Prof. Le Bon and kindred writers call the invisible "race soul." Racial activity produces race character, for "Function produces organism." I cannot agree with these writers in the view that the race soul is a given fixed entity. Social psychogenesis is a present and a progressive process. Japan is a capital illustration of it. In the development of races and civilizations involution is as continuous a process as evolution. Evolution is, indeed, only one-half of the process. Without involution, evolution is incomprehensible. And involution is the more interesting half, as it is the more significant. In modern discussion much that passes by the name of evolution is, in reality, a discussion of involution.

The attentive reader will have discovered that the real point of the discussion of Japanese characteristics given in the preceding chapters has been on the point of involution. How have these characteristics arisen? has been our ever-recurring question. The answer has invariably tried to show their relation to the social order. In this way we have traversed a large number of leading characteristics of the Japanese. We have seen how they arose, and also how they are now being transformed by the new Occidentalized social order. We have seen that not one of the characteristics examined is inherent, that is, due to brain structure, to biological heredity. We have concluded, therefore, that the psychical characteristics which differentiate races are all but wholly social.

It is incumbent on advocates of the biological view to point out in detail the distinguishing inherent traits of the Orient. Let them also catalogue the essential psychic characteristics of Occidentals. Such an attempt is seldom made. And when it is made it is singularly unconvincing. Although Prof. Le Bon states that the mental constitution of races is as distinctive and unaltering as their anatomical characteristics, he fails to tell us what they are. This is a vital omission. If the differences are as distinct as he asserts, it would seem to be an easy matter to describe them. Whatever the clothing adopted, it is an easy matter for one to distinguish a European from an Asiatic, an Englishman from an Italian, a Japanese from a Korean, a Chinaman from a Hindu. The anatomical characteristics of races are clear and easily described. If the psychic characteristics are equally distinct, why do not they who assert this distinctness describe and catalogue these differences?

Occasionally a popular writer makes something of an attempt in this direction, but with astonishingly slight results. A recent writer in the London *Daily Mail* has illustrated afresh the futility of all attempts to catalogue the distinguishing characteristics of the Oriental. He names the inferior position assigned to women, the licentiousness of men, licensed prostitution, lack of the play instinct among Oriental boys, scorn of Occidental civilization, and the rude treatment of foreigners. Many of his statements of facts are sadly at fault. But supposing them to be true, are they the differentiating characteristics of the Orient? Consider for a moment what was the position of woman in ancient times in the Occident, and what was the moral character of Occidental men? Is not prostitution licensed to-day in the leading cities of Europe? And is there not an unblushing prostitution in the larger cities of England and America which would put to shame the licensed prostitution of Japan? Are Orientals and their civilization universally esteemed and considerately treated in the Occident? Surely none of these are uniquely Oriental characteristics, distinguishing them from Occidental peoples as clearly as the anatomical characteristics of oblique eyes and yellow skin.

Mr. Percival Lowell has made a careful philosophical effort to discover the essential psychic nature of the Orient. He describes it, as we have seen, as "Impersonality." The failure of his effort we have sufficiently considered.

There remain a few other characterizations of the Orient that we may well examine briefly.

It has been stated that the characteristic psychic trait distinguishing the East from the West is that the former is intuitive, while the latter is logical. In olden times Oriental instruction relied on the intuitions of the student. No reliance was placed on the logical process. Religion, so far as it was not ceremony and magic, was intuitional, "Satori," "Enlightenment," was the keyword. Each man attains enlightenment by himself—through a flash of intuition. Moral instruction likewise was intuitional. Dogmatic statements were made whose truth the learner was to discover for himself; no effort was made to explain them. Teaching aimed to go direct to the point, not stopping to explain the way thither.

That this was and is a characteristic of the Orient cannot be disputed. The facts are abundant and clear. But the question is whether this is a racial psychic characteristic, such that it inevitably controls the entire thinking of an Oriental, whatever his education, and also whether the Occident is conspicuously deficient in this psychic characteristic. Thus stated, the question almost answers itself.

Orientals educated in Western methods of thought acquire logical methods of reasoning and teaching. The old educational methods of Japan are now obsolete. On the other hand, intuitionalism is not unknown in the West. Mystics in religion are all conspicuously intuitional. So too are Christian scientists, faith-healers, and spiritualists. Great preachers and poets are intuitionalists rather than logicians.

Furthermore, if we look to ancient times, we shall see that even Occidentals were dominated by intuitionalism. All primitive knowledge was dominated by intuitions, and was as absurd as many still prevalent Oriental conceptions of nature. The bane of ancient science and philosophy was its reliance on a priori considerations; that is, on intuition. Inductive, carefully logical methods of thought, of science, of philosophy, and even of religion, are relatively modern developments of the Occidental mind. We have learned to doubt intuitions unverified by investigation and experimental evidence. The wide adoption of the inductive method is a recent characteristic of the West.

Modern progress has consisted in no slight degree in the development of logical powers, and particularly in the power of doubting and examining intuitions. To say that the East is conspicuously intuitional and the West is conspicuously logical is fairly true, but this misses the real difference. The West is intuitional plus logical. It uses the intuitional method in every department of life, but it does not stop with it. An intuition is not accepted as truth until it has been subjected by the reason to the most thorough criticism possible. The West distrusts the unverified and unguided intuitive judgment. On the other hand, the East is not inherently deficient in logical power. When brought into contact with Occidental life, and especially when educated in Occidental methods of thought, the Oriental is not conspicuously deficient in logical ability.

This line of thought leads to the conclusion that the psychic characteristics distinguishing the East from the West, profound though they are, are sociological rather than biological. They are the characteristics of the civilization rather than of essential race nature.

A fact remarked by many thoughtful Occidentals is the astonishing difficulty—indeed the impossibility—of becoming genuinely and intimately acquainted with the Japanese. Said a professor of Harvard University to the writer some years ago: "Do you in Japan find it difficult to become truly acquainted with the Japanese? We see many students here, but we are unable to gain more than a superficial acquaintance. They seem to be incrusted in a shell that we are unable to pierce." The editor of the *Japan Mail*, speaking of the difficulty of securing "genuinely intimate intercourse with the Japanese people," says: "The language also is needed. Yet even when the language is added, something still remains to be achieved, and what that something is we have never been able to discover, though we have been considering the subject for thirty-three years. No foreigner has ever yet succeeded in being admitted into the inner circle of Japanese intercourse."

Is this a fact? If not, why is it so widespread a belief? If it is a fact, what is the interpretation? Like most generalizations it expresses both a truth and an error. As the statement of a general experience, I believe it to be true. As an assertion of universal application I believe it to be false. As a truth, how is it to be explained? Is it due to difference of race soul, and thus to racial antipathy, as some maintain? If so, it must be a universal fact. This, however, is an error, as we shall see. The explanation is not so hard to find as at first appears.

The difficulty under consideration is due to two classes of facts. The first is that the people have long been taught that Occidentals desire to seize and possess their land. Although the more enlightened have long since abandoned this fear and suspicion, the people still suspect the stranger; they do not propose to admit foreigners to any leading position in the political life of the land. They do not implicitly trust the foreigners, even when taken into their employ. That foreigners should not be admitted to the inner circle of Japanese political life, therefore, is not strange. Nor is it unique to Japan. It is not done in any land except the United States. Secondly, the diverse methods of social intercourse characterizing the East and the West make a deep chasm between individuals of these civilizations on coming into social relations. The Oriental bows low, utters conventional "aisatsu" salutations, listens respectfully, withholds his own opinion, agrees with his vis-à-vis, weighs every word uttered with a view to inferring the real meaning, for the genius of the language requires him to assume that the real meaning is not on the surface, and chooses his own language with the same circumspection. The Occidental extends his hand for a hearty shake—if he wishes to be friendly—looks his visitor straight in the eye, speaks directly from his heart, without suspicion or fear of being misunderstood, expresses his own opinions unreservedly. The Occidental, accustomed to this direct and open manner, spontaneously doubts the man who lacks it. It is impossible for the Occidental to feel genuinely acquainted with an Oriental who does not respond in Occidental style of frank open intercourse. Furthermore, it is not Japanese custom to open one's heart, to make friends with everyone who comes along. The hail-fellow-well-met characteristic of the Occident is a feature of its individualism, that could not come into being in a feudal civilization in which every respectable man carried two swords with which to take instant vengeance on whoever should malign or doubt him. Universal secretiveness and conventionality, polite forms and veiled expressions, were the necessary shields of a military feudalism. Both the social order and the language were fitted to develop to a high degree the power of attention to minutest details of manner and speech and of inferring important matters from slight indications. The whole social order served to develop the intuitional method in human relations. Reliance was placed more on what was not said than on what was clearly expressed. A doubting state of mind was the necessary psychological prerequisite for such an inferential system. And doubt was directly taught. "Hito wo mireba dorobo to omoye," "when you see a man, count him a robber," may be an exaggeration, but this ancient proverb throws much light on the Japanese chronic state of mind. Mutual suspicion—and especially suspicion of strangers—was the rule in Old Japan. Among themselves the Japanese make relatively few intimate friends. They remark on Occidental skill in making friends.

That the foreigner is not admitted to the inner social life of the Japanese is likewise not difficult of explanation, if we bear in mind the nature of that social life. Is it possible for one who keeps concubines, who takes pleasure in geisha, and who visits houses of prostitution, to converse freely and confidentially with those who condemn these practices? Can he who stands for a high-grade morality, who criticises in unsparing measure the current morality of Japanese society, expect to be admitted to its inner social circles? Impossible. However friendly the relations of Japanese and foreigners may be in business and in the diplomatic corps, the moral chasm separating the social life of the Occident from that of the Orient effectually prevents a foreigner from being admitted to its inner social life.

It might be thought that immoral Occidentals would be so admitted. Not so. The Japanese distinguish between Occidentals. They know well that immoral Occidentals are not worthy of trust. Although for a season they may hobnob together, the intimacy is shallow and short-lived; it rests on lust and not on profound sympathies of head and heart.

And this suggests the secret of genuine acquaintance. Men become profoundly acquainted in proportion as they hold in common serious views of life, and labor together for the achievement of great moral ends. Now a gulf separates the ordinary Japanese, even though educated, from the serious-minded Occidental. Their views of life are well-nigh antipodal. If their social intercourse is due only to the accident of business or of social functions, what true intimacy can possibly arise? The acquaintance can only be superficial. Nothing binds the two together beyond the temporary and accidental. Let them, however, become possessed of a common and a serious view of life; let them strive for the attainment of some great moral reform, which they feel of vital importance to the welfare of the nation and the age, and immediately a bond of connection and intercourse will be established which will ripen into real intimacy.

I dispute the correctness of the generalization above quoted, however, not only on theoretical considerations, but also as a matter of experience. Among Christians, the conditions are fulfilled for intimate relations between Occidentals and Orientals which result, as a matter of fact, in genuine and intimate friendship. The relations existing between many missionaries and the native Christians and pastors refute the assertion of the editor of the *Japan Mail* that, "no foreigner has ever yet succeeded in being admitted into the inner circle of Japanese intercourse." This assertion is doubtless true in regard to the relation of foreigners to non-Christian society. The reason, for the fact, however, is not because one is Occidental and the other Oriental in psychic nature, but solely because of diverse moral views, aims, and conduct.

It is not the contention of these pages, however, that intimate friendships between Occidental and Oriental Christians are as easily formed as between members of two Occidental nations. Although common views of life, and common moral aims and conduct may provide the requisite foundations for such intimate friendships, the diverse methods of thought and of social intercourse may still serve to hinder their formation. It is probably a fact that missionaries experience greater difficulty in making genuine intimate friendships with Japanese Christians than with any other race on the face of the globe. The reasons for this fact are manifold. The Japanese racial ambition manifests itself not only in the sphere of political life; it does not take kindly to foreign control in any line. The churches manifest this characteristic. It is a cause of suspicion of the foreign missionary and separation from him; it has broken up many a friendship. Intimacy between missionaries and leading native pastors and evangelists was more common in the earlier days of Christian work than more recently, because the Japanese church organization has recently developed a self-consciousness and an ambition for organic independence which have led to mutual criticisms.

Furthermore, Japanese Christians are still Japanese. Their methods of social intercourse are Oriental; they bow profoundly, they repeat formal salutations, they refrain from free expression of personal opinion and preference. The crust of polite etiquette remains. The foreigner must learn to appreciate it before he can penetrate to the kindly, sincere, earnest heart. This the foreigner does not easily do, much to the detriment of his work.

And on the other hand, before the Oriental can penetrate to the kindly, sincere, and earnest heart of the Occidental, he must abandon the inferential method; he must not judge the foreigner by what is left unsaid nor by slight turns of that which is said, but by the whole thought as fully expressed. In other words, as the Occidental must learn and must trust to Oriental methods of social intercourse, so the Oriental must learn and must trust to the corresponding Occidental methods. The difficulty is great in either case, though of an opposite nature. Which has the greater difficulty is a question I do not attempt to solve.

Another generalization as to the essential difference marking Oriental and Occidental psychic natures is that the former is meditative and appreciative, and the latter is active. This too is a characterization of no little truth. The easy-going, time-forgetting, dreaming characteristics of the Orient are in marked contrast to the rush, bustle, and hurry of the

179

Occident. One of the first and most forcible impressions made on the Oriental visiting the West is the tremendous energy displayed even in the ordinary everyday business. In the home there is haste; on the streets men, women, and children are "always on the run." It must seem to be literally so, when the walk of the Occidental is compared with the slow, crawling rate at which the Oriental moves. Horse cars, electric cars, steam cars, run at high speed through crowded streets. Conversation is short and hurried. Visits are curtailed—hardly more than glimpses. Everyone is so nervously busy as to have no time for calm, undisturbed thought. So does the Orient criticise and characterize the Occident.

In the Orient, on the contrary, time is nothing. Walking is slow, business is deliberate, visiting is a fine art of bows and conventional phrases preliminary to the real purpose of the call; amusements even are long-drawn-out, theatrical performances requiring an entire day. In the home there is no hurry, on the street there is no rush. To the Occidental, the Oriental seems so absorbed in a dream life that the actual life is to him but a dream.

If the characterization we are considering is meant to signify that the Orient possesses a power of appreciation not possessed by the West, then it seems to me an error. The Occident is not deficient in appreciation. A better statement of the difference suggested by the above characterization is that Western civilization is an expression of Will, whereas Eastern civilization is an expression of subordination to the superior—to Fate. This feature of Oriental character is due to the fact that the Orient is still as a whole communal in its social order, whereas the Occident is individualistic. In the West each man makes his own fortune; his position in society rests on his own individual energy. He is free to exert it at will. Society praises him in proportion as he manifests energy, grit, independence, and persistence. The social order selects such men and advances them in political, in business, in social, and in academic life. The energetic, active characteristics of the West are due, then, to the high development of individualism. The entire Occidental civilization is an expression of free will.

The communal nature of the Orient has not systematically given room for individual progress. The independent, driving man has been condemned socially. Submission, absolute and perpetual, to parents, to lord, to ancestors, to Fate, has been the ruling idea of each man's life. Controlled by such ideas, the easy-going, time-ignoring, dreaming, contemplative life—if you so choose to call it—of the Orient is a necessary consequence.

But has this characteristic become congenital, or is it still only social? Is dreamy appreciation now an inborn racial characteristic of Oriental mind, while active driving energy is the corresponding essential trait of Occidental mind? Or may these characteristics change with the social order? I have no hesitancy whatever in advocating the latter position. The way in which Young Japan, clad in European clothing, using watches and running on "railroad time," has dropped the slow-going style of Old Japan and has acquired habits of rapid walking, direct clear-cut conversation, and punctuality in business and travel (comparatively speaking) proves conclusively the correctness of my contention. New Japan is entering into the hurry and bustle of Occidental life, because, in contact with the West, she has adopted in a large measure, though not yet completely, the individualism of the West.

As time goes on, Japanese civilization will increasingly manifest the phenomena of will, and will proportionally become assimilated to the civilization of the West. But the ultimate cause of this transformation in civilization will be the increasing introduction of individualism into the social order. And this is possible only because the so-called racial characteristics are sociological, and not biological. The transformation of "race soul" therefore does not depend on the intermarriage of diverse races, but only on the adoption of new ideas and practices through social intercourse.

We conclude, then, that the only thoroughgoing interpretation of the differences characterizing Eastern and Western psychic nature is a social one, and that social differences can be adequately expressed only by contrasting the fundamental ideas ruling their respective social orders, namely, communalism for the East and individualism for the West.

The unity that pervades the Orient, if it is not due to the inheritance of a common psychic nature, to what is it due? Surely to the possession of a common civilization and social order. It would be hard to prove that Japanese, Koreans, Chinese, Siamese, Burmese, Hindus (and how many distinct races does the ethnologist find in India), Persians, and Turks are all descendants from a common ancestry and are possessed therefore by physical heredity of a common racial psychic nature. Yet such is the requirement of the theory we are opposing. That the races inhabiting the Asiatic continent have had from ancient times mutual social intercourse, whereby the civilization, mental, moral, and spiritual, of the most developed has passed to the other nations, so that China has dominated Eastern Asia, and India has profoundly influenced all the races inhabiting Asia, is an indisputable fact. The psychic unity of the Orient is a civilizational, a social unity, as is also the psychic unity of the Occident. The reason why the Occident is so distinct from the Orient in social, in psychic, and in civilizational characteristics is because these two great branches of the human race have undergone isolated evolution. Isolated biological evolution has produced the diverse races. These are now fixed physical types, which can be modified only by intermarriage. But although isolated social evolution has produced diverse social and psychic characteristics these are not fixed and unalterable. To transform psychic and social characteristics, intimate social intercourse, under special conditions, is needful alone.

If the characteristics differentiating the Eastern from the Western peoples are only social, it might be supposed that the results of association would be mutual, the East influencing the West as much as the West influences the East, both at last finding a common level. Such a result, however, is impossible, from the laws regulating psychic and social intercourse. The less developed psychic nature can have no appreciable effect on the more highly developed, just as undeveloped art cannot influence highly developed art, nor crude science and philosophy highly developed science and philosophy. The law governing the relations of diverse civilizations when brought into contact is not like the law of hydrostatics, whereby two bodies of water of different levels, brought into free communication, finally find a common level, determined by the difference in level and their respective masses. In social intercourse the higher civilization is unaffected by the lower, in any important way, while the lower is mightily modified, and in sufficient time is lifted to the grade of the higher in all important respects. This is a law of great significance. The Orient is becoming Occidentalized to a degree and at a rate little realized by travelers and not fully appreciated by the Orientals themselves. They know that mighty changes have taken place, and are now taking place, but they do not fully recognize their nature, and the multitudes do not know the source of these changes. In so far as the East has surpassed the West in any important direction will the East influence the West.

In saying, then, as we did in our first chapter, that the Japanese have already formed an Occidento-Oriental civilization, we meant that Japan has introduced not only the external and mechanical elements of Western civilization into her new social order, but also its inner and determinative principle—individualism. In saying that, as the Ethiopian cannot change his skin nor the leopard his spots, so Japan will never become thoroughly Occidentalized, we did not intend to say that she was so Oriental in her physiological nature, in her "race soul," that she could make no fundamental social transformation; but merely that she has a social heredity that will always and inevitably modify every Occidental custom and conception that may be brought to this land. Although in time Japan may completely individualize her social order, it will never be identical with that of the West. It will always bear the marks of her Oriental social heredity in innumerable details. The Occidental traveler will always be impressed with the Orientalisms of her civilization. Although the Oriental familiar with the details of the pre-Meiji social order will be impressed with what seems to him the complete Occidentalization of her new civilization and social order, although to-day communalism and individualism are the distinguishing characteristics respectively of the East and the West, they are not necessary characteristics due to inherent race nature. The Orient is sure to become increasingly individualistic. The future evolution of the great races of the earth is to be increasingly convergent in all the essentials of individual and racial prosperity, but in countless non-essential details the customs of the past will remain, to give each race and nation distinctive psychic and social characteristics.

XXXVII
GENERAL CONCLUSIONS

The aim of the present work has been to gain insight into the real nature of both Japanese character and its modern transformation.

In doing this we have necessarily entered the domain of social science, where we have been compelled to take issue with many, to us, defective conceptions. Our discussions of social principles have, however, been narrowly limited. We have confined our attention to the interpretation of those social and psychic characteristics differentiating the Japanese from other races. Our chief contention has been that these characteristics are due to the nature of the social order that has prevailed among them, and not to the inherent nature of the people; and that the evolution of the psychic characteristics of all races is due to social more than to biological evolution.

This position and the discussions offered to prove it imply more than has been explicitly stated. In this closing chapter it seems desirable to state concisely, and therefore with technical terminology, some of the more fundamental principles of social philosophy assumed or implied in this work. Brevity requires that this statement take the form of dogmatic propositions and unillustrated abstractions. The average reader will find little to interest him, and is accordingly advised to omit it entirely.

Let us first clearly see that we have made no effort to account for the origin or inherent nature of psychic life. That association or the social order is the original producing cause of psychic life is by no means our contention. Given the psychic nature as we find it in man, the problem is to account for its diverse manifestation in the different races and civilizations. This, and this alone, has been our problem.

Psychic nature is the sole and final cause of social life. Without psychic nature there could be no association. Personalized psychic nature is the sole and final cause of human social life. Numberless conditions determine by stimulation or imitation the manifestation of psychic life. These conditions differ for different lands, peoples, ages, and political relations, producing diverse social orders for each separated group. These diverse social orders determine the psychic characteristics differentiating the various groups. Social life and social order are objective expressions of a reality of which psychic nature is the subjective and therefore deeper reality. The two cannot be ruthlessly torn apart and remain complete, nor can they be understood, or completely interpreted, apart from each other. They are correlative and complementary expressions for the same reality.

Similarly physical and psychical life are to be conceived as profoundly interrelated, being respectively objective and subjective expressions of a reality incapable of separate interpretation. Yet each has markedly distinct characteristics and is the subject of distinct laws of activity and development.

Heredity is of two kinds, biological heredity, transmitting innate characters, and social heredity, transmitting acquired habits and their physiological results.

The innate characters transmitted by biological heredity are either physiological, anatomical, or psychical.

The acquired habits transmitted by social heredity are essentially psychical: but they may result in acquired physiological, or even anatomical, characters. Here belong the physiological effects of diet, housing, clothing, occupation, education, etc., which have not yet been taken up and incorporated into the innate physiological constitution by biological heredity. The physiological effects of social heredity are through the daily physical life and activity of each individual, in accordance with the requirements of the social order in which he is reared; and these are reached through its influence on the acquired psychical habits, which are transmitted through association, imitation, and the control of activities by language and education. In biological heredity the transmission is exclusively prior to birth, while in social heredity it is chiefly, if not entirely, after birth.

In social heredity the transmission is not determined by consanguinity, and therefore extends to members of alien races when they are incorporated in the social organization.

While the transmission of biological inheritance to each offspring is inevitable and complete, that of social inheritance is largely voluntary. It is also more or less complete, according to the knowledge, purpose, and effort of the individuals concerned. The transmission of acquired social and psychic characteristics even from parents to offspring depends on their association, and the imposition on their offspring by parents of their own modes of life. Sharing with parents their bodily activities, their language and their environment, both social and psychical, the offspring necessarily develop psychic and social characteristics similar to those of the parents.

Evolution takes place through the transformation of inheritance. The evolution of *innate* physiological, anatomical, and psychical characters takes place through the transformation of biological inheritance; and the evolution of society and of *acquired* characters chiefly through the transformation of social inheritance.

Nearly all biologists admit that change in the form of natural selection is one of the principles transforming biological inheritance; but whether the *acquired* characters of parents are even in the least degree inherited by the offspring, thus becoming *innate* characters, is one of the important biological problems of recent years. Into this problem we have not entered, though we recognize that it must have important bearings on sociological science. Briefly stated, it is this: Do social and psychic characteristics, acquired by individuals or by groups of individuals, affect the intrinsic inherited and transmissible psychic nature in such ways that offspring, by the mere fact of being offspring, necessarily manifest those characteristics, regardless of the particular social environment in which they may be reared? Into this problem, thus broadly stated, we do not enter. Limiting our view to those advanced races which manifest practically equal physiological development, we ask whether or not their differentiating psychic characteristics are due to modifications of their inherited and intrinsic psychic nature, such that those characteristics are necessarily transmitted to offspring through intrinsic biological heredity. Current popular and scientific sociology seems to give an affirmative answer to this question. The reply of this work emphasizes the negative. Although it is not maintained that there is absolutely no difference whatever in the psychic nature of the different races, or that the psychic differences distinguishing the races are entirely transmitted by social heredity, it is maintained that this is very largely the case—far more largely than is usually perceived or admitted. Such inherent differences, if they exist, are so vague and intangible as practically to defy discovery and clear statement, and may be practically ignored.

The only adequate disproof of the position here maintained would be about as follows. Let a Japanese infant be reared in an American home from infancy, not only fed and clothed as an American, but loved as a member of the family and trained as carefully and affectionately as one's own child. The full conditions require that not only the child himself, but everyone else, be ignorant of his parentage and race in order that he be thought to be, and be treated as though he were, a genuine member of his adopting home and people. What would be the psychic characteristics of that child when grown to manhood? If he should manifest psychic traits like those of his Japanese parents, if he should think in the Japanese order, if he should have a tendency to use prepositions as postpositions, if he should drop pronouns and should use honorific words in their place, if he should be markedly suspicious and inferential, if he should bow in making his salutations rather than shake hands, if he should show marked preference for sitting on the floor rather than on chairs, and for chopsticks to knives and forks, and if developing powers as an artist he should naturally paint Japanese pictures, Japanese landscapes, and Japanese faces, finding himself unable to draw according to the canons of Western art, if on developing poetic tastes he should find special pleasure in seventeen syllable or thirty-one syllable exclamatory poems, finding little interest in Longfellow or Shakespeare, if, in short, he should develop a predilection for any distinctive Japanese custom, habit of thought, method of speech, emotion or volition, it would evidently be due to his intrinsic heredity. If in all these matters, however, he should prove to be like an American, acquiring an American education like any American boy, and if on being brought to Japan, at, say, thirty years of age, still supposing himself to be an American, he should have equal difficulty with any American in mastering the language and adapting himself to and understanding the Japanese people, then it would follow that his psychic characteristics have been inherited socially and he is what he is, nationally, because of his social heritage. Such a result would show that the psychic traits differentiating races are social and not intrinsic.

We have limited our discussion to the advanced races because the problem is then relatively simple, the material abundant, and the issue clear. Much discussion in theology, psychology, and sociology is futile because it concerns that practically mythical being, the aboriginal man, about whose social and psychic life no one knows anything, and any theorizer can say what he chooses without fear of shipwreck on incontrovertible facts. Whether the lowest races known to-day are differentiated from the highest only by acquired social and psychic characteristics, or also by differences of psychic nature, may perhaps be an open question. However this may be, the case is fairly clear in regard to the higher races inhabiting the earth. Their differentiating psychic characteristics are, for the most part, not due to diverse psychic nature, but to diverse social orders, while the transmission of these characteristics takes place, as a matter of observation, through social heredity.

The discussions of this work are exclusively concerned with the evolution of society and of psychic characteristics. But even in this limited field we have not attempted to cover the whole ground. We have given our chief attention to the interdependence of social phenomena and psychic characteristics. The causes of evolution in the social order have not been the main subject under discussion.

Segregation is the essential condition on which divergent evolution is dependent. Many forms of segregation may be specified, under each of which evolution proceeds on a different principle. In brief, it may be said that biological segregation prevents the swamping of incipient organic divergences, by preventing the intermarriage of those possessing such divergences, while social segregation prevents the swamping of incipient social divergences and their corresponding incipient psychic characteristics by preventing the inter-association of those having such tendencies.

Biologically segregated groups undergo divergent biological evolution through segregated marriage, producing distinct physiological unities or racial types. These racial types are now relatively fixed and can be appreciably modified only by the intermarriage of different races.

Socially segregated groups undergo divergent social evolution through the segregated social intercourse of the members of each group, producing distinct civilizational and psychic unities. The differences between these social or psychic groups are relatively plastic and are the subject of constant variation. The modification of the social and psychic characteristics of a group takes place through a change in the physical or social environment of the group, or through the rise of strong personalities within the group.

Biologically distinct groups may thus be unified biologically only by intermarriage, while socially physically distinct groups may be unified socially and psychically without intermarriage, but exclusively through association.

The psychic defects of the offspring of interracial marriages may be largely due to the defective social heredity transmitted by the parents, rather than to mixed intrinsic inheritance.

The term "race soul" is a convenient, though delusive, because highly figurative, expression for the psychic unity of a social group. The unity is due entirely to the more or less complete possession by the individual members of the group, of common ideas, ideals, methods of thought, emotions, volitions, customs, institutions, arts, and beliefs.

Each individual is molded psychically to the type of the social group in which he is reared. The "race soul" is thus imposed on the individual by conscious and unconscious education.

The psychic evolution of social groups is divergent so long as isolation is fairly complete, but becomes convergent in proportion to association. Perfect association produces complete psychic unity, though it should be noted that perfect association of geographically separated social groups is practically unattainable.

The essential elements constituting national unity are psychic and social, not biological. Racial unity is biological. The same race may accordingly separate into different social and psychic groups. And members of different races may belong to the same social psychic group.

The so-called "race soul" of many sociologists is, therefore, a fiction and indicates mental confusion. The term refers not to the racial unity of inherent psychic nature, but only to the social unity of socially inherited psychic characteristics. Groups thus socially unified may or may not be racially homogeneous. In point of fact no race is strictly homogeneous biologically, nor is any social group completely unified psychically.

In sociology as in biology function produces organism, that is to say, activity produces the organ or faculty fitted to perform the activity.[DN] The psychic characteristics differentiating social groups are chiefly, and perhaps exclusively, due to diverse social activities. These activities are determined by innumerable causes, geographical, climatic, economic, political, intellectual, emotional, and personal.

The plasticity of a psychic group is due to the plasticity of the infant mind and brain, which is wonderfully capable of acquiring the language, thought forms, and differentiating characteristics of any group in which it may be reared. To what extent this plasticity extends only carefully conducted experiments can show. In the higher Asiatic and European races we find it to be much greater than is generally supposed to be the case, but it is not improbable that the lowest races possess it in a much lower degree.

The relative fixity of a psychic group is due to the fact that in full-grown adults, who form the majority of every group, function has produced structure. Body, brain, and mind have "set" or crystallized in the mold provided by the social order. Influences sufficiently powerful to transform the young have little effect on the adult. The relative fixity of a psychic group is also due to the difficulty—well-nigh impossibility—of bringing new psychic influences to bear on all members of the group simultaneously. The majority, being oblivious to the new psychic forces, maintain the old psychic régime. The difficulty of reform, of transforming a social order, is principally due to these two causes.

The "character" of a people (psychic group) consists of its more or less unconscious, because structuralized or incarnate, ideas, emotions, and volitions. Chief among them are those concerning the character of God, the nature and value of man and woman, the necessary relation of character to destiny, the nature and meaning of life and death, and the nature and the authority of moral law. In proportion as the social order incorporates high or low views on these vital subjects, is the character of the people elevated and strong, or debased and weak.

The destiny of a people, and the rôle it plays in history, are determined not by chance nor yet by environment, but in the last analysis by its own character. Yet this character is not something given it complete at the start, an intrinsic psychical inheritance, nor is it dependent for transmission on biological heredity, passing only from parents to offspring. Character belongs to the sphere of social psychic life and is the subject of social heredity. Through social intercourse the moral character dominating a psychic group may be transmitted to members of an alien psychic group. This usually takes place through missionary activity. The moral character of a psychic group may in this way be fundamentally transformed, and with character, destiny.

Floating ideas, not yet woven into the warp and woof of life, not yet incarnate in the individual or in the social order, have little influence on the character of the individual or the group, however beautiful, true, or elevating such ideas may be in themselves. The character of a people is to be judged, therefore, not by the beauty or elevation of every idea that may be found in its literature, but only by those ideas that have been assimilated, that have become incorporated into the social order. These determine a people's character and destiny. According as these ideas persist in the social order, is its character permanent.

Progress consists of expanding life, communal and individual, extensive and intensive, physical and psychical. True progress is balanced. High communal development, that is, highly organized society, is impossible without the wide attainment of highly developed individuals. Progressive mastery of nature likewise is impossible apart from growing psychic development in all its branches, emotional, intellectual and volitional, communal and individual.

Historically, communalism is the first principle to emerge in consciousness. To succeed, however, it must be accompanied by at least a certain degree of individualism, even though it be quite implicit. The full development of the communal principle is impossible apart from the correspondingly full development of the individual principle. These are complementary principles of progress. Each alone is impossible. In proportion as either is

185

emphasized at the expense of the other, is progress impeded. Arrested civilizations are due to the disproportionate and excessive development of one or the other of these principles.

Personality, expressing and realizing itself in communal and individual life, in objective and subjective forms, is at once the cause and the goal of progress. Social and psychic evolution are, therefore, in the last analysis, personal processes. The irreducible and final factor in social evolution and in social science is personality; for personality is the determinative factor of a human being.

Progress in personal development consists of increasing extent and accuracy of knowledge, refinement and elevation of emotions, and nobility and reliability of volitions. Progress in personal development requires the individual to pass from objective heterocratic to subjective autocratic or self-regulative ethical life. He must pass from the traditional to the enlightened, from the communal to the individualistic stage in ethics and religion. He must feel with increasing force the binding nature of the supra-communal sanctions for communal and individual life, accepting the highest dictates of the enlightened moral consciousness as the laws of the universe. But this means that the individual must secure increasing insight into the immutable and eternal laws of spiritual being and must identify his personal interests, his very self with those laws, with the Heart of the. Universe, with God himself. Only so will he become completely autonomous, self-regulative. Only thus will the individual become and remain an altruistic communo-individual, fitted to meet and survive the relaxation of the historic communal and supra-communal sanctions for communal and individual life, a relaxation induced by growing political liberty and growing intellectual rejection of primitive or defective religious beliefs.

Progress in personality is thus at bottom an ethico-religious process. The wide attainment of developed personality permits the formation of enlarging highly organized psychic groups, accompanied by increasing specialization of its individual members. This communal expansion, ramifying organization and individual specialization, secures increasing extensive and intensive intellectual understanding of the universe, and this in turn active mastery of nature, with all the consequences of growing ease and richness of life.

Ethico-religious, autonomous personality is thus the tap-root of highly developed and permanently progressive civilizations. Personality is, therefore, the criterion of progress. Mere ease of physical life, freedom from anxiety, light-hearted, care-free happiness, mastery of nature, material civilization, highly developed art, literature, and music, or even refined culture, are partial and inadequate, if not positively false, criteria.

Personality, as a nature, is an inherent psychic heritage shared by all human beings. It is transmitted only from parents to offspring, and its transmission depends only on that relation. Personality, as a varying psychic characteristic, is a matter of social inheritance, and is profoundly dependent, therefore, on the nature of the social order and the social evolution.

Religion, as incorporated in life, is the most important single factor determining the personality and character of its adherents, either hindering or promoting their progress.

Japanese social and psychic evolution have in no respects violated the universal laws of evolution. Japanese personal and other psychic characteristics are the product not of essential, but of social inheritance and social evolution. Japan has recently entered into a new social inheritance from which she is joyfully accepting new conceptions and principles of communal and individual life. These she is working into her social organism.

Already these are producing profound, and we may believe permanent, transformations in her social order and correspondingly profound and permanent transformations of her character and destiny.

THE END

INDEX

186

Dwarfed plants,—delight in the abnormal,

FOOTNOTES:

[A]
"Things Japanese," p. 156.

[B]
Let not the reader gather from the very brief glance at the attainments of New Japan, that she has overtaken the nations of Christendom in all important respects; for such is far from the case. He needs to be on his guard not to overestimate what has been accomplished.

[C]
Prof. B.H. Chamberlain.

[D]
Only since the coming of the new period has it become possible for a woman to gain a divorce from her husband.

[E]
Chapter xxix. Some may care to read this chapter at this point.

[F]
Cf. chapter ii.

[G]

"Kokoro," by L. Hearn, p. 31.

[H]
Japan Mail, September 30, 1899.

[I]
Part II. p. xxxii.

[J]
Japan Mail, June 4, 1898, p. 586.

[K]
If all that has been said above as to the relative lack of affection between husband and wife is true, it will help to make more credible, because more intelligible, the preceding chapter as to the relative lack of love for children. Where the relation between husband and wife is what we have depicted it, where the children are systematically taught to feel for their father respect rather than love, the relation between the father and the children, or the mother and the children, cannot be the same as in lands where all these customs are reversed.

[L]
The effect of Christian missions cannot be measured by the numbers of those who are to be counted on the church rolls; almost unconsciously the nation is absorbing Christian ideals from the hundreds of Christian missionaries and tens of thousands of Christian natives. The necessities of the new social order make their teachings intelligible and acceptable as the older social order did not and could not. This accounts for the astonishing change in the anti-Christian spirit of the Japanese. This spirit did not cease at once on the introduction of the new social order, nor indeed is it now entirely gone. But the change from the Japan of thirty years ago to the Japan of to-day, in its attitude toward Christianity, is more marked than that of any great nation in history. A similar change in the Roman Empire took place, but it required three hundred years. This change in Japan may accordingly be called truly miraculous, not in the sense, however, of a result without a cause, for the causes are well understood.

Among the Christians, especially, the old order is rapidly giving way to the new. Christianity has brought a new conception of woman and her place in the home and her relation to her husband. Japanese Christian girls, and recently non-Christian girls, are seeking an education which shall fit them for their enlarging life. Many of the more Christian young men do not want heathen wives, with their low estimate of themselves and their duties, and they are increasingly unwilling to marry those of whom they know nothing and for whom they care not at all. Already the idea that love is the only safe foundation for the home is beginning to take root in Japan. This changing ideal is bringing marked social changes. In some churches an introduction committee is appointed whose special function is to introduce marriageable persons and to hold social meetings where the young people may become acquainted. Here an important evolution in the social order is taking place before our eyes, but not a few of the world's wise men are too exalted to see it. Love and demonstrative affection between husband and wife will doubtless become as characteristic of Japan in the future as their absence has been characteristic in the past. To recapitulate: these distinctive characteristics of the emotional life of the Japanese might at first seem to be so deep-rooted as to be inherent, yet they are really due to the ideas and customs of the social order, and are liable to change with any new system of ideas and customs that may arise. The higher development of the emotional life of the Japanese waits now on the reorganization of the family life; this rests on a new idea as to the place and value of woman as such and as a human being; this in turn rests on the wide acceptance of Christian ideals as to God and their mutual relations. It involves, likewise, new ideals as to man's final destiny. In Japan's need of these Christian ideals we find one main ground and justification, if justification be needed, for missionary enterprise among this Eastern people.

[M]
Chapter v. p. 82.

[N]
P. 133

[O]
"Résumé Statistique l'Empire du Japan," published by the Imperial Cabinet, 1897.

[P]
As illustrating the point under discussion see portions of addresses reported in "The World's Parliament of Religions," vol. ii. pp. 1014, 1283.

[Q]
Japan Mail, December 10, 1898.

[R]
I have found it difficult to secure exact information on the subject of the Imperial concubines (who, by the way, have a special name of honor), partly for the reason that this is not a matter of general information, and partly because of the unwillingness to impart information to a foreigner which is felt to tarnish the luster of the Imperial glory. A librarian of a public library refused to lend a book containing the desired facts, saying that foreigners might be freely informed of that which reveals the good, the true, and the beautiful of Japanese history, customs, and character, but nothing else. By the educated and more earnest members of the nation much sensitiveness is felt, especially in the presence of the Occidental, on the subject of the Imperial concubinage. It is felt to be a blot on Japan's fair name, a relic of her less civilized days, and is, accordingly, kept in the background as much as possible. The statements given in the text in regard to the number of the concubines and children are correct so far as they go. A full statement might require an increase in the figures given.

[S]
P. 59.

[T]
P. 119.

[U]
Aston's "Japanese Literature," p. 29.

[V]
"Japanese Literature," p. 24.

[W]
Cf. chapter xxxiii.

[X]
Gustave Le Bon maintains, in his brilliant, but sophistical, work on "The Psychology of Peoples," that the "soul of a race" unalterably determines even its art. He states that a Hindu artist, in copying an European model several times, gradually eliminates the European characteristics, so that, "the second or third copy ... will have become exclusively Hindu." His entire argument is of this nature; I must confess that I do not in the least feel its force. The reason the Hindu artist transforms a Western picture in copying it is because he has been trained in Hindu art, not because he is a Hindu physiologically. If that same Hindu artist, taken in infancy to Europe and raised as a European and trained in European art,

should still persist in replacing European by Hindu art characteristics, then the argument would have some force, and his contention that the "soul of races" can be modified only by intermarriage of races would seem more reasonable.

[Y]
"The Human Species," p. 283.

[Z]
Ibid., p. 282.

[AA]
Ibid., p. 384.

[AB]
The manuscript of this work was largely prepared in 1897 and 1898. Since writing the above lines, a vigorous discussion has been carried on in the Japanese press as to the advantages and disadvantages of the present system of writing. Many have advocated boldly the entire abandonment of the Chinese character and the exclusive use of the Roman alphabet. The difficulties of such a step are enormous and cannot be appreciated by anyone not familiar with the written language of Japan. One or the strongest arguments for such a course, however, has been the obstacle placed by the Chinese in the way of popular education, due to the time required for its mastery and the mechanical nature of the mind it tends to produce. In August of 1900 the Educational Department enacted some regulations that have great significance in this connection. Perhaps the most important is the requirement that not more than one thousand two hundred Chinese characters are to be taught to the common-school children, and the form of the character is not to be taught independently of the meaning. The remarks in the text above are directed chiefly to the ancient methods of education.

[AC]
Griffis' "Religions of Japan," p. 272.

[AD]
P. 24.

[AE]
Far East for January, 1898.

[AF]
January 20, 1900.

[AG]
Japan Mail, November 12, 1898.

[AH]
P. 17.

[AI]
P. 18.

[AJ]
P. 18.

[AK]
"History of the Empire of Japan," compiled and translated for the Imperial Japanese Commission of the World's Columbian Exposition.

[AL]
"Japanese Literature," p. 4.

[AM]
Cf. chapter xvi. p. 199.

[AN]
Cf. chapter xvii.

[AO]
Quotations from "A Japanese Philosopher" will be found in chapters xxiv. and xxvi.

[AP]
"Things Japanese," p. 133.

[AQ]
P. 213.

[AR]
P. 30.

[AS]
Cf. chapter vii.

[AT]
Cf. chapter xv. pp. 186, 187.

[AU]
Cf. chapters xvi. and xvii.

[AV]
Chapter xv.

[AW]
Chapters xix. and xx.

[AX]
P. 39.

[AY]
P. 36.

[AZ]
Pp. 42, 43.

[BA]
P. 45.

[BB]
P. 61.

[BC]
P. 120.

[BD]

P. 129.

[BE]
P. 130.

[BF]
Dickenson's "Japan," chapter vii.

[BG]
Cf. chapter xxi.

[BH]
P. 163.

[BI]
P. 169.

[BJ]
It is interesting to observe that the contempt of Old Japan for trade, and the feeling that interest and profit by commerce were in their nature immoral, are in close accord with the old Greek and Jewish ideas regarding property profits and interest. Aristotle held, for instance, that only the gains of agriculture, of fishing, and of hunting are natural gains. Plato, in the Laws, forbids the taking of interest. Cato says that lending money on interest is dishonorable, is as bad as murder. The Old Testament, likewise, forbids the taking of interest from a Jew. The reason for this universal feeling of antiquity, both Oriental and Occidental, lies in the fact that trade and money were not yet essential parts of the social order. Positive production, such as hunting and farming, seemed the natural method of making a living, while trade seemed unnatural—living upon the labor of others. That Japan ranked the farmer higher in the social scale than the merchant is, thus, natural. In moral character, too, it is altogether probable that they were much higher.

[BK]
Cf. chapter ix. p. 103.

[BL]
Chapter vi.

[BM]
Chapter xxix. p. 339.

[BN]
An anonymous writer, in a pamphlet entitled "How the Social Evil is Regulated in Japan," gives some valuable facts on this subject. He describes the early history of the "Social Evil," and the various classes of prostitutes. He distinguishes between the "jigoku" (unlicensed prostitutes), the "shogi" (licensed prostitutes), and the "geisha" (singing and dancing girls). He gives translations of the various documents in actual use at present, and finally attempts to estimate the number of women engaged in the business. The method of reaching his conclusions does not commend itself to the present writer and his results seem absurdly wide of the mark, when compared with more carefully gathered figures. They are hardly worth quoting, yet they serve to show what exaggerated views are held by some in regard to the numbers of prostitutes in Japan. He tells us that a moderate estimate for licensed prostitutes and for geisha is 500,000 each, while the unlicensed number at least a million, making a total of 2,000,000 or 10 per cent. of the total female population of Japan! A careful statistical inquiry on this subject has been recently made by Rev. U.G. Murphy. His figures were chiefly secured from provincial officers. According to these returns the number of licensed prostitutes is 50,553 and of dancing girls is 30,386. Mr. Murphy's figures cannot

be far astray, and furnish us something of a basis for comparison with European countries. Statistics regarding unlicensed prostitutes are naturally not to be had.

[BO]
P. 148.

[BP]
June 25, 1898.

[BQ]
The last line of figures, those for 1897, is taken from Rev. U.G. Murphy's statistical pamphlet on "The Social Evil in Japan."

[BR]
It is stated that Mill's work on "Representative Government," which, translated, fills a volume of five hundred pages in Japanese, has reached its third edition.

[BS]
The *Japan Mail* for February 5, 1896; quoting from the *Jiji Shimpo*.

[BT]
The best summary of this discussion which I have seen in English is found in the *Japan Mail* for February 4, 1899.

[BU]
Japan Mail, January 14, 1899.

[BV]
Japan Mail, June 24, 1898.

[BW]
The constituency of the Doshisha consists principally of Kumiai Christians.

[BX]
"Occult Japan," p. 23.

[BY]
Cf. chapter xxiv.

[BZ]
"A Japanese Philosopher," p. 120.

[CA]
In immediate connection with this oft-quoted statement, however, I would put the following, as much more recent, and probably representing more correctly the Marquis's matured opinion. Mr. Kakehi, for some time one of the editors of the Osaka *Mainichi Shinbun* (Daily News), after an interview with the illustrious statesman in which many matters of national importance were discussed, was asked by the Marquis where he had been educated. On learning that he was a graduate of the Doshisha, the Marquis remarked: "The only true civilization is that which rests on Christian principles, and that consequently, as Japan must attain her civilization on these principles, those young men who receive Christian education will be the main factors in the development of future Japan."

[CB]
Chamberlain's "Things Japanese," p. 358.

[CC]
"Things Japanese," p. 70, and Murray's "Hand-book for Japan," p. 37.

[CD]
"Things Japanese," p. 93.

[CE]
P. 85.

[CF]
Cf. chapter xxiii. p. 271.

[CG]
By the term "centralization" I mean personal centralization. Political centralization is the gathering of all the lines of governmental authority to a single head or point. Personal centralization, on the contrary, is the development in the individual of enlarging and joyous consciousness of his relations with his fellow-countrymen, and the bringing of the individual into increasingly immediate relations of interdependence with ever-increasing numbers of his fellow-men, economically, intellectually, and spiritually. These enlarging relations and the consciousness of them must be loyally and joyfully accepted. They should arouse enthusiasm. The real unity of society, true national centralization, includes both the political and the personal phase. The more conscious the process and the relation, the more real is the unity. By this process each individual becomes of more importance to the entire body, as well as more dependent upon it. While each individual becomes with increasing industrial development more specialized in economic function, if his personal development has been properly carried on, he also becomes in mind and in character a micro-community, summing up in his individual person the national unity with all its main interests, knowledge, and character.

[CGa]
P. 14.

[CH]
P. 15.

[CI]
Pp. 88, 89.

[CJ]
Pp. 203, 204.

[CK]
Cf. chapter viii.

[CL]
See the *Rikugo Zasshi* for March, 1898.

[CM]
Cf. chapter xv.

[CN]
Buddhism is largely responsible for the wide practice of "joshi," through its doctrine that lovers whom fate does not permit to be married in this world may be united in the next because of the strength of their love.

[CO]

P. 88.

[CP]
P. 12.

[CQ]
P. 14.

[CR]
P. 15.

[CS]
In their relations with foreigners, the people, but especially the Christians, are exceedingly lenient, forgiving and overlooking our egregious blunders both of speech and of manner, particularly if they feel that we have a kindly heart. Yet it is the uniform experience of the missionary that he frequently hurts unawares the feelings of his Japanese fellow-workers. Few thoughts more frequently enter the mind of the missionary, as he deals with Christian workers, than how to say this needful truth and do that needful deed so as not to hurt the feelings of those whom he would help. The individual who feels slighted or insulted will probably give no active sign of his wound. He is too polite or too politic for that. He will merely close like a clam and cease to have further cordial feelings and relations with the person who has hurt him.

[CT]
Cf. chapter xiii.

[CU]
See chapter xxix.

[CV]
P. 201.

[CW]
Cf. chapter vii.

[CX]
It seems desirable to guard against an inference that might be made from what I have said about Hegel's "Nothing." Hegel saw clearly that his "Nothing" was only the farthest limit of abstraction, and that it was consequently absolutely empty and worthless. It was only his starting point of thought, not his end, as in the case of Brahmanism and of Buddhism. Only after Hegel had passed the "Nothing" through all the successive stages of thesis, antithesis, and synthesis, and thus clothed it with the fullness of being and character, did he conceive it to be the concrete, actual Absolute. There is, therefore, the farthest possible difference between Hegel's Absolute Being and Buddha's Absolute. Hegel sought to understand and state in rational form the real nature of the Christian's conception of God. Whether he did so or not, this is not the place to say.

[CY]
I remark, in passing, that Western non-Christian thought has experienced, and still experiences, no little difficulty in conceiving the ultimate nature of being, and thus in solving the problem, into which, as a cavernous tomb, the speculative religions of the Orient have fallen. Western non-Christian systems, whether materialism, consistent agnosticism, impersonal pantheism, or other systems which reject the Christian conception of God as perfect personality endowed with all the fullness of being and character, equally with philosophic Buddhism, fail to provide any theoretic foundation for the doctrine of the value

of man as man, and consequently fail to provide any guarantee for individualism in the social order and the wide development of personality among the masses.

[CZ]
Cf. chapter vi.

[DA]
Foot of chapter xxix.

[DB]
Chapter xxxiii. p. 498.

[DC]
It seems desirable to append a brief additional statement on the doctrine of the "personality of God," and its acceptability to the Japanese. I wish to make it clear, in the first place, that the difficulties felt by the Japanese in adopting this doctrine are not due primarily to the deficiency either of the Japanese language or to the essential nature of the Japanese mind, that is to say, because of its asserted structural "impersonality." We have seen how the entire thought of the people, and even the direct moral teachings, imply both the fact of personality in man, and also its knowledge. The religious teachings, likewise, imply the personality even of "Heaven."

That there are philosophical or, more correctly speaking, metaphysical difficulties attending this doctrine, I am well aware; and that they are felt by some few Japanese, I also know. But I maintain that these difficulties have been imported from the West. The difficulties raised by a sensational philosophy which results in denying the reality even of man's psychic nature, no less than the difficulties due to a thoroughgoing idealism, have both been introduced among educated Japanese and have found no little response. I am persuaded that the real causes of the doubt entertained by a few of the Christians in Japan as to the personality of God are of foreign origin. These doubts are to be answered in exactly the same way as the same difficulties are answered in other lands. It must be shown that the sensational and "positive" philosophies, ending in agnosticism as to all the great problems of life and of reality, are essentially at fault in not recognizing the nature of the mind that knows. The searching criticism of these assumptions and methods made by T.H. Green and other careful thinkers, and to which no answer has been made by the sensational and agnostic schools of thought, needs to be presented in intelligible Japanese for the fairly educated Japanese student and layman. So, too, the discussions of such writers and philosophical thinkers as Seth, and Illingworth, and especially Lotze, whose discussions of "personality" are unsurpassed, should be presented to Japanese thinkers in native garb. But, again I repeat, it seems to me that the difficulty felt in Japan on these subjects is due not to the "impersonality" of the language or the native mind, or to the hitherto prevalent religions, but wholly to the imported philosophies and sciences. The individuals who feel or at least express any sense of difficulty on these topics—so far at least as my knowledge of the subject goes—are not those who know nothing but their own language and their own native religions, but rather those who have had exceptional advantages in foreign study, many of them having spent years abroad in Western universities. They furnish a fresh revelation of the quickness with which the Japanese take up with new ideas. They did not evolve these difficulties for themselves, but gathered them from their reading of Western literature and by their mingling with men of unevangelical temper and thought in the West.

[DD]
"Sacred Books of the East," vol. xlix, part ii. p. 147.

[DE]
Cf. chapters xiii. and xxxi.

[DF]

It is not strange that in all the centers of this new learning Confucius was deified and worshiped. In connection with many schools established for the study of his works, temples were built to his honor, in which his statue alone was placed, before which a stately religious service was performed at regular intervals. Thus did Confucianism become a living and vitalizing, although, as we shall soon see, an incomplete religion.

[DG]

Writers on the history and philosophy of religion have much to say about the differences between national and universal religions. The three religions which they pronounce universal are Mahomedanism, Buddhism, and Christianity. The ground for this statement is the fact that each of these religions has developed strong individualistic characteristics. They are concerned with individual salvation. The importance of this element none will deny, least of all the writer. But I question the correctness of the descriptive adjective. Because of their individualistic character they are fitted to leap territorial boundaries and can find acceptance in every community; for this they are not dependent on the territorial expansion of the communities in which they arose.

[DH]
P. xvii.

[DI]
P. xviii.

[DJ]
P. 19.

[DK]
P. 6.

[DL]
P. 37.

[DM]
P. 83.

[DN]

Whether or not the activity modifies the transmissible nature is the problem as to the inheritance of acquired characteristics. The dictum that function produces organism does not say whether that organism is transmissible or not, either in biology or sociology.